SPEECHES OF THE
GOVERNORS OF MASSACHUSETTS
1765-1775

A Da Capo Press Reprint Series

THE ERA OF THE AMERICAN REVOLUTION

GENERAL EDITOR: LEONARD W. LEVY

Claremont Graduate School

SPEECHES OF THE
GOVERNORS OF MASSACHUSETTS
1765-1775

THE ANSWERS OF
THE HOUSE OF REPRESENTATIVES THERETO
With Their Resolutions and Addresses for That Period

And Other Public Papers Relating to the Dispute
Between This Country and Great Britain Which
Led to the Independence of the United States

Edited by Alden Bradford

DA CAPO PRESS • NEW YORK • 1971

A Da Capo Press Reprint Edition

This Da Capo Press edition of
Speeches of the Governors of Massachusetts,
1765-1775, is an unabridged republication of
the first edition published in Boston in 1818.
It is reprinted by permission from a copy owned by
the Harvard Law School Library.

Library of Congress Catalog Card Number 71-119048
SBN 306-71947-9

Published by Da Capo Press
A Division of Plenum Publishing Corporation
227 West 17th Street, New York, N.Y. 10011
All Rights Reserved

Manufactured in the United States of America

SPEECHES OF THE
GOVERNORS OF MASSACHUSETTS
1765-1775

SPEECHES

OF THE

GOVERNORS OF MASSACHUSETTS,

FROM

1765 TO 1775;

AND

THE ANSWERS

OF

THE HOUSE OF REPRESENTATIVES,

TO THE SAME;

WITH THEIR

RESOLUTIONS AND ADDRESSES

FOR THAT PERIOD.

AND OTHER

PUBLIC PAPERS,

RELATING TO THE

DISPUTE BETWEEN THIS COUNTRY AND GREAT BRITAIN,

WHICH LED

TO THE INDEPENDENCE OF THE UNITED STATES.

—

BOSTON:

PRINTED BY RUSSELL AND GARDNER,

PROPRIETORS OF THE WORK.

....

1818.

INTRODUCTORY REMARKS.

BY THE EDITOR.

THE Independence of the United States of America, with respect to the government of Great Britain, of which, from their first settlement, they had been colonies, thus making a part of that mighty empire, is an event of no ordinary magnitude. The principles, which operated to produce it, are, in a political view, of the highest moment to civilized society; and the consequences have been such, as not only to exceed all calculation, and astonish the most sanguine theorist, but to promote, in a wonderful degree, the freedom, the improvement, and the best interests of man. It cannot, then, be a useless labor to collate and preserve the documents, which serve to develope the characters, and to exhibit the views and principles of the individuals, who were instrumental in effecting that glorious event.

The English, who first settled in North America, were men of great hardihood and enterprize. And in addition to these lofty qualities, we may also justly attribute to them, with a very few exceptions, an unconquerable love of civil liberty. Perhaps, in a few instances, adventurers to this new world were actuated principally by a love of gain. It is particularly true, however, of the first English inhabitants of Plymouth, Massachusetts, Rhode Island and Connecticut, that they were not only brave and enterprizing, but strongly attached to the principles of civil and religious freedom. In truth, this sentiment in them was a passion; and this passion was often raised to enthusiasm. Perhaps, a love of religious liberty was their predominant trait of character. Yet they were scarcely less tenacious of their political, than of their reli-

gious rights.   Many of them were men of education and reflection.
They lived too in times when political subjects were much agitated ; and early imbibed a spirit of free inquiry on questions
relating to the end and design of civil government.

It may be well doubted, whether any people, who were advocates for religious freedom, ever discovered any indifference to
their political condition.   It is certain, however, that this inconsistency cannot be justly charged upon our ancestors, the first
inhabitants of New England.   To enjoy liberty of conscience in
religious worship, was their principal object in settling a wild and
savage territory, and submitting to the various privations and sufferings necessarily incident to their situation.   But it is abundantly evident from their history, that they early claimed and
exercised the powers of self government—made laws (as far as
was necessary to add to the common law) for the regulation, defence and support of the colonies, and openly opposed every
attempt to control their own authority in civil concerns, which a
mistaken or corrupt ministry in England ever dared to make.
They exercised the various prerogatives of sovereignty, by the
infliction of capital punishments ; maintaining courts of judicature, from which, in most cases, there was no appeal ; coining
money ; raising and disbanding troops at their own instance and
will ; and laying their taxes, without any addition or interference
from the government of Great Britain.   Yet they acknowledged
allegiance to the Crown of England.   They boasted of being subjects of the British King ; and readily yielded obedience to his
requisitions, though they claimed the merit of consenting, or of a
voluntary compliance.   The controling and paramount authority
of the King or Parliament even, was not indeed denied* on the one
hand, nor exercised, except in a few instances, on the other, but
with the assent and approbation of the colonists.

* Judge Marshall, in the introduction to his Life of Washington, says, " the authority
of Parliament to lay taxes on the colonies was denied by the General Court of Massachusetts Bay in 1692." An act of the Governor, Council and House of Representatives of this
colony in October, 1692, " setting forth general privileges, declared and enacted,"
among other things, as follows, (which is the only declaration we have been able to find to
that effect) " that no aid, tax, assessment, loan or imposition whatever, shall be laid, assessed, imposed or levied, on any of their Majesties subjects, on any color or pretence
whatever, *but by the act and consent of the Governor, Council and Representatives of the people,
assembled in General Court ;* and that no freeman shall be taken and imprisoned, or deprived of his freehold or liberty ; nor shall he be judged or condemned, *but by the lawful
judgment of his Peers, or the law of this Province.*"

The distinction, however, it must be acknowledged, was never fully settled, between the rights or claims set up by the colonists, and the authority asserted by the King and Parliament of Great Britain. There was no formal decision on the subject, and no opinion seems to have obtained, which was not denied, or assented to with reluctance, either by the advocates of the controling power of the parent country, or by individuals in the colonies. What the people in this country openly and explicitly contended for, was the sole right to lay internal taxes, while at the same time they admitted the authority of the British government to regulate trade and commerce. Whenever the question was agitated in England, it was there contended, that they might rightfully impose additional internal taxes, as well as raise a revenue for the Crown by duties on commercial enterprizes. The only inquiry with the ministry seems to have been, as to the policy and expediency of such measures.

In the reign of George II. an act of Parliament was passed imposing a duty on sugars, &c. But the duty was small, and the act was not very rigidly executed ; and was, therefore, submitted to without much complaint or opposition. But when, in the reign of George III. in 1764, the former act of George II. was continued and enforced, the duty increased, and an impost also laid on the article of molasses brought to the colonies from any other than British plantations in the West Indies, and the jurisdiction of vice admiralty courts was enlarged, by which the people were deprived of trial by juries in all cases relating to revenue arising from these duties, and made liable to unreasonable and oppressive suits—the question was presented, with new and peculiar interest, of the constitutional right of Parliament to lay any taxes or raise any revenue, in the colonies, except in so far as the same should be consented to and voted for by the representatives of the people.

It was abundantly evident to the apprehension of reflecting men here, that the British ministry of that period, were determined to raise a revenue from America, to enable them to meet the demands on that government, then greatly in debt, and the officers of which were supported at an enormous expense. The patriots in this country were resolved to resist this system at the very outset. Their first objections, however, went rather to the policy and equity of the measure, than to the right of Parliament to raise and collect a revenue from the colonies, as will be seen by some of the papers in the first part of this volume. They early contended, indeed, that their charter guaranteed to them the right to govern and tax themselves; and that they and their fathers had suffered much in settling and defending the country, and had incurred a heavy debt for their own protection and that of the other British settlements against the common enemy, which would be a great burden for them for many years of peace and commercial prosperity, which they had little reason to expect, so long as the duties, recently imposed, should be continued.

This opinion was advanced and urged from considerations suggested by some expressions in their charter, which seemed to admit of the construction, that the colonists were to enjoy the entire regulation of their own concerns; for they believed the charter, not so much a grant of privileges, revocable at the pleasure of Parliament, as a contract between the British government and the people who first settled this country, and submitted to various hardships and sufferings for the very purpose of having the right to legislate for themselves. They also pleaded, that they were originally and really Englishmen. They neither claimed nor wished, (at that period,) to be independent of the parent country, but acknowledged themselves as making a part of the British empire; and therefore contended for a participation of all the rights and privileges of British subjects; one of which, and that fundamental and unalienable, according to the constitution and charter of that free country, was, to be subject to taxation only by consent of their own representatives. It was not, however, till after much oppression, and some hesitancy on the part of the ministry, and the high claims they advanced for royal prerogative and parliamentary authority; not until the administration pretended to a right to legislate for and bind the colonies in all cases whatever; and did, in fact, impose heavy and new duties on all commercial enterprizes; that the colonists proceeded to deny the constitutional right of Parliament to tax them, and asserted, to the fullest extent, the principle, that all attempts to raise taxes here by the British government, without the consent of our own legislature, was arbitrary and tyrannical, and ought to be opposed by the real friends of liberty.

As early as 1765, resolutions were passed by the representatives of Massachusetts, and opinions were advanced in their replies to the speeches of the governors, who were then appointed by the Crown, claiming the exclusive right of laying taxes on the people in this colony; and denying the constitutional authority of Parliament to impose them. The year preceding, indeed, they had fully expressed their doubts of the authority of Parliament in this case, and the conclusion was very evident, from the claims set up, and the arguments then advanced, that they did not allow such a right in the government of the parent country. The ministry in England needed additional revenues to pay off the debt of the nation ; and being satisfied also of their right to raise it from the colonies, (though some individuals of great respectability in England doubted the right,* and many, the policy, of the measure) they persevered in their plan of laying and collecting imposts; and thus the administration in England, and the representatives of the people here, were completely and fully at issue. The papers published in this volume will shew the progress of the controversy, and furnish particularly the arguments and opinions advanced by the representatives here in support of the rights claimed for the colonies.

There appears not to have been any special causes in operation at this period, to produce the dispute between the colonies and the parent country. That such a dispute should, at some period, exist, was perhaps to be expected from the peculiar situation, the nature of the original charter, the growing population and prosperity, the spirit and character, of the colonists. But at the time of which we speak, and just previous to the controversy,

* At the time the stamp act passed, and others, providing for raising a revenue on the colonies, several members of the House of Commons opposed the measures, on the ground of their being inconsistent with the rights granted us by charter. And in 1689, when the Rev. Dr. Mather applied to King William, for a renewal of the charter of this Province, which had been a few years before vacated, under the arbitrary reign of the Stuarts, Dr. Burnet, then Bishop of Salisbury, is stated to have said, "that there was a greater sacredness in the charter of New England, than in the corporations in England ; because these were only acts of grace, whereas the charter of New England was a contract between the King and the first patentees. They promised the King to enlarge his dominions at their own charges, provided they and their posterity might enjoy such and such privileges. They had performed their part ; and for the King to deprive their posterity of the privileges therein granted them, would carry a face of injustice in it."

the attachment of the people here to the government and people of England was never more sincere and ardent. They had lately been united in a war for defence against those considered the natural enemies of the English. The promptness and bravery of the provincial troops, and the liberality of the colonial legislatures, in raising an army to act with British regulars, were highly commended by the English at home. They knew that the services and expenses of the colonists were of great extent, and served to promote the interests and honor of Great Britain herself. Our people also had been much conversant with the British, and could not but admire many traits of their character. Nor do we believe, that the opposition to the authority claimed by the British ministry, and the dispute agitated at this period, is to be attributed in any degree to a spirit of ambition or rivalship in those who were considered the leaders on the part of the colonies. It will not be pretended that the patriots of that day were not men of *like passions* with others of our race. And it is possible, that in a few cases, an envious or restless disposition had some influence. But we feel confident, that the remark is very generally true, when we attribute to the leading men in opposition to the measures of the British administration, sincerity, patriotism, and the most upright and disinterested intentions. It surely was not their object to strip others of power, that they might themselves tyrannize over their fellows. It was not their wish to obtain lucrative offices, then in the hands of others, that they might revel in opulence and luxury. Nor can it justly be said of them, that they were either visionary theorists, contending for a form of government which was impracticable ; or that they were advocates for a democratic and levelling system which would exclude all authority from legislators and rulers, and place men in a situation which they hold by nature. But they did contend for the rights given them by their charter, and to which they were constitutionally entitled as subjects of the free government of Great Britain ; and therefore bound by no laws, to which their representatives had not, in their name, assented. These rights they strenuously asserted ; for these they firmly and perseveringly contended.

We mean not to claim for Massachusetts all the merit of opposition to the arbitrary measures of Great Britain, nor all the influence which was exerted to effect the revolution. Other colonies were forward and decisive in disapproving of the power claimed by the British ministry, of that period, over the people in these provinces; and readily united with Massachusetts in measures of redress. Virginia, so early as 1765, passed resolutions, declaring their sense of charter rights and privileges, with which the authority then claimed by Parliament to impose taxes, on the colonies, was totally incompatible.

Before this, and some time in 1764, the Assemblies of New York and Pennsylvania, had presented memorials to the King and Parliament, stating objections to the acts of the British government for raising revenues in the colonies, and asserting their sole right to impose taxes on their constituents. These last, though prior, in point of time, to the Virginia resolutions, were not so direct and explicit in the denial of the right claimed by the British ministry to tax the colonists; but, like the memorial of Massachusetts, in November, 1764, contained a remonstrance against such a measure; and stated, that, by their charter, and according to ancient usage, no taxes ought to be laid, or duties collected in the colonies without the consent of the Representatives of the people here. We believe, however, that the history of those times will abundantly shew, that the House of Representatives in Massachusetts was the most firm, systematic and persevering in its efforts for the repeal of these oppressive acts, in exciting a just sense of our rights and our dangers, and in rousing the spirit of the people generally to make a solemn, decisive stand, which involved the alternative of liberty or death.

In January, 1764, the Council and House of Representatives of Massachusetts wrote to their agent in England, respecting the sugar act, before mentioned, as follows: "There are certain acts of Parliament, which contain clauses extremely detrimental to the trade and fishery of this province, the ill influence of which is not confined thereto, but extends to Great Britain itself, particularly an act made in the 6th year of his late Majesty, entitled an act for the better securing and encouraging the trade of his Majesty's sugar colonies in America; whereby, among other

2

things, is imposed a duty of six pence per gallon on all molasses or syrups, and five shillings per hundred weight on all sugars of foreign produce imported into any of the plantations of America. This act was originally obtained, and has been continued by the great influence of the sugar colonies, in Parliament, without any prospect of revenue or rational advantage resulting from it. The case, however, is now altered. The ministry have adopted this act, and seem disposed to raise a revenue from it; for, in pursuance of orders from the lords of the treasury, the officers of the customs here have lately given public notice, that said act, in all its parts, will be carried fully into execution; the consequences of which will be ruinous to the trade of this province, hurtful to all the colonies, and greatly prejudicial to the mother country. The cod fishery in this province will be wholly broken up, the yearly amount of which is upwards of £164,000. The loss of the fishery will occasion more than five thousand seamen to be immediately turned out of employment, who, with most of our shipwrights and other mechanics, will be under a necessity of quitting the province, being utterly unfit for the business of husbandry; and after them it is easy to see that a considerable part of our other inhabitants will follow; so that we shall make a retrogradation in our condition, and become what we were a century ago, a poor colony of husbandmen, unable to make use of the manufactures of our mother country, and under the necessity of living within ourselves.

"With regard to Great Britain, a prohibition of our trade to the foreign plantations will lessen her own trade, and increase that of France, her rival and natural enemy."

"It had been suggested," they observed, "that the original design of the act laying a duty on sugar, molasses, &c. had been altered; and that it was intended, not as a prohibition or restraint on the trade of the colonies in these articles, but to raise a revenue; and that other measures for that purpose had been proposed—we cannot, therefore, help expressing our concern upon this occasion. We are empowered by our charter (and his Majesty's other colonies are empowered by the commissions under which they are governed,) to raise monies for the support of our government. *If duties or taxes are to be laid upon us in any one instance, what assurance have we that they will not be so multi-plied as to render this privilege of no importance to us ?* We have at all times done every thing which could be expected of us in support of his Majesty's government. We are still disposed to do every thing in our power ; and *hope it will be thought as rea-sonable, that the assemblies of the colonies should determine what monies should be raised upon the inhabitants here, as that the Parliament of Ireland should determine the monies to be raised upon the inhabitants there. The growth of the colonies depends upon the enjoyment of their liberties and privileges."*

The views and dispositions of the people of Massachusetts may be fully perceived by this statement. In their petition and me-morial in November following, they speak more explicitly, and remonstrate against the authority of Parliament to impose taxes on the colonies with more firmness and precision. This memo-rial, however, was penned with great temperance and caution, and contained expressions of unshaken loyalty and allegiance to the King. Governor Bernard, in his speech, at the next session of the General Court, complimented them for their great modera-tion.

The phraseology used in the preamble of the bills for raising and granting taxes in the General Court in Massachusetts, would seem to imply very clearly, that the power and right to tax the colonies and to raise monies from them, were exclusively in the houses of assemblies here. It was called a grant to his Majesty, for the use and service of the colony. In February, 1765, two acts passed, in which, by way of preamble, this language and phraseology are used; one for imposing duties on wines and dis-tilled spirits, and the other, a duty of impost and tonnage. And there was always a readiness thus to raise monies by the repre-sentatives of the people here, to pay the troops of the colonies which had been enlisted by requisition of the King, and to pay debts incurred for the common defence.

It was soon evident, however, that the ministry were resolved to raise a revenue from the colonies for the support of govern-ment ; though it was pretended it was necessary and should be

---

* The committee who prepared this letter were T. Hutchinson, J. Bowdoin, Judge Rus-sell, O. Thacher, and Mr. Tyler.

applied to pay the troops stationed on our frontiers for the defence of the colonists, and to lessen the debt already incurred for our protection. The ministry, indeed, appeared willing to compromise with the colonies, when they objected to the acts imposing duties ; and proposed, that the tax should be such as they themselves should desire, provided they raised the amount required of them. The reply of the Representatives of Massachusetts was, that by paying the debt incurred by the colony in prosecuting the late war, we should be taxed to a very great amount, and fully equal, considering our population and wealth, to the tax which the parent country would have to raise for the same purpose. They declared their unwillingness to add to the burdens of the people, and expressed the opinion, that it would be arbitrary and unconstitutional, as well as oppressive in the Parliament, to impose any other taxes.*

The stamp act was not passed at the session, when first proposed ; so that the people here had time to consider its nature and consequences. And with this in apprehension and under the operation of those before mentioned, a great excitement was produced in the public feelings, and an open and decided opposition was generally expressed against the authority of Parliament thus assumed to tax the colonies. This act was considered, indeed, as the prelude to still more oppressive and despotic measures. The people refused to purchase or use the stamps ; and the persons appointed to distribute them were, in some instances, treated with gross insult. Some riots ensued, which were very unjustifiable ; and which the most decided advocates for colonial privileges did not attempt to excuse. But it was pretended by the officers and friends of the British ministry, that the men of influence here did not exert their influence to punish the authors of these disturbances ; and representations were made to those in authority in England, that an armed force was necessary to preserve the peace of the province. In April, 1765, the mutiny bill

* Mr. Agent Jackson, in a letter to Governor B   \ard, February, 1765, says, "In the course of the debates in both Houses, on repealing the stamp act, it has appeared, that it never was the practice of England, to lay internal taxes on her dominions which were not represented ; or that, if this practice was ever varied from, it was always complained of, and the practice either dropped, or a representation called to sit in Parliament soon after."

was introduced into Parliament, under the pretence of rebellion in Massachusetts, and to justify the sending and stationing of regular troops in the colonies. It was soon discovered that several men high in office and power here, had given exaggerated statements of the views and conduct of the people; and that the acts complained of, as destructive of our freedom, had been adopted in consequence of such representations. This increased the excitement among the people, and the situation of the country became more critical and alarming. In general, however, popular tumult was restrained, and the fervor of the people, sometimes greatly augmented by the measures of the British ministry at home, or of their officers here, was limited and controled.

That no greater extravagancies were committed, at that period of popular excitement and commotion, must be attributed to the sober and moral character of the people in the colony; who, though enthusiastically attached to civil liberty, were habituated to obedience of all lawful authority, and readily acknowledged the necessity of maintaining the legitimate power of government.

They opposed the measures of the British ministry from principle. And their conduct was firm, consistent and persevering in attaining the object for which they contended. The struggle was perilous, but the issue was successful and glorious. It is unnecessary, however, to narrate in detail the measures adopted, and the events which occurred from this time to the period when a resort was had to force, and war actually commenced between the colonies and Great Britain. This statement, concise and imperfect as it is, it was believed might be useful, as introductory to a perusal of the papers now given to the public in this volume.

NOTE.

As the question, agitated at the period, for which this volume furnishes public documents, viz. the authority of Parliament to make laws for the colonies, was one which occasioned the great collision between England and this country, and was, indeed, the principal matter in controversy, it is thought proper to add here, the following notices, which the Editor has collected, since preparing the foregoing remarks.

In 1640, a motion was made to Governor Winthrop and his Council, to send some person to England, to solicit favors and privileges of Parliament. But they declined ; observing, " that, if they should put themselves under the protection of Parliament, they should be subject to all such laws as might be imposed on them ; in which, though their good might be intended, great injury might really be done them." Referring to this, Governor Trumbull remarks, " as at that early period, so it hath been ever since, that the colonies, so far from acknowledging the Parliament to have a right to make laws binding on them in all cases, have denied [or rather not acknowledged] it in any case." In June, 1661, the General Court adopted the following resolutions, viz. " We conceive the patent, under God, to be the first and main foundation of our civil polity, by a Governor and Company. The Governor, Deputy Governor, Assistants, and Representatives, have full power and authority, both legislative and executive, for the government of the people here, concerning both ecclesiastics and in civils, without appeals, excepting laws repugnant to the laws of England. We conceive any imposition, prejudicial to the country, contrary to any just laws of ours, not repugnant to the laws of England, to be an infringement of our rights. This government hath also power to set up all sorts of officers, as well superior as inferior, and point out their power and places."

Governor Endicott, in the name of the General Court, about the same period, supplicated King Charles II. " for his gracious protection of the people here, in the *continuance* of civil privileges and religious liberties, the enjoyment of which was the known end of suing for the patent confirmed upon this plantation by his royal father ;" and " if the King or Parliament should demand what those privileges are, which we desire the continuance of, (the committee of the General Court say to their agents,) your answer may be, all those which are granted us by patent, which we have hitherto enjoyed, without any other power imposed over us, or any other infringement of them, which would be destructive to the end of our coming hither; as also that no appeals may be permitted from hence in any case, civil or criminal, which would be an intolerable burden, and render authority and government vain and ineffectual." Sir W. Jones, Attorney General, told King James, " that he could no more grant a commission to levy money on his subjects in Jamaica, (though a conquered island,) without their consent, than they could discharge themselves from their allegiance to the English Crown." Even in 1766, the very year Parliament declared their right to impose taxes, and to make laws for the colonies in all cases, the Governor here was instructed (by the British ministry, in the name of the King) to " *recommend*" to the General Court to make compensation to those who suffered by the riots in August, 1765.

In 1757, when Lord Loudon, then first in military command in the colonies, directed that some British troops should be quartered in Boston, and called also upon this province for more troops, the General Court did not consider themselve *obliged* to comply merely on this requisition. But they debated the matter ; they claimed the right of deciding on the request. They even refused, for a time, to quarter the troops in the town of Boston, and they insisted that a law of the province was necessary to legalize any such requisition. " We conceive," they said, " that when his Majesty's forces are to be quartered in the province, an act of the Legislature is requisite to empower the civil magistrates to do it."—" We beg leave further to observe, that the inhabitants of this province are entitled to the natural rights of English born subjects ; that by the royal charter, the powers and privileges of civil government are granted to them ; that the enjoyment of these rights, powers and privileges, is their support under all burdens and pressures ; the loss or hazard of them will deject and dispirit them." The charter did not allow even the King's Governor to carry the inhabitants out of the province, without the consent of the General Court. In 1761, Secretary Oliver, by order of the General Court, wrote to Mr. Agent Bollan, in England, that the Legislature here considered they had a right by charter to pass a law, which should suspend even a former law, assented to and approved by his Majesty, (which was necessary as to some particular acts passed here) until his Majesty's pleasure was known; and he was directed to defend to the utmost, the General Court's power of legislation, in its full extent, according to the charter.

MASSACHUSETTS STATE PAPERS.

1765.......1775.

SPEECH

OF GOVERNOR BERNARD, TO THE COUNCIL AND HOUSE OF
REPRESENTATIVES, OCT. 18, 1764.

Gentlemen of the Council, and
  Gentlemen of the House of Representatives.

IN the last session I informed you of my determination to
avoid frequent sessions as much as possible ; and therefore I desired that you would not postpone any public business, that could
not conveniently wait till the winter ; it not being my intention
to have another session before that time, unless something unexpected and unforeseen should require it. And accordingly, you,
gentlemen of the House of Representatives, made such provisions
as you thought sufficient, for instructing your agent, and otherwise supporting your interest at Great Britain, under the present
exigencies ; which have not, that I know, been materially altered
since that time.

Nevertheless, as several gentlemen of both Houses have signified to me their apprehension that some further provisions are
still necessary, for the maintaining the territorial rights and commercial interests of this Province, by a proper representation of
the same, I have thought fit to call you together at this time, inconvenient indeed in regard to the season of the year, but timely
for the business for which you are assembled.

And now you are met, I shall leave you to your own deliberations : It may be thought, perhaps, that I am not impartial and
independent enough to be your counsellor ; but I am sure, I am
truly and heartily a friend to your real interest. As such, I shall
take upon me to recommend to you, at this time more than ever,

3

unity, prudence, and moderation : the first is necessary to give your resolutions due weight ; the next to direct them to proper purposes ; and the last to obtain for them a favorable hearing.

FRA. BERNARD.

Council Chamber, October 18, 1764.

—

ANSWER

OF THE COUNCIL AND HOUSE OF REPRESENTATIVES, TO THE FOREGOING SPEECH, NOVEMBER 3, 1764.

May it please your Excellency.

YOUR Excellency's speech to the two Houses, gives us great pleasure, as it furnishes us with an opportunity of expressing our sentiments to your Excellency on a matter of the last importance, not only to this Province in particular, but to the colonies in general.   What we refer to, and what your Excellency's speech refers to, is the late act of Parliament for granting certain duties in the British colonies and plantations in America; to which act we humbly apprehend we may propose our objections, at the same time we acknowledge it to be our duty to yield obedience to it while it continues unrepealed.   With your Excellency's leave we shall here just touch upon the principal grievances which we apprehend ourselves under by means of said act, and would humbly submit them to the consideration of our superiors at home.   The most material are these, that said act essentially affects the civil rights and commercial interests of the colonies ; and affecting these last, will proportionally affect the commercial interests of Great Britain. The civil rights of the colonies are affected by it, by their being deprived, in all cases of seizures, of that inestimable privilege and characteristic of English liberty, a trial by jury.   The courts of admiralty, at which such cases are triable, are constituted without juries ; and not only so, but interested in the event of the trial. In all condemnations, the judge and officers, according to the practice of that court, have a twentieth part of the whole value of the articles condemned ; but in case of acquittal are entitled only to customary fees, which, in many instances, bear but a small proportion to the amount of said twentieth.   The manifest tendency of which is, to produce decrees of condemnation, where there is no just cause of seizure ; though with respect to the present judge for this Province, we apprehend he is not to be biassed by such a motive.

In regard of the commercial interests of the colonies, they are affected in a double respect—by the method of procedure in cases of forfeiture, and by the duty laid on some of the enumerated articles. With respect to the first, all forfeitures and penalties inflicted by said act, or any other act of Parliament relating to the trade and revenues of the colonies, and incurred here, may, at the election of the informer or prosecutor, be prosecuted, either in any court of admiralty in the said colonies where the offence shall be committed, or in any court of vice admiralty which may be appointed over all America.

The last mentioned court has been appointed and now exists ; and all prosecutions referred to in the act may be brought to it.— In which case, the claimant, as some construe the act, may have five hundred leagues to travel in order to enter his claim ; it being very supposable that the prosecutor would lay him under all possible difficulties to prevent his claiming ; in which case he would be sure of a decree in his favor. And though the claimant should be put to the difficulty and expense of going that distance, he will not be permitted to enter his claim until sufficient security be first given by persons of known ability, in the penalty of a certain sum, to answer the costs and charges of prosecution. And in default of giving such security, the ship or goods shall be adjudged forfeited, and condemned. After all this difficulty and expence, (however unreasonably) brought upon him, if sentence shall be given for the claimer, and it shall appear to the judge that there was a probable cause for seizure, he shall certify that there was such probable cause ; and in that case, the defendant shall not be entitled to any costs of suit whatever; nor shall the persons seizing be liable to any action on account of such seizure. This being very obvious, the grievances which must follow, need no illustration ; and therefore we shall proceed to mention wherein the commercial interests of the colonies are affected by the duty and restraint laid on some of the enumerated articles. We shall instance in the fishery and lumber trade only. In respect of the first, it will be greatly diminished by means of the duty on foreign molasses. Our pickled fish wholly, and a great part of the cod fish, are fit only for the West India market. The British Islands cannot take off one third of the quantity caught ; the other two thirds must be lost, or sent to the foreign plantations, where molasses are given in exchange. The duty on this article will greatly diminish its importation hither ; and being the only article allowed to be given in exchange for our fish, a less quantity of the latter will of course be exported. The obvious effect of which must be the diminution of the fish trade, not only to the West Indies, but to Europe ; fish suitable for both those markets being the produce of the same voyage. If, therefore, one of these markets be shut, the other cannot be supplied. The loss of one is the loss of both, as the fishery must fail with the loss of either.

In respect to lumber, it is not to be sent to any part of Europe, excepting Great Britain. The hardship of this restraint appears the greater, as that article does not interfere with the produce of

Britain ; and the colonies have an ample fund of it to supply every demand, not exclusive of her own.

Now these duties, restraints and regulations, we humbly apprehend will greatly affect the commercial interests of our mother country. It is certain they will lessen the trade of the colonies, which is the source of their ability to pay for the British manufactures they consume. In the proportion that this source fails, the importation and consumption of those manufactures will lessen.*

The national debt is heavy, and we suppose the American act was intended to lighten it. But, without entering into the consideration of the propriety of such a measure, it is probable it will not answer that intention. The only certain effect of it will be, the diminution of the trade of the colonies, and a proportionable diminution of the trade of Great Britain. The circumstances of the colonies, however opulent they may be represented, will not admit of money being drawn from them by taxes or duties ; and this is demonstrably evident from this single fact, that the balance of their trade with Great Britain has perpetually been and still is against them. And all the bills of exchange, and silver and gold, which are the product of their other trade, are not sufficient to pay this balance. This we know and feel to be fact with regard to this Province. Whatever, therefore, is taken from us by way of tax, will occasion just so much deficiency in the payment of said balance, and eventually will be just so much loss to the trade of Britain.

This being the case, with the utmost deference to our superiors, we humbly apprehend it would be for the interest of our mother country, instead of drawing money from the colonists by taxes, to encourage their trade, and to let it expand as far as their genius and inclination could carry it, with this limitation only, that it should not interfere with her own produce and manufactures. The encouragement of their trade would enable the colonists, not only to pay their balances to Britain, but to take larger quantities of her manufactures ; the demand for which would be continually increasing with their growth, till it would equal the present capacity of Britain to supply.

Thus we have given your Excellency some observations on the act, and here and also in our memorial to the honorable House of Commons upon the subject of said act, and the proposed stamp duty, represented how the colonies, and Great Britain will probably be affected by them. What we have to request is, that your Excellency would please to lay these observations, and also a copy of said petition before his Majesty's ministers, and represent to them their grievances which we have mentioned arising from the said act, and such as we apprehend would be caused by a stamp duty ; and in the name of the two Houses earnestly to beseech the

---

* In the original draft, the idea was suggested, that the colonists would be obliged to manufacture for themselves, which would soon operate to the injury of the British manufactures.

favor of their influence to ease us of the burden of the first, and remove from us the apprehensions of the latter.

[Signed, A. Oliver, Secretary, and S. White, Speaker. The committee who reported it, were B. Lincoln, I. Erving, I. Bowdoin, T. Hubbard, and H. Gray, of the Council; Col. Clap, Col. Waldo, Capt. Saunders, Mr. Hall, Gen. Winslow, and Mr. Lee, of the House.]

PETITION

OF COUNCIL AND HOUSE OF REPRESENTATIVES, TO THE HONORABLE
HOUSE OF COMMONS, NOVEMBER 3, 1764.

To the Honorable the Commons
of Great Britain, in Parliament assembled.

THE petition of the Council and House of Representatives of his Majesty's Province of Massachusetts Bay,
Most humbly sheweth,

That the act, passed in the last session of Parliament, entitled "an act for granting certain duties in the British colonies and plantations in America," &c.* must necessarily bring many burdens upon the inhabitants of these colonies and plantations, which your petitioners conceive would not have been imposed, if a full representation of the state of the colonies had been made to your honorable House—

That the duties laid upon foreign sugars and molasses by a former act of Parliament, entitled "an act for the better securing and encouraging the trade of his Majesty's sugar colonies in America," if the act had been executed with rigor, must have had the effect of an absolute prohibition—

That the duties laid on those articles by the present act still remain so great, that, however otherwise intended, they must undoubtedly have the same effect—

That the importation of foreign molasses into this Province in particular, is of the greatest importance, and a prohibition will be prejudicial to many branches of its trade, and will lessen the consumption of the manufactures of Great Britain—

That this importance does not arise merely, nor principally, from the necessity of foreign molasses in order to its being consumed or distilled within the Province—

---

* In the 4th year of George III. an act of Parliament was passed, granting certain duties in the British colonies and plantations in America; and for continuing, amending and making perpetual, an act passed in the 6th year of George II. entitled "an act for the better securing and encouraging the trade of his Majesty's sugar colonies in America," &c. By this act, the former duties on sugars and molasses, imported into the British provinces, in America, from any plantation or colony not under the dominion of Great Britain, (which must be very strictly collected,) were continued and increased. The most rigid regulations were imposed for collecting the duties; and courts of admiralty, and of vice-admiralty, in any part of America, were to take cognizance of all actions on seizures, complaints, &c.

That if the trade, for many years carried on, for foreign molasses, can be no longer continued, a vent cannot be found for more than one half the fish of inferior quality which. are caught and cured by the inhabitants of the Province, the French not permitting fish to be carried by foreigners to any of their islands, unless it be bartered or exchanged for molasses—

That if there be no sale of fish of inferior quality, it will be impossible to continue the fishery ; the fish usually sent to Europe will then cost so dear, that the French will be able to undersell the English at all the European markets ; and by this means one of the most valuable returns to Great Britain will be utterly lost, and that great nursery of seamen destroyed—

That the restraints laid upon the exportation of timber, boards, staves and other lumber from the colonies to Ireland and other parts of Europe, except Great Britain, must greatly affect the trade of this Province, and discourage the clearing and improving of the lands which are yet uncultivated—

That the powers given by the late act to the court of vice admiralty, instituted over all America, are so expressed as to leave it doubtful, whether goods seized for illicit importation in any one of the colonies may not be removed, in order to trial, to any other colony, where the judge may reside, although at many hundred miles distance from the place of seizure—

That if this construction should be admitted, many persons, however legally their goods may have been imported, must lose their property, merely from an inability of following after it, and making that defence which they might do, if the trial had been in the colony where the goods were seized—

That this construction would be so much the more grievous, seeing that in America the officers, by this act, are indemnified in case of seizure, whenever the judge of admiralty shall certify that there was probable cause ; and the claimant can neither have costs nor maintain an action against the person seizing, how much soever he may have expended in defence of his property—

That the extension of the powers of courts of vice admiralty has, so far as the jurisdiction of the said courts hath been extended, deprived the colonies of one of the most valuable of English liberties, trials by juries—

That every act of Parliament, which in this respect distinguishes his Majesty's subjects in the colonies from their fellow subjects in Great Britain, must create a very sensible concern and grief—

That there have been communicated to your petitioners sundry resolutions of the House of Commons, in their last session, for imposing stamp duties or taxes upon the inhabitants of the colonies, the consideration whereof was referred to the next session—

That your petitioners acknowledge with all gratitude, the tendencies of the legislature of Great Britain of the liberties of the subjects in the colonies, who have always judged by their representatives both of the way and manner, in which internal taxes should be raised within their respective governments, and of the ability of the inhabitants to pay them—

That they humbly hope the colonies in general have so demeaned themselves, more especially during the late war, as still to deserve the continuance of all those liberties which they have hitherto enjoyed—

That although, during the war, the taxes upon the colonies were greater than they have been since the conclusion of it, yet the sources by which the inhabitants were enabled to pay their taxes, having ceased, and their trade being decayed, they are not so able to pay the taxes they are subjected to in time of peace, as they were the greater taxes in time of war—

That one principal difficulty, which has ever attended the trade of the colonies, proceeds from the scarcity of money, which scarcity is caused by the balance of trade with Great Britain, which has been continually against the colonies—

That the drawing sums of money from the colonies, from time to time, must distress the trade to that degree, that eventually Great Britain may lose more by the diminution of the consumption of her manufactures, than all the sums which it is possible for the colonies thus to pay can countervail—

That they humbly conceive, if the taxes which the inhabitants of this Province are obliged annually to pay towards the support of the internal government, the restraint they are under in their trade for the benefit of Great Britain, and the consumption thereby occasioned of British manufactures be all considered, and have their due weight, it must appear, that the subjects of this Province are as fully burdened as their fellow subjects in Britain, and that they are, whilst in America, more beneficial to the nation, than they would be if they should be removed to Britain, and there held to a full proportion of the national taxes and duties of every kind.

Your petitioners, therefore, most humbly pray, that they may be relieved from the burdens, which they have humbly represented to have been brought upon them by the late act of Parliament, as to the wisdom of the honorable House shall seem meet, that the privileges of the colonies relative to their internal taxes, which they have so long enjoyed, may still be continued to them, or that the consideration of such taxes on the colonies may be referred, until your petitioners, in conjunction with the other governments, can have opportunity to make a more full representation of the state and condition of the colonies and the interest of Great Britain with regard to them.

Signed by

S. WHITE, Speaker.
A. OLIVER, Secretary.

November 3, 1764.

[This petition was altered several times, after it was first read and adopted in the House of Representatives. The Council objected

to two or three sentences, some of which were omitted. There
was finally a committee of conference of the House of Representatives and of the Council; and the result was to retain the words
"rights" and "liberties" in several places, instead of "privileges,"
which had been substituted by the Council. The committee were
J. Otis, jr. O. Thacher, and Col. Clap, of the House; T. Hutchinson, J. Otis, and E. Trowbridge, of the Council.]

*Extract of a letter from the Committee of Council and House of
Representatives, to their Agent in England, accompanying the
foregoing petition.*

In their letter to Agent Mauduit, accompanying this petition,
the committee of the Council and House of Representatives, observe, "that the late act of Parliament," imposing additional duties on molasses, &c. imported into the colonies, "affects this colony more than any other:" and they say, "that they have been
induced thus to petition and remonstrate," respecting said act, and
the bill for duties on stamp paper, &c. then pending before Parliament, in consequence of a suggestion made by the agent and another
gentleman in England, "that a decent remonstrance might procure
some relief." And in their petition they say, "we have endeavored to avoid giving offence, and have touched upon our rights in
such a manner, as that no inference can be drawn, that we have given them up, on the one hand, nor that we set up in opposition to
the Parliament, nor deny that we are bound to the observance of
acts of Parliament, on the other. But in a letter to you, we may
be more explicit on this point—a right, the people of the colonies
have undoubtedly by charter and commissions to tax themselves.
So far as the Parliament shall lay taxes on the colonies, so far they
will deprive them of this right. If the first settlers of the colonies
had not imagined that they were as secure of the enjoyment of this
right as of their titles to their lands, in all probability they would
never have left England, and no one colony could have been settled."

" Acts of Parliament, it will be said, are above charters, and
can annihilate them. It is true. So one act of Parliament may
infringe upon them. And, perhaps, there would be no greater
reason for complaint in that case, than when the rights of a corporation in England, or in the colonies are infringed : to be sure
not greater, than when what are deemed the fundamentals of the
English constitution are changed, with respect to any considerable
part of the subjects. Such fundamentals, we deem the right of
being taxed by our own representatives only ; and the rights to
trials by juries. Upon the latter, we have said the less in our petition, because, by the charter, the power of appointing courts of
admiralty, where no juries are in use, and which are the only occasions of our complaints upon that head, is reserved to the Crown.
But then it must be remembered, that all seizures for illicit trade

are tried in the exchequer in England by juries; and that we have no reason to suppose, that our ancestors, when they accepted the charter, imagined the powers of courts of admiralty would be extended beyond what they are in England—and as for the newly constituted court of admiralty, if the judge takes cognizance of all maritime matters and all offences which have been usually tried by courts of admiralty in America, and which may arise in any part of the colonies, it may bring such oppression upon the subjects as will be insupportable."

" In point of equity, we think we may well claim an exemption from taxes by Parliament. Our ancestors, and we believe the first settlers of every colony, except Nova Scotia and Georgia, occasioned but little, some of them, no expense, and yet have brought an amazing addition of wealth, territory and subjects, to the nation. They are burdened with the support of government within themselves : they are under restraints in their trade, which the subjects of Great Britain are not ; and what the colonies lose by that, Britain gains. The colonies find more employment for the manufactures in Britain, we believe, than all the world besides. And this is a matter which is not to be lightly considered." " In point of policy, it will certainly prove a mistake to lay further burdens on the colonies. You have now all we can spare from our necessary support, and the expense of clearing and cultivating a new country, and by this means increasing the dominions of Britain. In this way, the people pay to you cheerfully. In the other, it will ever be paid with grief and reluctance." " We are morally certain, that the molasses trade cannot be carried on, and the present duty paid."

[The committee to draft the letter, were T. Hutchinson and I. Bowdoin, of the Council ; J. Otis, O. Thacher, and T. Gray, of the House.]

Extracts from the statement of the services and expenses of the Province of Massachusetts, made by a Committee of the Council and House of Representatives, chosen for the purpose in October, 1764, and sent to the colony's agent in England, to furnish arguments why the colony should not be taxed, &c.

" One great cause alleged for imposing taxes on the colonies, not granted by their own representatives, by the mere authority of Parliament, being this, that they ought to contribute to defray the charges of a war undertaken for their defence, to which it is said they have never yet sufficiently contributed, the Province of Massachusetts Bay deem it proper briefly to set forth their own merits and services, their exertions and expenses in the common cause from the first incorporation to the present time.

" In the year 1620, the colony of New-Plymouth, now included in the present Province of Massachusetts Bay, was began to be

4

planted by Gov. Bradford and others, a small but vigorous number.
By their prudence and vigilance they supported themselves in a wild
desart, surrounded by Indians, without any assistance from the
Crown of Great Britain.

" In 1629, the colony of Massachusetts Bay was begun to be
planted, the adventurers having obtained from Charles I. an ample
charter, on the faith of which they made those beginnings in colo-
nizing, which have increased to this day, though the charter has
long since been lost to them.

" Whoever should read the records of the first settlements in
the colony cannot but pity a feeble number separated by an immense ocean from the capital of their government, surrounded by
savages, of whose good will they had no assurance, conflicting
with hunger, cold, nakedness, and every other hardship of a desart.

" Their first cares, under all their privations and sufferings, were
to train the inhabitants to arms, to build forts, &c.

" In 1635, Gov. Winslow offered to raise troops at the expense
of the colonies, under authority from the King of England, not
only to defend the settlements here against the Indians, French
and Dutch, but to extend the territory of the British government
in America. But the proposal was rejected through the influence
of Arch Bishop Laud, who hated the puritans of that period.

" In 1637, at their own expense the colonies raised one hundred
and sixty men, and subdued the Peguots, a powerful and dangerous tribe of Indians.

" In 1643, the colonies of Massachusetts, Plymouth, Connecticut
and New-Haven united for common defence; and thus probably
prevented the overthrow of the settlements of Connecticut and
New-Haven, if not of the others also.

" From 1675 to 1686, the colony of Massachusetts Bay, with
short intermissions, was engaged in wars with the Indians, who, at
that period, were numerous and powerful, and threatened to destroy all the English settlements : and for which they asked no assistance of the Crown, but bore the heavy load themselves.

" In 1690, this Province raised 800 men for the reduction of Nova
Scotia, under Sir W. Phips, who conquered the country, and subjected it to the English till the peace of Reswick.

" From this time to 1714, the colony was frequently engaged,
at their own charge, in wars against the French, for the defence of
English plantations, and for rescuing various places which had fallen
into the hands of those enemies of Great Britain. In 1744, the
Province also furnished a large number of men to assist the English
against the French in Nova Scotia.

" Afterwards, during the campaigns of 1755, 56, 58, 59, 60, &c.
the Province raised troops, at a very great expense, to co-operate
with the British in their expeditions against Crown Point, &c. The
whole cost of their expeditions from 1755 to 1762, was 943,839*l.*
The cost of scouting parties, for the same period, was 27,496*l.*

Their armed vessels for the protection of trade, cost 34,795*l.* All which amount to 1,039,390*l.* And these sums being much greater than could be raised on the people each year, the Province was annually obliged to take up large sums on interest, and often to anticipate and mortgage the revenues of the government. At the conclusion of the late war, the Province was and still is very much in debt; and it will take them many years, with all the resources in their power, even though their trade was allowed to continue on the footing it was at the close of the war, to clear their debts.

" The cost of many forts and garrisons on the frontiers is not included in the above sum. Nor can any estimate be made of the cost to individuals by the demand for personal service. For the numbers raised in these years, (from 1755 to 1762) being equal to the whole militia, it hath come to the turn of every enlisted soldier in the whole militia to serve once. And they who would not serve in person were obliged to hire, at a great premium.

" From small beginnings, through innumerable toils, hardships and sufferings, a rude desart is become a well-peopled and fruitful plantation. From its infancy to the present age, this colony, with no expense to the Crown, has defended the territory granted to it; and thereby mightily extended the British empire and immensely increased the British commerce. It has ever been ready to afford its utmost help, when the King's service called; has actually made divers valuable conquests for the Crown; and by its great exertions and expenses in the last war has impoverishsd and enfeebled itself so as it will not in many years recover the athletic state it was in at the beginning of the late French war.

" It is not intended, by any thing here said, to derogate from the merits of the other colonies; most of them have had their share in these great conquests; and without the joint and united vigor of so many, so much could never have been accomplished. Nor does Massachusetts desire to be distinguished from the other colonies by any new grants and immunities; neither are they seeking any further rewards. They desire only, that the privileges their ancestors purchased so dearly, and they have never forfeited, may be continued to them. Being conscious to themselves of entire loyalty to his most excellent Majesty, and dutiful respects to the parent state, they trust the wisdom and justice of the nation will allow them the possession of all the rights, privileges and immunities which the subjects of Great Britain do and ought to enjoy.

[The committee was appointed to make this statement, in Oct. 1764; and were T. Hutchinson, A. Oliver, J. Bowdoin, T. Flucker and J. Otis, of the Council; and T. Cushing, O. Thacher, T. Gray and E. Sheafe, of the House. In their letter sent to the agent enclosing it, the committee observe, " it will appear from the statement, that this Province has had its full share of the burdens of the British empire; and that, by its own representatives, it has ever cheerfully submitted to the heaviest taxes it was any how capable of bearing. The Province finds itself greatly exhausted by their exertions ; and it will be with the utmost difficulty we shall clear the heavy load of debt the last war has involved us in, though no new burdens were brought upon us, and our trade were left to its natural course. But if the severe regulations of the late act are continued and new taxes laid on us, these will drain us of our specie, the sinews of trade, and otherwise so distress us, that we shall neither be able to pay the public debt we owe as a community, nor individuals what they owe to the merchants of Great Britain ; a general bankruptcy, public and private, must ensue."]

====

SPEECH

OF GOVERNOR BERNARD, TO THE COUNCIL AND HOUSE OF REPRESENTATIVES, JANUARY 10, 1765.

Gentlemen of the Council, and
Gentlemen of the House of Representatives,

At the opening of this session, I have the pleasure to congratulate you upon the storms which threatened the peace of Great Britain being happily blown over: the hasty and ill advised encroachments upon our rights by some of the French and Spanish commanders have been disavowed by their respective courts ; and fresh assurances have been given that the acquisitions confirmed to us by the late peace, shall be enjoyed without interruption ; which will be further secured by the best of guarantees, a respectable British navy.

I have also to congratulate you upon the happy termination of the Indian war, in a manner both honorable and safe ; and which must effectually discourage such attempts for the future. We, who are at a distance from the scenes of action, should not be indifferent to this interesting event, as the welfare, and particularly the peace of every part of British America, is the concern of the whole.

I have, in pursuance of your request made to me last session, recommended to the favor of his Majesty's ministers, the petition which you prepared to be presented to the House of Commons ; and I flatter myself that these representations will have success, as they must receive great weight from the dutiful manner in which they are formed. I shall not neglect any other opportunity to promote the real welfare of this Province, consistently with its subordination to the King of Great Britain, and the common interest of the whole empire.

I have at present nothing to lay before you, but what arises within the Province, which I shall communicate to you at proper times.

In these, and in all other matters, I shall not doubt your attention to your duty, both to your King and to your country. The late exemplary instances of your unanimity, prudence, and moderation, in times of difficulty and distrust, will distinguish you to your advantage, will confirm the reputation you have hitherto acquired, and give assurance of your resolution to support it by your future conduct.   FRA. BERNARD.

Council Chamber, January 10, 1765.

ANSWER

OF THE COUNCIL AND HOUSE OF REPRESENTATIVES, TO THE FOREGOING SPEECH:

May it please your Excellency,

WITH great pleasure we received your Excellency's congratulations; and sincerely rejoice in every occurrence that tends to establish the peace and prosperity of Great Britain. The disavowal of the late encroachments upon our rights, and the fresh assurances given by the French and Spanish courts, that the acquisitions confirmed to us by the late peace shall be enjoyed without interruption, we hope are sincere; but the best guarantee of those acquisitions is the British navy, which we hope will ever be maintained on so respectable a footing, and be under such direction as to frustrate all attempts to invade them.

The happy termination of the Indian war, in which so many of our fellow-subjects have been massacred, and so extensive a frontier desolated, must give sincere joy to every breast susceptible of the feelings of humanity; at least to every one that bears any affection for British America. We in this Province in particular, though at a distance from the late scenes of cruelty, cannot be indifferent to this interesting event, having often experienced the severest effects of Indian rage. May this peace prove an honorable and lasting one.

We are much obliged to your Excellency for recommending to the favor of the ministry our petition to the House of Commons. We flatter ourselves the representations therein made, will have success, not only from the dutiful manner in which they are formed, but from the necessary connection there is between the interest of the nation, and the success of that petition; it will be a demonstrable truth, that the national interest will be best promoted and secured by encouraging the trade of the colonies. If that prospers or declines, so will the trade of Great Britain; but in a greater proportion. The wealth and power of Britain, however great, are still in their minority compared with what, it is probable, they will one day be, if the trade and growth of her colonies are not impeded.

We are also much obliged to your Excellency for your kind declaration, that you " shall not neglect any other opportunity to promote the real welfare of this Province, consistently with its subordination to the kingdom of Great Britain, and the common interest of the whole empire." It is in your Excellency's endeavors to promote the real welfare of this Province ; and in these endeavors our inclinations conspire with our duty to give your Excellency our best assistance.

In all matters your Excellency shall lay before us, we hope to make it evident that we are influenced by a principle of affection as well as duty to our sovereign and country. It is our honor to be in their employment, and we shall esteem it our happiness to render them any real service.

If we have exhibited any exemplary instances of unanimity, prudence and moderation, it gives us a real satisfaction that they meet with your Excellency's approbation.

We agree with your Excellency that the times are difficult : but we hope they are not times of distrust. We distrust not the wisdom and goodness of Parliament, having with the colonies in general, often experienced the happy effects of both. On the same wisdom and goodness, next to the Supreme, we still rely. As that respectable body has power, we humbly trust their wisdom and goodness will exert it, to remove the embarrassments upon our trade, to which the difficulty of the times is owing.

═══

Letter from J. Mauduit, Esq. agent in England, for the Province of Massachusetts, to the Secretary. London, Feb. 9, 1765.

I HAVE now to acquaint the great and General Court, that a stamp duty was proposed in the House of Commons, on the 6th instant. It was opened, by shewing, that as the colonies have a right to protection, so the Parliament has a right to tax them in aid thereof. Their several charters were referred to, and declared to be all under the control of Parliament. To this right of Parliament, every member who approved the measure, declared his assent ; so that the only question was, whether a stamp duty should now be laid ; and this was carried, on a decision of fourteen. Petitions from Virginia and New-York, were offered, by their agents to be presented, but no member would take them : and Mr. Jackson, who had ours in his pocket, agreeably to what he and I had settled, plainly saw it was, at that time, fittest to remain there. At present, I can only say, that I am taking every rational measure I can think of, to support your petition, which is to be presented to the House on Tuesday, by Mr. Jackson, and is the day appointed for the first reading of the bills.

Letter from Mr. Agent Mauduit, to the Committee of the House of Representatives of Massachusetts. London, Feb. 19, 1765.

I RECEIVED your several letters of Nov. 27th and 28th, and Dec. 17th, to all of which I shall attend as my infirmities will permit. At present I have to acquaint you, that I have employed my whole time in favor of your petition; and to remove impressions and dislike to the humors and disposition of the Province. A week before the stamp duty was to be proposed, I sent a pamphlet (I had prepared,) to the houses of most of the members. I plainly saw, some time ago, that right, founded in charters or custom, could not be supported by any one in the House, against the right of Parliament to tax the colonies. I therefore endeavored, (though I never gave up that point) to soften the hands of power, and prevent a resentment shown, as was first intended : and so far hitherto I have succeeded.

Mr. Grenville opened the fitness of laying this tax on the colonies, and the incontestible right of Parliament to do it, without noticing the New-York address, or the House of Assembly's letter to me ; both which papers were tacked together, and intended to be laid before the House, as proof of an undutiful temper. Only one member, in the warmth of his speech, glanced at it ; but in this he had no second. After about seven hours debate, there was no other question, (nor indeed could be) but whether a stamp duty should now be laid. The House divided upon it, and it was carried by four to one.

I hope the interest of Parliament, for imposing this tax, was only to convince the colonies that it had the right, which was by them contested ; and that the House will now rather attend to mitigate or take off some of those burdens laid on your trade by the last act. Several petitions were offered, but were all rejected ; and even Connecticut, which was more moderate than ours, with respect to the stamp duty, received the negative. Ours was offered last, by Mr. Jackson, but mentioned in such a manner, that no vote of rejection was put, so that I may possibly present a petition at another time, leaving out only what relates to the stamp duty : and this I think to do by Mr. Jackson, in concert with all the aid I can procure.

Letter from Secretary Oliver, to Mr. Agent Jackson, written by order of the General Court, June, 1765.

BY several of the papers, directed to be delivered you by Mr. Mauduit, the late agent, you will observe the opinion of the two Houses with regard to some of the probable ill effects of the last year's act of Parliament for granting certain duties in the colonies, and some of them with respect to trade have been already verified, as will appear by the petitions and statements of Messrs. Patrick Tracy, Thomas Boylston and Fortesque Vernon, merchants, within this Province. In consequence of said act, three vessels, belonging to them severally, have been seized and condemned—with respect to which matter, they in their petitions in general declare, that their vessels sailed hence before said act took place, viz. before Sept. last ; that no bond was required of them at the respective custom houses, at which their vessels were cleared out ; and that said act did not then require any bond ; that said vessels proceeded to the French islands, and loaded with molasses ; that on their return they were forced by stress of weather, two of them into New-Providence, and the other into Bermuda ; that these were the first English ports which Tracy's and Boylston's vessels had put in at, after sailing hence ; that Wm. Vernon's vessel had only touched at Barbadoes, and sailed again before the 29th of Sept. ; that at Providence and Bermuda said vessels were seized, and with their cargoes, by the court of admiralty finally adjudged and condemned forfeited for a want of certificates that bonds had been given pursuant to said act ; that the vessels and cargoes were appraised at a rate much below their value, with a view (they say) that in case they should be able to reverse the decree, they should notwithstanding recover a small part of the value of their vessels and cargoes. This is a brief state of the representation they make, as you will see by their petitions. If this representation be just, their case is really hard, and merits the notice of those who have power to relieve them.

====

SPEECH

OF GOVERNOR BERNARD, TO THE TWO HOUSES, MAY 30, 1765.

Gentlemen of the Council, and
   Gentlemen of the House of Representatives,

BEING always desirous of making your attendance at the General Court as agreeable to you as may be, I thought it proper to appoint the meeting of it at this town, that you may be free, not only from real danger, but also from the apprehension of it. And as I have nothing to propose to you for his Majesty's immediate service, your deliberations will be chiefly employed upon the affairs of your own Province.

Among these, the state of the eastern country deserves most particular regard : the augmentation of the garrisons made at the last session was a seasonable provision, and happily has not been too late. But defence alone is not sufficient ; prevention of hostilities is equally necessary to the preservation of that country. To this I have given particular attention with all my power, and have hitherto succeeded. But it has served to convince me that there still remains much undone, which I have not had the power, or at least have not chose to take upon me to do.

You shall be made acquainted with my sentiments upon this subject, which are partly drawn from information received from others, and partly from observations made by myself. And I doubt not but you will concur with me in every measure necessary for the security and support of that country, which is now, as it were, an infant colony. We who rest in the bosom of safety should not neglect the protection of our brethren exposed to daily perils ; nor while we enjoy the blessings of an old colony, be unmindful of the imbecility and necessities of a new one.

Gentlemen,

As I suppose the season of the year will make you desirous of a recess as soon as well may be, it is my intention not to continue this session beyond what the present exigencies of the government shall absolutely require : And therefore I must recommend to you to postpone unnecessary business, and to expedite such as cannot be postponed. In this, as in all matters tending to the service of the Province and to your convenience, you may depend upon my assistance and concurrence.

FRA. BERNARD.

Council Chamber, at Concord, May 31, 1764.

[This speech was printed through the inadvertence of a compositor in the office ; and was not intended by the editor to be printed at all.]

———

SPEECH

OF GOVERNOR BERNARD, TO THE COUNCIL AND HOUSE OF
REPRESENTATIVES, MAY 30, 1765.

Gentlemen of the Council, and
Gentlemen of the House of Representatives,

At the opening of this General Court, I have no orders from his Majesty to communicate to you ; nor any thing to offer myself but what relates to your internal policy : I shall therefore take this opportunity to point out such domestic business as more immediately deserves your attention.

Soon after my arrival to this government, I formed in my mind an idea of three improvements which this country was capable of making profitable to itself and convenient to Great Britain : I mean pot ash, hemp, and the carrying lumber to the British markets. They are all proper staples for New England ; and must be very acceptable to Great Britain, as she is at present supplied with them from foreigners, by a losing trade.

5

I have already had the pleasure to see the first of these established with effect, and wanting now nothing but care to preserve its credit, and prevent the general quality of the goods, which is of a superior kind, being rendered doubtful and suspicious by the fraudulent practices of particulars. This is a necessary caution at the commencement of a new trade; for upon its first reputation depends its future success. There is already a law for the regulation of this trade; but it wants to be carried into execution: this I must desire may be done this session, as it is now become immediately wanting.

You have lately given a public testimony of your desire to promote the production of hemp: I am equally persuaded of your good intentions to the improvement of the lumber trade; as you must be sensible of the insufficiency of the present markets for the reception of the great quantity of lumber which is now produced, and which will be continually increasing. The Parliament of Great Britain has already given encouragement to the one; and it is hoped it will also extend its bounty to the other.

These are proper objects of your concern; works which naturally arise in your own country, strengthen your connection with Great Britain, may easily be confined within yourselves, and will soon be superior to those of foreign rivals. When these are added to your other resources, they will form a fund, which, with the blessing of God upon your industry and frugality, will be adequate to the expense of all necessary imports: and you will have no occasion, as you have hitherto shewn no disposition, vainly to attempt to transfer manufactories from their settled abode; an undertaking at all times difficult, but, under the disadvantage of high priced labor, impracticable.

Gentlemen of the House of Representatives,

I shall order the treasurer to lay before you the present state of the treasury, that you may consider of further means for reducing and finally discharging the provincial debt with ease to the people. I shall be ready to concur with you in all necessary measures for that purpose, that shall be agreeable to the laws and instructions by which I must form my conduct.

Gentlemen,

The general settlement of the American Provinces, which has been long ago proposed, and now probably will be prosecuted to its utmost completion, must necessarily produce some regulations, which, from their novelty only, will appear disagreeable. But I am convinced, and doubt not but experience will confirm it, that they will operate, as they are designed, for the benefit and advantage of the colonies. In the mean time a respectful submission to the decrees of the Parliament, is their interest, as well as their duty.

In an empire, extended and diversified as that of Great Britain, there must be a supreme legislature, to which all other powers must

be subordinate. It is our happiness that our supreme legislature, the Parliament of Great Britain, is the sanctuary of liberty and justice; and that the Prince, who presides over it, realizes the idea of a patriot King. Surely, then, we should submit our opinions to the determinations of so august a body; and acquiesce in a perfect confidence, that the rights of the members of the British empire will ever be safe in the hands of the conservators of the liberty of the whole.   FRA. BERNARD.
    Council Chamber, May 30, 1765.

[Committees were appointed to consider that part of the Governor's speech, respecting pot ash, the manufacture of hemp, and lumber. But the journal furnishes no evidence that any reply was made to that part of the speech, which referred to the state of the Province, though Mr. White, (the Speaker,) J. Otis, T. Cushing, S. Dexter, and Col. Worthington, were chosen a committee to consider it.]

Proceedings of the House of Representatives, respecting sending a Committee to New York, to consult with Committees from other colonies, on the state of the country, June 6, 1765.

THE House taking into consideration the many difficulties to which the colonies are and must be reduced by the operation of some late acts of Parliament; after some time spent,
    On a motion made and seconded, ordered that Mr. Speaker, Brigadier Ruggles, Col. Partridge, Col. Worthington, Gen. Winslow, Mr. Otis, Mr. Cushing, Col. Saltonstall, and Capt. Sheafe, be a committee to consider what measures had best be taken, and make report.
    The committee appointed for that purpose, reported as follows. The committee appointed to consider what dutiful, loyal, and humble address may be proper to make to our gracious Sovereign and his Parliament, in relation to the several acts passed, for levying duties and taxes on the colonies, have attended that service, and are humbly of opinion :
    That it is highly expedient there should be a meeting as soon as may be, of committees from the Houses of Representatives or Burgesses in the several colonies on this continent, to consult together on the present circumstances of the colonies, and the difficulties to which they are and must be reduced by the operation of the late acts of Parliament for levying duties and taxes on the colonies, and to consider of a general and humble address to his Majesty and the Parliament to implore relief.
    And the committee are further of opinion that a meeting of such committees should be held at New York, on the first Tuesday of

October next, and that a committee of three persons be chosen by this House on the part of this Province, to attend the same.

And that letters be forthwith prepared and transmitted to the respective Speakers of the several Houses of Representatives or Burgesses in the colonies aforesaid, advising them of the resolution of this House thereon, and inviting such Houses of Representatives or Burgesses to join this with their committees, in the meeting, and for the purposes aforesaid.

And that a proper letter be prepared and forwarded to the agent of the Province on these matters in the mean time.

Read and accepted, and ordered, that Mr. Speaker, Mr. Otis, and Mr. Lee, be a committee to prepare a draft of letters to be sent to the respective Speakers of the several Houses of Representatives in the colonies, and make report.

The committee appointed for that purpose, reported the following draft.

Province of Massachusetts Bay.   *Boston, June 8, 1765.*

Sir—The House of Representatives of this Province in the present session of the General Court, have unanimously agreed to propose a meeting, as soon as may be, of committees from the Houses of Representatives or Burgesses, of the several British colonies on this continent, to consult together on the present circumstances of the colonies, and the difficulties to which they are and must be reduced by the operation of the acts of Parliament for levying duties and taxes on the colonies ; and to consider of a general and united, dutiful and humble representation of their condition to his Majesty and the Parliament, to implore relief. The House of Representatives of this Province have also voted to propose that such meeting be at the city of New York, on the first Tuesday of October next, and have appointed a committee of three of their members to attend that service, with such as the other Houses of Representatives or Burgesses in the several colonies may think fit to appoint to meet them : And the committee of the House of Representatives of this Province are directed to repair to said New York, on said first Tuesday of October next, accordingly. If, therefore, your honorable House should agree to this proposal, it would be acceptable, that as early notice of it as possible might be transmitted to the Speaker of the House of Representatives of this Province.

SAMUEL WHITE, Speaker.

[The Committee was chosen by the House, June, 1765, and were James Otis, Col. Partridge, of Hatfield, and Timothy Ruggles ; but Ruggles did not consent to the doings of the convention, which met at New York, in Oct. 1765 ; and was afterwards censured for it by the House of Representatives.]

PETITION

*Of the freeholders and other inhabitants of the Massachusetts Bay,
Rhode Island, and Providence Plantations, New Jersey, Pennsyl-
vania, the government of the counties of New Castle, Kent and
Sussex, upon Delaware, Province of Maryland, &c.*

MOST HUMBLY SHEWETH,

THAT the inhabitants of these colonies, unanimously devoted
with the warmest sentiments of duty and affection to your Majesty's sacred person and government, inviolably attached to the
present happy establishment of the protestant succession in your
illustrious house, and deeply sensible of your royal attention to
their prosperity and happiness, humbly beg leave to approach the
throne by representing to your Majesty, that these colonies were
originally planted by subjects of the British Crown, who, animated
with the spirit of liberty, encouraged by your Majesty's royal predecessors, and confiding in the public faith for the enjoyment of
all the rights and liberties essential to freedom, emigrated from
their native country to this continent, and by their successful perseverance in the midst of innumerable dangers and difficulties, together with a profusion of their blood and treasure, have happily
added these vast and valuable dominions to the empire of Great
Britain.

That for the enjoyment of these rights and liberties several governments were early formed in the said colonies, with full power
of legislation agreeably to the principles of the English constitution.

That under those governments these liberties thus vested in
their ancestors and transmitted to their posterity, have been exercised and enjoyed, and by the inestimable blessings thereof, under
the favor of Almighty God, the inhospitable deserts of America
have been converted into flourishing countries ; science, humanity
and the knowledge of divine truth, diffused through remote regions
of ignorance, infidelity and barbarism, the number of British subjects wonderfully increased, and the wealth and power of Great
Britain proportionably augmented.

That by means of these settlements, and the unparalleled suc
cess of your Majesty's arms, a foundation is now laid for rendering the British empire the most extensive and powerful of any recorded in history ; our connection with this empire, we esteem
our greatest happiness and security, and humbly conceive it may
now be so established by your royal wisdom, as to endure to the latest
period of time. This with most humble submission to your Majesty, we apprehend will be most effectually accomplished, by fixing
the pillars thereof, on liberty and justice, and securing the inherent
rights and liberties of your subjects here, upon the principles of
the English constitution. To this constitution these two principles
are essential, the right of your faithful subjects freely to grant to

your Majesty such aids as are required for the support of your government over them, and other public exigencies, and trials by their peers. By the one they are secured from unreasonable impositions, and by the other, from arbitrary decisions of the executive power. The continuance of these liberties, to the inhabitants of America, we ardently implore, as absolutely necessary to unite the several parts of your widely extended dominions, in that harmony so essential to the preservation and happiness of the whole. Protected in these liberties, the emoluments Great Britain receive from us, however great at present, are inconsiderable, compared with those she has the fairest prospect of acquiring. By this protection, she will for ever secure to herself the advantage of conveying to all Europe the merchandizes which America furnishes; and of supplying, through the same channel, whatever is wanted from thence. Here opens a boundless source of wealth and naval strength; yet these advantages, by the abridgment of those invaluable rights and liberties, by which our growth has been nourished, are in danger of being forever lost, and our subordinate legislatures, in effect, rendered useless by the late acts of Parliament, imposing duties and taxes on the colonies, and extending the jurisdiction of the courts of admiralty here, beyond its ancient limits; statutes by which your Majesty's Commons, in Britain, undertake absolutely to dispose of the property of their fellow subjects, in America, without their consent; and for the enforcing whereof, they are subjected to the determination of a single judge, in a court unrestrained by the wise rules of the common law; the birthright of Englishmen, and the safeguard of their persons and property.

The invaluable rights of taxing ourselves, and of trial by our Peers, of which we implore your Majesty's protection, are not, we humbly conceive, unconstitutional, but confirmed by the great charter of English liberty. On the first of these rights, the honorable the House of Commons found their practice of originating money bills, a right enjoyed by the kingdom of Ireland, by the clergy of England, until relinquished by themselves; a right, in fine, which all other, your Majesty's English subjects, both within and without the realm, have hitherto enjoyed.

With hearts, therefore, impressed with the most indelible characters of gratitude to your Majesty, and to the memory of the kings of your illustrious house, whose reigns have been signally distinguished by their auspicious influence on the prosperity of the British dominions; and convinced, by the most affecting proofs of your Majesty's paternal love to all your people, however distant, and your increasing and benevolent desires to promote their happiness, we most humbly beseech your Majesty, that you will be graciously pleased to take into your royal consideration, the distresses of your faithful subjects, on this continent; and to lay the same before your Majesty's Parliament; and to afford them such relief, as in your royal wisdom their unhappy circumstances shall be judged to require.

And your petitioners, as in duty bound, will pray, &c.

Signed,

JAMES OTIS, OLIVER PARTRIDGE,	*Commissioners from Massachusetts Bay.*
HENRY WARD, METCALF BOWLER,	*Commissioners from Rhode Island.*
HENDRICK FISHER, JOSEPH BORDEN,	*Commissioners from New Jersey.*
JOHN MORTON, GEORGE BRYAN,	*Commissioners from Pennsylvania.*
CÆSAR RODNEY, THOMAS M'KEAN,	*Commissioners from Delaware.*
WILLIAM MURDOCK, EDWARD TILGMAN, THOMAS RINGGOLD,	*Commissioners from Maryland.*

[A similar petition was addressed to each House of Parliament; but containing no new arguments, nor advancing any new principles, it is thought unnecessary to publish them.]

====

SPEECH

OF GOVERNOR BERNARD, TO THE COUNCIL AND HOUSE OF
REPRESENTATIVES, SEPT. 25, 1765.

Gentlemen of the Council, and
Gentlemen of the House of Representatives,

I HAVE called you together at this unusual time, in pursuance of the unanimous advice of a very full Council, that you may take into consideration the present state of the Province, and determine what is to be done at this difficult and dangerous conjuncture. I need not recount to you the violences which have been committed in this town, nor the declarations which have been made and still subsist, that the act of Parliament for granting stamp duties in the British colonies shall not be executed within this Province. The ordinary executive authority of this government is much too weak to contradict such declarations, or oppose the force by which they are supported. It has therefore been found necessary to call the whole legislative power in aid of the executive government. From this time this arduous business will be put into your hands, and it will become a provincial concern.

Upon this occasion it is my duty to state to you what will probably be the consequences, if you should suffer a confirmed disobedience of this act of Parliament to take place. I am sensible how dangerous it is to speak out at this time, and upon this subject; but my station will not allow me to be awed or restrained in what I have to say to the General Court. Not only my duty to the King, but my duty to the Province, my love of it, my concern for it, oblige me to be plain and explicit upon this occasion. And I hope no advocate for liberty will violate that essential and constitutional right, freedom of speech in General Assembly.

As I desire not to dictate to you, and would avoid all appearances of doing it, I shall resolve what I have to recommend to your consideration into mere questions, and avoid assertions of my own in matters which are doubtful. I shall not enter into any disquisition of the policy of the act. It has never been a part of my business to form any judgment of it; and as I have not hitherto had any opportunity to express my sentiments of it, I shall not do it now. I have only to say, that it is an act of the Parliament of Great Britain, and as such ought to be obeyed by the subjects of Great Britain. And I trust that the supremacy of that Parliament over all the members of their wide and diffused empire, never was and never will be denied within these walls.

The right of the Parliament of Great Britain to make laws for the American colonies, however it has been controverted in America, remains indisputable at Westminster. If it is yet to be made a question, who shall determine it but the Parliament? If the Parliament declares that this right is inherent in them, are they like to acquiesce in an open and forcible opposition to the exercise of it? Will they not more probably maintain such right, and support their own authority? Is it in the will or in the power, or for the interest of this Province to oppose such authority? If such opposition should be made, may it not bring on a contest which may prove the most detrimental and ruinous event which could happen to this people?

It is said that the gentlemen who opposed this act in the House of Commons, did not dispute the authority of Parliament to make such a law, but argued from the inexpediency of it at this time, and the inability of the colonies to bear such an imposition. These are two distinct questions, which may receive different answers. The power of the Parliament to tax the colonies may be admitted, and yet the expediency of exercising that power at such a time, and in such a manner, may be denied. But if the questions are blended together so as to admit of but one answer, the affirmation of the right of Parliament will conclude for the expediency of the act. Consider, therefore, gentlemen, if you found your application for relief upon denying the Parliament's right to make such a law, whether you will not take from your friends and advocates the use of those arguments which are most like to procure the relief you desire?

You, gentlemen of the House of Representatives, have proposed a Congress of committees from the representatives of the several colonies, to consider of a general, united, dutiful, loyal and humble representation to his Majesty and the Parliament. Are the late proceedings consistent with the dutiful, loyal and humble representation which you have proposed ? Will the denying the power and authority of the King and Parliament, be the proper means to obtain their favor ? If the Parliament should be disposed to repeal this act ; will they probably do it whilst there subsists a forcible opposition to the execution of it ?. Is it not more probable that they will require a submission to their authority, as a preliminary to their granting you any relief ? Consider then, whether the opposition to the execution of the act, has not a direct tendency to defeat the measures you have taken to procure a repeal of it, if you do not interpose to prevent it.

By this act, all papers which are not duly stamped, are to be null and void ; and all persons who shall sign, engross or write any such papers, will forfeit for each fact ten pounds. If therefore, stamps are not to be used, all public offices must be shut up ; for it cannot be expected that any officer should incur penalties much beyond all he is worth, for the sake of doing what will be null and void when it is done. I would therefore desire you to consider what effects the stopping two kinds of offices only, the courts of justice and the custom houses, will have upon the generality of the people. When the courts of justice are shut up, no one will be able to sue for a debt due to him, or an injury done him. Must not then all credit and mutual faith cease of course, and fraud and rapine take their place ? Will any one's person or property be safe, when their sole protector of the law is disabled to act ? Must not the hand of violence be then let loose, and force of arms become the only governing power ? Is it easy to form an adequate idea of a state of general outlawry ? And may not the reality exceed the worst idea you can form of it.

If trade and navigation shall cease by the shutting up the ports of this province for want of legal clearances, are you sure that all other ports which can rival these, will be shut up also ? Can you depend upon recovering your trade again entire and undiminished, when you shall be pleased to resume it ? Can the people of this province subsist without navigation for any long time ? What will become of the seamen who will be put out of employment ? What will become of the tradesmen who immediately depend upon navigation for their daily bread ? Will these people endure want quietly without troubling their neighbors ? What will become of the numberless families which depend upon fishery ? Will they be able to turn the produce of their year's work into the necessaries of life, without navigation ? Are there not numberless other families who do not appear immediately concerned in trade, and yet ultimately depend upon it ? Do you think it pos-

6

sible to provide for the infinite chain of the dependents upon trade who will be brought to want by the stopping it ? Is it certain that this province has a stock of provisions within itself sufficient for all its inhabitants without the usual imports ? If there should be a sufficiency in general, can it be distributed among all the individuals without great violence and confusion ? In short, can this province bear a cessation of law and justice, and of trade and navigation, at a time when the business of the year is to be wound up, and the severe season is hastily approaching ? These are serious and alarming questions, which deserve a cool and dispassionate consideration.

I would not willingly aggravate the dangers which are before you ; I do not think it very easy to do it : this province seems to me to be upon the brink of a precipice ; and that it depends upon you to prevent its falling. Possibly I may fear more for you than you do for yourselves ; but in the situation you now stand, a sight of your danger is necessary to your preservation ; and it is my business to open it to you. But I do not pretend to enumerate all the evils which may possibly happen ; several, and some of no little importance will occur to you, though they have been omitted by me. In a word, gentlemen, never were your judgment and prudence so put to a trial, as they are like to be upon the present occasion.

I am aware that endeavors have been or may be used to lessen my credit with you, which I have hitherto always studied to improve to the advantage of the province. Violences seldom come alone : the same spirit which pulls down houses attacks reputations. The best men in the province have been much injured in this way : I myself have not escaped this malignity. But I shall not lower myself so as to answer such accusers : to you I shall always owe such explanations as shall be necessary to the improvement of a good understanding between us. However, I will take this opportunity to declare publicly, that ever since I have set in this chair, I have been constantly attentive to the true interests of this province, according to the best of my understanding, and have endeavored to promote them by all means in my power. The welfare of this people is still uppermost in my heart ; and I believe no man feels more for them than I do at this present time.

Gentlemen of the House of Representatives,

I must recommend to you to do an act of justice, which at the same time will reflect credit on yourselves : I mean to order a compensation to be made to the sufferers by the late disturbances. Their losses are too great for them to sit down with ; one of them amounts to a very large sum. You must be sensible that it will be expected that the damages be made good ; and it will be better for you to do it of your own accord before any requisition is made to you. An estimate of these damages is made by a committee of the Council pursuant to order, which will be laid before you.

Gentlemen,

I am sensible of the difficulty of the part you have to act ; it may not be sufficient for you to be convinced of the necessity of a submission to the law for the present, unless the same conviction shall be extended to the people in general. If this should be so, I can only desire you to use all means to make yourselves well acquainted with the exigencies of the present time ; and if you shall be persuaded that a disobedience of the act is productive of much more evil than a submission to it can be ; you must endeavor to convince your constituents of the truth of such persuasion. In such case I shall readily grant you a recess for a sufficient time, and I shall be ready to concur with you in all other legal measures to provide for the safety of the people in the best manner.

FRA. BERNARD.

Council Chamber, September 25, 1765.

[It may be proper to observe here, that a riot took place in Boston, in August, 1765, in which the custom house officers were insulted and threatened, and some of their property destroyed.]

ANSWER

OF THE HOUSE OF REPRESENTATIVES, TO THE GOVERNOR'S SPEECH,
OCTOBER 23, 1765.

May it please your Excellency,

THE House of Representatives have entered into a due consideration of your speech to both houses at the opening of this session ; and should have earlier communicated to your Excellency our sentiments thereupon, had not the late sudden and unexpected adjournment prevented it.

We must confess, that after your Excellency had called us together in pursuance of the unanimous advice of a very full Council, we were in hopes you would have given the assembly time then to have considered the critical state of the province, and determined what was proper to be done at so difficult and dangerous a conjuncture.

Your Excellency tells us, that the province seems to be upon the brink of a precipice ! A sight of its danger is then necessary for its preservation. To despair of the commonwealth, is a certain presage of its fall. Your Excellency may be assured, that the representatives of the people are awake to a sense of its danger, and their utmost prudence will not be wanting to prevent its ruin.

We indeed could not have thought that a weakness in the executive power of the province had been any part of our danger, had not your Excellency made such a declaration in your speech. Certainly the General Assembly have done every thing incumbent on them ; and laws are already in being for the support of his Majesty's authority in the province. Your Excellency doth not point out to us any defect in those laws ; and yet you are pleased to say, that the executive authority is much too weak. Surely you cannot mean, by calling the whole legislative, in aid of the executive authority, that any new and extraordinary kind of power should by law be constituted, to oppose such acts of violence as your Excellency may apprehend from a people ever remarkable for their loyalty and good order ; though at present uneasy and discontented. If, then, the laws of the province for the preservation of his Majesty's peace are already sufficient, your Excellency, we are very sure, need not to be told, to whose department it solely belongs to appoint a suitable number of magistrates to put those laws in execution, or remove them in case of failure of their duty herein. And we hope this important trust will remain with safety to the province, where the constitution has lodged it.

Your Excellency is pleased to tell us, that declarations have been made and still subsist, that the act of Parliament for granting stamp duties in the colonies, shall not be executed within this province. We know of no such declarations. If any individuals of the people have declared an unwillingness to subject themselves to the payment of the stamp duties, and choose rather to lay aside all business than make use of the stamped papers, as we are not accountable for such declarations, so neither can we see any thing criminal in them. This House has no authority to control their choice in this matter ; the act does not oblige them to make use of the papers ; it only exacts the payment of certain duties for such papers as they may incline to use. Such declarations may possibly have been made, and may still subsist, very consistently with the utmost respect to the King and Parliament.

Your Excellency has thought proper to enumerate very minutely the inconveniencies that may arise from the stamped papers not being distributed among the people ; with respect to some of which your love and concern for the province leads you to fear more for us than we do for ourselves. We cannot think your Excellency would willingly aggravate our dangers ; we are not in particular so alarmed, as your Excellency seems to be, with the apprehension of the hand of violence being let loose. Your Excellency, upon recollection, will find that all papers relative to crown matters are exempt from stamps. The persons of his Majesty's good subjects will still remain secure from injury. That spirit which your Excellency tells us attacks reputations and pulls down houses, will yet be curbed by the law. The estates of the people will remain guarded from theft or open violence. There will be no danger of force of arms becoming the only governing power. Nor shall we realize what your Excellency is pleased to call a state of general outlawry. This we think necessary to be observed, without a particular consideration of ll the consequences which your Excellency fears, to prevent, if possible, any wrong impressions from fixing in the minds of ill disposed persons, or remove them if already fixed.

You are pleased to say, that the stamp act is an act of Parliament, and as such ought to be observed. This House, sir, has too great a reverence for the supreme legislature of the nation, to question its just authority: It by no means appertains to us to presume to adjust the boundaries of the power of Parliament; but boundaries there undoubtedly are. We hope we may without offence, put your Excellency in mind of that most grevious sentence of excommunication, solemnly denounced by the church, in the name of the sacred trinity, in the presence of King Henry the Third, and the estates of the realm, against all those who should make statutes, or observe them, being made contrary to the liberties of the Magna Charta. We are ready to think that those zealous advocates for the constitution usually compared their acts of Parliament with Magna Charta; and if it ever happened that such acts were made as infringed upon the rights of that charter, they were always repealed. We have the same confidence in the rectitude of the present Parliament; and therefore cannot but be surprized at an intimation in your speech, that they will require a submission to an act as a preliminary to their granting relief from the unconstitutional burdens of it; which we apprehend includes a suggestion in it far from your Excellency's design, and supposes such a wanton exercise of mere arbitrary power, as ought never to be surmised of the patrons of liberty and justice.

Furthermore, your Excellency tells us that the right of the Parliament to make laws for the American colonies remains indisputable in Westminster. Without contending this point, we beg leave just to observe that the charter of the province invests the General Assembly with the power of making laws for its internal government and taxation; and that this charter has never yet been forfeited. The Parliament has a right to make all laws within the limits of their own constitution; they claim no more. Your Excellency will acknowledge that there are certain original inherent rights belonging to the people, which the Parliament itself cannot divest them of, consistent with their own constitution: among these is the right of representation in the same body which exercises the power of taxation. There is a necessity that the subjects of America should exercise this power within themselves, otherwise they can have no share in that most essential right, for they are not represented in Parliament, and indeed we think it impracticable. Your Excellency's assertion leads us to think that you are of a different mind with regard to this very material point, and that you suppose we are represented; but the sense of the nation itself seems always to have been otherwise. The right of the colonies to make their own laws and tax themselves has been never, that we know of, questioned ; but has be in constantly recognized by the King and Parliament. The very supposition that the Parliament, though the supreme power over the subjects of Britain universally, should yet conceive of a despotic power within themselves, would be most disrespectful ; and we leave it to your Excellency's consideration, whether to suppose an indisputable right in any government, to tax the subjects without their consent, does not include the idea of such a power.

May it please your Excellency,

Our duty to the King, who holds the rights of all his subjects sacred as his own prerogative ; and our love to our constituents and concern for their dearest interests, constrain us to be explicit upon this very important occasion. We beg that your Excellency would consider the people of this province as having the strongest affection for his Majesty, under whose happy government they have felt all the blessings of liberty : They have a warm sense of honor, freedom and independence of the subjects of a patriot King : they have a just value for those inestimable rights which are derived to all men from nature, and are happily interwoven in the British constitution : They esteem it sacrilege for them ever to give them up ; and rather than lose them, they would willingly part with every thing else.   We deeply regret it, that the Parliament has seen fit to pass such an act as the stamp act : we flatter ourselves that the hardships of it will shortly appear to them in such a point of light as shall induce them in their wisdom to repeal it : In the mean time we must beg your Excellency to excuse us from doing any thing to assist in the execution of it : Were we, in order to avoid assertions, to resolve what we have to say on this head into mere questions, we should with all humility ask, whether it would be possible for us to add any weight to an act of that most august body the Parliament ? whether it would not be construed as arrogance and presumption in us to attempt it ? whether your Excellency can reasonably expect that the House of Representatives should be active in bringing a grievous burden upon their constituents ? Such a conduct in us would be to oppose the sentiments of the people whom we represent, and the declared instruction of most of them.   They complain that some of the most essential rights of Magna Charta, to which as British subjects they have an undoubted claim, are injured by it : that it wholly cancels the very conditions upon which our ancestors settled this country, and enlarged his Majesty's dominions, with much toil and blood, and at their sole expense : that it is totally subversive of the happiest frame of subordinate, civil government, expressed in our charter, which amply secures to the Crown our allegiance, to the nation our connection, and to ourselves the indefeasible rights of Britons : that it tends to destroy that mutual confidence and affection, as well as that equality which ought ever to subsist among all his Majesty's subjects in his wide and extended empire : that it may be made use of as a precedent for their fellow subjects in Britain for the future, to demand of them what part of their estates they shall think proper, and the whole if they please : that it invests a single judge of the admiralty, with a power to try and determine their property in controversies arising from internal concerns, without a jury, contrary to the very expression of Magna Charta ; that no freeman shall be amerced, but by the oath of good and lawful men of the vicinage : that it even puts it in the power of an informer to carry a supposed offender more than two thousand miles for trial ; and what is the worst of all evils, if his Majesty's American subjects are not to be governed, according to the known stated rules of the constitution, as those in Britain are, it is greatly to be feared that their minds may in time become disaffected ; which we cannot even entertain the most distant thought of without the greatest abhorrence. We are truly sorry that your Excellency has never made it a part of your business to form any judgment of this act ; especially as you have long known what uneasiness the most distant prospect of it gave to his Majesty's good subjects in America, and of this province, of which you are substituted to be the head and father. Had your Excellency thought it proper to have seasonably entered into a disquisition of the policy of it, you would, we doubt not, have seen that the people's fears were not without good foundation ; and the love and concern which you profess to have for them, as well as your duty to his Majesty, whose faithful subjects they are, might have been the most powerful motives to your Excellency to have expressed your sentiments of it early enough to those whose influence brought it into being.

We cannot help expressing our great uneasiness, that after mentioning some violences committed in the town of Boston, your Excellency should ask this House, whether such proceedings are consistent with the dutiful, humble and loyal representations which we propose should be made. We are sure your Excellency will not expressly charge us with encouraging the late disturbances ; and yet to our unspeakable surprise and astonishment, we cannot but see, that by fair implication it may be argued from the manner of expression, that an odium was intended to be thrown on the province. We inherit from our ancestors the highest relish for civil liberty ; but we hope never to see the time when it shall be expedient to countenance any methods for its preservation but such as are legal and regular. When our sacred rights are infringed, we feel the grievance, but we understand the nature of our happy constitution too well, and entertain too high an opinion of the virtue and justice of the supreme legislature, to encourage any means of redressing it, but what are justifiable by the constitution. We must therefore consider it as unkind for your Excellency to cast such a reflection on a province whose unshaken loyalty and indissoluble attachment to his Majesty's most sacred person and government was never before called in question, and we hope in God never will again. We should rather have thought your Excellency would have expressed your satisfaction in presiding over so loyal a people, who in that part of the government where the violences were committed, before there was time for them to be supported by the arm of civil power, and even while the supreme magistrate was absent, by their own motion raised a spirit and diffused it through all ranks, successfully to interpose and put a stop to such dangerous proceedings.

Your Excellency is pleased to recommend a compensation to be made to the sufferers by the late disturbances. We highly disapprove of the acts of violence which have been committed ; yet till we are convinced that to comply with what your Excellency recommends, will not tend to encourage such outrages in time to come, and till some good reason can be assigned why the losses those gentlemen have sustained should be made good, rather than any damage which other persons, on any other different occasions, might happen to suffer, we are persuaded we shall not see our way clear to order such a compensation to be made. We are greatly at a loss to know who has any right to require this of us, if we should differ from your Excellency in point of its being an act of justice, which concerns the credit of the government. We cannot conceive why it should be called an act of justice, rather than generosity, unless your Excellency supposes a crime committed by a few individuals, chargeable upon a whole community.

We are very sorry that your Excellency should think it needful to intimate that any endeavors have been, and may be used, to lessen your credit with this House. Your Excellency cannot but be sensible that when the popular pulse beats high for privileges, it is no unusual thing for a clamor to be raised against gentlemen of character and eminence. We can assure you that our judgment of men, especially those in high stations, is always founded upon our experience and observation. While your Excellency is pleased to make your duty to our most gracious Sovereign, and a tender regard to the interest of his subjects of this province, the rule of your administration, you may rely upon the readiest assistance that this house shall be able to afford you. And you will have our best wishes that you may have wisdom to strike out such a path of conduct, as, while it secures to you the smiles of your Royal Master, will at the same time conciliate the love of a free and loyal people.

[The Session in September lasted only three days; and the Court met again October 21. The answer was prepared by S. White, (the speaker,) T. Cushing, S. Dexter, J. Lee, Capt. Sheaffe, Gen. Winslow, T. Gray, and Mr. Foster, of Plymouth.]

MESSAGE

OF GOVERNOR BERNARD, TO THE TWO HOUSES, RESPECTING
STAMPS, SEPTEMBER 26, 1765.

Gentlemen of the Council, and
 Gentlemen of the House of Representatives,

A. SHIP is arrived in this harbor with stamped papers on board
for the King's use in this province ; and also with other papers
for the like use in the province of New Hampshire and colony of
Rhode Island.

As Mr. Oliver has declined the office. of distributor of stamped
papers, and cannot safely meddle with what are arrived, the care
of them devolves to this government, as having a general charge of
the King's interest within it.

I have. already laid this matter before the Council, and they have
referred it to the General Court. I therefore now apply to you,
jointly, to desire your advice and assistance, in order to preserve
the stamped papers designed for this government, being the King's
property of 'very considerable value, safe and secure for his Majesty's further orders.

I must also desire you at the same time to consider of the like
preservation of the stamped papers designed for New Hampshire
and Rhode Island, if the distributors appointed for those governments should decline taking charge of them, as in such case the
care of them will devolve to this government equally with the others.

FRA. BERNARD.

Council Chamber, September 25, 1765.

——

ANSWER

OF THE TWO HOUSES, TO THE FOREGOING MESSAGE,
SEPTEMBER 26, 1765.

May it please your Excellency,

THE House having given all due attention to your Excellency's
message of this day, beg leave to acquaint your Excellency, that
as the stamped papers, mentioned in your message, are brought
here without any directions to this government, it is the sense of
the House that it may prove of ill consequence for them any ways
to interest themselves in this matter. We hope, therefore, your
Excellency will excuse us if we cannot see our way clear to give
you any advice or assistance herein.

7

Resolutions of the House of Representatives, expressive of their sense of the rights of the colonies, October 25, 1765.

1. *Resolved,* That there are certain essential rights of the British constitution of government, which are founded in the law of God and nature, and are the common rights of mankind; Therefore,

2. *Resolved,* That the inhabitants of this province are unalienably entitled to those essential rights, in common with all men; and that no law of society can, consistent with the law of God and nature, divest them of those rights.

3. *Resolved,* That no man can justly take the property of another, without his consent; and that upon this original principle, the right of representation in the same body which exercises the power of making laws for levying taxes, which is one of the main pillars of the British constitution, is evidently founded.

4. *Resolved,* That this inherent right, together with all other essential rights, liberties, privileges, and immunities of the people of Great Britain, have been fully confirmed to them by Magna Charta, and by former and later acts of Parliament.

5. *Resolved,* That his Majesty's subjects, in America, are, in reason and common sense, entitled to the same extent of liberty with his Majesty's subjects in Britain.

6. *Resolved,* That by the declaration of the royal charter of this province, the inhabitants are entitled to all the rights, liberties, and immunities of free and natural subjects of Great Britain, to all intents, purposes and constructions whatever.

7. *Resolved,* That the inhabitants of this province appear to be entitled to all the rights aforementioned, by an act of Parliament, 13th of George II.

8. *Resolved,* That those rights do belong to the inhabitants of this province, upon principles of common justice: their ancestors having settled this country at their sole expense, and their posterity having constantly approved themselves most loyal and faithful subjects of Great Britain.

9. *Resolved,* That every individual in the colonies is as advantageous to Great Britain, as if he was in Great Britain, and held to pay his full proportion of taxes there. And as the inhabitants of this province pay their full proportion of taxes, for the support of his Majesty's government here, it is unreasonable for them to be called upon to pay any part of the charges of the government there.

10. *Resolved,* That the inhabitants of this province are not, and never have been, represented in the Parliament of Great Britain; and that such a representation there, as the subjects in Britain do actually and rightfully enjoy, is impracticable for the subjects in America. And further, that in the opinion of this House, the several subordinate powers of legislation, in America, were constituted upon the apprehensions of this impracticability.

11. *Resolved,* That the only method, whereby the constitutional rights of the subjects can be secure, consistent with a subordination to the supreme power of Great Britain, is by the continued exercise of such powers of government as are granted in the royal charter, and a firm adherence to the privileges of the same.

12. *Resolved,* As a just conclusion from some of the foregoing resolves, that all acts, made by any power whatever, other than the General Assembly of this province, imposing taxes on the inhabitants, are infringements of our inherent and unalienable rights, as men and British subjects; and render void the most valuable declarations of our charter.

13. *Resolved,* That the extension of the powers of the court of admiralty within this province, is a most violent infraction of the right of trials by juries: A right which this House, upon the principles of their British ancestors, hold most dear and sacred; it being the only security of the lives, liberties, and properties of his Majesty's subjects here.

14. *Resolved,* That this House owe the strictest allegiance to his most sacred Majesty King George the Third; that they have the greatest veneration for the Parliament; and that they will, after the example of all their predecessors, from the settlement of this country, exert themselves to their utmost, in supporting his Majesty's authority in the province; in promoting the true happiness of his subjects; and in enlarging the extent of his dominion.

Ordered, That all the foregoing resolves be kept in the records of this House; that a just sense of liberty, and the firm sentiments of loyalty may be transmitted to posterity.

[These resolutions passed unanimously; and the committee who reported them, were S. White, (the Speaker,) Cushing, Adams, Dexter, Bowers, Sheaffe, Witt, Saunders, and Humphrey.]

[The following communications between the House of Representatives and the Council, will shew how tenacious the former were of their rights.]

MESSAGE

FROM THE HOUSE OF REPRESENTATIVES TO THE COUNCIL, ON THE SUBJECT OF DRAWING MONEY FROM THE TREASURY BY THE GOVERNOR AND COUNCIL, WITHOUT CONSENT OF THE HOUSE; NOVEMBER, 6, 1765.

In the House of Representatives, Resolved, that the following Remonstrance be sent up to his Majesty's Council.

May it please your Honors,

AT a time when all this continent are groaning under the burden of taxes necessarily laid on them, by their own Representatives, to discharge the arrearages incurred by the late war; at a time when they are justly complaining that very heavy additional taxes, external and internal, have been imposed on them by the British Parliament, without their consent, and in which they neither are nor can be represented; at a time when the establishment of Castle William was kept up to the same number of men that his Excellency required in the height of the war, besides four independent companies, excused from all other military duty but that of defending that fortress: At such a time, it is to the last degree astonishing to this House, that the Governor and Council should go about to make an additional establishment of a new company there; and that the sum of £116,17 has been actually drawn out of the treasury, for that purpose, by a warrant from the Governor and Council. There is no principle of the British constitution more clearly and firmly established, than that impositions, neither in time of war, or other the greatest necessity or occasion that may be, much less in the time of peace, neither upon foreign or inland commodities of what nation soever, be they never so superfluous or unnecessary, neither upon merchants, strangers, or denizens, may be laid by the King's absolute power, without the assent of Parliament, be it for never so short a time. If the Governor and Council have a right, in any case, to raise and pay one company, they may raise ten or an hundred; and at their pleasure subject this people to be governed by a standing army. We, therefore, in duty to ourselves, our constituents, and to posterity, declare the said procedure to be an high infraction of the rights of this House, with whom the originating and granting all taxes on the freeholders and inhabitants of this province, is indubitably and constitutionally lodged. We are the more alarmed at this extraordinary step in the Governor and Council, as, besides that it implies a very injurious distrust of the independent companies assigned for the more immediate defence of Castle William; a similar instance of misapplying the public monies in relation to fitting out a sloop of war, was not long since remonstrated against.

We earnestly beseech your honors that no measures of this kind be taken for the future, and that you would be pleased to order that the said sum be replaced in the treasury for the public service.

[A remonstrance conceived in the same terms with the above, mutatis mutandis, was presented to the Governor.]

MESSAGE

FROM THE COUNCIL TO THE HOUSE OF REPRESENTATIVES, IN ANSWER
TO THE ABOVE, NOVEMBER 7, 1765.

In Council, Resolved unanimously, that the following Message be sent to the House of Representatives.

Gentlemen of the House of Representatives,

AT a time when union of councils and unity of measures are so necessary to the welfare and peace of the community, the Board are very sorry that any thing should take place to interrupt the harmony which ought to subsist between the several branches of the legislature.

The Board agree with the honorable House that no principle of the British constitution is more clearly and firmly established, than that no impositions upon foreign or inland commodities. or upon merchants, strangers or denizens, may be laid by the King's absolute power, without assent of Parliament. And the Board apprehend, that they have not, either in their separate capacity, or in conjunction with the Governor, acted inconsistently with that principle.

It seems necessary to the well being of society, that there should be subsisting within it a power at all times ready to provide against sudden and unexpected emergencies, that by an immediate exertion a positive good may be produced, or a threatened evil prevented. If the General Court could be always sitting, that power would always reside therein ; but when this cannot be the case, it would argue great defect in the constitution, to suppose such a power not to exist ; and if it exists at all, it must be in the Governor and Council. From the very nature of government, which is formed for the good of the people, it seems necessary that the Governor and Council, in cases of emergency, should have a power (when the General Court cannot be sitting) to provide for the good of the people. And such a power is deducible from the province charter, which declares, " that the Governor, with the Assistants or Counsellors, or seven of them at the least, shall and may, from time to time, hold and keep a Council for the ordering and directing of the affairs of the Parliament." And the same power is implied in the oath, which each Counsellor is by law obliged to take, upon his admission to the Board, viz. " that he will, to the best of his judgment, at all times, freely give his advice to the Governor for the good encouragement of the public affairs of this government." The Board, however, are by no means fond of exercising such a power ; and wish the occasions for it had never arisen, and may never arise again. And in justice to themselves, they must declare, that they are not chargeable with making wanton use of any power entrusted with them.

What the honorable House mention as exceptional in their conduct, the Board came into with great reluctance. The minds of
the people were so agitated at that time about the stamps, that it
was generally apprehended that if they were not lodged in some
place of security, they would be infallibly destroyed ; in which
case the province might have been answerable at least for the
amount of them.   Upon this reason, without being more particular,
the conduct of the Board stands.   It did not proceed from any affection for the stamps, to which they have as great an aversion as
the honorable House ; nor from a disposition to put the province
to a needless expense ; for as soon as they judged it might be done
with propriety, they unanimously advised, " that his Excellency
give orders to stop any further enlistment, and to discharge the
men already enlisted as soon as may be ;" which his Excellency
accordingly did.

The Board are embarked in the same bottom with the honorable
House—we must both sink or swim together ; and any expense or
injury to the province is suffered proportionally by both. The
Board are therefore led by interest as well as principle, to prevent
the one, if unnecessary, and to ward off the other ; and in what
they did, they thought they were doing what their duty required
of them ; the using means to prevent an injury happening to the
province, or to prevent the people in the warmth of their temper
from hurting themselves.   The Board may have misjudged in this
matter, they pretend not to be infallible.   This, however, they can
say, they have been actuated by upright principles ; and so far
was it from their intention to make a high infraction, or any infraction at all on the rights of the honorable House (with whom they
are fully sensible all taxes should constitutionally originate) that
their sole aim was the prevention of an evil to the province.   And
the Board think it their duty, at this time, to declare, that when the
government is more immediately devolved on the Governor and
Council, they ought not to leave the Commonwealth at hazard, so
long as any endeavors of their's consistent with the Constitution
can avail to preserve it.

In the House of Representatives, November 8, 1765 : Resolved,
that the following Message be sent to the Honorable Board, in reply to their answer of yesterday.

Mr. President,

THE answer of the Honorable Board to the remonstrance of
the House, gives us very sensible concern, as it contains, not only
a justification of the measure complained of ; but is, in effect, a
declaration of the Honorable Board, that, in the recess of the Gen-

eral Court, all the powers of government are devolved on and vested in the Governor and Council, at their discretion to be exercised and executed. As the legislative power of Great Britain is by the constitution lodged in the King, Lords and Commons, so the subordinate provincial legislative power is here lodged in the Governor, Council and House of Representatives ; and it would be quite as constitutional to assert, that in the recess of Parliament, the Supreme Legislative of Great Britain is devolved on his Majesty and the House of Lords, or the Privy Council, as to affirm, that in the recess of the General Court, all the powers of the Legislature here are devolved on the Governor and Council. It seems to be conceded by the Honorable Board, that if the General Assembly had been sitting, the Governor and Council could not have rightly taken the measures complained of. This is a concession, that it was properly a legislative act. And will the Honorable Board assert, that the Governor and Council are a complete Legislature, in the recess of the General Court, while it is manifest they have no such distinct power when the General Court is sitting ? Many have been the attempts to make the people of England easy under taxes, imposition and the levies of troops without any parliamentary establishment, but in vain. The nation could never be brought to so visible an infraction of their native right of giving and granting only such part and proportion of their property to the public service as they might think fit.

The clause in the province charter, recited by the Honorable Board in their answer, can, by the rules of good construction, only relate to the executive powers lodged by the said charter in the Governor and Council, ever subject to the just limitation and control of the fundamental principles and laws of the constitution. The capital of these is, that, under no color or pretext whatever, can the subject be directly or indirectly taxed, but by his own consent, in person, or by his representative. There can be no necessity for so strange an exertion of power and prerogative in the Governor and Council in any emergency that may happen in the recess of the General Court, as very great military powers are by charter lodged in the Governor, who with advice of his Council may ever proclaim the law martial. But should that be done, the *pay* of the army would depend on the legislative power ; and all grants for that purpose must originate with the representatives of the people. There is nothing more certain than that the Governor and Council of this province, in the recess of the General Court, can rightfully claim only executive powers ; and as they represent the Supreme Executive in Great Britain, we would cheerfully admit, that so far as is necessary for the good of the whole, they may, in cases of urgent necessity exercise the just prerogatives of the Crown, which are, by royal charter, devolved upon them. And, both there and here, as the legislative and executive powers are in different hands, the good of society, for obvious reasons, requires that several things should be left to the discretion of him or them, who have the executive power. But this hinders not but that the prerogative should in certain instances be expressly limited and bounded. All who are acquainted with the laws and constitution of Great Britain, very well know that the prerogative there is thus limited, and that since the revolution there have been no successful attempts to leap the bounds firmly fixed at that glorious era. One of those bounds was the appropriation of the several branches of the revenue granted by the Commons, which are in no case to be broken in upon. When any extraordinary exigency takes place, it is to be provided for as well as may be ; and that in confidence of the Parliament ; and the first opportunity is taken to lay the matter before the Commons. Have we ever had even a compliment of this kind ? If the Sheriff cannot in any case raise the posse comitatus, or if the standing militia answer not the ends of their institution, and in consequence thereof it becomes needful to raise new levies, the House should be called upon for their approbation, at least ex post facto ; but we have not heard a syllable to this purpose. We entertain no doubt of the uprightness and good intentions of the Honorable Board, but have only to desire them seriously to consider what the people of this province will have left them worthy the great name of freedom, if it should be conceded that an unlimited power is devolved on and lodged with the Governor and Council in the recess of the General Court, which recess, with or without the advice of the Council, may, at the pleasure of the Commander in Chief, be continued from the day of one general election to that of another. If the Governor and Council can, at their discretion, dispose of the public monies when raised, a direct assessment by them on the freeholders and inhabitants of the province, without admiting the House to an opportunity of originating or assenting to the taxes imposed on the subject, would be a very unimportant step. It is impossible the Honorable Board should more sincerely wish for peace and harmony in government than the House. But this is a point we must not, we cannot give up.

SPEECH

OF GOVERNOR BERNARD, TO THE COUNCIL AND HOUSE OF
REPRESENTATIVES, NOVEMBER 8, 1765.

Gentlemen of the Council, and
    Gentlemen of the House of Representatives,

I was so determined to let the business of this part of the session pass on without any interruption from me, that I have postponed doing myself justice in a matter in which I think I have been much injured. But as it has not been my intention to pass it over in silence, and therefore seem to admit the justice of the charge, I take this opportunity to make the following expostulation.

Gentlemen of the House of Representatives,

Your answer to my speech is conceived in terms so different from what you have been used to address me with, that I know not how to account for it, but from the disordered state of the province, which affects its very councils. I shall therefore avoid reasoning upon the unfair arguments and groundless insinuations which have been made use of to misrepresent me. Time and their own insufficiency will effectually confute them. Time will make you, gentlemen, sensible how much you were deceived when you were prevailed upon to give a sanction to so injurious a treatment of me.

What have I done to deserve this? I have happened to be the Governor of this province at a time when the Parliament has thought proper to enact a taxation of the colonies. It is not pretended that I have promoted this tax; nor can it with any truth be pretended that I have had it in my power to have opposed it by any means whatsoever. However, when the act was passed it brought upon me a necessary duty, which, it seems, did not coincide with the opinions of the people. This is my offence; but it is really the offence of my office; and against that, you should have expressed your resentment, and not against my person. If I could have dispensed with my duty, perhaps I might have pleased you; but then I must have condemned myself, and been condemned by my Royal Master. I cannot purchase your favor at so dear a rate.

I will however own, if it will please you, that I acted with more zeal for you, than prudence towards myself: I have thought it your duty to submit to this act until you could get it repealed; I have thought that a submission to it would be the readiest means to obtain a repeal; I have thought that a disobedience of it would be productive of more hurt to you than a submission to it; I have urged these things earnestly, because I thought them of great importance to you; but still I have acted with a regard to truth and with an upright intention. I may be mistaken in my apprehension of this matter; but the time is yet to come when it shall appear that I am so. If it should be so, as I heartily wish it may, an error of judgment, with a good will and fair meaning, does not deserve a severe reprehension; much less does it deserve it before it really appears to be an error.

You seem to be displeased with my making the opposition to the execution of the act of Parliament a business of the provincial legislature. But gentlemen, you should consider that it was in pursuance of the unanimous advice of a very full Council that I called you together for this very purpose. It was necessary for me to explain the cause of your meeting; and I could not avoid being explicit upon the subject, consistent with my sense of duty.

8

I should have thought myself very inexcusable if I had foreseen danger to the province like to arise from the behavior of the people and not have warned you against them ; but I could not be so indifferent about the welfare of this government. I have therefore acquitted myself ; I have delivered my own soul ; and you will remember, that, if any consequences disagreeable to you shall happen, I have not been wanting in guarding you against them. If there shall be none such, so much the better ; I shall be well pleased to find myself mistaken.

To justify your unkind treatment of me, you charge me with unkindness towards the province. This is no uncommon practice ; but let us see in the present case how it is founded. You intimate that if I had had the love and concern for the people which I profess, I should have expressed my sentiments of the act early enough to those whose influence brought it into being. But from whence do you learn that I have had any opportunity to express such sentiments ? Do you imagine that I take the liberty of obtruding my advice to his Majesty's ministers unasked and unexpected, and in a business belonging to a department with which I have not the honor to correspond ? I have never neglected any opportunity to serve the province in those offices to which I have a right to apply, and have taken as great liberty in so doing as perhaps any Governor whatsoever ; but in this business I have had no pretence to interpose ; nor do I believe any Governor in America has presumed to express his sentiments against the act in question.

You charge me with casting a reflection on the loyalty of the province, by wresting my words to a meaning which it is not easy to conceive how they could be thought to bear. No one, gentlemen, has been louder in proclaiming the loyalty of this province than I myself have. I have boasted of it ; I have prided myself in it ; and I trust the time will come when I shall do so again ; for I hope the estimate of this people will not be formed from a review of the present times, which, in my opinion, have been made much more difficult than they need have been. But this fermentation must subside, though it is not easy to say when, or in what manner ; and the province will be restored to its former peace and reputation.

If I wanted to apologize for my general conduct in this government, I need only to apply to your registers, where I shall find frequent instances of the approbation of my administration. And, so far as an upright intention, and a diligent exercise of my abilities will go, I have deserved them. It is not much above a year since you thought proper, by a special request, to desire me to be your advocate for particular purposes. If I was at liberty to make public my execution of that commission, I should make those blush who would persuade you that I am not a real friend to the interests, and especially to the trade of this people. Nothing is better understood at home than my attachment to this province. The public offices, where my letters are filed, are full of proofs of it ; and there is not a minister of state, whom I have had the honor to correspond with, who does not know I am far from being unfriendly to the province, or indifferent to its interests.

But, gentlemen, you will make me cautious how I force my services upon you. Not that I intend to desert the cause of the province ; I shall still serve it by all means in my power. And really, gentlemen, if you will permit me to give you one piece of advice more, you may possibly stand in such need of advocates as to make it not prudent for you to cast off any of your natural and professed friends : for such I am, and shall always be, in wishes and private offices, whether you will allow me to appear publicly in that character or not. The pains which are taken to disunite the General Court, must have bad consequences, more or less ; but they shall not prevent me pursuing such measures as I shall think most conducive to the general welfare of the province.

FRA. BERNARD.

Council Chamber, November 8, 1765.

ANSWER

OF THE HOUSE OF REPRESENTATIVES, TO THE GOVERNOR'S SPEECH
OF NOVEMBER 8, 1765, PRESENTED JANUARY 17, 1766.

May it please your Excellency,

As you was pleased to close the last session of the General Assembly with a speech to both Houses, there was no time for the House of Representatives then to take it under their consideration. Thinking it our duty, however, to give all attention to what your Excellency is pleased at any time to say to us, we have made it the first business of this session carefully to peruse it ; and should have been glad if we could have passed it over in silence.

The House, sir, has no disposition to dispute your Excellency's right to deliver your speech to the Assembly at what time you think proper ; yet, if at any time, you are pleased to express yourself in terms which bear hard upon ourselves or our constituents, we cannot help observing to your Excellency, that it appears to us an undue exercise of the prerogative to lay us under the necessity, either of silence, or of being thought out of season in making a reply.

Our answer to your former speech might have been " conceived in terms different from what you have been used to ;" and yet be unexceptionable. We are very sorry your Excellency has been pleased to charge it with " unfair arguments and groundless insinuations to misrepresent you," without pointing out the justice of the charge.

You tell us, that in order to justify our construction of your words, as being designed to cast an odium on the province, we have " wrested them to a meaning, which it is not easy to conceive they could bear." To vindicate ourselves, we need only recite your own words. Your Excellency asked the House, " whether the late proceedings (meaning the violences which had been committed in Boston, to which you particularly referred) were consistent with the humble, dutiful and loyal representations to his Majesty and the Parliament, which they had proposed." If your Excellency did not intend to have it understood, that the whole province had abetted those violent proceedings, we are utterly at a loss to apprehend the pertinence of the question.

The House, however, would not have insisted on this, had not your Excellency expressed as much in your last speech before the prorogation, wherein you say, " that the disordered state of the province, (meaning, as the House apprehend, those violent proceedings,) had affected its very councils;" and allege this as the cause or occasion of the unusual terms, in which they had addressed you. And, indeed, what other meaning can we put upon what your Excellency further says in the same speech, " that the House had been prevailed upon to give a sanction to an injurious treatment of you." From all which, this House cannot think it would be putting a forced construction upon your words to conclude, that it is your Excellency's opinion, that the whole body of the people had justified the violences committed by a few persons in the town of Boston, (though publicly detested by its inhabitants) that they were upon the very borders of rebellion, that their representatives had adopted their spirit, and had been prevailed upon, by your enemies out of doors, to give a sanction to an injurious treatment of you. The House expressed their concern, that your Excellency should entertain such an opinion of a people, whom you have heretofore been pleased to characterise as the most loyal of his Majesty's American provinces. And they are very sorry that you should think you have reason to use such severity of language towards themselves, especially after they had assured you, that their judgment of men, particularly of those in high stations, and consequently of your Excellency, was always formed on their own experience and observation.

Your Excellency's manner of expression, in another part of your speech, fully shews that you have in some measure altered, or at least suspended, your opinion of the people of this province in point of their loyalty : in speaking of which you make use of the time past and future, without mentioning the present. " No one," you tell us, " has been louder in proclaiming the loyalty of this people than yourself. You have boasted of it ; you have prided yourself in it." And then you add, " that you trust the time will come when you shall do so again." Your present sentiments of them you hide in silence, for which a reason seems to be implied in the hopes you express, " that an estimate of this people will not be formed from a review of the present times." Of the present times, may it please your Excellency, impartial history will record, that the people of this continent, after giving the strongest testimonies of their loyalty to his Majesty, particularly by making their utmost exertions in defending his territories and enlarging his dominion in this part of the world, upon a motion made in this House, gave an equal testimony of a love of liberty and regard to those principles, which are a basis of his Majesty's government, by a glorious stand, even against an act of Parliament; because they plainly saw, that their essential, unalienable right of representation and of trials by jury, the very foundation of the British constitution, was infringed, and even annihilated by it. But that they had knowledge and virtue enough to regulate their opposition to it by the law, and steadily to persevere in such steps as the constitution has prescribed to obtain its repeal; that is, by humble, dutiful and loyal representations to his Majesty and the Parliament. And we take this occasion to acquaint your Excellency and all the world, that the House of Representatives of this province have in general been expressly instructed by their constituents to endeavor to obtain a repeal by all means consistent with their loyalty to their Sovereign, and a due veneration to the Parliament of Great Britain. An estimate, formed from this view, can never be to the disadvantage of the present times.

Your Excellency says, that these times have been made more difficult, than they need have been; which is also the opinion of this House. Those who have made them so, have reason to regret the injury they have done to a sincere and honest people. We are glad, however, to find, that the difficulty of the times is, in a great measure, removed; and we trust, that the province will be soon restored to its former tranquillity—your Excellency is pleased to add, "reputation." The custom houses are now open, and the people are permitted to do their own business. The courts of justice must be open—open immediately, and the law, the great rule of right in every county in the province, executed.* The stopping the course of justice is a grievance which this House must inquire into. Justice must be fully administered through the province, by which the shocking effects, which your Excellency apprehended from the people's non-compliance with the stamp act, will be prevented. Nothing now remains but to support the King's executive authority in this province, for which there is sufficient provision in the laws; and patiently to wait in hope that the humble, dutiful and loyal application, jointly made by the people of

* The courts had been suspended for some months, because they would not proceed to do business without stamps; and the people declined using them. See doings of the General Court on the subject, Feb. 1766.

the continent for the repeal of the act, will be succeeded. And though your Excellency has told us, that you never thought it proper to express your sentiments against the act, we have reason to expect, that as it is " a business in which you have no pretence to interpose," you have never taken any steps to prevent its repeal.

You are pleased to say, that "nothing is better understood at home than your attachment to this province—that the public offices, where your letters are filed, are full of proofs of it : and that there is not a minister of state, whom you have the honor of corresponding with, who does not know you are far from being unfriendly to the province, or indifferent to its interests." This House would, by no means, dispute the sincerity of your Excellency's declarations ; and we think we might from hence conclude, that though " you have happened to be the Governor of this province, at a time when the Parliament has thought proper to enact a taxation of the colonies," you did not promote this tax ; your Excellency indeed is not pleased so expressly to declare this ; yet as you have the honor of corresponding with ministers of state, we might have been at least induced to believe, had not your Excellency said, that it could not with any truth be pretended, that you had it in your power, by some means, to have prevented it. And it was upon the presumption of your great interest in the British Court, that the House took the liberty of saying, that the love and concern you profess to have for the people of your province might have been powerful motives to your Excellency to have expressed your sentiments of the act early enough to those whose influence brought it into being. But your Excellency has fully satisfied us with regard to this matter, by intimating in your speech, " that you never had an opportunity to express such sentiments ;" that it was a business belonging to a department, " with which you have not the honor to correspond, and in which you had no pretence to interpose ;" and " that your sentiments delivered to his Majesty's ministers unasked," upon an affair, which most nearly affected the liberties of his subjects under your government, "would be deemed an obtrusion." Upon all which, the House forbear to make any remarks ; and thank your Excellency for assuring us, that you have never neglected any opportunity of serving the province in those offices, to which you have a right to apply.

You are pleased to remind us of the frequent instances, in our registers, of the approbation of your administration. Your Excellency will allow them to be testimonies of the justice of this people and of their good disposition towards you. We wish you were at liberty to make public your execution of that commission, which your Excellency mentions, wherein you were specially requested by a former House to be their advocate for particular purposes. For your Excellency may be assured that this House is at all times ready to acknowledge, with gratitude, the wisdom and fidelity of your administration, as well as any kind offices which you are pleased to do the province in a more private manner, whenever you shall make us sensible of them. We shall always think the province happy in your real friendship, and should be very sorry, should you think it necessary " for the future to be cautious in the exercise of it."

The pains which your Excellency mentions, as having been taken to disunite the General Court, have not been within our observation. And you may rely upon it, that nothing on our part will be wanting to cultivate that harmony which is ever necessary, and especially at this dangerous conjuncture, while your Excellency shall pursue such measures as shall be most conducive to the general welfare of the province.

[This answer was reported by J. Otis, J. Bowers, S. Adams, Gen. Winslow, Capt. Sheaffe, T. Cushing and Col. Gerrish.]

———

SPEECH

OF GOVERNOR BERNARD, TO THE COUNCIL AND HOUSE OF REPRESENTATIVES, JANUARY 16, 1766.

Gentlemen of the Council, and

Gentlemen of the House of Representatives,

You are met together at the usual time for opening the winter session : I have no immediate commands from his Majesty to propose to you ; nor any thing of myself to recommend, but the dispatch of the ordinary business of the session with all proper expedition.

Whenever the time shall come when my service can be made acceptable to you, it will not be wanting. At present I have only to desire, that in framing such matters as must be sent up to me for my consent, you will duly consider the nature of my office and the obligations I am under not to dispense with the duties of it.

FRA. BERNARD.

Council Chamber, January 16, 1766.

———

ANSWER

OF THE HOUSE OF REPRESENTATIVES TO THE ABOVE, JANUARY 16, 1766.

May it please your Excellency,

HAVING considered your speech at the opening of this session, the House of Representatives beg leave to say, that they have the utmost reason to confide in the paternal care of our most gracious

Sovereign, who ever makes the happiness of all his subjects the great rule of his government. That, as it is their indispensable duty, so it is their fixed determination, in every part of their conduct, to make the honor of his Majesty, and the welfare of his subjects of this province, the grand objects of their attention. That while they persevere in such steps, as have a manifest tendency to promote these most valuable purposes, they cannot possibly counteract the nature and design of your office, nor interfere with your obligations not to dispense with the duties of it; and that they have therefore just reason to expect your countenance and consent when it shall be necessary.

We thank you, sir, for the kind assurance you are pleased to give us, that "whenever the time shall come when your service can be acceptable to us, it shall not be wanting;" and we only add, that since his Majesty was pleased to honor you with the government of this his province, we have never known the time when your Excellency's service would not have been very acceptable to us.

[The committee were Mr. Otis, Mr. Dexter, Col. Bowers, Mr. Adams, Major Humphrey, Capt. Sheaffe, and Mr. Cushing.]

━━

REPORT

OF THE HOUSE OF REPRESENTATIVES, ON GRIEVANCES, JANUARY 21, 1766.

The committee to whom was referred the examination into, and consideration of, the grievances the people of this province labor under, reported as follows, and desired leave to sit again.

1. The Governor and Council printing the stamp act and the mutiny act, especially against the known sense of this House, who had refused to be at the expense of printing the stamp act, is a grievance.

2. The printing acts of Parliament at any time at the expense of this province, and more especially when the sense of this House is known to be against it, as was the case in the late printing the stamp act, is bringing an unconstitutional expense on this people, and a grievance.

3. The Governor's holding a private Council weekly without the warning for the general Council, required by charter, and with their advice exercising a legislative power, as has been of late frequently, particularly in taking upon them to regulate and stop the interest of the public securities, is a great grievance, and of very dangerous tendency.

4. The shutting up the Courts of Justice in this province, particularly the superior court, which is not yet open, nor like to be

as we can learn, has a manifest tendency to dissolve the bonds of civil society; is unjustifiable on the principles of law and reason, dangerous to his Majesty's Crown and dignity, and in disherison thereof, and an intolerable grievance on the subject, to be forthwith redressed.

PROCEEDINGS

OF THE COUNCIL AND HOUSE OF REPRESENTATIVES, RESPECTING SITTING OF COURTS, JANUARY AND FEBRUARY, 1766.

IN the House of Representatives, October 26, 1765, ordered, that the Speaker, (Mr. White,) Gen. Winslow, Mr. Cushing, Mr. Adams, Mr. Gray, Col. Clap, Mr. Brown, and Capt. Sheaffe, with such as the Honorable Board shall join, be a committee to consider and report some proper methods to prevent difficulties which may arise in the proceedings of courts of justice through the province, and any other matters.—In Council, read and concurred ; and I. Erving, W. Brattle, Nathaniel Sparhawk, Harrison Gray, Thomas Flucker, and R. Tyler, are joined in the affair.

October 30th. The committee of both Houses appointed the 26th instant, to consider and report some proper methods to prevent the difficulties which may arise, reported the following resolve :

Whereas his Excellency the Governor has informed the two Houses, that A. Oliver, Esq. lately appointed to distribute the stamped papers within this province, has in manner and form declined the office, and his Excellency has also declared that he has no warrant, order or authority whatever to distribute the stamped papers, or to unpack the bales, or separate the parcels, or order any person whatever so to do. In consequence of which, his Excellency further says, that he has, in pursuance of the advice of Council, ordered the stamped papers to be deposited at Castle William ; there to be preserved entire and without being unpacked for his Majesty's further orders ; and whereas the stamp act is looked upon, even by the most sensible and judicious persons in the colonies, to be so grievous and unconstitutional, as that it is not supposed, that any person will think it consistent with his own reputation to act in said office. In order, therefore, to prevent the interruption of the courts of justice through the province, and many evils which may arise, unless such remedy is provided as the great necessity and importance of the case immediately requires ;

Be it resolved, that the Justices of the Superior Court, the Justices of the Courts of Common Pleas for the respective counties, Judges of Probate, Clerks of all Courts, Registers of Deeds and of Probate, Sheriffs, Coroners, and all others, who by said act are re-

9

quired to make use of stamped papers, be, and they are hereby ordered and directed to proceed in the same manner in the execution of their respective offices, as if the said act had never passed ; and all papers whatever, which are subject to be stamped by said act shall, without the stamp, be deemed valid, during this emergency. In Council read and sent down.

In the House of Representatives, read and ordered that this report be recommitted ; and that the committee be directed to sit forthwith.

In the House of Representatives, January 23, 1766 : Resolved, that the shutting up of the Courts of Justice in this province, particularly the Superior Court, has a manifest tendency to dissolve the bonds of civil society, is unjustifiable on the principles of law and reason, and dangerous to his Majesty's Crown and dignity, a very great grievance on the subject that requires immediate redress ; and that, therefore, the Judges and Justices and all other public officers in this province, ought to proceed in the discharge of their several functions as usual.

In Council, January 30 : Resolved, that the vote of the House of Representatives of the 23d instant, relative to the opening of the several Courts of the province, be further referred for consideration—and that it be recommended to the Justices of the Superior Court of Judicature to meet together as soon as may be, and determine whether they will open the said Court at the next term and proceed upon the trial of civil actions, and all other business as usual, or not ; and that they communicate such their determination to this Board—and the Secretary is directed to write to each of said Judges immediately by express, and enclose to each a copy of this resolve.

In the House of Representatives, February 14, 1766 : Resolved, that the shutting up of the Courts of Justice in this province, particularly the Superior Court, has a manifest tendency to dissolve the bonds of civil society, is unjustifiable on the principles of law and reason, and dangerous to his Majesty's Crown and dignity, a very great grievance on the subject that requires immediate redress.   And that, therefore, the Judges and Justices and all other public officers in this province, ought to proceed in the discharge of their several functions as usual.

In Council, read and non-concurred ; and ordered, that the grounds of the Board's proceeding herein, be subjoined as follows :—The Board are sensible, that the shutting of the Courts of Justice in this province, would be attended with fatal consequences, as the Honorable House are ; but on the Board's recommending it to the Justices of the Superior Court to consider and determine whether they would, at the next term, proceed to try civil actions, and do other business as usual, the Justices took the matter into consideration, and returned their answer thereon in writing to the Board ; by which answer, and the verbal declaration since made by some of the Justices, the Board are fully satisfied, that the Superior Court will, at the next term, be open and proceed as usual to do business. And the Board are, from other evidence, likewise satisfied, that the other Courts will, at their respective terms, be open and proceed to business as usual.

———

Extract of a letter from W. Bollan, Esquire, Agent for the province, in England, to the Secretary, dated April 30, 1766.

SIR,

My time, since the receipt of your last letter, as well as some months before, having been employed in strenuous endeavors to promote directly or indirectly the province service, every possible mean of advancing the public welfare in those, so difficult times, being very desirable, I hope the General Court will pardon my not answering it sooner. Prejudice, the powerful enemy of truth and justice, preventing, in a great measure, in my opinion, a true sense of your just constitutional rights taking place ; for this, and other reasons, in order to its extirpation, or a diminution of its force, I attempted, in a public essay, to expose the malignity of its nature, at the same time endeavoring to strengthen and secure that freedom of speech and writing upon public affairs, which have, in times past, been so severely restrained, and which is so necessary to the defence of your rights and interests, which in some respects will ever be best defended here, when the advocate for them, who spares no pains or expense, may not only consult and use the records of the kingdom relative to the foundation of the colonies, or that of the state whereof they are members ; but likewise being provided with proper preparatory knowledge, may be ready effectually to support his own propositions against all objections, and refute the many erroneous notions which are from time to time advanced to your prejudice ; apprehending, that, sooner or later, attempts might be made to take away the necessary freedom. But, indeed, not expecting that any of our politicians would so soon endeavor to subject persons, in any case, to the pains and penalties of a præmunire for their use of this freedom in behalf of the colonies. And offences relative to the interior transactions of the colonies, respecting their lands, monies, goods, and domestic concerns, having been made cognizable in the court of admiralty, which proceeds according to the civil law, I set forth, in part, the introduction and nature thereof, together with the great mischiefs and dangers that have ensued on taking away trials by juries, with the severities of the Court of Star Chamber, and other arbitrary proceedings; for the avoidance whereof your ancestors settled New England. My original plan was so large, and in point of execution so difficult, in many particulars, that though I pursued it with diligence, it was impossible to execute it within the desirable season, in its full extent, and I was extremely hurried in despatching the last and most important part which relates to the nature and rights of the colonies, and their firm, proper and perpetual union with their mother country, which I have ever had much at heart; together with matters preparatory to the repeal of the stamp act. After having, I believe, examined all the records in the kingdom which relate to the settlement of America, by various searches at the tower, and the offices wherein the Parliament rolls are kept, three records, mentioned in my essay, were found, whereof two relate to *Calais.* The act which provided for its sending members to Parliament, and which contains a very great variety of regulations for that place, remain in the office at Westminster; and the writ that issued thereupon remains in the tower, as well as the ordinance of Edward I. This act, I believe, was never published. On the publication of this essay, several judicious persons, friends of the colonies, some of whom were men of consequence, being of opinion that publishing immediately a proper number of copies of such part as related directly to the colonies would be serviceable, I thereupon got five hundred copies despatched, which were chiefly given to the members at the doors of the House of Commons and House of Lords, the remainder being given to other persons. And during the violence of those contests which took place pending the repeal of the stamp act, when it was believed by intelligent persons, that the ministry would be changed, and a persuasion prevailed, that this act would consequently be enforced, I directly wrote a more spirited piece, touching trial by juries, and other interesting points, which had the approbation of an able judge, one of the principal friends and promoters of the repeal, as well as others. But the ministerial revolution, which was so much feared, not taking place, and matters taking a desirable turn, he thought it advisable not to publish it; and not to mention other particulars, I have since done every thing which lay in my power for the service of the province.

Extract of a letter from Secretary Conway to Governor Bernard, dated October 24, 1765, and by the Governor communicated to the House of Representatives, January 22, 1766.

It is with the greatest concern his Majesty learns the disturbances which have lately arisen in your province; the general confusion that seems to reign there; and the total languor and want of energy in your government to exert itself with any dignity or efficacy, for the suppression of tumults, which seem to strike at the very being of all authority and subordination amongst you.

Nothing can certainly exceed the ill advised and intemperate conduct held by a party in your province, which can in no way contribute to the removal of any real grievance they might labor under, but may tend to impede and obstruct the exercise of his Majesty's benevolent attention to the ease and comfort, as well as to the welfare of all his people.

It is hoped and expected, that this want of confidence in the justice and tenderness of the mother country, and this open resistance to its authority, can only have found place among the lower and more ignorant of the people. The better and wiser part of the colonies will know that decency and submission may prevail, not only to redress grievances, but to obtain grace and favor, while the outrage of a public violence can expect nothing but severity and chastisement.

These sentiments you, and all his Majesty's servants, from a sense of your duty to, and love of your country, will endeavor to excite and encourage. You will, in the strongest colors, represent to them the dreadful consequences that must inevitably attend the forcible and violent resistance to acts of the British Parliament, and the scene of misery and distraction to both countries, inseparable from such a conduct.

For, however unwillingly his Majesty may consent to the exertion of such powers as may endanger the safety of a single subject, yet can he not permit his own dignity, and the authority of the British legislature, to be trampled on by force and violence, and in avowed contempt of all order, duty and decorum.

If the subject is aggrieved, he knows in what manner legally and constitutionally to apply for relief; but it is not suitable either to the safety or dignity of the British empire, that any individuals, under the pretence of redressing grievances, should presume to violate the public peace.

———

Extracts from letters written by R. Jackson, Esq. Agent for the Colony, in England, to Governor Bernard, dated November and December, 1765, *February and March,* 1766.

[Though these are not precisely some of the papers promised in the title page, as they discover the views and opinions of men in power in England, it was thought proper to insert them here.]

"NOVEMBER 8, 1765.

" I CONFESS I cannot foresee what government will do here, but am informed they are determined to support the stamp act, and not to give way to its repeal. How far they may be right in this,

I dare not judge yet ; but I am sure great moderation and temper, and even some strong proofs of regard are necessary, to conciliate the affections of the Americans, which I find are universally tainted. It is impossible to excuse the lower class in America, or the indiscretion of those who set them on, even for a man who has American affections only ; for this indiscretion and extravagance, cannot but be highly prejudicial to America. At the same time I shall always condemn and lament the conduct of those in Great Britain, who by their stations and interest in the welfare of the British empire, should neither have wanted wisdom to direct them, nor anxious concern to have disposed them to have listened to it. I heartily disapproved of the stamp act before it passed : I voted against it, and doubt not I shall vote for the repeal. I know your sentiments were the same as mine on this subject, as well as those of Lieutenant Governor Hutchinson, however the misguided rabble have chose him as an object of their resentment. What will be the consequences of the misconduct on both sides the water, I cannot foresee : I assure you I have no greater hopes than from the very wise speech you have left the country to meditate on.

" When I began this, and when I wrote by the packet, I was inclined to think there was no chance of the repeal of the stamp act ; I well knew that many men, who are among the most necessary to the new administration, were always the strongest advocates for this tax, and indeed for taxes in general in America ; and I had pretty good intelligence, that there was a resolution to carry it through. I believe long before you receive this, you will have had some proofs of it from this side the water ; yet the day after I wrote my last letter, I collected from conversation I had with several persons (some of whom may be said to have a share in the administration, and others I know have a great portion of the confidence of those who have,) that if any reasonable and moderate conduct of the colonies give us an opportunity of decently stepping back, we shall probably repeal the act. I confess when I see what has happened here, already, and in America, I am in the utmost anxiety about the event, and am little relieved by the assurances I speak of."

"NOVEMBER 9, 1765.

" I cannot express my concern for what has happened in America ; God knows what the consequences will be ; sure I am that the conduct of the Americans will weaken the power of friends here to serve them. I wish the leading men knew a little more of this country ; no man in England is more disposed to serve them than myself. I sincerely think that in serving them, I serve the interests of the whole British empire. I shall heartily contribute all that lies in my power to bring about a repeal of the stamp act ; I sincerely think, that whatever be the power of Parliament, in discretion, *it ought not to exercise that power, in laying taxes on America, while it has no share in the election of the members of the House of Commons ;* yet I cannot think that resistance to an act of the British Legislature is justifiable on any principle that will not overturn any government in the world.

" Nothing can be more unjust than the treatment of the worthy and unfortunate Lieutenant Governor, nothing can be a greater proof of the blindness of the rabble. I know that he has urged the weightiest arguments against the obnoxious acts, and that they have been used at home from his materials."

" NOVEMBER 26, 1765.

" I cannot yet guess what are the intentions of administration on the subject of America ; I have received encouragement to hope the best, not from ministers, but from some closely connected with them. My own conduct has been, and will continue uniformly the same ; I shall always oppose Parliamentary taxes in America, and wish to see Parliaments seldom interfere in American affairs. If they are to do it, I shall dread the worst, unless America has a choice of members given her. At all events, I think acts of the Legislature are to be obeyed. I should be glad to hear some good news from New York, such as may found the most favorable resolutions for America."

" DECEMBER 26, 1765.

" I am unwilling to let slip any opportunity of writing to you, though I know of little new since I wrote last, for ministry wear the same appearances it did then. Upon the two divisions we have had in the House of Commons, and one in the House of Lords, they have carried every thing before them. For my own part, though I have nothing to expect from them, and indeed want nothing, I heartily wish them continuance of power, that nothing may retard the wished for measures in American affairs."

" FEBRUARY 16, 1766.

" What will become of the stamp act, I dare not guess ; no labor of mine has been spared to obtain its repeal ; which is however strongly opposed, and at present by an apparent majority in the House of Lords, as far as one can apply that majority to the stamp act. For we have yet come to no resolution on that subject in our House ; we have been perusing letters, public papers, and examining witnesses, and now and then debating a little for near three weeks, besides coming to some resolution on the right of Parliament. Your public letters have justly done you great honor in both, especially our House. I think there can be no objection to my saying, (as I intend to do when the debate on the bill comes on) that I know both you and Mr. Hutchinson's opinion, were against passing the bill ; though you have both so well done your duty in supporting it, as far as in your power."

"MARCH 3, 1766.

"I cannot let this vessel sail without acquainting you that the stamp act is probably on the point of being repealed ; since we have ventured to conclude that the House of Lords will hardly throw out the bill. The repeal, however, could not have been obtained without another act for declaring the right of Parliament to bind the colonies by laws in all cases whatsoever ; which will probably as little prejudice them, as the power we claim in Ireland, the manner of exercising which you are acquainted with.

" The carrying the repeal of the stamp act is miraculous. I say not this to get any credit for myself. I have in truth done all in my power, but this is very little indeed ; though I have never been a minute out of the House of Commons for above six weeks whilst it has been on, often till ten at night, not seldom till three in the morning. This I should have done, had I been agent to no province or colony in America."

"MARCH 15, 1766.

" I have the pleasure to inform you, that you have great credit here ; and that there can be no difficulty in your obtaining a confirmation of Mount Desert in any form. I shall forthwith concert measures with Mr. J. Pownall for that purpose. The confirmation of the other grants has been postponed at the earnest desire of the Lords of Trade, who are overwhelmed with other business, as well as attendance on Parliament ; but I have promises that they may pass at or soon after Easter.

" I say you are in great credit here ; because you are always mentioned with great respect in both Houses of Parliament, and from thence, elsewhere ; not but some reports have been spread to your disadvantage ; *particularly, that you might at the beginning, by acting with vigor, have nipped the spirit of sedition in the bud;* though they acknowledge it was impracticable after the first day. I mention this to you, because it may be of service to you to know it ; though hardly worth your while to attempt to refute it, as it seems almost forgot, or at least drowned in the general approbation your conduct, sentiments, and opinion have found here.

I sincerely believe the moderation and good sense of your letters, as well as your express opinion have contributed much to the repeal of the stamp act ; as well as to the ease we expect on the head of molasses and foreign sugar ; the duty on the former will be reduced I believe to one penny ; and though the duty on the latter cannot be brought to a reduction, the warehousing it will be permitted in order to bring it to an European market.

" With regard to the stamp act, it will probably be repealed on Monday or Tuesday, in the House of Lords ; where there has been a strong opposition, and where there will be another debate. This opposition has been chiefly built on the resistance of the Americans to the authority of Parliament ; on the principles this resistance has been supposed to be founded ; and on the expectation of future resistance to acts of all sorts on these principles.

"In the course of the debates in both Houses, it has appeared that it never was the practice of England to lay internal taxes on her dominions, that were not represented ; or that if this practice ever was occasionally varied from, it was always complained of ; and the practice either dropped, or a representation called to sit in Parliament soon after. I endeavored to shew in the House of Commons, that in all ages and nations a difference has been made and felt, (though, perhaps not distinguished by a line,) between external and internal taxes, as well as between all taxation and general legislation. In all times laws have been made affecting all the English dominions ; sometimes external taxes imposed by a representation not general. In England itself, laws have been continually (down to the civil wars) enacted by proclamation, and external taxes levied without consent of Parliament ; but though these have been occasionally condemned and questioned in the reign of James I. and Charles I., they never were before, unless it were by being granted by Parliament, after they had some time been levied for years without grant. Whereas the statute book abounds with judgments of the Parliament, that internal taxes ought not to be levied without consent of Parliament, that is, the representation of that part of the kingdom that paid, for the others were not taxed ; though being excepted, it looks as if the Parliament thought they would have been charged by general words.

"I hope all difficulties arising from the stamp act will be soon removed ; it was, I think, in effect, repealed in the House of Lords yesterday ; for on a division upon the second reading, the majority, Lords and Proxies, was thirty-four. I assure you, your opinion has much contributed to this, and that opinion has received weight from all your letters read in both Houses of Parliament. The present ministry and their friends have to a degree made themselves responsible for the future conduct of the Americans, who would certainly be guilty of the basest ingratitude, if they should abuse the confidence put in them by their friends, after those who they deem their enemies, have built so much on the expectation that they will. But I hope this will not be so."

10

SPEECH

Gentlemen of the Council, and

  Gentlemen of the House of Representatives,

 I HAVE great pleasure in being able to open this General Court with congratulating you upon the repeal of the stamp act. When I consider the difficulties, with which this business has labored, and the causes from whence they arose ; when I look back upon the dangers which this people have so narrowly escaped, I cannot but earnestly wish, that a proper improvement may be made of this happy event, so as to restore this province to the public reputation, and the domestic peace, which it happily enjoyed before the late distractions.

 In times of public calamity, it is not unusual for private interests and resentments to intermix themselves with popular discontent, and execute their purposes under the borrowed mask of patriotic zeal. This has been the primary cause of that unlimited abuse which has been cast upon the most respectable characters in this province ; at a time when integrity and ability should rather have been solicited to the aid of the people, than deterred from serving them. Of this I have no little experience myself ; but it has not abated my concern for the welfare of the conntry, nor prevented my endeavors to promote it.

 To such a degree of injustice has the late infatuation been carried, that the principal object of the fury of the people, was a gentleman to whom they were most highly indebted for his services in the very cause for which they rose against him.* And it is remarkable that those persons, who framed and conducted the only American petition, which was read and well received in Parliament, and was of real use in procuring the repeal, have been proscribed by the invidious name of friends to the stamp act ; when in truth such a character did not exist in the province, unless it was in the persons of the accusers themselves, whose violent and precipitate measures created all those difficulties, which the united efforts of every friend of America, in every rank and station, were but just able to surmount.

 It were to be wished, that a veil could be drawn over the late disgraceful scenes. But that cannot be done, till a better temper and understanding shall prevail in general, than seems to be at present, if we can judge from some proceedings, which I fear, when known at home, will afford matter of triumph to those who were for maintaining the stamp act ; and sorrow and concern to

---

* Lieutenant Governor Hutchinson, no doubt.

those who procured its repeal. But the inflammation of this country has been a grand object with some persons, and neither the indulgence of Parliament, nor the moderation of government, nor the exigency of the times, have as yet been able to put a stop to that pursuit.

However, I have given my testimony against these proceedings, in a manner very disagreeable to me, and very contrary to my disposition. Whilst the business of the General Court was carried on in good humor and with good understanding, I have been unwilling to interrupt the general harmony by too great an attention to my own sentiments, and have frequently given up my opinion to what has in any degree appeared to be the voice of the people. Every person who hears me, can, more or less, give testimony of the mildness and moderation of my administration; how much I have endeavored to remove and prevent distinctions of men and divisions of parties; and how little I have interposed my judgment against the sense of the councils over which I have presided.

But when the government is attacked in form; when there is a profest intention to deprive it of its best and most able servants, whose only crime is their fidelity to the Crown,* I cannot be indifferent; but find myself obliged to exercise every legal and constitutional power to maintain the King's authority against this ill judged and ill timed oppugnation of it. At the same time, I publicly declare, that whenever an opportunity shall offer to restore to the provincial councils, that harmony and union which not long ago it was my pride to cultivate, I will embrace it most cordially; and will use my utmost endeavors to heal the divisions and bury the animosities, which the late distractions have created. In the mean time, as I have appeared before the British Parliament a true friend to the province, as well as a faithful servant to the Crown, I shall leave it to this good people to recognise me in that united character, at their own time and in their own manner.

Gentlemen,

I am in continual expectation to receive his Majesty's commands to lay before you matters of importance; and whenever they shall arrive I shall be obliged to call you together again. I therefore think it advisable to make this session as short as well may be; and recommend it to you, not to engage in any business, which does not require present despatch. The consideration of the terms upon which the stamp act has been repealed; of the expectations of the Parliament, that the Americans will not abuse the

---

* In electing Counsellors, the following gentlemen, who had been of the Board for several years, were not chosen, viz. Tho. Hutchinson, A. Oliver, P. Oliver, and Edmund Trowbridge. The Governor also gave a negative to the election of J. Otis, as Speaker, and of Col. Otis, J. Gerrish, Tho. Saunders, J. Bowers, N. Sparhawk, and S. Dexter, who had been chosen Counsellors,

indulgencies granted them ; and of the assurances which the promoters of the repeal have publicly given, that it will be most gratefully and humbly received, is a subject which I could well enlarge upon ; but I shall reserve it to another opportunity, when I shall probably be assisted by special instructions for that purpose, and I hope shall be able to speak to you with greater authority than my own.   FRA. BERNARD.

Council Chamber, May 29, 1766.

===

ANSWER

OF THE HOUSE OF REPRESENTATIVES TO THE FOREGOING SPEECH.

JUNE 3, 1766.

May it please your Excellency,

THE House of Representatives of this province, beg leave to return to your Excellency our congratulations upon the repeal of the stamp act ; a most interesting and happy event, which has diffused a general joy among all his Majesty's loyal and faithful subjects throughout this extensive continent.

This is a repeated and striking instance of our most gracious Sovereign's paternal regard for the happiness and welfare of all his subjects. We feel upon this occasion, the deepest sense of loyalty and gratitude. We are abundantly convinced that our legal and constitutional rights and liberties will always be safe under his propitious government. We esteem the relation we have ever stood in with Great Britain, the mother country, our happiness and security. We have reason to confide in the British Parliament, from this happy instance, that all his Majesty's faithful subjects, however remote, are the objects of their patronage and justice.

When we reflect on the difficulties under which this important business labored, and the causes from whence they arose, we are truly astonished that they have been surmounted ; and we gratefully resent the noble and generous efforts of those illustrious patriots who have distinguished themselves in our cause. Indeed, when we look back upon the many dangers from which our country hath, even from its first settlement, been delivered, and the policy and power of those, who have to this day sought its ruin, we are sensibly struck with an admiration of Divine goodness, and would religiously regard the arm which has so often shielded us.

Upon so joyful an occasion, we were in hopes your Excellency would have spread a veil over every disagreeable scene in the late times of public calamity ; but to our surprise and astonishment, we find your Excellency declaring in your speech, at the opening of the General Court, that this cannot be done till a better temper and understanding shall prevail in general, than there seems to be at present. Though your Excellency has seen reason to form so unfavorable an opinion of the present times, we beg leave, with all humility, to ask, whether so great a liberality as you have shown, in your strictures upon them, has a tendency to make them better ? " Private interests and resentments," "popular discontent," " unlimited abuse on the most respectable characters." These and such like expressions, run through a considerable part of your speech. We should have been glad if your Excellency had given some intimation, at least, that you did not mean to cast reflections on either of the two Houses, to whom your speech was immediately addressed. We have reason to fear, that whatever were your intentions, this construction will be put upon it by those who would be glad to improve the authority of your Excellency to our disadvantage. Upon this account, we find ourselves under a necessity, explicitly to declare to your Excellency, that no private resentments of ours, have intermixed with popular discontent. We have no interest detached from, or inconsistent with, the common good ; we are far from having any " ill purposes" to execute, much less under the " borrowed mask of patriotic zeal," or any other hypocritical disguise. It has ever been our pride to cultivate harmony and union, upon the principles of liberty and virtue, among the several branches of the legislature, and a due respect and reverence for his Majesty's representative in the province. We have endeavored to solicit integrity and ability to the aid of the people, and are very sorry if gentlemen of character have, by any means, been deterred from serving their country, especially in time of danger, when the eyes of all might have been upon them for deliverance. At such a time, for true patriots to be silent, is dangerous. Your Excellency tells us of an unlimited abuse which has been cast upon the most respectable characters, of which you have had no little experience yourself ; but you assure us that it has not abated your concern for the welfare of the country, nor prevented your endeavors to promote it. We thank your Excellency ; and upon this assurance we have reason to hope you have employed your influence in behalf of this people, at a time when they so much stood in need of it, in representing their behavior, in general, in the most candid and favorable view. In this light his Majesty, his Ministry and Parliament, have been desirous of viewing it, and when this good people shall find that your Excellency has served them in so essential a point, they will, we are sure, be ready " to recognize you in the united character of a true friend to the province, and a faithful servant of the Crown."

But, may it please your Excellency, we cannot forbear observing, that when you are speaking, as we conceive, of the injustice done his Honor the Lieutenant Governor, the last year, your manner of expression would lead a stranger to think that so horrid an act of villany was perpetrated, by the body of this people. The infatuation, you tell us, " has been carried to such a degree of injustice, that the principal object of the fury *of the people,* was a gentleman to whom they were most highly indebted for his services in the very cause for which they rose against him. Your Excellency, no doubt, means that the whole people, and not a part only, were most highly indebted to this gentleman for his services, and that the particular cause in which he had been engaged, concerned them all ; and yet, so infatuated have the body of the people been, that they even rose against this very gentleman, and made him the object of their fury ! Is not this the natural meaning of your words ? And will it not, sir, afford matter of triumph to the unrelenting enemies of this province, to hear the Governor himself declaring that this was the " prevailing temper of the people ;" that such was their " violent and precipitate measures," and that a veil cannot, even now, be drawn over so " disgraceful a scene," because the same temper among the people in general still prevails. There may, sir, be a general popular discontent upon good grounds. The people may sometimes have just reason to complain ; your Excellency must be sensible, that in such a circumstance, evil minded persons may take the advantage, and rise in tumult. This has been too common in the best regulated and best disposed cities in Europe. Under cover of the night a few villains may do much mischief. And such, sir, was the case here ; but the virtue of the people themselves finally suppressed the mob ; and we have reason to believe, that the unaffected concern which they discover at so tragical a scene, their united detestation of it, their spirited measures to prevent further disorders, and other circumstances well known to the honorable gentleman himself, have fully satisfied him, that such an imputation was without reason. But for many months past there has been an undisturbed tranquillity in general, in this province, and for the greater part of the time, merely from a sense of good order in the people, while they have been in a great measure deprived of the public tribunals, and the administration of justice, and so far thrown into a state of nature.*

We are at a loss to conceive your Excellency's meaning, when you allude to some proceedings which " when known at home you fear will afford matter of triumph to those who were for maintaining the stamp act, and sorrow and concern to those who procure its repeal ;" and when you tell us that " the inflammation of the country has been a grand object with some persons," we cannot suppose your Excellency would make a public declaration of a matter of such importance without good grounds. An attempt to inflame a country is a crime of very dark complexion. You tell us that a stop has not yet been put to that pursuit ; we hope you

---

* The courts had been suspended for some months. See proceedings on that subject, page 65 of this volume.

have taken every prudent and legal step in your own department to prevent it. Permit us however, to say, that it is possible you may have been misinformed, by persons not well affected to this people, and who would be glad to have it thought that we were turbulent and factious, and perpetually murmuring, even after every cause of complaint is removed. Such characters may still exist in the persons of some who have taken all occasions from the just resentment of the people, to represent them as inflammatory, disaffected and disloyal. Should there be any persons so abandoned, as to make it the object of their policy, to inflame the minds of the people against a wise, a good, a "mild and moderate administration," they may be assured of the severest censures of this House as soon as they are known.

But the manner in which you are pleased to explain the grounds of your testimony against the elections of the present year, seems to imply that it is your opinion that the two Houses have been so far influenced by an inflammatory spirit in particular persons, as even to make an attack upon the government in form. The two Houses proceeded in these elections with perfect good humor and good understanding ; and as no other business had been transacted when we were favored with your speech, it is astonishing to us, that you should think this a time to "interrupt the general harmony." We are wholly at a loss to conceive how a full, free-and fair election can be called "an attack upon the government in form," "a professed intention to deprive it of its best and most able servants," "an ill-judged and ill timed oppugnation of the King's authority." These, may it please your Excellency, are high and grievous charges against the two Houses, and such as we humbly conceive, no crowned head since the revolution has thought fit to bring against two Houses of Parliament. It seems to us to be little short, if any thing, of a direct impeachment of the two Houses of high treason. Oppugnation of the King's authority is but a learned mode of expression, which reduced to plain English, is fighting against the King's most excellent Majesty. But what, sir, is the oppugnation which we have been guilty of ? We were summoned and convened here to give our free suffrages at the general election, directed to be annually made by the royal charter. We have given our suffrages according to the dictates of our consciences, and the best light of our understanding. It was certainly our right to choose, and as clearly a constitutional power in your Excellency to disapprove, without assigning a reason either before or after your dissent. Your Excellency has thought proper to disapprove of some. We are far even from suggesting that the country has by this means been deprived of its best and ablest servants. We have released those of the Judges of the Superior Court who had the honor of a seat at the Board, from the cares and perplexities of politics, and given them opportunity to make still farther advances in the knowledge of the law, and to administer right and

justice within this jurisdiction. We have also left other gentlemen more at leisure to discharge the duties and functions of their
important offices. This surely is not to deprive the government
of its best and ablest servants, nor can it be called an oppugnation
of any thing, but a dangerous union of legislative and executive
power in the same persons; a grievance long complained of by
our constituents, and the redress of which some of us had special
instruction, to endeavor at this very election to obtain.

Your Excellency is pleased to say, that only one of all the
American petitions "was well received and of real use in producing the repeal;" that petition was forwarded from this province
in season, to be presented to the Parliament, before the stamp act
was passed; by whose influence the presentation of it was so
long delayed by Mr. Agent Jackson, and omitted through that
whole session of parliament, it is needless for us at present to inquire. If it was so well received, as your Excellency tells us it
was, and of real use in procuring the repeal, there is reason to
think it might have had its designed effect to prevent the passing
that act, and saved this continent from that distress and confusion
in which it has been involved. But your Excellency is under a
mistake, in supposing that this petition, alone, was well received
and of real use. Those from the late general congress, we are informed by our agent Mr. Deberdt, were early laid before the Ministry, and were well received by them. He tells us, that Mr. Secretary Conway kindly undertook to present that, which was prepared for his Majesty; and as the royal ear is always open to the
distresses of his people, we have not the least reason to doubt but
that so united a supplication of his American subjects was graciously considered by him; and with regard to those to the two
Houses of Parliament, one of them at least we know was highly
approved of by the chairman of the committee for American affairs,
was read in the House of Commons, and supported by Mr. Pitt;
it was never rejected, and we cannot suppose it failed of due attention merely for want of form. In truth sir, we look back with
the utmost pleasure upon the wisdom of the last House of Representatives, in proposing such a union of the colonies; and although
some have taken great pains to lessen the weight and importance
of the late congress in the minds of the people, we have the
strongest reason to believe that their firm and prudent measures
had a very great influence in procuring this happy repeal.

You are pleased to make a declaration that " whenever an opportunity shall offer to restore harmony and union to the provincial
councils, you will most cordially embrace it." The time, sir, is
already come; never was there so happy a juncture, in which to
accomplish so desirable an end; and it will be the pride of this
House to improve it; with this disposition we come together. If
any expression or sentiment in your speech should have a contrary
effect, as it will so far defeat our honest intention, it will fill us

with real concern. Permit us also to say, that it will disappoint the expectations of his Majesty and the Parliament in repealing the stamp act ; for it is most reasonable in them to expect that the restoration of the colonies to domestic peace and tranquillity will be the happy effect of the establishment of their just rights and liberties.

When your Excellency shall " be assisted by special instruction, and speak to us with greater authority than your own," we shall be all attention ; being assured, from past experience, that every thing coming from his Majesty will be full of grace and truth.

[This answer was prepared by T. Cushing, (the Speaker,) J. Otis, S. Adams, Col. O. Partridge, Maj. Hawley, Mr. Saunders, and Mr. Dexter.]

———

SPEECH

OF GOVERNOR BERNARD, TO THE COUNCIL AND HOUSE OF
REPRESENTATIVES, JUNE 3, 1766.

Gentlemen of the Council, and
Gentlemen of the House of Representatives,

I HAVE received a letter from the right honorable Mr. Secretary Conway, enclosing two acts of Parliament ; one for securing the dependency of the colonies on the mother country, and the other for the repeal of the stamp act. At the same time he is pleased to signify what his Majesty and his Parliament expect from the colonies, in return for the indulgence shewn them. I am also ordered to recommend to you, that full and ample compensation be made to the late sufferers by the madness of the people ; and for that purpose I am directed to lay before you the votes of the House of Commons, expressing their sense upon that subject ; whose humanity and justice, it is hoped, it will be your glory to imitate. The whole of this letter is conceived in such strong, patriotic and conclusive terms, that I shall not weaken it by a representation of my own, other than this short capitulation necessary to introduce what I have to say on the subject.

I cannot but lament, that this letter did not arrive before the meeting of the General Court. If it had, I flatter myself, it would have prevented a transaction, which must now be regretted more than ever. I mean your excluding from the King's Council the principal Crown Officers ; men, not only respectable in themselves for their integrity, their abilities, and their fidelity to their country, as well as to their King ; but also quite necessary to the adminis-

11

tration of government in the very station from whence you have displaced them. By this you have anticipated the expectations of the King and Parliament, and disappointed them, before they have been communicated to you. It is not in your power, in so full a manner as will be expected, to shew your respectful gratitude to the mother country, or to make a dutiful and affectionate return to the indulgence of the King and Parliament. It must and will be understood, that these gentlemen are turned out for their deference to acts of the British Legislature. Whilst this proceeding has its full effect, you will not, you cannot avoid being chargeable with unthankfulness and dissatisfaction on ground of former heat and prevailing prejudice. It is impossible to give any tolerable coloring to this proceeding. If it should be justified, by asserting a right ; that it is a legal power to choose whom you please, without regard to any considerations whatever ; the justification itself will tend to impeach the right. But if your right is ever so absolute, the distinction between a right, and the propriety of exercising it, is very obvious ; as this distinction has so lately been used with great effect to your own interest. Next to wishing, that this had never happened, it is to be wished, that some measures might be formed to draw a veil over it ; or at least to palliate it, and prevent its bad effects ; which surely must be very hurtful to this province, if it should be maintained and vindicated. If any expedients can be found out for this purpose, I will heartily concur in them ; and, in general, I will make the best use of all means, which you shall put into my hands, to save the credit of the province upon this unhappy emergency ; and I will set off to the best advantage I can, all other methods which you shall take to demonstrate those sentiments which are expected from you in the most effectual manner.

Gentlemen of the House of Representatives,

The requisition contained in this letter is of a most singular nature ; and the only one of the kind which I have known since I have served his Majesty in America. It is founded upon a resolution of the House of Commons, formed after a full consideration of the matter, and represented to his Majesty by the address of that House. The justice and humanity of this requisition is so forcible, that it cannot be controverted. The authority, with which it is introduced, should preclude all disputation about complying with it. I hope, therefore, you will add to the merit of your compliance by the readiness of it, and assume to yourselves the honor which now offers itself, of setting the first example of gratitude and dutiful affection to the King and Parliament, by giving those proofs of it, which are now pointed out to you. I must observe, that it is from the Provincial Assembly, that the King and Parliament expect this compensation should be made to the sufferers, without referring them to any other person whatever. Who ought finally to be charged with this expense, may be a proper consideration for you ; and I shall readily concur with you in your resolutions thereon, after the sufferers have been fully satisfied.

Gentlemen,

Both the business and the time are most critical ; and let me intreat you to recollect yourselves, and consider well what you are about. When the fate of the province is put in a scale, which is to rise or fall, according to your present conduct, will you suffer yourselves to be influenced by party animosities, or domestic feuds ? Shall this fine country be ruined, because every person in government has not been gratified with honors or office, according to the full of his pretensions ? Shall the private interests, passions or resentments of a few men, deprive this whole people of the great and manifold advantages, which the favor and indulgence of their Sovereign and his Parliament are even now providing for them ? There never was, at any time whatever, so fair a prospect of the improvement of the peace and welfare of this province, as is now opening to you. , Will you suffer this pleasant view to be intercepted or overclouded by the ill humors of particulars ? When wealth and happiness are held out to you, will you refuse to accept them ? Surely after his Majesty's commands are known, and the terms in which they are signified, well considered, the very persons who have created the prejudices and prepossessions, which I now endeavor to combat, will be the first to remove them, and prevent their ill effects.

It is now declared, that " such is the magnanimity of the King and his Parliament, that they seem disposed, not only to forgive, but to forget those unjustifiable marks of an undutiful disposition too frequent in the late transactions of the colonies." It is my desire to render this grace as beneficial and extensive within this province as can well be made. But it must be expected that whoever intends to take the benefit of it, should entitle themselves to it by a departure from that offensive conduct which is the object of it. Here, then, it will be necessary to draw a line, to distinguish who are, and who are not, the proper objects of the gracious intention of the King and Parliament. And if, after this proffered grace, any person shall go beyond this line ; and still endeavor directly or indirectly to foment a division between Great Britain and her colonies, and prevent that connexion of policy and union of interests, which are now in so fair a way of being established to perpetuity, surely that man will have much to answer for to both countries, and will probably be called to answer.

But I hope it will not be so, not in a single instance ; but that every person, even they who have given the greatest offence, will embrace this opportunity to restore peace to their country, and obtain indemnity for themselves. And all such who shall really desire to reconcile themselves to the King's government, either at home or here, may be assured, that without a future deliquency, every thing past will, as fast as can be, be buried in total oblivion. No one can suspect me of want of sincerity, in making this declaration ; as too ready a forgetfulness of injuries has been said to be my weakness. However, it is a failing, which I had rather suffer by, than be without.

I have spoken to you with sincerity, openness and earnestness, such as the importance of the subject deserves. When the fate of the province seems to hang upon the result of your present deliberations, my anxiety for the event, I hope, will make my warmth excusable. If I have let drop any word, which may seem severe or unkind, let the cause I am engaged in, apologize for it ; and where the intention is upright, judge of what I say, not by detached words or syllables, but by its general purport and meaning. I have always been desirous of cultivating a good understanding with you. And when I recollect the former happy times, when I scarce ever met the General Court, without giving and receiving testimonies of mutual approbation, I cannot but regret the interruption of that pleasant intercourse, by the successful artifices of designing men, enemies to the country, as well as to me. But now, that my character for affection to the province, and attention to its interests, is confirmed by the most authentic testimonials, I hope that at the same time, you renew your duty to the King, you will resume a confidence in his representative.

FRA. BERNARD.

ANSWER

OF THE COUNCIL TO THE GOVERNOR'S SPEECH, AT THE OPENING OF THE
PRESENT SESSION, AND TO HIS SPEECH OF THE THIRD INSTANT,
JUNE 7, 1766.

May it please your Excellency,

THE Board having taken into consideration your two speeches, beg leave to return our warmest congratulations on the repeal of the stamp act ; an event that has created the greatest and most universal joy which was ever felt on the continent of America ; and which promises the most happy fruits to Great Britain, from the growing prospect and grateful affection of her colonies. Not insensible of the difficulties which have attended this important affair, and the dangers, which, not only this province, but all

America have escaped, we assure your Excellency, that nothing shall be wanting on our part, which may contribute towards a proper improvement of this happy event, and the promoting so desirable an object as domestic peace. From such a disposition, we cannot but take notice, with regret, of any thing, which threatens to draw the least cloud over the present general joy. It is with pain we express our apprehension, that your Excellency's speech may tend to lead some, who are not acquainted with the state of the province, to entertain such an opinion of the government, or the people, or both, as they do not deserve. When your Excellency is pleased to mention " inflammations, distractions, infatuations, and the fury of the people," you seem to refer to some enormities committed by unknown and abandoned persons, in a time of universal uneasiness and distress. But your Excellency cannot mean to impute these enormities, justly abhorred by all ranks among us, to the body of this people, or any branch of the government. Detestable as they are, they can never lessen the reputation of this province; nor doth it need a veil on this occasion. Villains are to be found in the best communities on earth; and whatever excesses may have happened in America, under our late distressing apprehensions, the relief kindly granted us, demonstrates that our most gracious Sovereign, and the British Parliament, knew how to distinguish the complaints and dutiful remonstrances of loyal subjects, who thought themselves aggrieved, from the violences of a profligate rabble. Notwithstanding the intimations dropped from your Excellency, we are sure no ill temper generally prevails among us; nothing that can lead the Parliament to repent its indulgence to us; nothing that can afford just matter of triumph to those who were for maintaining the stamp act, nor of sorrow and concern to those who procured its repeal.

Your Excellency is pleased further to say, " when the government is attacked in form, when there is a professed intention to deprive it of its best and most able servants, whose only crime is their fidelity to the Crown, I cannot be indifferent; but find myself obliged to exercise every legal and constitutional power to maintain the King's authority against this ill judged and ill timed oppugnation of it." Whatever might have been your Excellency's intention, this is, according to the more obvious meaning of your expressions, a heavy charge, in which no particular persons, or any order of men are specified, delivered in a speech to both Houses of Assembly, and which the world is left to place where it pleases.

Your Excellency expressly says, there has been an attack upon government in form; and an ill judged and ill timed oppugnation of the King's authority. A regard to our own character, to truth and justice, and the reputation of the province, in which we have the honor to serve his Majesty, oblige us to speak upon this point with a freedom, in which we are far from meaning the least disrespect to your Excellency. Silence, upon such an occasion, would merit the imputation, which some may be ready, from your manner of expression, to lay upon us, and would prove us equally unworthy of the choice which has been made of us, and your Excellency's approbation. Have, then, the people of this province been guilty of an attack upon government in form, or of any oppugnation of the King's authority ? We declare to your Excellency, we know of no such thing. The people, ever loyal to the best of Sovereigns, and sensible of their felicity in connexion with, and subordination to, the mother country, have given new and unaffected testimony that these happy dispositions have increased in all orders, upon the indulgence granted to them. They have rejoiced, with the highest marks of honor and gratitude to the King, to both Houses of Parliament, and to our friends and patrons in Great Britain. They continually demonstrate a natural and warm affection to the country from which they derive, and by which they have been protected and cherished. It has been no small addition to the joy of the wise and sober upon the late great occasion, that quite through the province good order and decorum have happily been preserved ; and it is to the honor of that gracious Prince, under whose government, all ranks among us account themselves happy. And we think it of peculiar importance, at the present season, to the people of this province, that they be viewed in this light. Your Excellency will, therefore, allow us to bear this public testimony ; a testimony which may perhaps appear the more disinterested, as it comes from those who are not their more immediate representatives. In the above cited passage, and in a great part of your speech, if your Excellency had a particular reference to the transaction of both Houses in the late election of Counsellors, we beg leave to assure your Excellency, that we know of nothing done by the General Assembly on that day, which can, with any shadow of propriety, be deemed an attack upon government, or an oppugnation of the King's authority. Every part of the Legislature has acted in its proper place, and exerted those powers only with which they were entrusted by charter. No branch has usurped, or interfered with, the right of another. Diversity of sentiment respecting men and measures, and collisions of parties are common in all free governments. Some elections have been made, which your Excellency has signified your disapprobation of ; and it has had its effect. No one having called in question your right to negative such elections, or opposed you in the exercise of this branch of your authority. It would be improper to deliver our opinion of the expediency of any instances in which your Excellency and the two Houses of Assembly have exerted the several powers which respectively belonged to each. But we are obliged to assert, that nothing has taken place but what has been constitutional and according to the charter. And we are persuaded your Excellency, upon reflection, will not think that an election duly made, though disagreeable to the chair, deserves to be called a formal attack upon government, or an oppugnation of the King's authority. And should any thing like this be ever attempted, your Excellency would find this Board zealous to defend our Sovereign's honor and the constitutional power of his representative. We beg leave to assure your Excellency, that we shall heartily join with you in healing divisions and burying animosities, should they arise ; and that we shall cheerfully contribute all our power to the peace and honor of your administration.

May it please your Excellency,

The letter from the right honorable Mr. Secretary Conway, to your Excellency, accompanying your second speech from the chair, affords us a most agreeable occasion of repeatedly declaring the strong sentiments of respect and gratitude, with which we regard the lenity and tenderness already so remarkably manifested on the part of his Majesty and the Parliament, to the American colonies, and the prospect given us of some additional indulgencies ; for all which it will be our pleasure, as it must be our glory, to make the most dutiful and affectionate returns. These are the dispositions which have uniformly influenced this Board, before we saw this letter, so happily adapted to confirm us in them. And we beg leave to assure your Excellency, that from these dispositions we shall continue to act.

There are several paragraphs in your Excellency's speeches, which have been construed to bear hard on the gentlemen, who now constitute the Board ; but your explanation of them in Council, and your repeated declarations, that you had no such intention, have given satisfaction to the Board.

We again beg leave to assure your Excellency, that our best abilities shall be faithfully employed in promoting his Majesty's honor and interest, and in making every part of your administration easy and happy ; and such testimonies of your conduct, as are contained in Mr. Secretary Conway's letter, will not suffer us to conclude, without recognizing your Excellency in the united character of a true friend to the province, and a faithful servant to the Crown.

[The committee who reported the above, were W. Brattle, J. Bowdoin, H. Gray, N. Ropes, and R. Tyler ; and the committee who presented it, were W. Brattle, G. Bradford, T. Flucker, J. Powell, and J. Pitts.]

ANSWER

OF THE HOUSE OF REPRESENTATIVES, TO THE GOVERNOR'S SPEECH,
JUNE 5, 1766.

May it please your Excellency,

THE House have fully considered your Excellency's speech
of the third instant, and beg leave to observe, that as on the one
hand no consideration shall ever induce us to remit in the least our
loyalty and gratitude to the best of Kings, so on the other, no un-
provoked asperity of expression on the part of your Excellency
can deter us from asserting our undoubted charter rights and privileges. One of the principal of those is, that of annually choosing
his Majesty's Council for this province.

Had the most excellent letter from one of his Majesty's principal Secretaries of State, which has been communicated to the
House, arrived sooner, it could not have prevented the freedom
of our elections ; nor can we, on the strictest examination of the
transactions of the day of our general election, so far as the House
was concerned, discover the least reason for regret. So long as
we shall have our charter privileges continued, we must think ourselves inexcusable, if we should suffer ourselves to be intimidated
in the free exercise of them. This exercise of our rights can never,
with any color of reason, be adjudged an abuse of our liberty.

Lest we should be at a loss for the proceedings and transactions which have given your Excelleucy so much uneasiness, you
have been pleased to inform us, in express terms, that you " mean
the excluding from the King's Council the principal Crown Officers ; men not only respectable in themselves for their integrity,
their abilities and their fidelity to their country, as well as to their
King, but also quite necessary to the administration of government
in the very station from whence we have displaced them." Had
your Excellency thought fit to have favored us with your sentiments and opinion of the candidates previously to the election, it
could not have more arrested our attention as a breach of our privileges ; and it would surely be as proper to give intimations of this
kind before, as now the business is past a remedy, for this year at
least. The Assembly of another year will act for themselves, or
under such influence and direction as they may think fit. The
two Crown Officers who were of the Honorable Board the last
year, and not chosen this, are the Lieutenant Governor and Secretary. The other gentlemen of the Board last year, who are not
chosen this, hold only provincial commissions. This province has
subsisted and flourished, and the administration of government
has been carried on here entirely to the royal approbation, when
no Crown Officers had a seat at the Board, and we trust this may

be the case again. We find not in the Secretary of State's letter
the least intimation that it was expected by his Majesty or his
Ministry, that we should elect into his Majesty's Council the
principal, or indeed any other Crown Officers. For any thing
that appears in the letter, we are left entirely to the exercise of
our own judgment and best discretion in making our elections
agreeably to the royal charter.

If it is not now in our power in so full a manner, as will be expected, to show our respectful gratitude to the mother country, or
to make a dutiful, affectionate return to the indulgence of the
King and Parliament, it shall be no fault of ours; for this we intend and hope, we shall be able fully to effect.

We cannot persuade ourselves that it must and will be understood that those gentlemen were turned out, as your Excellency
is pleased to express it, for their deference to acts of the British
Legislature. We have given the true reason of this proceeding
in our answer to your Excellency's first speech of this session.
We are under no apprehension that when the true grounds and
reasons of our proceedings are known and candidly considered,
we shall be in the least degree chargeable with unthankfulness
and dissatisfaction on ground of former heat and prevailing prejudice, or on any other ground.

Your Excellency says, " it is impossible to give any tolerable
coloring to this proceeding." The integrity and uprightness of
our intentions and conduct is such, that no coloring is requisite,
and therefore we shall excuse ourselves from attempting any.
We hold ourselves to be quite free in our suffrages; and provided
we observe the directions of our charter, and the laws of the land,
both which we have strictly adhered to, we are by no means accountable but to God and our own consciences for the manner in
which we give them. We believe your Excellency is the first
Governor of this province that ever formally called the two Houses
of Assembly to account for their suffrages, and accused them of
ingratitude and disaffection to the Crown, because they had not
bestowed them on such persons as in the opinion of the Governor,
were quite necessary to the administration of government. Had
your Excellency been pleased in season to have favored us with a
list, and positive orders whom to choose, we should, on your principles have been without excuse. But even the most abject slaves
are not to be blamed for disobeying their master's will and pleasure when it is wholly unknown to them.

Your Excellency says, " If it should be justified by asserting a
right, that is, a legal power to choose whom we please, without regard to any considerations whatever, the justification itself will tend
to impeach the right." We clearly assert our charter rights of a
free election. But for your Excellency's definition of this right,
viz. " a legal power to choose whom we please, without regard to
any considerations whatever," we contend not. We made our

12

elections after the most mature and deliberate consideration, and had special regard to the qualifications of the candidates, and all circumstances considered, chose those we judged most likely to serve his Majesty, and promote the welfare and prosperity of his people. We cannot conceive how the assertion of our clear charter right of free election can tend to impeach that right or charter. We would hope that your Excellency does not mean open and publicly to threaten us with a deprivation of our charter privileges, merely for exercising them according to our best judgment and discretion. As to us, as our charter is, we should think it of very little value, if it should be adjudged that the sense and spirit of it require the electors should be under the absolute direction and control of the Chair, even in giving their suffrages. For whatever may be our ideas of the wisdom, prudence, mildness and moderation of your administration, of your forgiving spirit, yet we are not sure your successor will possess those shining virtues.

We are very sensible that be our right of election ever so clear and absolute, there is a distinction between a right and the propriety of exercising it. This distinction we hope, will apply itself with full force, and all its advantage to your Excellency's reluctant exertion of the prerogative in disapproving six of the gentlemen chosen by the two Houses of Assembly. But this being a matter of discretion, is solely within your Excellency's breast, and we are taught by your just distinction, that such is the gift of suffrages. It therefore gives us great pain to have our discretion questioned, and our public conduct thus repeatedly arraigned.

Your Excellency has intimated your readiness to concur with us in any palliative or expedient to prevent the bad effects of our elections, which you think must surely be very hurtful to the province, if it should be maintained and vindicated. But, as we are under no apprehensions of any such effects, especially when we reflect on the ability and integrity of the Council your Excellency has approved of, we beg leave to excuse ourselves from any unnecessary search after palliatives or expedients.

We thank your Excellency for your kind assurances of " using all means to save the credit of this province." But we conceive that when the true state of the province is represented and known, its credit can be in no kind of danger. The recommendation enjoined by Mr. Secretary Conway's letter, and in consequence thereof made to us, we shall embrace the first convenient opportunity to consider and act upon. In the mean time cannot but observe, that it is conceived in much higher and stronger terms in the speech than in the letter. Whether in thus exceeding, your Excellency speaks by your own authority, or a higher, is not with us to determine.

However, if this recommendation, which your Excellency terms a requisition, be founded on " so much justice and humanity that it cannot be controverted :" If " the authority with which it is introduced should preclude all disputation about complying with it," we should be glad to know what freedom we have in the case.

In answer to the questions which your Excellency has proposed with so much seeming emotion, we beg leave to declare, that we will not suffer ourselves to be in the least influenced by party animosities or domestic feuds, let them exist where they may : that if we can possibly prevent it, this fine country shall never be ruined by any person : that it shall be through no default of ours, should this people be deprived of the great and manifest advantages which the favor and indulgence of our most gracious Sovereign and his Parliament are even now providing for them. On the contrary, that it shall ever be our highest ambition, as it is our duty, so to demean ourselves in public and private life, as shall most clearly demonstrate our loyalty and gratitude to the best of Kings, and thereby recommend this people to further gracious marks of the royal clemency and favor.

With regard to the rest of your Excellency's speech, we are sorry we are constrained to observe, that the general air and style of its savors much more of an act of free grace and pardon, than of a parliamentary address to the two Houses of Assembly ; and we most sincerely wish your Excellency had been pleased to reserve it (if needful) for a proclamation.

[The committee who prepared this answer, were T. Cushing, (the Speaker,) Mr. Otis, Major Hawley, Mr. Saunders, Col. O. Partridge, S. Adams, and Col. Bowers.]

ADDRESS OF THANKS

FROM THE HOUSE OF REPRESENTATIVES TO THE KING, FOR IIIS ASSENT TO THE REPEAL OF THE STAMP ACT, JUNE 19, 1766.

Most Gracious Sovereign,

Your Majesty's most faithful subjects, the Representatives of your province of Massachusetts Bay, in New England, under the deepest sense of duty and loyalty, beg leave humbly to approach the throne, and to express their warmest gratitude, that your Majesty has been pleased, in Parliament, to give your royal assent to the repeal of the American stamp act.

This is a repeated instance of your royal clemency, and affords a fresh and affecting testimony of your Majesty's unremitted and indulgent attention to the welfare and happiness of all your subjects.

Your Majesty will allow us, with the greatest grief and anxiety, to express our apprehension, that your American subjects may have been represented to your Parliament as having manifested some kind of disaffection to their constitutional dependence on the parent country; and as disposed to take occasion from the lenity and tenderness of your Majesty and the Parliament, to abate of their respect and submission to the supreme legislative authority of Great Britain.

Permit us, with all humility, to assure your Majesty of the great injustice of any such representations. Your subjects of this province, and we doubt not of the whole continent of America, are too sensible of the blessings they enjoy under your mild and gracious government, to admit the idea of such a temper and conduct, without abhorrence. They esteem their connexion with their fellow subjects in Great Britain, and a constitutional subordination to your Parliament, their great privilege and security. Happy in the full possession of our rights and liberties under your Majesty's propitious government, we never can be wanting in returns of duty and the most grateful affection.

Such, may it please your Majesty, are our dispositions; and we beg leave to assure your Majesty, that we shall ever esteem it our glory to cultivate, as far as our influence may extend, all sentiments of loyalty and affection to your Majesty's personal government, and to maintain a happy harmony between your subjects of Great Britain and those of your American colonies.

(Signed)   T. CUSHING, Speaker.

[The committee by whom this address was prepared, were the Speaker, (Mr. Cushing,) Mr. Otis, Mr. Worthington, Mr. Adams, Mr. Dexter, and O. Partridge.]

═══

VOTE OF THANKS

OF THE HOUSE OF REPRESENTATIVES TO DIVERS NOBLEMEN AND GEN-
TLEMEN, IN ENGLAND, FOR THEIR EFFORTS IN PROCURING A REPEAL
OF THE STAMP ACT, JUNE 20, 1766.

UPON a motion made and seconded, resolved, unanimously, that the most grateful acknowledgments of this House be made to the right honorable William Pitt, Esq. for his noble and generous efforts, in the present session of Parliament, in favor of the British colonies; and particularly for the display of his great abilities, and his assiduous and successful endeavors, in procuring an act for the repeal of the stamp act; and that the Speaker be desired, by the first opportunity, to transmit to him a letter accordingly.

Resolved, unanimously, that the most sincere thanks of this House be given to his grace, Augustus Henry, Duke of Grafton, one of his Majesty's principal Secretaries of State, &c. for his noble and generous patronage of the British colonies. And that a copy of this vote be transmitted to his grace, in the most respectful manner, by the Speaker.

The House also unanimously passed a vote of thanks, in the same tenor, severally to,

His grace, Philip Dorsett, Earl of Chesterfield, Lord Stanhope; his Grace, Thomas Pelham, Duke of Newcastle; his Grace, Charles, Duke of Richmond; the right honorable Robert Earl, of Northington, Lord High Chancellor of Great Britain; the right honorable Henry Seymore Conway, Esq. one of his Majesty's principal Secretaries of State; the right honorable Charles Watson, Marquis of Rockingham, first Lord Commissioner of his Majesty's treasury; the right honorable George Onslow; the right honorable Charles Townsend; the right honorable William, Earl of Shelburne; the right honorable Charles, Earl of Campden; the right honorable William, Earl of Dartmouth; the right honorable John, Earl of Egmont; the right honorable George, Duke of Pomfret; the right honorable Vere Poulett, Earl Poulett; the right honorable George, Lord Edgcumb; the right honorable William Dowdswell, Esq. Chancellor of his Majesty's Exchequer; Sir George Saville, Baronet, member of Parliament, for Yorkshire; Sir William Meredith, Knight, member of Parliament, for Liverpool; the right honorable Arthur Onslow, Esq.; the honorable George Howard, Esq. member of Parliament, and General in his Majesty's army; the honorable Isaac Barre, Esq. member of Parliament, and Colonel in his Majesty's army; Sir William Baker, Knight, member of Parliament; and George Cooke, Esq. member of Parliament.

―――――

ANSWER

OF THE HOUSE OF REPRESENTATIVES TO THE GOVERNOR'S SPEECH OF JUNE 3, RESPECTING COMPENSATION TO THOSE WHO SUFFERED IN THE RIOTS OF AUGUST 1765....JUNE 25, 1766.

[The Governor's speech of May 29, and of June 3, 1766, refer to the subject, and recommend the House of Representatives to provide for their remuneration; as will be seen by a perusal of those speeches. June 24, 1766, the House appointed a committee to prepare a message to the Governor in answer to that part of his speech which recommends such compensation. The committee consisted of Mr. Cushing, (the Speaker,) S. Adams, S. Dexter,

Col. Richmond, and Capt. Saunders.   On the 25th of June the committee reported the following, which was adopted.]

May it please your Excellency,

THE House of Representatives have duly attended to that part of your Excellency's speech which had reference to a full and ample compensation to be made to the sufferers in the late disturbances.

We are sensibly affected with the loss they have sustained, and have the greatest abhorrence of the madness and barbarity of those persons who were the instruments of their sufferings.   Nothing shall be omitted by us, in our department, to bring the perpetrators of so horrid a fact to exemplary justice ; and if it be in their power, to a pecuniary restitution of all damages.   But, may it please your Excellency, as a compliance with your Excellency's recommendation to the Provincial Assembly, to make up their losses, appears to this House, not as an act of justice, but rather of generosity, they are in doubt, whether they have any authority to make their constituents chargeable with, without their express consent.   The House, therefore, beg leave to acquaint your Excellency, that they have thought it their duty to refer the consideration of this matter to the next sitting of the General Court, that the members may have the opportunity of taking the minds and instructions of their several towns thereon.

═══

MESSAGE

OF GOVERNOR BERNARD, TO THE HOUSE OF REPRESENTATIVES,
JUNE 27, 1766.

Gentlemen of the House of Representatives,

As your reasons for not complying at present with what has been recommended to you by order of the King, with the advice of his Parliament, on the behalf of the sufferers in the late disturbances, will probably be canvassed with great precision, it will be proper that the intendment of them should be as certain as may be.   I should, therefore, be glad to know whether I must understand from your message of yesterday, that it is your opinion that a detection of the perpetrators of the late mischiefs is necessary to entitle the sufferers to a compensation for their losses.

It appears to be the gracious intention of the King and Parliament, that a veil should be cast over the late disturbances, provided it be covered by a general and uniform dutiful behavior for the future. But it is certainly no less their firm and resolute purpose, that the sufferers by these disturbances shall have a full and ample indemnification made to them. And this business has been committed to you upon principles of humanity and justice, rather than of mere generosity.

If you think, that an inquiry into the promotion and perpetration of the late disorders a necessary preliminary to determine, from whom the charge of the compensation shall finally come, and shall pronounce for the expediency of such an inquiry, you will certainly be assisted by the Governor and Council in the prosecution of it. And I dare say it will be no difficult work to trace this matter to the bottom.*

But in the mean time, I fear the King and Parliament will think their intimations disregarded, by your proposing an inquiry now, after it has been neglected for nine months past : during all which time the House have had this very business of indemnifications under their consideration. They expect from you, that the sufferers shall be indemnified at all events, whether the offenders are discovered or not, or whether they are able to pay the damages or not ; and seem to be more intent upon indemnification than upon punishment.

I, therefore, wish for the sake of the province, whose interests, and especially those of its trade, are now in a very nice balance, and for the sake of this town, whose respectable inhabitants have already suffered much in the opinion of the world, for having been tame spectators of the violences committed in it ; that you would remove this disgrace without the least delay, by ordering the indemnification immediately to be made upon the credit of those whom you shall hereafter judge to be chargeable with it. When this is done, there can be no objection to your postponing the consideration, on whom this money ought ultimately to be laid, to what time you please. And there is no doubt but that any inquiry, which you shall think fit to make for this purpose, will be as efficacious as you can desire.

FRA. BERNARD.

* The House appointed a committee, viz. Gen. Ruggles, Mr. Hall, Mr. Sheaffe, and Mr. Hancock, to wait on the Governor, and desire him to acquaint them whether he had any light whereby the House might come to a knowledge of the rioters of last year ; who reported, that the Governor was pleased to inform them, that he heard many hints and some few persons named ; that he had not taken any minutes respecting the matter ; but if the House were disposed to sit into the next week, he would recollect what had occurred to him on the subject, and acquaint such a committee of secrecy, as the House might think proper to appoint, with all he knew of the matter. A committee was accordingly appointed by the House, to sit in the recess of the Court, and make inquiry into the riots committed in August, 1765, with power to send for persons and papers ; and that the matter of their inquiry be kept a secret, till they should make a report to the House. The Court was adjourned, June 28, and convened again by the Governor, October 29 ; and on the 30th, the committee aforementioned reported, that July 9th, they waited on his Excellency to receive that assistance, which he was pleased to propose to the House, in his message, last session. He, therefore, called the Council together. The committee offered to hear and receive any information from the Governor and Council, respecting the riots. But none was communicated ; and the Council was adjourned without day.

ANSWER

May it please your Excellency,

THE House have duly attended to your Excellency's message of the 27th inst. We are fully sensible of the goodness of the King and Parliament; and agree with your Excellency, that it appears to be their gracious intention that a veil should be drawn over the late disturbances. And we hope our behavior will always be such as to merit their approbation.

Sir, the House are ever attentive to the applications of persons of every rank, whose case justly claims their consideration. But as the sufferers, whom we apprehend your Excellency refers to, have never applied to this House in a parliamentary way for relief, we are humbly of opinion, that we have done all at present that our gracious Sovereign and his Parliament can reasonably expect from us. But to shew our regard to every thing recommended by the King and Parliament, we have appointed a committee to sit in the recess of the Court, to make a thorough inquiry into the riots committed in August last, and to discover the persons concerned therein, as far as may be. For the effectuating which business, we doubt not but we shall be aided by your Excellency and his Majesty's Council.

And further, would acquaint your Excellency, that the House have passed a resolve to take the report of this committee under consideration, at the beginning of the next session of this Court, and act thereon what shall appear to them to be just and reasonable.

Your Excellency is pleased to enforce the immediate compliance of the House with this requisition, by an argument drawn from a regard to the town of Boston, the reputation of whose inhabitants your Excellency says has already suffered much for having been tame spectators of the violences committed, and that this disgrace would be removed thereby. We see no reason why the reputation of that town should suffer in the opinion of any one, from all the evidence which has fallen under the observation of the House. Nor does it appear to us how a compliance would remove such disgrace, if that town had been so unhappy as to have fallen under it.

SPEECH

OF GOVERNOR BERNARD, TO THE COUNCIL AND HOUSE OF
REPRESENTATIVES, OCTOBER 29, 1766.

Gentlemen of the Council, and
    Gentlemen of the House of Representatives,

I HAVE thought proper to call you together, that you may have an opportunity to give a positive answer to what I recommended to you, by order of his Majesty, last session; as it will be expected of me that it be reported to his Majesty before the opening of the business of the next year; and I heartily wish it may be such as will answer the expectations and desires of your friends in Great Britain. For my own part, I shall upon this occasion, as upon all others, make the best use of the means you shall put in my hands to promote the honor and reputation of the province.

As you are called together for this business only, when it is finished, I shall have no objection to your returning home, until the usual time of opening the winter session.

FRA. BERNARD.

Council Chamber, October 29, 1766.

ANSWER

OF THE HOUSE OF REPRESENTATIVES TO THE ABOVE SPEECH,
NOVEMBER 11, 1766.

May it please your Excellency,

YOUR speech to both Houses at the opening of the present session, has been repeatedly under the most deliberate consideration of the House of Representatives.

It was indeed, sir, with great reluctance, that the House found themselves under the necessity of having recourse to your former speech and message upon this occasion; but as you are pleased to refer us to them without saying any thing to qualify them, the House cannot help observing, that the manner in which your Excellency has repeatedly proposed a compensation to the sufferers, has been derogatory to the honor of the House, and in breach of the privileges thereof. That the terms you have made use of, have been essentially different from those, dictated to you, by his Majesty's express command, signified in a letter from his Secretary of State. That they tended to weaken the inherent, uncon-

13

trolable right of the people, to dispose of their own money to such purposes as they shall judge expedient, and to no other. And that, under these apprehensions, it is not improbable, some of the towns may have framed their instructions to their Representatives against a compensation out of the public treasury.

The House, however, with the most dutiful and profound respect, have attended to his Majesty's most gracious and mild recommendation ; and observe that it is his pious and benevolent intention, that not only a compensation should be made to the sufferers, in the late times, but also that a veil be drawn over every disgraceful scene, and to forgive, and even to forget, the undutiful behavior of any of his subjects, in those unhappy times.

Confirmed in the opinion, that an indemnification of the offenders is of equal importance and necessity with the making compensation to the sufferers, and being ever ready, with the utmost cheerfulness, to unite their endeavors in promoting the wise and gracious purposes of their rightful Sovereign ; in conformity to the spirit of Mr. Secretary Conway's letter, the House have framed a bill, entitled " An act for granting compensation to the sufferers, and general pardon, indemnity and oblivion to the offenders, in the late times."*

This bill they have ordered to be published for the consideration of the several towns, and humbly pray your Excellency would please to give them a recess for that purpose.

[Major Hawley, Mr. Dexter, Col. Bowers, Mr. Adams, and Major Johnson, were the committee who prepared the above answer.]

SPEECH

OF GOVERNOR BERNARD TO THE HOUSE OF REPRESENTATIVES,
NOVEMBER 13, 1766.

Gentlemen of the House of Representatives,

In the letter of the Earl of Shelburne, which I laid before you, you have a second testimony from another of his Majesty's Secretaries of State, of the tenderness and affection towards the people under my government, with which I have conducted myself during

---

* The said bill passed to be enacted, December 6, 1766. The preamble was as follows : " Whereas the King's most excellent Majesty, from a hearty and pious desire that the sufferers in the late riots should be compensated, and that a veil may be drawn over the late unhappy excesses, has been graciously pleased to signify his intention to forgive and forget them ; at the same time of his abundant clemency, recommending a compensation to the sufferers, &c. from a grateful sense of his Majesty's grace and clemency, in order to promote peace and safety, to make compensation to said sufferers, and thus to demonstrate to the world our sense of the happiness we enjoy, in being a part of the British empire, and being entitled to the rights, liberties and privileges of British subjects ; we, his Majesty's most dutiful and loyal subjects, the Representatives of the Commons of this province, in the great and General Court assembled, of our free and good will, have resolved to give and grant, and pray that it may be enacted," &c.

the late disputes, and therefore I shall make no other answer to the ungenerous insinuations in your message of yesterday, than by referring to your own journals, from whence it will evidently appear, that it is from among yourselves, and not from me, that the difficulties which have prevented your making a compensation to the sufferers, have arose.

I am very sorry that you have not already complied with what has been recommended to you; but it is some satisfaction to me, that you have laid a foundation for completing this business, which I hope will not fail of success. The importance of the affair, and the hasty approach of the new year, will not allow the loss of a day which can be saved; and therefore, I shall make the recess which you desire, as short as possible. And that you may do the business with as much credit to yourselves as may be, I shall continue the session until you can come to a final determination.

FRA. BERNARD.

Council Chamber, November 13, 1766.

—————

LETTER

OF LORD SHELBURNE TO GOVERNOR BERNARD, AND BY HIM LAID BEFORE THE GENERAL COURT.

Whitehall, September 13, 1766.

SIR,

I HAVE had the honor to lay before the King, your letters of the 29th of June, and 19th of July last, together with the enclosures therein contained; and I have received his Majesty's commands to communicate them to such of his servants, as he thinks proper usually to consult upon his most important affairs, as soon as the season of the year will conveniently admit of this meeting, for this and other purposes. In the mean time, his Majesty is extremely sorry to observe any degree of ill temper remaining in his colony of Massachusetts Bay, or, that points should be so improperly agitated, as to tend to the revival of disputes, which every friend to America must wish to be forgotten. They have seen the Parliament of Great Britain give due attention to all well founded complaints of the province, notwithstanding they appeared to them, in some parts, not so properly urged, and though the legislature will, certainly, on all just occasions, exercise and enforce its legislative power over the colonies, yet, it cannot be doubted, but it will exert it with a due regard to the nature of their connexion with the mother country.

Upon this occasion it is proper to observe, in general, that the ease and honor of his Majesty's government in America, will greatly depend on the temper and wisdom of those who are trusted with the administration there ; and that they ought to be persons disdaining narrow views, private combinations, and partial attachments. It is with great pleasure, sir, that I have observed the manner in which you have conducted yourself, during the disputes of the last year, which I cannot do, without highly approving your attention and watchfulness on the one hand, to support the authority of government, and on the other, the tenderness and affection which appeared in all your letters, toward the people under your government. A temperate conduct, founded on the true basis of public good, avoiding all the unnecessary reserve, where nothing arbitrary is thought of, and nothing unreasonable is required, must carry conviction to the hearts of the deluded, conciliate the minds of all, and ensure the confidence of his Majesty's loyal and loving subjects of America.

Upon these considerations, I am persuaded that the Assembly will, immediately upon their meeting, fall upon measures to terminate all local difficulties, which appear, by your accounts, to have hitherto prevented that compliance which will be expected by Parliament, with the *recommendations* you have been required to make, in consequence of the resolutions of both Houses. It is impossible to conceive that they will suffer any private considerations to interfere with their desire of shewing a proper sense of that paternal regard, which they have experienced from his Majesty, and of the attention which Parliament has given to their complaints ; which can never be done with more propriety, than by granting, with the utmost cheerfulness, a just compensation to those who have suffered by the late disorders.

I am, with truth and regard, sir, your most obedient, humble servant,   SHELBURNE.

RESOLVES

OF THE HOUSE OF REPRESENTATIVES ON THE SUBJECT OF COMPENSATION
TO THE SUFFERERS BY THE RIOTS IN 1765.

ORDERED, That Major Hawley, Mr. Otis, and Mr. Adams, be a committee to prepare a resolve, setting forth the motives which induced this House to pass the bill for granting compensation, &c. who reported thereon as follows :

Resolved, That this House, in passing the bill for granting compensation to the sufferers, and of free and general pardon, indemnity and oblivion, to the offenders in the late times, were influenced by a loyal and grateful regard to his Majesty's most mild and gracious recommendation ; by a deference to the opinion of the illustrious patrons of the colonies in Great Britain ; and for the sake of internal peace and order, without regard to any interpretation of his Majesty's recommendation into a requisition, precluding all debate and controversy ; and under a full persuasion that the sufferers had no just claim or demand on the province ; and that this compliance ought not hereafter to be drawn into a precedent.

After which the House passed the two following resolutions, viz.

1. Resolved, That it was the indispenasble duty of the sufferers to have applied to the government here, rather than to the government at home ; and that the neglect of any of them to petition to this Assembly till October last, while they were complaining at home, is very reprehensible.

2. Whereas it appears to this House, by the resolutions of the honorable the House of Commons of Great Britain, that it was their opinion that the resolutions of divers assemblies in America, had a tendency to encourage the riots that happened there, Resolved, that this cannot be said of the resolutions of the House of Representatives of this province, as the said riots happened about two months before any such resolutions were made.*

—

LETTER

FROM DENNYS DE BERDT, ESQ. AGENT FOR THE PROVINCE, IN ENGLAND, TO THE SPEAKER OF THE HOUSE OF REPRESENTATIVES, DATED AT LONDON, AUGUST 6. 1766.

SIR,

SINCE my last, I received a few lines from Lord Dartmouth, in which he says, " I am sorry to hear that the Assembly of Boston has *refused* to make the indemnification *recommended* by Parliament. New York has complied."

Had you been here to be fully apprized of the long debate which your friends supported in the House, to obtain the word " *recommend*," as a term entirely consistent with your liberty, it must have left a grateful impression on your mind, which your address is so full of, both to the King and Parliament, that I can hardly believe you should come to such a conclusion. If the report be a slander on the province, I shall be glad if you will put it in my power to refute it ; as I am ambitious your Assembly, who I have the honor to be employed by, should stand high in the esteem of the King, Ministry, and Parliament, as well as in the esteem of all the real friends of America, which such a refusal will abate.

* The riots were in August, 1765, and the resolutions in October after.

LETTER

FROM THE SAME, SEPTEMBER 19, 1766.

Since my last to you, I have received several letters from your friends, in answer to your vote of thanks, (which I enclose,) and the universal approbation it has met with, proves it a very well judged measure : and Lord Chesterfield and the old Speaker Onslow, whose hearts were warm in your cause, were very particularly pleased; and the latter desired me to assure your House, he esteemed it the highest honor which could be conferred on him.

Yesterday I waited on Lord Shelburne, our new Secretary of State ; and his Lordship expressed himself in such terms as gave me great satisfaction, and desired me to assure your House, he had the highest regard for America, wished their prosperity, and would make it his care to promote it. That you might be perfectly easy about the enjoyment of your rights and privileges under the present administration. But on the other hand, the dignity of government must be maintained, as well as due regard to the administration here ; which I assured them was your real disposition, as was manifest by the tenor of the addresses, two of which came through my hands, yours and from the lower counties of Pennsylvania.

He desired you would finish the affair of the damages sustained, because it gave occasion to your and the enemies of the administration to upbraid them for the gentle measures they adopted ; on the other hand, he had also written to every Governor on the continent to behave with moderation to the several provinces over which they preside ; and had written to your Governor in particular, to pursue healing measures. And added, that whatever new Governors were appointed, he would take care to send such men as should act on the most generous principles, and thereby secure the affections of the people.

SPEECH

OF GOVERNOR BERNARD, TO THE COUNCIL AND HOUSE OF REPRESENTATIVES, JANUARY 28, 1767.

Gentlemen of the Council, and
    Gentlemen of the House of Representatives,

At the opening of this session, I have nothing by command of his Majesty to lay before you. What I have to propose from myself, shall be communicated by separate papers. At present, I have only to recommend to you, that the support of the authority of the government, the maintenance of the honor of the province, and the promotion of the welfare of the people, may be the chief objects of your consultations. These are duties common to us all; and whilst they are truly pursued, there can be no room for disagreement or dissatisfaction.

FRA. BERNARD.

Council Chamber, January 28, 1767.

=====

ANSWER

OF THE HOUSE OF REPRESENTATIVES TO THE ABOVE,
JANUARY 31, 1767.

May it please your Excellency,

Your speech to both Houses of the General Assembly at the opening of the present session, has been duly considered by the House of Representatives.

Your Excellency is pleased to recommend " the support of the authority of the government, the maintenance of the honor of the province, and the promotion of the welfare of the people, as the chief objects of our consultations."

By the authority of the government, this House understand, the charter rights and powers of the Great and General Court or Assembly of this province, and the several branches of the same ; and the powers with which the civil officers of the province are by law vested. While the members of that Assembly firmly maintain those rights and powers, and the body of the people steadily and vigorously sustain and protect the civil officers in the exercise of their respective powers, in the full execution of the good laws of the province, and the discharge of their several trusts, whether judiciary or ministerial, we apprehend the authority of the government is then supported. It is necessary for the support of this authority, that the House of Representatives well inform themselves of the true extent of those rights and powers, and sacredly adhere to their own rights as one branch of the legislature. That they zealously assert the rights of their constituents, the people of this province ; without transgressing the bounds of their own power, or invading the rights and prerogatives of the other branches of the Assembly. And that they endeavor, that the body of the people be well acquainted with their own natural and constitutional rights and privileges ; and the liberty, safety, peace and happiness which they will not fail to enjoy, while the General Assembly is protected in the due exercise of their rights and powers, and the

laws of the land have their free course, and are faithfully and impartially executed. This, may it please your Excellency, being
our own apprehension of the authority of the government, and its
support, we shall always greatly rejoice to find your Excellency
exciting and animating us in the discharge of this important duty.
As it would be unpardonable in us ever to lose sight of it, your
Excellency may be assured, that we shall always make the support
of the authority of the government one great object of our consultations.

Upon this occasion, we cannot forbear to observe to your Excellency, with concern, that when the two Houses were directed
to attend your Excellency in the Council Chamber, at a time when
none but the General Assembly and their servants are intended to
be present, his Honor the Lieutenant Governor was pleased to appear in General Assembly, and there to continue till the House
returned to their chamber, while your Excellency was not only in
the province, but actually in the chair.   We are of opinion that
this conduct is not supportable by any precedent ; but should there
be found, upon searching ancient records, an instance of the
kind, it is not only in itself an impropriety, but repugnant to the
constitution, and the letter of the charter ; which declares the
great and General Court to consist of the Governor and Council,
or Assistants, for the time being, and such freeholders of the province, as shall be from time to time elected or deputed, by the
major part of the freeholders and other inhabitants, qualified by
the royal charter, to give their votes. If the honorable gentleman
was introduced by your Excellency, we apprehend that the happiest means of supporting the authority of the government, or
maintaining the honor of the province, were not consulted therein.
But if he came in and took a seat, of his own motion, we are constrained to say, that it affords a new and additional instance of
ambition, and a lust of power, to what we have heretofore observed.*

If your Excellency in recommending to our consultations the
support of the authority of the government, intends that executive
power is become weak, and calls for the aid of the legislative ;
and that an ill temper and a factious spirit so far prevails in the

* The Governor replied to this part of the Message from the House, and contended for
the propriety of the Lieutenant Governor's conduct in this case. The House replied to the
Governor's Message, and insisted that it was highly improper in the Lieutenant Governor
to take a seat in Council, as he had not been chosen a member, and as the Chair of the Governor was not vacant. They acknowledged, that there had been an instance of this kind in
1702, when Povey was Lieutenant Governor. But they stated, that Governor Belcher had
expressly excluded Tailor and Phips, at the time they were Lieutenant Governors, from a
seat in the Council, when they had not been elected thereto by the General Court. The Governor still insisted the conduct of Mr. Hutchinson in the affair, was correct ; and the latter
gentleman also addressed a letter to the Governor, (which was communicated to the House,)
complaining of the severity and partiality of the House, in objecting to his taking a seat at
the Council Board. The House then referred the subject to the Council, and requested them
to give an opinion whether they thought the Lieutenant Governor had a right to a seat at
the Board. They decided, unanimously, that he had not, " by charter, a constitutional
right to a seat at the Board, either with or without a voice." And they added, " the
Board assure the House, that they will sincerely endeavor to preserve the constitutional and
charter rights of his Majesty's most loyal and dutiful subjects of this province."

province, as to require severer methods, we can, with great satisfaction, inform you otherwise. Your Excellency may be assured that a disposition in the people to yield all due obedience to his Majesty's authority and the laws of this province, renders it altogether unnecessary that any extraordinary methods should be taken for that purpose. And as the welfare of the people so much depends upon it, we have just reason to expect that every branch of the legislature will take the most effectual measures to remove from the mind of our Sovereign such unfavorable sentiments of the province, as may have been occasioned by the malignant whispers of its enemies.

We cannot promise your Excellency that there shall be no disagreement or diversity of sentiments in matters of importance that may come before the General Court; this is scarcely to be expected in a free assembly. In such cases, this House, as they ever have, will still consider their own honor concerned, to debate with candor, and to decide with judgment. While the true end of government is kept in view, and invariably pursued in the several departments of it, the honor of the province and the welfare of the people will be maintained and promoted, and there can be no room for dissatisfaction.

Had your Excellency any command from his Majesty to lay before us, we should attend to it with the utmost loyalty and respect; being fully persuaded that our gracious Sovereign will require of us nothing but what is just and wise. When you shall be pleased to communicate to us any proposal of your own, we shall duly consider its nature, importance and tendency, and act agreeably to the best light of our own understanding.

MESSAGE

FROM THE HOUSE OF REPRESENTATIVES, TO THE GOVERNOR,
JANUARY 30, 1767.

The House of Representatives beg to be informed by your Excellency, whether any provision has been made, at the expense of this government, for his Majesty's troops lately arrived in this harbor, and by whom? And also whether your Excellency has reason to expect the arrival of any more to be quartered in this province?

14

THE FOLLOWING MESSAGE WAS RECEIVED FROM HIS EXCELLENCY,
IN ANSWER TO THE ABOVE.

Gentlemen of the House of Representatives,

In answer to your message of this day, I send you a copy of the minutes of Council, by which provision for the artillery company at the Castle, in pursuance of the late act of Parliament, was made.

I intended to lay the matter before you, and had given orders for an account of the present expenses to be made out for that purpose, which, having received since your message came to me, I hereby communicate.

I have received no advice whatever of any other troops being quartered in this province; nor have I any reason to expect the arrival of such, except from common report, to which I give little credit.   FRA. BERNARD.

———

MESSAGE

FROM THE HOUSE OF REPRESENTATIVES, TO THE GOVERNOR,
FEBRUARY 4, 1767.

May it please your Excellency,

In reply to your message of the 30th of January, the House of Representatives beg leave to observe, that it is by virtue of the royal charter alone, that the Governor and Council have any authority to issue money out of the treasury, and that only according to such acts as are, or may be, in force within this province. This clause was intended to secure to the House of Representatives the privilege of originating, granting, and disposing of taxes. But we apprehend it would be of very little value and importance, if it should become a settled rule that the House are obliged to impose and levy assessments, rates, and taxes upon the estates or persons of their constituents, for the payment of such expenses as may be incurred by virtue of an order of the Governor and Council, without the knowledge and consent of the House. Your Excellency, therefore, in giving orders, with the advice of the Council, for making provision for the artillery companies at the Castle, acted, in an essential point, contrary to the plain intention of the charter of the province, wherein the powers of the several branches of the General Assembly are declared and limited. If, however, there was an urgent necessity for this procedure, in the recess of the Court, we are very much surprised, that your Excellency should suffer the whole of the last session of the General Assembly to pass over without laying this matter before us; and that it was again omitted, in the present session, till the House had waited upon your Excellency with their message. It is the just expectation of this House, founded in the principles of the constitution, to have the earliest notice of a matter of this nature; and we cannot but remonstrate to your Excellency, that the omission of it was a breach of our privileges.

But, may it please your Excellency, it is still more grievous to us to find your Excellency making mention of a late act of Parliament, in pursuance of which your Excellency and the Council have created this expense to the province. One great grievance in regard to the stamp act was, that it deprived us of the advantage of a fundamental and most essential part of the British constitution, the unalienable right of freedom from all taxation, but such as we shall voluntarily consent to and grant. While we feel a sense of the worth and importance of this right, we cannot but express concern that an act of Parliament should yet be in being, which appears to us to be as real a grievance, as was that which so justly alarmed this continent. Your Excellency and the Council, by taking this step, have unwarrantably and unconstitutionally subjected the people of this province to an expense without giving this House an opportunity of passing their judgment upon it; and have also put it out of our power, by an act of our own, to testify the same cheerfulness which this Assembly has always shown in granting to his Majesty of their free accord, such aids as his Majesty's service has from time to time required.

[The committee who reported this message, were Mr. Cushing, (the Speaker,) Mr. Otis, Maj. Hawley, Capt. Sheaffe, Mr. Adams, Mr. Dexter, and Col Ward.]

MESSAGE

OF GOVERNOR BERNARD, TO THE HOUSE OF REPRESENTATIVES, FEBRUARY 17, 1767.

Gentlemen of the House of Representatives,

THE charges against me and the Council, contained in your message of the 4th instant, have had a full consideration; the result of which is, that the proceedings in making provisions for the King's troops, lately arrived here, appear to be constitutional and warrantable; and are justified not only by the usage of this government, but by the authority of the General Court itself.

The barracks at the Castle were built by order of the General Court, for the reception of the King's troops, when they should arrive here, that there might be no occasion for quartering them upon the inhabitants. Fuel and candles are necessary to the occupation of barracks; without them, no troops could go in, or stay there; it being an allowance always incidental to their living in barracks. When, therefore, the General Court ordered these barracks to be built for troops, it must have been implied, that the incidental necessaries should be provided for the troops, when they went into them. Otherwise, we must suppose, that the General Court did not intend that the barracks should be applied to the use for which they were built.

The manner of making the provision, and the provision itself, were agreeable to the usage of this government, in the like cases. It consisted of fuel and candles only, which are absolutely necessary, and always have been allowed in these barracks; and it did not include several articles prescribed by the act of Parliament; and therefore, it was wholly conformable to the usage of the government and the necessity of the case, but to the act only, as it coincided with it. If there had been no such act, the Council would have thought themselves obliged to advise the ordering this provision, as it was necessary to the use of the barracks; it being their duty, in the recess of the General Court, to assist me in carrying into execution, by the usual means, an establishment provided for the convenience of the people.

As to your complaint against me, for not laying this matter before you, during the whole of the last session, and part of this, I shall only state the facts, and leave it there. What you call the whole of the last session, was only the six last days of it, when you met after an adjournment, to pass upon the compensation bill, As soon as you had finished that business, you desired me to grant you a recess. I did so; and told you at the same time, that, upon that account, I had postponed all other business to the next session. As to the part of this session, it was not forty-eight hours; and within that time, I had given orders for making out an account of the expense of the provision, in order to lay it before you, and I actually received it within two hours after I had your message. This is the whole of what you call an omission in breach of your privileges.   FRA. BERNARD.

SPEECH

OF GOVERNOR BERNARD, TO THE COUNCIL AND HOUSE OF REPRESENTATIVES, MAY 28, 1767.

Gentlemen of the Council, and
Gentlemen of the House of Representatives,

AT the opening of this session, I have nothing from the immediate command of his Majesty to lay before you. I therefore cannot employ the present opportunity better than by recommending to you to endeavor to restore to this General Court the mutual confidence and unanimity which prevailed in it until they were interrupted by the late popular uneasiness. And I must, at the same time, assure you, that I shall heartily concur with you in all measures which shall be conducive to so salutary an end.

I do not, however, mean to decline the full exercise of the constitutional powers with which I am vested : they are derived from the same fountain with your own privileges ; and therefore I trust that the free use of them can never give just cause of offence. But, as I desire to temper my authority with all possible moderation, I shall be obliged to you for every opportunity you shall give me to make evident this disposition.

The business of this session is generally short, and the season of the year requires that it should be so. You must have observed how very expensive unnecessary disputation is ; and therefore, I hope you will avoid it, that the public business may be done with all proper despatch, and you may return to your homes as soon as well may be. FRA. BERNARD.

[The Governor objected to J. Gerrish, T. Saunders, Col. Otis, J. Bowers, and S. Dexter, who had been elected Counsellors. The House immediately appointed them a committee to introduce to the Governor two gentlemen chosen Counsellors from their body.]

———

MESSAGE

FROM THE GOVERNOR TO THE HOUSE OF REPRESENTATIVES, MAY 28, 1767.

Gentlemen of the House of Representatives,

THIS morning Ensign Dalrymple, of the 14th regiment of foot, informed me that he was just arrived from Scotland, with twenty-seven recruits for said regiment, and praying that I would order quarters to be assigned for them. I accordingly ordered, that they should be received into the barracks at the Castle; and I laid the matter before the Council, and asked their advice concerning the ordering the usual allowances for these men, while they remain in the barracks. The Council have advised me, as the House is now sitting, to communicate this matter to the House, which I do, accordingly ; and desire that you will take order that proper provision be made for these men, while they remain in the barracks.

FRA. BERNARD.

ANSWER

OF THE HOUSE OF REPRESENTATIVES TO THE GOVERNOR'S SPEECH,.
JUNE 2, 1767.

May it please your Excellency,

Having duly considered your speech at the opening of this session, the House of Representatives beg leave, with great sincerity, to say, that there is nothing which they more ardently wish for, than a mutual confidence in the several branches of the General Assembly, and a happy unanimity in such measures as shall best promote the prosperity of his Majesty's government, and the peace and welfare of his subjects of this province. At the same time, we must freely declare to your Excellency, that during the whole period of that general calamity and distress, which you chose to denominate a popular uneasiness, we do not recollect a single act done by the representative body of this province, which could have the least tendency to interrupt a general harmony, so essentially necessary for the valuable purposes of government. Nor can it, in our opinion, without great injustice, be supposed, that had there been, in reality, nothing more than a groundless, popular uneasiness, it would have been suffered to intermix with their public councils, and occasion a breach of confidence.

We are obliged to say that there is the deepest concern among the people of this province ; that after they have shewn every possible mark of loyalty, it has yet been represented to his Majesty, that a degree of ill temper remains in his colony of Massachusetts Bay. The letter from the Secretary of State, (Lord Shelburne) which your Excellency communicated to the last Assembly, leaves no room to doubt but that such representation has been made.* Permit us, sir, just to observe, that nothing will tend more to conciliate the minds of this people, than to give us the opportunity

---

* Governor Bernard had often complained to the British ministry, before this period, as he continued afterwards to do, that the province was in a state of rebellion, and could not be governed, but by a military force. He recommended arbitrary measures, and urged to the appointment of Counsellors by the Crown, &c.

to make it evident to our constituents, that you have had no hand in such representation. Such a measure might tend to remove that concern, and to restore unanimity to this General Court ; and we rely on that assurance you have given us, that you will *heartily* concur with us in all measures which shall be conducive to so salutary a purpose.

You are pleased to make an open and express declaration, that you do not mean to decline the full exercise of the constitutional powers with which you are vested. We are fully convinced of it ; nor have we the least desire that you should ever decline the full exercise of those powers. Your Excellency, however, will allow us to say, that there is such a thing as an indiscreet use of legal power, of which this House have a right to form their own judgment.

Your Excellency tells us, you desire to temper your authority with all proper moderation. Whether you have not already, since the opening of this session, missed the fairest opportunity of making evident such a disposition, is a matter that is now open to the judgment of the world.

You have not been pleased to point out the business of this session, but strongly recommend to us to shorten it, as the season of the year requires. We are sensible there are matters that immediately concern his Majesty's government of this province, which properly now come before us. These we shall despatch in as short a time as will admit of a due deliberation upon them. Unnecessary disputation we shall avoid. Your Excellency tells us, we must have observed how very expensive it is. If you refer to the disputes of the last year, we do not judge them, so far as we have observed, to have been unnecessary, or protracted beyond due bounds. We are sorry there was occasion given for them ; but, in our opinion, the late House of Representatives are not chargeable with it. As the rights of this people are now entrusted to us, it is our indispensable duty to maintain and defend them. We hope none of them will be drawn into question ; but should that be the case, we are bound in conscience to contend for them ; and therefore we shall not think the dispute on our part unnecessary, or the time employed in it mispent.

[The committee who reported this answer were, Major Hawley, Mr. Otis, Col. Brown, Col. Bowers, Mr. Adams, Col. Partridge, and Mr. Dexter.]

RESOLVE

OF THE GENERAL COURT, MAKING PROVISION FOR THE REGULAR TROOPS,
REFERRED TO IN THE GOVERNOR'S MESSAGE, MAY 18, JUNE 16, 1767.

In the House of Representatives ; his Excellency the Governor having, by a message of the 28th of May last, acquainted the House of the arrival of twenty-seven recruits, under the command of Ensign Dalrymple, of his Majesty's fourteenth regiment of foot, now at Halifax, and having desired that the House would take order that proper provision might be made for them—

Resolved, that such provision be made for these men, while they remain here, as has *been heretofore usually* made for his Majesty's regular troops, when *occasionally* in this province ; and that the Commissary General be, and he is hereby directed to see that this resolve be put in execution.

====

[The speech of Governor Bernard, at the opening of the January session, 1768, related entirely to the running of the line between this province and New York ; and New Hampshire and Maine.]

====

RESOLVE

OF THE HOUSE, CONCERNING THEIR CIRCULAR LETTER TO THE ASSEMBLIES OF OTHER COLONIES, FEBRUARY 13, 1768.

WHEREAS this House has directed, that a letter be sent to the several Houses of Representatives and Burgesses of the British colonies on the continent, setting forth the sentiments of the House, with regard to the great difficulties that must accrue by the operation of divers acts of Parliament, for levying duties and taxes on the colonies, with the sole and express purpose of raising a revenue, and their proceedings thereon, in a humble, dutiful and loyal petition to the King, and such representations to his Majesty's ministers,* as they apprehend may have a tendency to obtain redress : and whereas, it is the opinion of this House, that all effectual methods should be taken to cultivate harmony between the several branches of this government, as being necessary to promote the prosperity of his Majesty's government in the province ;

Resolved, That Mr. Otis, Col. Preble, Col. Brown, Mr. Say-

---

* These documents will be found below in this volume.

ward, and Mr. Hall, be a committee to wait on his Excellency the
Governor, and acquaint him that a copy of the letter aforesaid,
will be laid before him, as well as of all the proceedings of this
House relative to said affair, if he shall desire it: and that said
committee humbly request, that his Excellency would be pleased
to favor the House with a copy of the letter from the right honorable the Earl of Shelburne, lately read to the House by order of his
Excellency, and his own letters to which it refers.*

MESSAGE

FROM GOVERNOR BERNARD, TO THE HOUSE OF REPRESENTATIVES, IN REPLY TO THE FOREGOING, FEBRUARY 16, 1768.

Gentlemen of the House of Representatives,

   In answer to your message of the 13th instant, I find it necessary to inform you, that soon after the letter of the Earl of Shelburne was read in your House, I ordered a copy of it to be given
to the Speaker, to be used as he should think fit, upon condition that
no other copy should be taken thereof.   I am very willing that
the copy in the Speaker's hands should be communicated to you,
in any manner which is consistent with that restriction.
   I know of no letters of my own which I think can be of any use
to you upon this occasion.
   I quite agree with you, in opinion, that all effectual methods
should be taken to cultivate harmony between the several branches
of the legislature of this government, as being necessary to promote
the prosperity of the province ; and I shall cheerfully join with
you in all proper measures for so salutary a purpose.

                                             FRA. BERNARD.

ANSWER

OF THE HOUSE OF REPRESENTATIVES, TO THE GOVERNOR'S MESSAGE, FEBRUARY 18, 1768.

May it please your Excellency,

   Your message of the 16th instant has been read, and duly considered, in the House of Representatives.   The manner in which
your Excellency was pleased to introduce into this House the let-

* This letter was afterwards reluctantly laid before the House by the Governor, and will
be found in this volume below.

ter from the right honorable the Earl of Shelburne by giving orders
to the Secretary to read it without leaving a copy, appeared to be
unprecedented and unparliamentary.· But this made but a light
impression on the House, when the members recollected, as far as
they could, the unfavorable sentiments his Lordship thought himself necessitated to entertain of the two Houses of this Assembly,
and of some particular members in this House, whose characters in
the opinion of the House, stand unimpeachable. Under this apprehension, they thought it necessary, for their own vindication,
humbly to request your Excellency to favor them with a copy of
his Lordship's letter ; and as it appeared to them that his Lordship
had formed his sentiments of the two Houses, and their members,
from your own letters to which he referred, the House thought they
could not do themselves and their members justice, unless they
could be favored with a sight of them also, and accordingly requested it of your Excellency.

You are pleased to say that you know of no letters of your " own
that you think can be of any use to the House upon this occasion."
The House did not in their vote or message say what occasion
they had to request them. But when his Lordship expressly says,
that it appears from your several letters, that your negativing counsellors in the late elections was done with due deliberation and
judgment, it is natural for the House to conclude that your Excellency had thought it convenient to give his Lordship the particular
reasons you had for a measure so rare and extraordinary. These
reasons seem to have prevailed to justify your Excellency ; for his
Lordship acquaints you that his Majesty is graciously pleased to
approve of your having exerted the power lodged in you by the
constitution of the province. But unfortunately for the two Houses,
his Lordship passes a different judgment upon their conduct, and
takes occasion to applaud the wisdom of those who framed the
charter, in providing that a power should be placed in the Governor as an occasional check upon any *indiscreet use* of the right
of electing counsellors. It evidently appears from this passage
that his Majesty's minister has conceived an opinion of the two
Houses as having made an indiscreet use of a charter right. The
House were willing to be convinced that this opinion and other
sentiments expressed in his Lordship's letter, which imply an high
censure upon the two Houses, and upon particular members of
this House, were rather inferences drawn from your letters, in
which his Lordship might be liable to mistake, than the direct expressions of it. Had your Excellency been pleased to have favored
them with the copies, they might have been of use upon the occasion, and satisfactory to the House. But as you have thought
proper to refuse them, they are left to conjecture with all possible
candor, and appeal to the world.

His Lordship is induced to believe that the Assembly have made
an indiscreet use of their right of choosing counsellors to the ex-

clusion of the principal officers of government from the Board, whose presence there as counsellors, so manifestly tends to facilitate the course of public business, and who have therefore been before this period usually elected ; and that they have thus exerted their right with a far different intention from that of promoting the reestablishment of tranquility, and evincing the duty and attachment of the colony towards Great Britain. The House would be glad to justify this construction of his Lordship's letter, which is nearly in the words of it, by publishing it in their journals, but that is inconsistent with your Excellency's restrictions. This is not the first time that his Majesty's ministers, and even his Majesty himself, after having had before him your Excellency's letters and the inclosures, has thought it necessary to form an opinion of his loyal subjects of this province, as having a degree of ill temper prevailing among them. And your Excellency cannot be insensible that the present House have heretofore, for the sake of conciliating the minds of the people, and restoring a unanimity to this General Conrt, requested your Excellency to give them the opportunity of making it evident to their constituents that your letters had no tendency to induce such an opinion : and the House still think that nothing would tend more to promote the salutary purpose of cultivating an harmony between the several branches of this legislature, in which your Excellency expresses a disposition cheerfully to join with the House, than an open aud unreserved explanation to each other. For this purpose the House, in their message, assured you that they were ready to lay before you their humble petition to his Majesty, and their representations to his ministers, with all their other proceedings upon the important matters that have been before them, at the same time they made their reasonable request of your Excellency's letters.

After having recited so great a part of the sentiments of his Lordship's letter, no one can be astonished at the conclusion he is pleased to make ; that under such circumstances it cannot be surprising, that his Majesty's Governor exerts the right entrusted to him by the same constitution, to the purpose of excluding those from the council, whose mistaken zeal may have led them into improper excesses, and whose private resentments (and his Lordship adds, he should be sorry to ascribe to them motives still more blameable) may in your opinion further lead them to embarrass the administration, and endanger the quiet of the province. Surely his Lordship would never have passed such a censure upon the two Houses of Assembly, nor upon particular gentlemen, altogether strangers to him, but upon what he thought to be the best authority. It is far beneath his character and dignity to give credit, or even to hearken to any account so prejudicial to the reputation of the province, and of particular persons, but what he receives from gentlemen in the highest stations in it. Your Excellency, then, must allow the House to believe, until they shall be convinced to the contrary, that your several letters, to which his Lordship refers, are so fully expressed, as to have lef this Lordship no room to suspect that he could be mistaken.

In such a case, your Excellency cannot think that the House can remain in silence. They recommend to their injured members a becoming calmness and fortitude ; and take this occasion to bear testimony to their zeal for the honor of their King, and the rights of their constituents. But the character of the people whom this House represent, as well as their own honor, is at stake, and requires them to take every prudent measure for their own vindication. The House are truly sorry that this new occasion of mistrust and jealousy has happened; but they can never be so wanting to themselves, as to omit the opportunity of removing from his Lordship's mind, the unfavorable impressions which appear by his letter; and what is of much greater importance to them, of standing before their Sovereign in their own just character of loyal subjects.

═══

MESSAGE

FROM THE GOVERNOR, BY THE SECRETARY, TO THE HOUSE OF REPRE-
SENTATIVES, IN REFERENCE TO THE ABOVE, FEBRUARY 22, 1768.

Mr. Speaker,

I AM ordered by his Excellency to inform you, that, as this House has thought fit to permit their message of February 18th, containing extracts from the Secretary of State's letter, with observations upon it, to be printed in a common newspaper, it is to no purpose to continue the restriction against granting copies of such letters. He therefore, consents, that it may be entered on the journals of the House.*

---

* February 24. The House passed the following resolve : Whereas his Excellency the Governor, in his message to this House, by the Secretary, the 16th inst. was pleased to signify his apprehension, that the House thought fit to permit their message of the 18th, containing extracts from the Secretary of State's letter, with observations upon it, to be published in a common newspaper ; which, if it be not explained, may induce his Excellency further to apprehend, that the House are in breach of confidence with regard to the restrictions he was pleased to lay them under, when he consented that the said letter should be perused in the House : Resolved, as the opinion of this House, that in order to make a pertinent and full answer to his Excellency's message of the 16th, it was necessary to recite some parts of his Lordship's letter : but that this House took no order with regard to the publishing of their message containing such recital, in a common newspaper.

LETTER

FROM LORD SHELBURNE, TO GOVERNOR BERNARD, COMMUNICATED TO THE HOUSE, FEBRUARY, 1768.

Whitehall, September 17, 1767.

SIR,

I HAVE the pleasure to signify to you his Majesty's approbation of your conduct, and to acquaint you that he is graciously pleased to approve of your having exerted the power lodged in you, by the constitution of the province of Massachusetts Bay, of negativing counsellors in the late election, which appears from your several letters, to have been done with due deliberation and judgment.

Those who framed the present charter, very wisely provided, that this power should be placed in the Governor, as an occasional check upon any indiscreet use of the right of electing counsellors, which was given by charter, to the Assembly, which might, at certain periods, by an improper exercise, have a tendency to disturb the deliberations of that part of the legislature, from whom the greatest gravity and moderation is more peculiarly expected. As long, therefore, as the Assembly shall exert their right of election, to the exclusion of the principal officers of government from the Council, whose presence there, as counsellors, so manifestly tend to facilitate the course of public business, and who have therefore been, before this period, usually elected, and while in particular, they exclude men of such unexceptionable characters, as both the present Lieutenant Governor and Secretary, undoubtedly are, and that too, at a time when it is more peculiarly the duty of all parts of the government to promote the reestablishment of tranquility, and not forego the least occasion of evincing the duty and attachment of the colony towards Great Britain. It cannot, under such circumstances, be surprising, that his Majesty's Governor exerts the right entrusted to him by the same constitution, to the purpose of excluding those from the Council, whose mistaken zeal may have led them into improper excesses, and whose private resentments (I should be sorry to ascribe to them motives still more blameable,) may, in your opinion, further lead them to embarrass the administration, and endanger the quiet of the province.

The dispute, which has arisen about the Lieutenant Governor's being present, without a voice, at the deliberations of the Council, is no otherwise important, than as it tends to show a warmth in the House of Representatives, which I am very sorry for. The question concerning his admission, seems to lie in the breasts of the Council only, as being the proper judges of their own privileges, and as having the best right to determine whom they will admit to be present at their deliberations.

I am to inform you, sir, that it is his Majesty's resolution to extend to you his countenance and protection in every constitutional measure, that shall be found necessary for the support of his government in the Massachusetts Bay : And it will be your care and your duty, to avail yourself of such protection, in *those cases only*, where the *honor* and *dignity* of *his Majesty's government* is *really*, either mediately, or immediately, concerned.

It is unnecessary to observe, that the nature of the English constitution is such as to furnish no real ground of jealousy to the colonies ; and where there is so large a foundation of confidence, it cannot be, but that accidental jealousies must subside, and things again return to their proper and natural course. The extremes, even of legal right, on either side, though sometimes necessary, are always inconvenient; and men of real property, who must be sensible that their own prosperity is connected with the tranquility of the province, will not be inactive, and suffer their quiet to be disturbed, and the peace and safety of the state endangered by the indiscretion or resentment of any.

I am, with great regard, your obedient servant,
                                        SHELBURNE.

====

MESSAGE

FROM GOVERNOR BERNARD, TO THE HOUSE OF REPRESENTATIVES, CONCERNING A LIBELLOUS PARAGRAPH IN A NEWSPAPER, MARCH 1, 1768.

Gentlemen of the House of Representatives,

I HAVE been used to treat the publications in the Boston Gazette, with the contempt they deserve ; but when they are carried to a length, which, if unnoticed, must endanger the very being of government, I cannot, consistently with the regard which I profess, and really have, for this province, excuse myself from taking notice of a publication in the Boston Gazette, of yesterday ; I have, therefore, consulted the Council thereupon, and have received their unanimous advice, that I should lay the said libellous paper before your House, as well as their Board. I have, therefore, ordered the Secretary to communicate to you the said libellous paper, that you may take the same, with the circumstances attending it, into your serious consideration ; and do therein, as the majesty of the King, the dignity of his government, the honor of this General Court, and the true interest of this province shall require.*

                                        FRA. BERNARD.

* The paragraph alluded to, was a low and scurrilous reflection on the Governor, similar to those which often appear in free countries, in times of high political excitement. It represented some one, (meaning Governor Bernard, no doubt,) as a tyrant, aiming to enslave the people, &c. but charging him with no personal immorality.

ANSWER

May it please your Excellency,

IN duty and great respect to his Majesty's representative and Governor of the province, this House have given all due attention to your message, of the first instant. You are pleased to recommend to their serious consideration, a publication in the Boston Gazette, of Monday last, as being carried to a length, which, if unnoticed, must endanger the very being of government. In this view, your Excellency, in the notice you have taken of it, without doubt, acted consistently with the regard to this province, which you profess.

We are sorry that any publication in the newspapers, or any other cause, should give your Excellency an apprehension of danger to the being or dignity of his Majesty's government here. But this House, after examination into the nature and importance of the paper referred to, cannot see reason to admit of such conclusion as your Excellency has formed. No particular person, public or private, is named in it. And as it does not appear to the House, that any thing contained in it, can affect the majesty of the King, the dignity of the government, the honor of the General Court, or the true interest of the province, they think they may be fully justified in their determination to take no further notice of it.

The liberty of the press is the great bulwark of the liberty of the people. It is, therefore, the incumbent duty of those who are constituted the guardians of the people's rights, to defend and maintain them. This House, however, as one branch of the legislature, in which capacity alone they have any authority, are ready to discountenance an abuse of this privilege, whenever there shall be occasion for it. Should the proper bounds of it, at any time, be transgressed, to the prejudice of individuals, or the public, it is their opinion, at present, that provision is already made for the punishment of offenders, in the common course of the law. This provision, the House apprehend, in the present state of tranquillity in the province, is sufficient, without the interposition of the General Assembly; which, however, it is hoped, will, at all times, be both ready and willing to support the executive power in the due administration of justice, whenever any extraordinary aid shall become needful.

SPEECH

OF GOVERNOR BERNARD, TO THE COUNCIL AND HOUSE OF
REPRESENTATIVES, MARCH 4, 1768.

Gentlemen of the House of Representatives,

THE moderation and good temper which appeared to regulate your conduct at the opening of this session, so flattered me, that I promised myself that the like disposition would have continued to the end of it. But I am sorry to find that the lovers of contention have shewed themselves not so intent upon preventing it, as upon waiting for a fit opportunity to revive it. The extraordinary and indecent observations which have been made upon the Secretary of State's letter, wrote, as I may say, in presence of the King himself, will fully justify this suggestion. The causes of the censure therein contained, have been specifically assigned, and set forth in the letter itself. These causes, are facts universally known, and no where to be denied; they are considered in the letter as the sole causes of the censure consequent thereto; and there was no occasion to resort to my letters, or any other letters for other reasons for it. If you think that this censure is singular, you deceive yourselves; and you are not so well informed of what passes at Westminster as you ought to be, if you do not know that it is as general and extensive as the knowledge of the proceedings to which it is applied; and, therefore, all your insinuations against me, upon false suppositions of my having misrepresented you, are vain and groundless, when every effect is to be accounted for from a plain narrative of facts, which must have appeared to the Secretary of State, from your own journals. It is not, therefore, me, gentlemen, that you call to account; it is the noble writer of the letter himself, the King's minister of state, who has taken the liberty to find fault with the conduct of a party in your Assembly.

Nor am I less innocent of the making this letter a subject of public resentment. When, upon the best advice, I found myself obliged to communicate it to you, I did it in such a manner, that it might not, and would not, if you had been pleased, have transpired out of the General Court. Prudent men, moderate men, would have considered it as an admonition, rather than a censure, and have made use of it as a means of reconciliation, rather than of further distraction. But there are men to whose being, (I mean the being of their importance) everlasting contention is necessary. And by these has this letter been dragged into public, and has been made the subject of declamatory observations; which, together with large extracts of the letter itself, have immediately after been carried to the press of the publishers of an infamous newspaper; notwithstanding the letter had been communicated in confidence, that no copy of it should be permitted to be taken.

So little have availed the noble Lord's intention of pointing out the means of restoring peace and harmony to this government, and my desire to pursue such salutary purpose, to the utmost of my power.

Having said thus much to vindicate myself, which every honest man has a right to do, I must add, that I have done nothing on my part to occasion a dispute between me and your House; it has been forced upon me, by particular persons, for their own purposes. I never will have any dispute with the Representatives of this good people, which I can prevent, and will always treat them with due regard, and will render them real service, when it is in my power. Time and experience will soon pull the masks off those false patriots, who are sacrificing their country to the gratification of their own passions. In the mean while I shall, with more firmness than ever, if it is possible, pursue that steady conduct, which the service of the King, and the preservation of this government, so forcibly demand of me. And I shall, above all, endeavor to defend this injured country from the imputations which are cast upon it, and the evils which threaten it, arising from the machinations of a few, very few, discontented men, and by no means to be charged on the generality of the people.

Gentlemen of the Council,

I return you thanks for your steady, uniform, and patriotic conduct during this whole session, which has shewn you impressed with a full sense of your duty, both to your King and to your country. The unanimous example of men of your respectable characters, cannot fail of having great weight to engage the people, in general, to unite in proper means to put an end to the dissention which has so long harrassed this province in its internal policy, and disgraced it in its reputation abroad. I shall not fail to make a faithful representation to his Majesty of your merit upon this occasion.

FRA. BERNARD.

PETITION TO THE KING,

FROM THE HOUSE OF REPRESENTATIVES OF THE PROVINCE OF MASSACHU-
SETTS BAY, SIGNED BY THEIR SPEAKER, BY THEIR ORDER,
JANUARY 20, 1768.

Most Gracious Sovereign,

Your Majesty's faithful subjects, the Representatives of your province of the Massachusetts Bay, with the warmest sentiments of loyalty, duty, and affection, beg leave to approach the throne;

16

and to lay at your Majesty's feet, their humble supplications, in behalf of your distressed subjects, the people of this province.

Our ancestors, the first settlers of this country, having, with the royal consent, which, we humbly apprehend, involves the consent of the nation, and at their own great expense, migrated from the mother kingdom, took possession of this land, at that time a wilderness, the right whereof they purchased, for a valuable consideration, of the council established at Plymouth, to whom it had been granted by your Majesty's royal predecessor, King James the First.

From the principles of loyalty to their Sovereign, which will ever warm the breast of a true subject, though remote, they acknowledged their allegiance to the English Crown: And your Majesty will allow us, with all humility to say, that they and their posterity, even to this time, have afforded frequent and signal proofs of their zeal for the honor and service of their Prince, and their firm attachment to the parent country.

With toil and fatigue, perhaps not to be conceived by their brethren and fellow subjects at home, and with the constant peril of their lives, from a numerous, savage and war-like race of men, they began their settlement, and God prospered them.

They obtained a charter from King Charles the First, wherein his Majesty was pleased to grant to them, and their heirs and assigns forever, all the lands therein described, to hold of him and his royal successors, in fee and common soccage; which we humbly conceive, is as absolute an estate, as the subject can hold under the Crown. And in the same charter, were granted to them and their posterity, all the rights, liberties, privileges, and immunities of natural subjects, born within the realm.

This charter they enjoyed, having, as we most humbly conceive, punctually complied with all the conditions of it, till in an unhappy time, it was vacated. But after the revolution, when King William and Queen Mary, of glorious and blessed memory, were established on the throne—in that happy reign, when to the joy of the nation and its dependencies, the crown was settled in your Majesty's illustrious family, the inhabitants of this province shared in the common blessing. They then were indulged with another charter, in which their Majesties were pleased, for themselves, their heirs and successors, to grant and confirm to them as ample estate in the lands or territories, as was granted by the former charter, together with other the most essential rights and liberties contained therein; the principal of which is, that which your Majesty's subjects within the realm have held a most sacred right, of being taxed only by representatives of their own free election.

Thus blessed with the rights of Englishmen, through the indulgent smiles of Heaven, and under the auspicious government of your Majesty and your royal predecessors, your people of this province have been happy, and your Majesty has acquired a numerous increase of loyal subjects, a large extent of dominion, and a new and inexhaustible source of commerce, wealth and glory.

With great sincerity, permit us to assure your Majesty, that your subjects of this province, ever have, and still continue to acknowledge your Majesty's High Court of Parliament the supreme legislative power of the whole empire; the superintending authority of which is clearly admitted in all cases, that can consist with the fundamental rights of nature and the constitution; to which your Majesty's happy subjects, in all parts of your empire, conceive they have a just and equitable claim.

It is with the deepest concern, that your humble suppliants would represent to your Majesty, that your Parliament, the rectitude of whose intentions is never to be questioned, has thought proper to pass divers acts, imposing taxes on your Majesty's subjects in America, with the sole and express purpose of raising a revenue. If your Majesty's subjects here shall be deprived of the honor and privilege of voluntarily contributing their aid to your Majesty, in supporting your government and authority in the province, and defending and securing your rights and territories in America, which they have always hitherto done with the utmost cheerfulness; if these acts of Parliament shall remain in force, and your Majesty's Commons in Great Britain shall continue to exercise the power of granting the property of their fellow subjects in this province, your people must then regret their unhappy fate in having only the name left of free subjects.

With all humility we conceive that a representation of your Majesty's subjects of this province in the Parliament, considering their local circumstances, is utterly impracticable. Your Majesty has heretofore been graciously pleased to order your requisitions to be laid before the Representatives of your people in the General Assembly, who have never failed to afford the necessary aid, to the extent of their ability, and sometimes beyond it; and it would be grievous to your Majesty's faithful subjects to be called upon in a way, that should appear to them to imply a distrust of their most ready and willing compliances.

Under the most sensible impressions of your Majesty's wise and paternal care for the remotest of your faithful subjects, and in full dependence on the royal declarations in the charter of this province, we most humbly beseech your Majesty to take our present unhappy circumstances under your royal consideration, and afford us relief in such a manner as in your Majesty's great wisdom and clemency shall seem meet.

LETTER

FROM THE HOUSE OF REPRESENTATIVES, TO D. DE BERDT, ESQ. AGENT
FOR THE PROVINCE, IN ENGLAND, JANUARY 12, 1768.

SIR,

SINCE the last sitting of the General Court, divers acts of Parliament, relating to the colonies, have arrived here; and as the people of this province had no share in the framing those laws, in which they are so deeply interested, the House of Representatives, who are constitutionally entrusted by them, as the guardians of their rights and liberties, have thought it their indispensable duty, carefully to peruse them; and having so done, to point out such matters in them, as appear to be grievous to their constituents, and to seek redress.

The fundamental rules of the constitution are the grand security of all British subjects; and it is a security which they are all *equally* entitled to, in all parts of his Majesty's extended dominions. The supreme legislative, in every free state, derives its power from the constitution; by the fundamental rules of which, it is bounded and circumscribed. As a legislative power is essentially requisite, where any powers of government are exercised, it is conceived, the several legislative bodies in America were erected, because their existence, and the free exercise of their power, within their several limits, are essentially important and necessary, to preserve to his Majesty's subjects in America, the advantages of the fundamental laws of the constitution.

When we mention the rights of the subjects in America, and the interest we have in the British constitution, in common with all other British subjects, we cannot justly be suspected of the most distant thought of an independency on Great Britain. Some, we know, have imagined this of the colonists, and others may, perhaps, have industriously propagated it, to raise groundless and unreasonable jealousies of them; but it is so far from the truth, that we apprehend the colonies would refuse it if offered to them, and would even deem it the greatest misfortune to be obliged to accept it. They are far from being insensible of their happiness, in being connected with the mother country, and of the mutual benefits derived from it to both. It is, therefore, the indispensable duty of all, to cultivate and establish a mutual harmony, and to promote the intercourse of good offices between them; and while both have the free enjoyment of the rights of our happy constitution, there will be no grounds of envy and discontent in the one, nor of jealousy and mistrust in the other.

It is the glory of the British constitution, that it hath its foundation in the law of God and nature. It is an essential, natural right, that a man shall quietly enjoy, and have the sole disposal of his own property. This right is adopted into the constitution. This natural and constitutional right is so familiar to the American subjects, that it would be difficult, if possible, to convince them, that any necessity can render it just, equitable and reasonable, in the nature of things, that the Parliament should impose duties, subsidies, talliages, and taxes upon them, internal or external, for the sole purpose of *raising a revenue*. The reason is obvious ; because, they cannot be represented, and therefore, their consent cannot be constitutionally had in Parliament.

When the Parliament, soon after the repeal of the stamp act, thought proper to pass another act, declaring the authority, power, and right of Parliament, to make laws that should be binding on the colonies, in all cases, whatever, it is probable that acts for levying taxes on the colonies, external and internal, were included ; for the act made the last year, imposing duties on paper, glass, &c. as well as the sugar acts and the stamp act, are, to all intents and purposes, in form, as well as in substance, as much revenue acts, as those for the land tax, customs and excises in England. The necessity of establishing a revenue in America, is expressly mentioned in the preambles ; they were originated in the honorable House of Commons, as all other money and revenue bills are ; and the property of the colonies, with the same form, ceremony and expressions of loyalty and duty, is thereby given and granted to his Majesty, as they usually give and grant their own. But we humbly conceive, that objections to acts of this kind, may be safely, if decently made, if they are of dangerous tendency in point of commerce, policy, and the true and real interest of the whole empire. It may, and if it can, it ought to be made to appear, that such acts are grievous to the subject, burthensome to trade, ruinous to the nation, and tending on the whole to injure the revenue of the Crown. And surely, if such mighty inconveniencies, evils, and mischiefs, can be pointed out with decency and perspicuity, there will be the highest reason not only to hope for, but fully to expect redress.

It is observable, that though many have disregarded life, and contemned liberty, yet there are few men who do not agree that property is a valuable acquisition, which ought to be held sacred. Many have fought, and bled, and died for this, who have been insensible to all other obligations. Those who ridicule the ideas of right and justice, faith and truth among men, will put a high value upon money. Property is admitted to have an existence, even in the savage state of nature. The bow, the arrow, and the tomahawk ; the hunting and the fishing ground, are species of property, as important to an American savage, as pearls, rubies and diamonds are to the Mogul, or a Nabob in the East, or the lands, tenements, hereditaments, messuages, gold and silver of the Europeans. And if property is necessary for the support of savage life, it is by no means less so in civil society. The Utopian schemes of levelling, and a community of goods, are as visionary and impracticable, as those which vest all property in the Crown, are arbitrary, despotic, and in our government unconstitutional. Now, what property can the colonists be conceived to have, if their money may be granted away by others, without their consent? This most certainly is the present case; for they were in no sense represented in Parliament, when this act for raising a revenue in America was made. The stamp act was grievously complained of by all the colonies; and is there any real difference between this act and the stamp act? They were both designed to raise a revenue in America, and in the same manner, viz. by duties on certain commodities. The payment of the duties imposed by the stamp act, might have been eluded by a total disuse of the stamped paper; and so may the payment of these duties, by the total disuse of the articles on which they are laid; but in neither case, without difficulty. Therefore, the subjects here, are reduced to the hard alternative, either of being obliged totally to disuse articles of the greatest necessity, in common life, or to pay a tax without their consent.

The security of right and property, is the great end of government. Surely, then, such measures as tend to render right and property precarious, tend to destroy both property and government; for these must stand and fall together. It would be difficult, if possible, to show, that the present plan of taxing the colonies is more favorable to them, than that put in use here, before the revolution. It seems, by the event, that our ancestors were, in one respect, not in so melancholy a situation, as we, their posterity, are. In those times, the Crown, and the ministers of the Crown, without the intervention of Parliament, demolished charters, and levied taxes on the colonies, at pleasure. Governor Andross, in the time of James II. declared, that wherever an Englishman sets his foot, all he hath is the King's; and Dudley declared, at the Council Board, and even on the sacred seat of justice, that the privilege of Englishmen, not to be taxed without their consent, and the laws of England, would not follow them to the ends of the earth. It was, also, in those days, declared in Council, that the King's subjects in New England did not differ much from slaves; and that the only difference was, that they were not bought and sold. But there was, even in those times, an excellent Attorney General, Sir William Jones, who was of another mind; and told King James, that he could no more grant a commission to levy money on his subjects in Jamaica, though a conquered island, without their consent, by an Assembly, than they could discharge themselves from their allegiance to the English Crown. But the misfortune of the colonists at present is, that they are taxed by Parliament, without their consent. This, while the Parliament continues to tax us, will ever render our case, in one respect, more deplorable and remediless, under the best of Kings, than that of our ancestors was, under the worst. They found relief by the interposition of Parliament. But by the intervention of that very power, we are taxed, and can appeal for relief, from their final decision, to no power on earth; for there is no power on earth above them.

' The original contract between the King and the first planters here, was a royal promise in behalf of the nation, and which till very lately, it was never questioned but the King had a power to make; namely, that if the adventurers would, at their own cost and charge, and at the hazard of their lives and every thing dear to them, purchase a new world, subdue a wilderness, and thereby enlarge the King's dominions, they and their posterity should enjoy such rights and privileges as in their charters are expressed; which are, in general, all the rights, liberties and privileges of his Majesty's natural born subjects within the realm. The principal privilege implied, and in some of their charters expressed, is a freedom from all taxes, but such as they shall consent to in person, or by representatives of their own free choice and election. The late King James broke the original contract of the settlement and government of these colonies; but it proved happy for our ancestors in the end, that he had also broken the original compact with his three kingdoms. This left them some gleam of hope; this very thing, finally, was the cause of deliverance to the nation and the colonies, nearly at the same time; it was the Parliament, the supreme legislative and constitutional check on the supreme executive, that in time operated effects worthy of itself; the nation and her colonies have since been happy, and our princes patriot Kings. The law and reason teaches, that the King can do no wrong; and that neither King nor Parliament are otherwise inclined than to justice, equity and truth. But the law does not presume that the King may not be deceived, nor that the Parliament may not be misinformed. If, therefore, any thing is wrong, it must be imputed to such causes. How far such causes have taken place and operated against the colonies, is humbly submitted to the revision and reconsideration of all.

By the common law, the colonists are adjudged to be natural born subjects. So they are declared by royal charter; and they are so, by the spirit of the law of nature and nations. No jurist, who has the least regard to his reputation in the republic of letters, will deny that they are entitled to all the essential rights, liberties, privileges and immunities, of his Majesty's natural subjects, born within the realm. The children of his Majesty's natural born subjects, born passing and repassing the seas, have, by sundry acts of Parliament, from Edward the Third to this time, been declared natural born subjects; and even foreigners, residing a certain time in the colonies, are, by acts of Parliament, entitled to all the rights and privileges of natural born subjects. And it is remarkable, that the Act of 13 Geo. II. chap. 7, presupposes that the colonists are natural born subjects; and that they are entitled to all the privileges of such; as appears by the preamble, which we shall now recite. "Whereas the increase of people is the means of advancing the wealth and strength of any nation or country; and whereas many foreigners and strangers, from the lenity of our government and purity of our religion, the benefit of our laws, the advantages of our trade, and the security of our property, might be induced to come and settle in some of his Majesty's colonies in America, if they were made partakers of the advantages and privileges which natural born subjects of this realm do enjoy." Which plainly shows it to be the sense of the nation, that the colonies were entitled to, and did actually enjoy, the advantages and privileges of natural born subjects. But if it could be admitted as clearly consistent with the constitution, for the Parliament of Great Britain to tax the property of the colonies, we presume it can be made to appear to be utterly inconsistent with the rules of equity that they should, at least at present. It must be considered, that by acts of Parliament, the colonies are prohibited from importing commodities of the growth or manufacture of Europe, except from Great Britain, saving a few articles. This gives the advantage to Great Britain of raising the price of her commodities, and is equal to a tax. It is too obvious to be doubted, that by the extraordinary demands from the colonies of the manufactures of Britain, occasioned by this policy, she reaps an advantage of at least twenty per cent. in the price of them, beyond what the colonies might purchase them for at foreign markets. The loss, therefore, to the colonists, is equal to the gain which is made in Britain. This in reality is a tax, though not a direct one; and admitting that they take annually from Great Britain, manufactures to the value of two millions sterling, as is generally supposed, they then pay an annual tax of four hundred thousand pounds, besides the taxes which are directly paid on those manufactures in England. The same reasoning will hold good with respect to the many enumerated articles of their produce, which the colonies are restrained, by act of Parliament, from sending to any foreign port. By this restraint, the market is glutted, and consequently the produce sold, is cheaper; which is an advantage to Great Britain, and an equal loss to, or tax upon, the colonists. Is it reasonable, then, that the colonies should be taxed on the British commodities here? especially when it is considered, that the most of them settled a wilderness, and, till very lately, defended their settlements without a farthing's expense to the nation. They bore their full proportion of the charges of securing and maintaining his Majesty's rights in America, in every war from their first settlement, without any consideration; for the grants of Parliament in the last war were compensations for an overplus of expense on their part. Many of them, and this province in particular, have always maintained their own frontiers at their own expense; and have also frequently defended his Majesty's garrison at Annapolis, when it must otherwise have been unavoidably lost. The nation, in the late war, acquired lands equal in value to all the expense she has been at in America, from its settlement; while the trade of the colonies has been only "secured and restricted;" it has not been enlarged, though new avenues of beneficial commerce have been opened to the mother country. The colonies have reaped no share in the lands which they helped to conquer, while millions of acres of those very lands have been granted, and still are granting, to people who, in all probability, will never see, if they settle them.

The appropriation of the monies, to arise by these duties, is an objection of great weight. It is, in the first place, to be applied for the payment of the necessary charges of the administration of justice, and the support of civil government, in such colonies where it shall be judged necessary. This House apprehends it would be grievous, and of dangerous tendency, if the Crown should not only appoint Governors over the several colonies, but allow them such stipends as it shall judge proper, at the expense of the people, and without their consent. Such a power, under a corrupt administration, it is to be feared, would introduce an absolute government in America; at best, it would leave the people in a state of utter uncertainty of their security, which is far from being a state of civil liberty. The Judges in the several colonies do not hold their commissions during good behavior. If then they are to have salaries independent of the people, how easy will it be for a corrupt Governor to have a set of Judges to his mind, to deprive a bench of justice of its glory, and the people of their security. If the Judges of England have independent livings, it must be remembered, that the tenure of their commission is during good behavior, which is a safeguard to the people. And besides, they are near the throne, the fountain of right and justice; whereas American Judges, as well as Governors, are at a distance from it. Moreover, it is worth particular notice, that in all disputes between power and liberty in America, there is danger that the greatest credit will always be given to the officers of the Crown, who are the men in power. This we have sometimes found by experience; and it is much to be feared, that the nation will fall into some dangerous mistake, if she has not already, by too great attention to the representations of particular persons, and a disregard to others.

But the residue of these monies is to be applied by Parliament, from time to time, for defending, protecting and securing the colonies. If the government at home is apprehensive that the colonists will be backward in defending themselves and securing his Majesty's territories in America, it must have been egregiously misinformed. We need look back no farther than the last war, for evidence of a contrary disposition. They always discovered the most cheerful compliance with his Majesty's requisitions of men and money for this purpose. They were then treated as free Brit-

17

ish subjects, and never failed to grant aid to his Majesty of their own free accord, to the extent of their ability, and even beyond it; of which the Parliament were then so sensible, that they made them grants, from year to year, by way of compensation for extra services. It is not at all to be doubted, but if they are still considered upon the footing of subjects, they will always discover the same disposition to exert themselves for his Majesty's service and their own defence; which renders a standing army in the colonies a needless expense. Or, if it be admitted that there may be some necessity for them in the conquered province of Canada, where the exercise of the Romish religion, so destructive to civil society, is allowed, surely there can be no need of them in the bowels of the old colonies, and even in cities, where there is not the least danger of a foreign enemy, and where the inhabitants are as strongly attached to his Majesty's person, family and government, as in Great Britain itself. There is an *English* affection in the colonists towards the mother country, which will forever keep them connected with her, to every valuable purpose, unless it shall be erased by repeated unkind usage on her part. As Englishmen, as well as British subjects, they have an aversion to an unnecessary standing army, which they look upon as dangerous to their civil liberties; and considering the examples of ancient times, it seems a little surprising, that a mother state should trust large bodies of mercenary troops in her colonies, at so great a distance from her, lest, in process of time, when the spirits of the people shall be depressed by the military power, another Cæsar should arise and usurp the authority of his master.

The act enabling his Majesty to appoint Commissioners of the Customs to reside in America, has also been read in the House. It declares an intention to facilitate the trade of America, of which we cannot have any great hopes, from the tenor of the commission. In general, innovations are dangerous; the unnecessary increase of Crown Officers is most certainly so. These gentlemen are authorized to appoint as many as they shall think proper, without limitation. This will probably be attended with undesirable effects. An host of pensioners, by the arts they may use, may in time become as dangerous to the liberties of the people as an army of soldiers; for there is a way of subduing a people by art, as well as by arms. We are happy and safe under his present Majesty's mild and gracious administration; but the time may come, when the united body of pensioners and soldiers may ruin the liberties of America. The trade of the colonies, we apprehend, may be as easily carried on, and the acts of trade as duly enforced, without this commission; and, if so, it must be a very needless expense, at a time when the nation and her colonies are groaning under debts contracted in the late war, and how far distant another may be, God only knows.

There is another act, which, this House apprehends, must be alarming to all the colonies; which is the act for suspending the legislative power of the Assembly of New York on a certain condition. A legislative body, without the free exercise of the powers of legislation, is to us incomprehensible. There can be no material difference between such a legislative and none at all. It cannot be said, that the Assembly of New York hath the free exercise of legislative power, while their very existence is suspended upon their acting in conformity to the will of another body. Such a restriction throughout the colonies, would be a short and easy method of annihilating the legislative powers in America, and by consequence of depriving the people of a fundamental right of the constitution, namely, that every man shall be present in the body which legislates for him.

It may not be amiss to consider the tendency of a suspension of colony legislation for non compliance with acts of Parliament, requiring a Provincial Assembly to give and grant away their own and their constituents money for the support of a standing army. We cannot but think it hard enough to have our property granted away without our consent, without being ordered to deal it out ourselves, as in the case of the mutiny act. It must be sufficiently humiliating to part with our property in either of those ways, much more in both; whereby, as loyal subjects as any under his Majesty's government, and as true lovers of their country as any people whatever, are deprived of the honor and merit of voluntarily contributing to the service of both. What is the plain language of such a suspension ? We can discover no more nor less in it than this : If the American assemblies refuse to grant as much of their own and their constituents money, as shall from time to time be enjoined and prescribed by the Parliament, besides what the Parliament directly taxes them, they shall no longer have any legislative authority ; but if they comply with what is prescribed, they may still be allowed to legislate under their charter restrictions. Does not political death and annihilation stare us in the face as strongly on one supposition as the other ? Equally, in case of compliance as of non compliance.

But let us suppose, for a moment, a series of events taking place, the most favorable in the opinion of those who are so fond of these new regulations ; that all difficulties and scruples of conscience were removed, and that every Representative in America should acknowledge a just and equitable right in the Commons of Great Britain, to make an unlimited grant of his and his constituents property ; that they have a clear right to invest the Crown with all the lands in the colonies, as effectually as if they had been forfeited. Would it be possible for them to conciliate their constituents to such measures ? Would not the attempt suddenly cut asunder all confidence and communication between the representative body and the people ? What, then, would be the consequence? Could any thing be reasonably expected but discontent, despair and rage, against their representatives, on the side of the people, and on the part of government, the rigorous exertion of civil and military power? The confusion and misery, after such a fatal crisis, cannot be conceived, much less described.

The present regulations and proceedings, with respect to the colonies, we apprehend to be opposite to every principle of good and sound policy. A standing army, in time of profound peace, is naturally productive of uneasiness and discontent among the people ; and yet the colonies, by the mutiny act, are ordered and directed to provide certain enumerated articles ; and the pains and penalties, in case of non compliance, are evident, in the precedent of New York. It also appears, that revenue officers are multiplying in the colonies, with vast powers. The Board of Commissioners, lately appointed to reside here, have ample discretionary powers given them, to make what appointments they please, and to pay the appointees what sums they please. The establishment of a Protestant Episcopate, in America, is also very zealously contended for ; and it is very alarming to a people, whose fathers, from the hardships they suffered, under such an establishment, were obliged to fly their native country into a wilderness, in order peaceably to enjoy their privileges, civil and religious. Their being threatened with the loss of both at once, must throw them into a disagreeable situation. We hope in God such an establishment will never take place in America, and we desire you would strenuously oppose it. The revenue raised in America, for ought we can tell, may be as constitutionally applied towards the support of prelacy, as of soldiers and pensioners. If the property of the subject is taken from him, without his consent, it is immaterial whether it be done by one man, or five hundred ; or whether it be applied for the support of ecclesiastic or military power, or both. It may be well worth the consideration of the best politician in Great Britain or America, what the natural tendency is of a vigorous pursuit of these measures. We are not insensible that some eminent men, on both sides the water, are less friendly to American charters and assemblies, than could be wished. It seems to be growing fashionable to treat them, in common conversation, as well as in popular publications, with contempt. But if we look back a few reigns, we shall find that even the august assembly, the Parliament, was, in every respect, the object of a courtier's reproach. It was even an aphorism with King James the First, that the Lords and Commons were two very bad copartners with a Monarch ; and he and his successors broke the copartnership as fast as possible. It is certainly unnatural for a British politician to expect, that ever the supreme executive of the nation can long exist, after the supreme legislative shall be depressed and destroyed, which may God forbid. If the supreme executive cannot exist long in Britain, without the support of the supreme legislative, it should seem very reasonable, in order to support the same supreme executive, at the distance of a thousand transmarine leagues from the metropolis, there should be, in so remote dominions, a free legislative, within their charter limitations, as well as an entirely free representative of the supreme executive of his Majesty, in the persons of Governors, Judges, Justices, and other executive officers; otherwise strange effects are to be apprehended; for the laws of God and nature are invariable. A politician may apply or misapply these to a multiplicity of purposes, good or bad; but these laws were never made for politicians to alter. Should the time ever come, when the legislative assemblies of North America shall be dissolved and annihilated, no more to exist again, a strange political phenomenon will probably appear. All laws, both of police and revenue, must then be made by a legislative, at such a distance, that without immediate inspiration, the local and other circumstances of the governed, cannot possibly be known to those who give and grant to the Crown, what part of the property of their fellow subjects they please. There will then be no Assemblies to support the execution of such laws: and, indeed, while existing, by what rule of law or reason, are the members of the Colony Assemblies executive officers? They have, as Representatives, no commission but from their constituents; and it must be difficult to show, why they are more obliged to execute acts of Parliament, than such of their constituents as hold no commissions from the Crown. The most that can be expected from either, is submission to acts of Parliament; or to aid the officers, as individual, or part of the posse comitatus, if required. It would seem strange to call on the Representatives, in any other way, to execute laws against their constituents and themselves, which both have been so far from consenting to, that neither were consulted in framing them. Yet it was objected by some, to the American Assemblies, that they neglected to execute the stamp act; and that their resolves tended to raise commotions; which certainly was not the case here. For all the disorders in Boston, in which any damage was done to property, happened long before the resolves of the House of Representatives here were passed.

We have reason to believe, that the nation has been grossly misinformed with respect to the temper and behavior of the colonists; and it is to be feared that some men will not cease to sow the seeds of jealousy and discord, till they shall have done irreparable mischief. You will do a singular service to both countries, if possible, in detecting them. In the mean time, we desire you would make known to his Majesty's ministers the sentiments of this House, contained in this letter, and implore a favorable consideration of America.

CIRCULAR LETTER,

**FROM THE HOUSE OF REPRESENTATIVES OF MASSACHUSETTS BAY, AD-
DRESSED TO THE SPEAKERS OF THE RESPECTIVE HOUSES OF REPRE-
SENTATIVES AND BURGESSES ON THIS CONTINENT.**

Province of Massachusetts Bay, February 11, 1768.

SIR,

THE House of Representatives of this province, have taken
into their serious consideration, the great difficulties that must accrue to themselves and their constituents, by the operation of several acts of Parliament, imposing duties and taxes on the American
colonies.*

As it is a subject in which every colony is deeply interested,
they have no reason to doubt but your House is deeply impressed
with its importance, and that such constitutional measures will be
come into, as are proper. It seems to be necessary, that all possible care should be taken, that the representatives of the several
assemblies, upon so delicate a point, should harmonize with each
other. The House, therefore, hope that this letter will be candidly
considered in no other light than as expressing a disposition freely
to communicate their mind to a sister colony, upon a common concern, in the same manner as they would be glad to receive the
sentiments of your or any other House of Assembly on the continent.

The House have humbly represented to the ministry, their own
sentiments, that his Majesty's high court of Parliament is the supreme legislative power over the whole empire ; that in all free
states the constitution is fixed, and as the supreme legislative derives its power and authority from the constitution, it cannot over-
leap the bounds of it, without destroying its own foundation ; that
the constitution ascertains and limits both sovereignty and allegiance, and, therefore, his Majesty's American subjects, who acknowledge themselves bound by the ties of allegiance, have an
equitable claim to the full enjoyment of the fundamental rules of
the British constitution ; that it is an essential, unalterable right,
in nature, engrafted into the British constitution, as a fundamental
law, and ever held sacred and irrevocable by the subjects within
the realm, that what a man has honestly acquired is absolutely his
own, which he may freely give, but cannot be taken from him without his consent ; that the American subjects may, therefore, exclusive of any consideration of charter rights, with a decent firmness,
adapted to the character of free men and subjects, assert this
natural and constitutional right.

It is, moreover, their humble opinion, which they express with

---

* In addition to former acts, one passed in 1767, imposing a duty on paper, glass, tea, &c.

the greatest deference to the wisdom of the Parliament, that the acts made there, imposing duties on the people of this province, with the sole and express purpose of raising a revenue, are infringements of their natural and constitutional rights ; because, as they are not represented in the British Parliament, his Majesty's Commons in Britain, by those acts, grant their property without their consent.

This House further are of opinion, that their constituents, considering their local circumstances, cannot, by any possibility, be represented in the Parliament ; and that it will forever be impracticable, that they should be equally represented there, and consequently, not at all ; being separated by an ocean of a thousand leagues. That his Majesty's royal predecessors, for this reason, were graciously pleased to form a subordinate legislature here, that their subjects might enjoy the unalienable right of a representation : also, that considering the utter impracticability of their ever being fully and equally represented in Parliament, and the great expense that must unavoidably attend even a partial representation there, this House think that a taxation of their constituents, even without their consent, grievous as it is, would be preferable to any representation that could be admitted for them there.

Upon these principles, and also considering that were the right in Parliament ever so clear, yet, for obvious reasons, it would be beyond the rules of equity that their constituents should be taxed, on the manufactures of Great Britain here, in addition to the duties they pay for them in England, and other advantages arising to Great Britain, from the acts of trade, this House have preferred a humble, dutiful, and loyal petition, to our most gracious sovereign, and made such representations to his Majesty's ministers, as they apprehended would tend to obtain redress.

They have also submitted to consideration, whether any people can be said to enjoy any degree of freedom, if the Crown, in addition to its undoubted authority of constituting a Governor, should appoint him such a stipend as it may judge proper, without the consent of the people, and at their expense ; and whether, while the judges of the land, and other civil officers, hold not their commissions during good behaviour, their having salaries appointed for them by the Crown, independent of the people, hath not a tendency to subvert the principles of equity, and endanger the happiness and security of the subject.*

In addition to these measures, the House have written a letter to their agent, which he is directed to lay before the ministry ; wherein they take notice of the hardships of the act for preventing mutiny and desertion, which requires the Governor and Council to provide enumerated articles for the King's marching troops, and

---

* A plan was already proposed (and afterwards adopted by the British ministry) to have the salaries of the Governor and Judges of the Supreme Court, fixed by the Crown, though paid by the people here. This was an innovation which justly alarmed the citizens of this province.

the people to pay the expenses ; and also, the commission of the gentlemen appointed commissioners of the customs, to reside in America, which authorizes them to make as many appointments as they think fit, and to pay the appointees what sum they please, for whose mal-conduct they are not accountable ; from whence it may happen, that officers of the Crown may be multiplied to such a degree as to become dangerous to the liberty of the people, by virtue of a commission, which does not appear to this House to derive any such advantages to trade as many have supposed.

These are the sentiments and proceedings of this House ; and as they have too much reason to believe that the enemies of the colonies have represented them to his Majesty's ministers, and to the Parliament, as factious, disloyal, and having a disposition to make themselves independent of the mother country, they have taken occasion, in the most humble terms, to assure his Majesty, and his ministers, that, with regard to the people of this province, and, as they doubt not, of all the colonies, the charge is unjust. The House is fully satisfied, that your Assembly is too generous and liberal in sentiment, to believe that this letter proceeds from an ambition of taking the lead, or dictating to the other assemblies. They freely submit their opinions to the judgment of others ; and shall take it kind in your House to point out to them any thing further, that may be thought necessary.

This House cannot conclude, without expressing their firm confidence in the King, our common head and father ; that the united and dutiful supplications of his distressed American subjects, will meet with his royal and favorable acceptance.*

[The Committee by whom the foregoing, and also Petition to the King, Letter to the Agent, to Lord Shelburne. &c. were, Mr. Cushing, (the Speaker,) Col. Otis, Mr. Adams, Major Hawley, Mr. Otis, Mr. Hancock, Capt. Sheaffe, Col. Bowers, and Mr. Dexter.]

* The Editor cannot but observe, that this *circular* was one of the most effectual measures to call the attention of the colonists to their real situation, in a political view, to disseminate correct sentiments on their constitutional and charter rights, to inspire a resolution to defend those rights, and to shew to the British administration, that the opposition in Massachusetts, to the late acts of Parliament, was the efforts of men who knew how both to appreciate and defend their political freedom. This will appear by the subsequent conduct of administration ; for it was soon required that this circular should be rescinded ; and when the General Court refused to do it, it was most arbitrarily ordered that it be dissolved. This, however, was only one, in a *series* of measures adopted, to resist the encroachments of despotic power, and to maintain the liberty long enjoyed by our ancestors.

LETTER

FROM THE HOUSE OF REPRESENTATIVES, TO THE RIGHT HONORABLE THE
EARL OF SHELBURNE, ONE OF HIS MAJESTY'S PRINCIPAL
SECRETARIES OF STATE.

Province of Massachusetts Bay, January 15, 1768.

MY LORD,

THE House of Representatives of this his Majesty's province, having had experience of your Lordship's generous sentiments of his Majesty's most loyal, though remote subjects in America, and of your noble exertions in their behalf, in the late time of their distress, beg leave to lay before your Lordship's view the new scenes of difficulty which are again opened upon us, and to implore your repeated interposition.

Your Lordship is not insensible that our forefathers were, in an unhappy reign, driven into this wilderness by the hand of power. At their own expense they crossed an ocean of three thousand miles, and purchased an inheritance for themselves and their posterity, with the view of propagating the christian religion, and enlarging the English dominion in this distant part of the earth. Through the indulgent smiles of Heaven upon them, though not without hardship and fatigue; unexperienced, and perhaps hardly to be conceived by their brethren and fellow subjects in their native land; and with the constant peril of their lives from a numerous race of men, as barbarous and cruel, and yet as warlike as any people upon the face of the earth, they increased their numbers, and enlarged their settlement. They obtained a charter from King Charles the First, wherein his Majesty was pleased to recognize to them a liberty to worship God according to the dictates of their conscience; a blessing which in those unhappy times was denied to them in their own country; and the rights, liberties, privileges and immunities of his natural born subjects within the realm. This charter they enjoyed, having punctually fulfilled the conditions of it, till it was vacated, as we conceive arbitrarily, in the reign of King Charles the Second. After the revolution, that grand era of British liberty, when King William and Queen Mary, of glorious and blessed memory, were established on the throne, the inhabitants of this province obtained another charter, in which the most essential rights and privileges, contained in the former, were restored to them. Thus blessed with the liberties of Englishmen, they continued to increase and multiply, till, as your Lordship knows, a dreary wilderness is become a fruitful field, and a grand source of national wealth and glory.

By the common law, my Lord, as well as sundry acts of Parliament, from the reign of Edward the Third, the children of his

18

Majesty's natural born subjects, born passing and repassing the seas, are entitled to all the rights and privileges of his natural subjects born within the realm. From hence the conclusion appears to be indisputable, that the descendants of his Majesty's subjects in the realm, who migrated with the consent of the nation, and purchased a settlement with their own treasure and blood, without any aid from the nation; who early acknowledged their allegiance to the Crown of England, and have always approved themselves faithful subjects, and in many instances given signal proofs of their loyalty to their King, and their firm attachment and affection to their mother country; the conclusion is strong, that exclusive of any consideration of their charter, they are entitled to the rights and privileges of the British constitution, in common with their fellow subjects in Britain. And it is very remarkably the sense of the British nation, that they are so, as appears by an act of Parliament, made in the 13th of his late Majesty, King George the Second.* The preamble of that act plainly presupposes it ; and the purview of the same act enables and directs the Superior Court of Judicature of this province, a court erected by the authority of the General Court, to naturalize foreigners, under certain conditions ; which it is presumed, the wisdom of the Parliament would not have empowered any people to do, who were not themselves deemed natural born subjects.

The spirit of the law of nature and nations, supposes, that all the free subjects of any kingdom, are entitled equally to all the rights of the constitution ; for it appears unnatural and unreasonable to affirm, that local, or any other circumstances, can justly deprive any part of the subjects of the same prince, of the full enjoyment of the rights of that constitution, upon which the government itself is formed, and by which sovereignty and allegiance are ascertained and limited. But your Lordship is so thoroughly acquainted with the extent of the rights of men and of subjects, as to render it altogether improper to take up any more of your time on this head.

There are, my Lord, fundamental rules of the constitution, which it is humbly presumed, neither the supreme legislative nor the supreme executive can alter. In all free states, the constitution is fixed; it is from thence, that the legislative derives its authority; therefore it cannot change the constitution without destroying its own foundation. If, then, the constitution of Great Britain is the common right of all British subjects, it is humbly referred to your Lordship's judgment, whether the supreme legislative of the empire may rightly leap the bounds of it, in the exercise of power over the subjects in America, any more than over those in Britain.

When mention is made of the rights of American subjects, and the interest they have in the British constitution, in common with

*See page 128, Letter to De Berdt.

all other British subjects, your Lordship is too candid and just in your sentiments, to suppose that the House have the most distant thought of an independency of Great Britain. They are not insensible of their security and happiness in their connexion with, and dependence on the mother state. These, my Lord, are the sentiments of the House, and of their constituents ; and they have reason to believe, they are the sentiments of all the colonies. Those who are industriously propagating in the nation a different opinion of the colonists, are not only doing the greatest injustice to them, but an irreparable injury to the nation itself.

It is the glory of the British constitution, that it has its foundation in the law of God and nature. It is essentially a natural right, that a man shall quietly enjoy, and have the sole disposal of his own property. This right is ingrafted into the British constitution, and is familiar to the American subjects. And your Lordship will judge, whether any necessity can render it just and equitable in the nature of things, that the supreme legislative of the empire, should impose duties, subsidies, talliages and taxes, internal or external, for the sole purpose of raising a revenue, upon subjects that are not, and cannot, considering their local circumstances, by any possibility, be equally represented, and consequently, whose consent cannot be had in Parliament.

The security of right and property, is the great end of government. Surely, then, such measures as tend to render right and property precarious, tend to destroy both property and government, for these must stand or fall together. Property is admitted to have an existence in the savage state of nature ; and if it is necessary for the support of savage life, it by no means becomes less so in civil society. The House intreat your Lordship to consider, whether a colonist can be conceived to have any property which he may call his own, if it may be granted away by any other body, without his consent. And they submit to your Lordship's judgment, whether this was not actually done, when the act for granting to his Majesty certain duties on paper, glass, and other articles, for the sole and express purpose of raising a revenue in America, was made. It is the judgment of Lord Coke, that the Parliament of Great Britain cannot tax Ireland " *quia milites ad Parliamentum non mittant.*" And Sir William Jones, an eminent jurist, declared it as his opinion, to King Charles the Second, that he could no more grant a commission to levy money on his subjects in Jamaica, without their consent, by an assembly, than they could discharge themselves from their allegiance to the Crown. Your Lordship will be pleased to consider that Ireland and Jamaica were both conquered ; which cannot be said of any of the colonies, Canada excepted ; the argument therefore, is stronger in favor of the colonies.

Our ancestors, when oppressed in the unfortunate reign of James the Second, found relief by the interposition of the Parliament. But it is the misfortune of the colonies at present, that by the intervention of that power they are taxed ; and they can appeal for relief from their final decision to no power on earth, for there is no power on earth above them. Your Lordship will indulge the House in expressing a deep concern upon this occasion ; for it is the language of reason, and it is the opinion of the greatest writers on the law of nature and nations, that if the Parliament should make any considerable change in the constitution, and the nation should be voluntarily silent upon it, this would be considered as an approbation of the act.

But the House beg leave to represent to your Lordship, that although the right of the Parliament to impose taxes on the colonies, without a representation there, was indisputable, we humbly conceive it may be made fully to appear to be unequal that they should, at least at present. Your Lordship will be pleased to remember, that by an act of Parliament, the colonists are prohibited from importing commodities and manufactures of the growth of Europe, saving a few articles, except from Great Britain. This prohibition not only occasions a much greater demand upon the mother country for her manufactures, but gives the manufacturers there the advantage of their own price ; and can it be questioned, my Lord, but the colonists are obliged by means of this policy, to purchase the British manufactures at a much dearer rate, than the like manufactures would be purchased at, if they were allowed to go to foreign markets ? It is a loss to the colonists, and an equal gain to Great Britain. The same reasoning holds good with respect to the many articles of their produce, which the colonies are restrained by act of Parliament from sending to foreign ports. This is in reality a tax, though an indirect one, on the colonies ; besides the duties of excise and customs laid on the manufactures in Great Britain. A celebrated British writer on trade, computes the artificial value arising from these duties, to be no less than fifty per cent. Your Lordship will then form an estimate of the part that is paid by the colonies upon the importation into America, which is generally said to be at least the value of two millions sterling.

The House is not, at this time, complaining of this policy of the mother state ; but beg your Lordship's impartial and candid consideration, whether it is not grievous to the colonies to be additionally taxed upon the commodities of Great Britain here, and to be solely charged with the defending and securing his Majesty's colonies, after they have cheerfully borne their full proportion of maintaining his Majesty's rights in this part of his dominions, and reducing his enemies to terms of peace.

Your Lordship will allow the House to express their fears, that the colonies have been misrepresented to his Majesty's ministers and Parliament, as having an undutiful disposition towards his Majesty, and a disaffection to the mother kingdom. It has, till a few years past, been the usage for his Majesty's requisitions to be laid before the Representatives of his people in America ; and we may venture to appeal to your Lordship, that the people of this province have been ready to afford their utmost aid for his Majesty's service. It would be grievous to his most faithful subjects, to be called upon for aid in a manner which implies a mistrust of a free and cheerful compliance. And the House intreat your Lordship's consideration whether our enemies at least, would not infer a want of duty and loyalty in us, when the Parliament have judged it necessary to compel us by laws for that purpose ; as by the late acts for raising a revenue in America, and the act for preventing mutiny and desertion ; in the latter of which the Governor and Council are directed to supply the King's troops with enumerated articles, and the people are required to pay the expense. But besides, your Lordship will judge whether the execution of this act can comport with the existence of a free legislative in America.

It is unnatural to expect, that the supreme executive power can long exist, if the supreme legislative should be depressed and destroyed. In order, therefore, to support the supreme executive of his Majesty, at so great a distance, in the person of his Governor, Judges, and other executive officers, it seems necessary that there should be a legislative in America as perfectly free, as can consist with a subordination to the supreme legislative of the whole empire. Such a legislative is constituted by the royal charter of this province. In this charter, my Lord, the King, for himself, his heirs and successors, grants to the General Assembly full power and authority to impose and levy proportionable and reasonable assessments, rates and taxes, upon the estates and persons of the inhabitants, to be issued and disposed of, by warrant under the hand of the Governor, with the advice and consent of the Council, for the service of his Majesty, in the necessary defence and support of his government of the province, and the protection and preservation of the inhabitants, according to such acts as are, or shall be, in force in the province. And the House are humbly of opinion, that the legislative powers in the several colonies in America, were originally erected upon a conviction, that the subjects there could not be represented in the supreme legislative, and consequently that there was a necessity that such powers should be erected.

It is, by no means, my Lord, a disposition in the House to dispute the just authority of the supreme legislative of the nation, that induces them thus to address your-Lordship ; but a warm sense of loyalty to their Prince, and, they humbly apprehend, a just concern for their natural and constitutional rights. They beg your Lordship would excuse their trespassing upon your time and attention to the great affairs of state. They apply to you, as a friend to the rights of mankind, and of British subjects. As *Americans*, they implore your Lordship's patronage, and beseech you to represent their grievances to the King, our Sovereign, and employ your happy influence for their relief.

LETTER

FROM D. DE BERDT, ESQ. AGENT FOR THE PROVINCE, IN ENGLAND, TO THE
SPEAKER OF THE HOUSE OF REPRESENTATIVES.

London, May 16, 1768.

SIR,

SINCE my last, I received your several letters, which I delivered, as directed ; and at Lord Shelburne's desire, sent him your
judicious observations on British liberty, which sentiments are exactly my own; but have not been admitted to converse with his
Lordship on that head ; nor has he returned me the papers.

It is, at present a time of great confusion ; the heats and ani-
mosity of electing new members of Parliament are not yet subsi-
ded ; universal discontent, on account of the dearness of provisions, which spreads itself throughout the kingdom, and will take
up the whole attention of the legislature, that I do not apprehend
any thing will be done on American affairs. However, you may
rely on my watching the most favorable opportunity to throw in
your petition, which, at present, will be by no means proper.

It gives me concern, as the prosperity of America, in conjunction with her mother country, lies near the heart of

Your obedient servant,

D. DE BERDT.

LETTER

FROM THE HOUSE OF REPRESENTATIVES OF THE PROVINCE OF MASSACHU-
SETTS BAY, SIGNED BY THEIR SPEAKER, BY THEIR ORDER, TO THE
RIGHT HONORABLE THE MARQUIS OF ROCKINGHAM,
JANUARY 22, 1768.

My Lord,

THE House of Representatives of this his Majesty's province,
have had the honor of your letter of the 7th of May last, communicated to them by their Speaker ; and thank your Lordship for
your condescension, in the kind sentiments you are pleased to express of his Majesty's good subjects of America, and of this province. The establishing the harmony between Great Britain and
her colonies, is a subject which your Lordship has judged worthy
of your particular attention ; and the exertions which you have
made for this very important purpose, claims the most grateful acknowledgments of this House. Your sentiments are so nobly ex-

tended beyond the most distant partial considerations, as must distinguish you as a patron of the colonies, a friend to the British constitution, and the rights of mankind.

Your Lordship is pleased to say, that you will not adopt a system of arbitrary rule over the colonies ; nor do otherwise than strenuously resist, where attempts shall be made to throw off that dependence, to which the colonies ought to submit. And your Lordship, with great impartiality, adds, " not only for the advantage of Great Britain, but for their own real happiness and safety."

This House, my Lord, have the honor heartily to join with you in sentiment; and they speak the language of their constituents. So sensible are they of their happiness and safety, in their union with, and dependence upon, the mother country, that they would by no means be inclined to accept of an independency, if offered to them. But, my Lord, they intreat your consideration, whether the colonies have not reason to fear some danger of arbitrary rule over them, when the supreme power of the nation have thought proper to impose taxes on his Majesty's American subjects, with the sole and express purpose of raising a revenue, and without their consent.

My Lord, the superintending power of that high court over all his Majesty's subjects in the empire, and in all cases which can consist with the fundamental rules of the constitution, was never questioned in this province, nor, as the House conceive, in any other. But, in all free states, the constitution is fixed ; it is from thence, that the supreme legislative, as well as the supreme executive derives its authority. Neither, then, can break through the fundamental rules of the constitution, without destroying their own foundation.

It is humbly conceived, that all his Majesty's happy subjects, in every part of his wide extended dominions, have a just and equitable claim to the rights of that constitution, upon which government itself is formed, and by which sovereignty and allegiance are ascertained and limited. Your Lordship will allow us to say, that it is an essential right of a British subject, ingrafted into the constitution, or, if your Lordship will admit the expression, a sacred and unalienable, natural right, quietly to enjoy and have the sole disposal of his own property. In conformity to this, the acts of the British Parliament declare, that every individual in the realm is present in his Majesty's high court of Parliament, by himself, or his representative, of his own free election. But, my Lord, it is apprehended that a just and equal representation of the subjects, at the distance of a thousand transmarine leagues from the metropolis, is utterly impracticable. Upon this opinion, this House humbly conceive his Majesty's royal predecessors thought it equitable to form subordinate legislative powers in America, as perfectly free as the nature of things would admit, that so their remote subjects might enjoy a right, which those within the realm have ever held sacred, of being taxed only by representatives of their own free election.

The House beg leave to observe to your Lordship, that the monies which shall arise by the act for granting to his Majesty certain duties on paper, glass and other articles, passed in the last session of Parliament, are to be applied, in the first place, for the payment of the necessary charges of the administration of justice, and the support of civil government in such colonies as shall be judged necessary; and the residue for defending, protecting and securing the colonies. They intreat your Lordship's consideration, what may be the consequences, in some future time, if the Crown, in addition to its right of appointing Governors over the colonies, which this House cheerfully recognize, should appoint them such stipends as it shall judge fit, without the consent of the people, and at their expense. And as the Judges of the land here do not hold their commissions during good behavior, your Lordship will judge, whether it may not hereafter happen, that at so great a distance from the throne, the fountain of justice, for want of an adequate check, corrupt and arbitrary rule may take place, even within the colonies, which may deprive a bench of justice of its glory, and the people of their happiness and safety.

Your Lordship's justice and candor will induce you to believe, that what our enemies may have taken occasion to represent to his Majesty's ministers and the Parliament, as an undutiful disposition in the colonies, is nothing more than a just and firm attachment to their natural and constitutional rights. It is humbly submitted to your Lordship, whether these ideas are well founded. And while this province and the colonies shall continue, in your Lordship's judgment, to be faithful and loyal subjects to his Majesty, they rely upon it, that your happy influence will ever be employed to promote the sentiments of tenderness, as well as justice, in the parent country.

[Letters were written by a committee of the House of Representatives, the same session, and sent to the right honorable Henry S. Conway, one of his Majesty's principal Secretaries of State; to the right honorable the Earl of Camden, Lord High Chancellor of England; the right honorable the Earl of Chatham; and to the Lords Commissioners of the Treasury. These letters are written with great ability, and breathe a noble spirit of freedom, and present some new views of the subject, at that time controverted; but as they are in substance like those here given, it was thought unnecessary to insert them in this volume. It is obvious, however, to remark, that these papers shew the diligence, the interest and zeal, which the patriots of that period exhibited in reference to the dispute between Great Britain and the colonies, and their unwearied efforts to secure the rights and liberties of the people.]

SPEECH

OF GOVERNOR BERNARD, TO THE COUNCIL AND HOUSE OF REPRESENTATIVES, MAY 26, 1768.

Gentlemen of the Council, and
Gentlemen of the House of Representatives,

As the chief intention of this session is to constitute the General Court for the year ensuing, and the season makes a long continuation of it very inconvenient, I must recommend to you, to avoid all business, that can well be postponed, to the next session.

Among those matters which will demand your immediate attention, will be the providing for the solicitation of the cause of this province, with regard to the boundary line with New York. As you are contented with that line which has heretofore been reported by the Lords Commissioners for trade and plantations ; and the province, in general, has hitherto acquiesced in it, there is great reason to expect that it will be confirmed. I have sent copies of the papers relating to the treaty between the two provinces, concerning the line, to the Secretary of the Board of Trade ; and have prayed that this province may have time to appoint an agent, or solicitor, before their cause is brought into judgment. I shall write more fully on the subject, as occasion shall serve, and shall give this business all the assistance, which my station and ability will afford. FRA. BERNARD.

[The Governor objected to T. Saunders, J. Hancock, J. Gerrish, A. Ward, Col. Otis, and J. Bowers, who were chosen Counsellors.]

MESSAGE

FROM THE GOVERNOR TO THE HOUSE OF REPRESENTATIVES, JUNE 21, 1768.

Gentlemen of the House of Representatives,

I HAVE his Majesty's orders to make a requisition to you, which I communicate in the very words in which I have received it. I must desire you to take it into immediate consideration, and I assure you, that your resolution thereon, will have most important consequences to the province. I am, myself, merely ministerial in this business, having received his Majesty's instruction for all I have to do in it. I heartily wish that you may see how forcible

19

the expediency of your giving his Majesty this testimonial of your
duty and submission is, at this time. If you should think otherwise, I must nevertheless do my duty.   FRA. BERNARD.

———

MESSAGE

FROM THE HOUSE OF REPRESENTATIVES, TO THE GOVERNOR,
JUNE 22, 1768.

May it please your Excellency,

THE House of Representatives humbly request your Excellency to lay before them a copy of his Majesty's instructions, referred to in your message of the 21st instant ; a copy of the letter
to your Excellency, from the right honorable the Earl of Hillsborough, dated the 22d of April, 1768 ; a copy of a letter from his
Lordship, communicated lately, by your Excellency to the honorable Board ; and copies of letters written by your Excellency to
his Lordship, relating to the subject of your aforesaid message.

———

ANSWER.

THE FOLLOWING MESSAGE WAS RECEIVED FROM HIS EXCELLENCY,
IN ANSWER TO THE ABOVE, JUNE 24, 1768.

Gentlemen of the House of Representatives,

I SHOULD have communicated the whole of the Earl of Hillsborough's letter, relating to the business which I laid before you
the 21st instant, if I had not been desirous that your compliance
with his Majesty's requisition, might have its fullest merit, by its
appearing to be entirely dictated by a sense of your duty.
But since you desire to know what my further orders are, I
hereby send you a copy of the other part of the letter, relative to
this business, which contains all my instructions thereupon.   And
as I know you will not expect that I should disobey the King's
positive commands, I must desire, that, if you should resolve to
oblige me to execute them, you will, previously to your giving
your final answer, prevent the inconveniences which must fall
upon the people, for want of the annual tax bill, which, I understand, is not yet sent up to the Board.   For, if I am obliged to
dissolve the General Court, I shall not think myself at liberty to

call another, till I receive his Majesty's commands for that purpose ; which will be too late to prevent the Treasurer issuing his warrants for the whole tax, granted by the act of the last year.

As to the letter of the Earl of Hillsborough, which I communicated to the Council, I must beg leave to be the proper judge of the time and occasion of communicating any papers I receive, to the Council or the House. If I had then thought it expedient to lay it before the House, I should have done it ; when I shall think it so, I shall do it.

As to your request of the copies of my letters to the Secretary of State, you may assure yourselves, that I shall never make public my letters to his Majesty's ministers, but upon my own motion, and for my own reasons.   FRA. BERNARD.

MESSAGE

FROM THE HOUSE OF REPRESENTATIVES, TO THE GOVERNOR,

JUNE 30, 1768.

May it please your Excellency,

THE House of Representatives of this his Majesty's ancient and loyal province of the Massachusetts Bay, have, with the greatest deliberation, considered your messages of the 21st and 24th instant, with the several extracts from the letter of the right honorable the Earl of Hillsborough, his Majesty's principal Secretary of State for North American affairs, dated the 22d of April last, which your Excellency has thought fit to communicate. We have also received the written answer which your Excellency was pleased to give the committee of this House, directed to wait on you the 29th instant, with a message, humbly requesting a recess, that the members might be favored with an opportunity to consult their constituents, at this important crisis, when a direct and peremptory requisition is made, of a new and strange constructure, and so strenuously urged, viz. that we should immediately rescind the resolution of the last House, to transmit circular letters to the other British colonies on the continent of North America, barely intimating a desire that they would join in similar dutiful and loyal petitions to our most gracious Sovereign, for the redress of the grievances occasioned by sundry late acts of Parliament, calculated for the sole purpose of raising a revenue in America.

We have most diligently revised, not only the said resolution, but also the circular letter, written and sent in consequence thereof; and after all, they both appear to us to be conceived in terms not only prudent and moderate in themselves, but respectful to that truly august body, the Parliament of Great Britain, and very dutiful and loyal in regard to his Majesty's sacred person, crown and dignity ; of all which, we entertain sentiments of the highest reverence and most ardent affection ; and should we ever depart from these sentiments, we should stand self condemned as unworthy the name of British subjects, descended from British ancestors, intimately allied and connected in interest and inclination with our fellow subjects, the commons of Great Britain.   We cannot but express our deep concern, that a measure of the late House, in all respects so innocent, in most, so virtuous and laudable, and as we conceive, so truly patriotic, should have been represented to administration in the odious light of a party and factious measure, and that pushed through by reverting in a thin House to, and reconsidering, what in a full assembly, had been rejected.   It was, and is a matter of notoriety, that more than eighty members were present at the reconsideration of the vote against application to the other colonies.   The vote for reconsideration was obtained by a large majority.   It is, or ought to be well known, that the presence of eighty members makes a full House, this number being just double that, by the royal charter of the province, required to constitute the third branch of our Colony Legislature.   Your Excellency might have been very easily informed, if you was not, that the measures of the late House, in regard to sundry acts of the late Parliament, for the sole purpose of raising a North American revenue, were generally carried by three to one ; and we dare appeal to your Excellency for the truth of this assertion, namely, that there were many persons in the majority, in all views, as respectable as the very best of the minority ; that so far from any sinister views, were the committee of the late House, appointed and directed to take into their most serious consideration, the then present state of the province, from going into any rash or precipitate measures, that they, for some days, actually delayed their first report, which was a letter to Mr. Agent De Berdt, on this candid and generous principle, that those who were reasonably presupposed to be most warmly attached to all your Excellency's measures, especially those for furthering, and, by all means, enforcing the acts for levying the North American revenue, might be present, and a more equal contest ensue.   It would be incredible, should any one assert that your Excellency wanted a true information of all these things, which were not done, or desired to be hid in a corner, but were notoriously transacted in the open light, at noon day.   It is, to us, altogether incomprehensible, that we should be required, on the peril of a dissolution of the great and General Court, or Assembly of this province, to rescind a resolution of a former House of Representatives, when it is evident, that resolution has no existence, but as a mere historical fact.

Your Excellency must know, that the resolution referred to, is, to speak in the language of the common law, not now "executory," but, to all intents and purposes, "executed."   The circular letters have been sent, and many of them have been answered; those answers are now in the public papers; the public, the world, must and will, judge of the proposals, purposes and answers. We could as well rescind those letters as the resolves; and both would be equally fruitless, if, by rescinding, as the word properly imports, is meant a repeal and nullifying the resolution referred to. But, if, as most probable, by the word rescinding, is intended a passing a vote of this House, in direct and express disapprobation of the measure above mentioned, as " illegal, inflammatory, and tending to promote unjustifiable combinations against his Majesty's peace, crown, and dignity," we must take the liberty to testify, and publicly to declare, that we take it to be the native, inherent, and indefeasible right of the subject, jointly or severally, to petition the King for the redress of grievances; provided always, that the same be done in a decent, dutiful, and constitutional way, without tumult, disorder, or confusion. Furthermore, we are also humbly, but very clearly and very firmly of opinion, that the petition of the late dutiful and loyal House to his Majesty, and their other very orderly applications for the redress of grievances, have had the most desirable tendencies and effects to keep men's minds in ease and quiet. We must be excused, in thinking that the people were, in truth, patiently waiting for the meeting of a new Parliament, and their measures, and his Majesty's pleasure; and it is probable, they would every where have thus waited the event, had it not been revealed here, that the late provincial application for redress of grievances, were somehow, strangely obstructed, and the province, in consequence of misinformation and misrepresentation, most unfortunately fallen under the royal displeasure; and to complete this misfortune, it was not only divulged to the other colonies, but some of them actually received the information before it was made known here, that the House had been accused to his Majesty, or his ministers, or fallen under the displeasure of the one, or the censure of the other.

On the whole, sir, we will consider his most sacred Majesty, under God, as our King, and best protector, and common father, and shall ever bear him true and faithful allegiance.

We also regard your Excellency as the representative of the greatest potentate on earth; and at all times have been, and shall be, as far as was, or is, or could consist with the indefeasible purposes of preserving life, liberty and property, most ready and willing, to treat you with all that respect, justly due to your high rank and station. But we are constrained to say, that we are disagreeably convinced, that your Excellency entertains not that paternal regard for the welfare of the good people of this province, which you have sometimes been pleased to profess, and which they have at all times, an irrefragable right to expect from their Governor. Your Excellency has thought fit, not only to deny us a recess, to consult our constituents in regard to the present requisition, but hath assured us, in effect, that you shall take silence, at least a'delay, not as usual, for a consent, but for a denial. You have also thought fit to inform us, that you cannot think yourself at liberty, in case of the dissolution of this,'to call another Assembly, without the express orders of his Majesty, for that purpose; and at the same time, your Excellency has been pleased to assure us, that you have communicated the whole of Lord Hillsborough's letter, and your instructions, so far as relates to the requisition. In all this, however, we cannot find, that your Excellency is more than directed to dissolve the present Assembly, in case of a non-cómpliance on the part of the House. If the votes of the House are to be controlled by the direction of a minister, we have left us but a vain semblance of liberty. We know it to be the just prerogative of the Crown, at pleasure to dissolve a Parliament; we are also sensible, that, consistently with the great charter of this province, your Excellency, when you shall think fit, with or without the intervention of a minister, can dissolve the great and General Court of this colony, and that, without the least obligation to convene another within the year. But, should it ever grow into use, for any ill disposed Governor of the province, by means of a mistaken or wilful wrong state of facts, to procure orders for a dissolution, the same charter will be of no value.

We take this opportunity, faithfully to represent to your Excellency, that the new revenue acts and measures, are not only disagreeable to, but in every view, are deemed an insupportable burthen and grievance, with a very few exceptions, by all the freeholders and other inhabitants of this jurisdiction. And we beg leave, once for all, to assure your Excellency, that those of this opinion, are of "no party, or expiring faction." They have, at all times, been ready to devote their time and fortunes to his Majesty's service. Of loyalty, this majority could as reasonably boast, as any who may happen to enjoy your Excellency's smiles. Their reputation, rank and fortune, are, at least, equal to those who may have been sometimes considered as the only friends to good government; while some of the best blood in the colony, even in the two Houses of Assembly, lawfully convened, and duly acting, have been openly charged with the unpardonable crime of oppugnation against "the royal authority." We have, now, only to inform your Excellency, that this House have voted not to rescind, as required, the resolution of the last House; and that, on a division on the question, there were ninety-two nays, and seventeen yeas. In all this, we have been actuated by a conscientious, and, finally, a clear and determined sense of duty to God, to our King, our country, and our latest posterity; and we most ardently wish, and humbly pray, that in your future conduct, your Excellency may be influenced by the same principles.

[Governor Bernard prorogued the General Court, the day the House sent him the above message; and the next day, by proclamation, dissolved it.]

LETTER

FROM THE HOUSE OF REPRESENTATIVES, TO LORD HILLSBOROUGH,
JUNE 30, 1768.

My Lord,

His Excellency the Governor of this province, has been pleased to communicate to the House of Representatives, extracts of a letter he had received from your Lordship, dated Whitehall, 22d of April, 1768; wherein it is declared to be the royal pleasure, that he should require of them, in his Majesty's name, to rescind the resolution, which gave birth to a circular letter from the Speaker of the last House, and to declare their disapprobation of, and dissent to, that rash and hasty proceeding.

The House are humbly of opinion, that a requisition from the throne, of this nature, to a British House of Commons, has been very unusual; perhaps there has been no such precedent since the revolution. If this be the case, some very aggravated representations of this measure, must have been made to his Majesty, to induce him to require of *this* House, to rescind a resolution of a former House, upon pain of forfeiting their existence. For, my Lord, the House of Representatives, duly elected, are constituted by the royal charter, the representative body of his Majesty's faithful commons of this province, in the General Assembly. Your Lordship is pleased to say, that his Majesty considers this step " as evidently tending to create unwarrantable combinations, and to excite an unjustifiable opposition to the constitutional authority of Parliament." The House, therefore, thought it their indispensable duty, immediately to revise the letter referred to; and carefully to recollect as far as they were able, the sentiments which prevailed in the House, to induce them to revert to, and resolve on the measure.

It may be necessary to observe, that the people in this province have attended, with a deep concern, to the several acts of the British Parliament, which impose duties and taxes on the colonies; not for the purpose of regulating the trade, but with the sole intention of raising a revenue. This concern, my Lord, so far from being limited within the circle of a few inconsiderate persons, is become universal. The most respectable for fortune, rank and station, as well as probity and understanding, in the province, with very few exceptions, are alarmed with apprehensions of the fatal consequences of a power exercised in any one part of the British empire, to command and apply the property of their fellow subjects at discretion. This consideration prevailed on the last House of Representatives, to resolve on a humble, dutiful, and loyal petition to the King, the common head and father of all his people, for his gracious interposition, in favor of his subjects of this province. If your Lordship, whom his Majesty has honored with the American department, has been instrumental in presenting a petition, so interesting to the well being of his loyal subjects here, this House beg leave to make their most grateful acknowledgments, and to implore your continued aid and patronage.

As all his Majesty's North American subjects are alike affected by these parliamentary revenue acts, the former House very justly supposed, that each of the Assemblies on the continent, would take such methods of obtaining redress, as should be thought by them respectively, to be regular and proper. And being desirous, that the several applications should harmonize with each other, they resolved on their circular letter ; wherein their only view seems to be, to advertise their sister colonies of the measures *they* had taken upon a *common* and important concern, without once calling upon them to adopt those measures, or any other.

Your Lordship, surely, will not think it a crime in that House, to have taken a step, which was perfectly consistent with the constitution ; and had a natural tendency to compose the minds of his Majesty's subjects of this and his other colonies, until, in his royal clemency, he should afford them relief, at a time, when it seemed to be the evident design of a party, to prevent calm, deliberate, rational and constitutional measures from being pursued ; or to stop the distresses of the people from reaching his Majesty's ear, and consequently to precipitate them into a state of desperation, and melancholy extremity. Thus, my Lord, it appears to this House ; and your Lordship will impartially judge, whether a representation of it to his Majesty as a measure "of an inflammatory nature"— as a step evidently tending "to create unwarrantable combinations," and, "to excite an unjustifiable opposition to the constitutional authority of the Parliament," be not injurious to the representatives of this people, and an affront to his Majesty himself.

An attempt, my Lord, to impress your royal mind, with a jealousy of his faithful subjects, for which there are no just grounds, is a crime of the most malignant nature ; as it tends to disturb and destroy that mutual confidence between the Prince and the subjects, which is the only true basis of public happiness and security ; your Lordship, upon inquiry, may find that such base and wicked attempts have been made.

It is an inexpressible grief to the people of this province, to find repeated censures falling upon them, not from ministers of state alone, but from majesty itself, grounded on letters and accusations from the Governor, a sight of which, though repeatedly requested of his Excellency, is refused. There is no evil of this life, which they so sensibly feel, as the displeasure of their Sovereign. It is a punishment, which they are assured, his Majesty would never inflict, but upon a representation of the justice of it, from his servants, whom he confides in. Your Lordship will allow the House to appeal to your own candor, upon the grievous hardship of their being made to suffer so severe a misfortune, without ever being called to answer for themselves, or even made acquainted with the matters of charge alleged against them: A right, which, by the common rules of society, founded in the eternal laws of reason and equity, they are justly entitled to. The House is not willing to trespass upon your patience. They could recite numbers of instances, since Governor Bernard has been honored by his Majesty, to preside over this province, of their suffering the King's displeasure, through the instrumentality of the Governor, intimated by the Secretary of State, without the least previous notice, that they had ever deviated from the path of their duty. This, they humbly conceive, is just matter of complaint, and it may serve to convince your Lordship, that his Excellency has not that tender feeling for his Majesty's subjects, which is characteristic of a good Governor, and of which the Sovereign affords an illustrious example.

It is the good fortune of the House, to be able to show, that the measure of the last House, referred to in your Lordship's letter to the Governor, has been grossly misrepresented, in all its circumstances. And it is matter of astonishment, that a transaction of the House, the business of which, is constantly done in the open view of the world, could be thus colored ; a transaction which, by special order of the House, was laid before his Excellency, whose duty to his Majesty is, at least, not to misinform him.

His Excellency could not but acknowledge, in justice to that House, that moderation took place in the beginning of the session. This is a truth, my Lord. It was a principle with the House, to conduct the affairs of government in this department, so as to avoid the least occasion of offence. As an instance of their pacific disposition, they granted a further establishment for one of his Majesty's garrisons in the province, rather to gratify his Excellency, who had requested it, than from a full conviction of its necessity. But your Lordship is informed, that this moderation " did not continue ;" and that, " instead of a spirit of prudence and respect for the constitution, which seemed at that time to influence the conduct of a large majority of the members, a thin House at the end of the session, presumed to revert to, and resolve on a measure of an inflammatory nature ;" that it was an "unfair proceeding"—" contrary to the real sense of the House ;" and " procured by surprise." My Lord, the journals and minutes of the House will prove the contrary of all this. And to convince your Lordship, the House beg leave to lay before you, the several resolutions relating to these matters, as they stand recorded.

The House having finished their petition to the King, and their letters to divers of his Majesty's ministers ; a motion was regularly made on the 21st of January, which was the middle of the session, and a resolution was then taken, to appoint a time to consider the expediency of writing to the Assemblies of the other colonies on this continent, with respect to the importance of their joining with them, in petitioning his Majesty at this time. Accordingly, on the day assigned, there being eighty-two members present, a number always allowed to be sufficient to make a full House, the question was debated; in consequence of which, a motion took place, that letters be wrote to the several Assemblies of the provinces and colonies on the continent, acquainting them, that the House had taken into consideration, the difficulties to which they are, and must be reduced, by the operation of the late acts of Parliament, for levying duties and taxes on the colonies ; and have resolved on a humble, dutiful and loyal petition to his Majesty, for redress ; and also upon proper representations to his Majesty's ministers on the subject. And to desire, that they would severally take such constitutional measures thereupon, as they should judge most proper. And the question upon the motion, passed in the negative. On Thursday, the 4th of February, it was moved in the House, that the foregoing question be considered, so far as to leave it at large ; and conformable to a standing rule of the House, that no vote or order shall be reconsidered at any time, unless the House be as full, as when such vote or order was passed ; the number in the House was called for, and it appearing that eighty-two members were present,* the question was put, and passed in the affirmative, by a large majority ; and by an immediately subsequent resolve, the first vote was ordered to be erased. The same day, the resolution which gave birth to the circular letter, took place, a question being regularly moved and fairly debated, whether the House would appoint a committee to prepare a letter, to be sent to each of the Houses of Representatives and Burgesses on the continent, to inform them of the measures which this House has taken, with regard to the difficulties arising from the acts of Parliament for levying duties and taxes on the American colonies, and report to the House, which passed in the affirmative ; and a committee was appointed accordingly. This committee, after deliberating a week, reported the letter, which was read in the House, and accepted, almost unanimously ; and fair copies of the same were ordered to be taken, for the Speaker to sign, and forward as soon as might be. And this day, there were eighty-three members in the House.

The day following, an order passed, that a fair copy of the letter be transmitted to Dennis De Berdt, Esq. in London. The design of which was, that he might be able to produce it, as necessity might require, to prevent any misrepresentation of its true spirit and design.

* The same number as before. It is to be observed, that the House, at that time, consisted of about one hundred and ten members. By the royal charter, forty makes a quorum. Hence it appears, that eighty-two members are more than double the number, sufficiently legal, to transact business, and were then three quarters of the whole House.

On Saturday, the 13th of February, in order that no possible occasion might be taken by the Governor, to think, that the debates and resolutions were designed to be kept a secret from his Excellency, the House came to the following resolution, viz. : Whereas this House hath directed, that a letter be sent to the several Houses of Representatives and Burgesses of the British colonies on the continent, setting forth the sentiments of this House, with regard to the great difficulties that must accrue by the operation of divers acts of Parliament, for levying duties and taxes on the colonies, with the sole and express purpose of raising a revenue ; and their proceedings thereon, in a humble, dutiful, and loyal petition to the King, and such representations to his Majesty's ministers, as they apprehend, may have a tendency to obtain redress : And whereas it is the opinion of this House, that all effectual methods should be taken, to cultivate harmony between the several branches of this government, as being necessary to promote the prosperity of his Majesty's government in this province ; Resolved, That a committee wait on his Excellency the Governor, and acquaint him, that a copy of the letter aforesaid, will be laid before him, as soon as it can be drafted ; as well as of all the proceedings of this House, relative to said affair, if he shall desire it. And a committee was appointed, who waited on his Excellency accordingly. On Monday following, the House resolved on the establishment already mentioned, which is observed, only to shew your Lordship, that there was, at this time, no disposition in the House, "to revive unhappy divisions and distractions, so prejudicial to the true interest of Great Britain and the colonies."

The House beg leave to apologize to your Lordship, for the trouble given you in so particular a narration of facts ; which they thought necessary to satisfy your Lordship, that the resolution of the last House, referred to by your Lordship, was not an unfair proceeding, procured by surprise in a thin House, as his Majesty has been informed ; but the declared sense of a large majority, when the House was full : That the Governor of the province was made fully acquainted with the measure ; and never signified his disapprobation of it to the House, which it is presumed, he would have done, in duty to his Majesty, if he had thought it was of evil tendency : And, therefore, that the House had abundant reason to be confirmed in their own opinion of the measure, as being the production of moderation and prudence. And the House humbly rely on the royal clemency, that to petition his Majesty will not be deemed by him to be inconsistent with a respect to the British constitution, as settled at the revolution, by William the Third : That to acquaint their fellow subjects, involved in the same distress, of their having done so, in full hopes of success, even if they had invited the union of all America in one joint supplication, would not be discountenanced by our gracious Sovereign, as a measure of an inflammatory nature ; That when your Lordship shall, in justice, lay a true statement of these matters before his Majesty, he will no longer consider them as tending to create unwarrantable combinations, or excite an unjustifiable opposition to the constitutional authority of the Parliament :   That he will then clearly discern, who are of that desperate faction, which is continually disturbing the public tranquility ; and, that while his arm is extended for the protection of his distressed and injured subjects, he will frown upon all those, who, to gratify their own passions, have dared even to attempt to deceive him !

The House of Representatives of this province, have more than once, during the administration of Governor Bernard, been under a necessity of intreating his Majesty's ministers to suspend their further judgment upon such representations of the temper of the people, and the conduct of the Assembly, as they were able to make appear to be injurious.   The same indulgence, this House now beg of your Lordship ; and beseech your Lordship to patronize them so far, as to make a favorable representation of their conduct to the King our Sovereign ; it being the highest ambition of this House, and the people whom they represent, to stand before his Majesty in their just character, of affectionate and loyal subjects.

====

REPORT AND RESOLUTIONS

OF THE COUNCIL, JUNE 30, 1768,

THE committee appointed the 13th instant, to inquire into the state of the province, made report, as follows, viz :—

The committee appointed by the foregoing order, find, on inquiry, that there is great uneasiness among the people of this province, arising from the several causes referred to in the resolves herewith presented ; which, with the unusual proceedings relative to the seizure made in Boston, the 10th instant, gave occasion for the tumultuous and unwarrantable assembling of a number of persons on the same evening, and the consequent disorders that took place.

The committee have agreed upon the following resolves, to be passed upon this occasion, by the two Houses, if they think proper, and herewith humbly submit them to their consideration.

In the name of the committee,
JOHN ERVING.

Whereas there has been, for some time past, a general uneasiness among the people of this province, occasioned by the late act of Parliament imposing duties upon sundry articles, for the purpose of raising a revenue, as also by the appointment of a Board of

Commissioners; and the inhabitants of the province, by the act and appointment aforesaid, having been drained of their money, and greatly distressed in their trade and business; and it being apparent, that the money collected, has been applied for the increasing of officers, to a number, that has a very disagreeable aspect on the future welfare of this people:

Resolved, That the two Houses will immediately take under consideration, and make strict inquiry into all the grievances complained of as aforesaid; and into the new and unprecedented procedure of the custom house officers, with regard to the seizure below mentioned; and take such measures, and make such representations to his Majesty and his Parliament, as may tend to procure the redress of said grievances.

And whereas, on Friday, the 10th instant, towards the evening, a vessel was seized in Boston, by several of the officers of the customs, and immediately after, upon a signal given by one of the said officers, one or more armed boats from the Romney man of war, took possession of her, cut her fasts, and carried her from the wharf where she lay, into the harbor, alongside the Romney, which occasioned a number of people to be collected, who, from the violence and unprecedentedness of the procedure, with regard to the carrying off said vessel, and the reflection thereby, upon the inhabitants of the town, as disposed to rescue any seizure that might be made, took occasion to insult and abuse said officers, and afterwards to break some of the windows of their dwelling houses, and commit other disorders, in disturbance of the peace of his Majesty's subjects, and in breach of the good and wholesome laws of this province:

Resolved, That, although the extraordinary circumstances attending the said seizure, may in some measure, extenuate the criminality of the riotous proceedings aforesaid; yet being, notwithstanding, of a very criminal nature, and of dangerous consequence, the two Houses do hereby declare their utter abhorrence and detestation of them. And in order to bring the perpetrators to justice;

Resolved, That his Excellency the Governor be desired to direct the Attorney General to prosecute all persons guilty of the riot aforesaid; or, that any way aided or abetted the same, to the end, that they may be punished agreeably to law. And for discovering and detecting of the said rioters and their abettors, his Excellency the Governor, is hereby desired to issue forthwith, a proclamation, offering a reward of   to such person or persons, as shall make such discovery, so as that said rioters and abettors may be brought to condign punishment.

[The House of Representatives was engaged on some very interesting subject, when the above was sent down to them, from the Council, and did not admit the message. And the same day, the House was prorogued, and the day following, dissolved; so that they never acted on the subject.]

NOTE OF THE EDITOR.

[June 30, 1768, the day the General Court was prorogued, the Council being in session, a committee of the Board was appointed, composed of the following gentlemen : W. Brattle, J. Bowdoin, J. Russell, T. Flucker, and R. Tyler, to consider the state of the province, and to report what they should consider proper to be laid before his Majesty, respecting the same. July 7th, Mr. Bowdoin, from the aforesaid committee, reported the draft of an address to the King, which was accepted ; and Governor Bernard was requested to forward the same to his Majesty's Secretary of State. In this address, the Council state the services and expenses of the province, for many former years ; they complain of the acts of Parliament, laying duties, as extremely burdensome, as the debt of the province, incurred chiefly to pay the troops who had lately joined with the British in defending, securing and extending his Majesty's dominions, was very great. They declared their readiness to submit to all lawful authority ; acknowledged their allegiance, and professed their sincere loyalty to the King ; and prayed that the charter rights and privileges of the people might not be wrested from them, on account of any representations made as to their disaffection to the Crown, or opposition to constitutional statutes.* Soon after this, the Council was convened by the Governor, when he stated to the Board, that a riot had taken place, in which some of the officers of the customs were insulted, in consequence of their having seized a vessel belonging to a merchant of Boston, on a suggestion of her having goods liable to impost, but which there was an attempt to secrete, and thus avoid the payment of duties. It will be seen above, in this volume, what were the views and feelings of the Council, in reference to this affair. The Council expressed their disapprobation of the riot, and declared their readiness, in all regular and proper methods, to assist in bringing the authors of it to punishment. They, however, stated, that the seizure of the vessel was attended with circumstances highly insulting and irritating to the feelings of the citizens ; and gave it as their opinion, that the officers of the customs would not have been insulted, but for the unprecedented manner in which the seizure was made ; which was by several barges of armed men, from a British man of war, then lying in the harbor. The officers of the customs, affected to believe, that they could not safely remain in Boston ; and they retired to the ship of war, lying near the Castle, and afterwards to that fortress, then commanded by British regular troops, where they remained for many weeks. Considering the great irritation of the people, produced by recent oppressive and arbitrary measures, they were, perhaps, liable for

---

* In November following, the Council forwarded a petition to Parliament, very similar, in its spirit and arguments, to the address before presented to the King.

a time, to some insults. But the Council uniformly appeared ready to support the government and the laws, and decidedly expressed their disapprobation of all riots. The subject was long in agitation, between the Governor and Council. He endeavored to bring them into the dilemma of justifying the conduct of the officers of the customs, and interposing, directly, by an executive act, for their protection, or of countenancing the riot which had taken place, and being identified with those who meant to oppose, forcibly and overtly, the King's authority. He endeavored, by the letters he wrote to Lord Hillsborough, to have it believed in England, that the latter was true; and that even the Council was a factious, disorderly body, unwilling to support the authority of government, and aiding the people in their opposition to the laws. In their proceedings, however, they were temperate and prudent, yet firm and judicious. They resisted the intrigues of Governor Bernard, who strove to make them acquiesce in the arbitrary measures of the British ministry, and appealed to constitutional principles, as paramount to the temporary statutes of Parliament, as well as to particular orders from the King's Privy Council. Another important question was, at this period, discussed by the Council of this province, in consequence of an application from Governor Bernard, for quarters for two British regiments, which were ordered here from Halifax, and two more from Ireland. The Council consented, and advised that the two first be quartered in the barracks, at Castle Island; and that the municipal authority of the town of Boston, be consulted as to the other two regiments. The Selectmen declined doing any thing on the subject. The Governor then requested the Council to furnish quarters for one regiment, in the Manufactory House, in Boston, belonging to the province. The Council did not consent to the proposal, assigning as a reason, for not complying, that the act of Parliament, in relation to the subject, provided, that the regular troops of the Crown should be placed in the public barracks; and that no military officer, nor even the civil executive, was competent to oblige any town, or the Council, to furnish other quarters for them; and they expressed the opinion, that it belonged to the municipal authority, and not to the Board, to decide as to the quartering the troops in Boston. One regiment, however, was landed in Boston, notwithstanding this opposition, both of the town and the Executive Council of the province; and the Governor, then demanded of the Council, certain articles of provisions for the troops. The Council advised, after some hesitation and delay, that the troops be furnished with the articles needed, provided it were not done at the particular expense of the province. This decision was not pleasing to the Governor; and he took occasion to represent the conduct of the Council very unfavorably to the British ministers; and stated anew the imbecility of the executive, while thus composed of men chosen by the people in the province. To his statements, it was also, undoubtedly owing, that the administration ordered so many regular troops to be sent and stationed here; whose presence was intended to awe the people into submission to the arbitrary measures which had been adopted by Parliament, in relation to the government of the colonies. In April, 1769, the Council addressed a long letter to Lord Hillsborough, vindicating their conduct, with reference, both to the riot, and quartering of the British regulars; in which they discovered their attachment to the rights of the people, and their loyalty to the King; and exposed the intrigues, and the misrepresentations of Governor Bernard. When a new General Court met in May, 1769, the following resolve was passed by the House of Representatives, expressing their sense of the zeal and attention of the Council to the public interest.]

Resolve of the House of Representatives, June, 1769.

The House having taken into consideration, certain copies of letters, written by Governor Bernard, to the Earl of Hillsborough, one of his Majesty's principal Secretaries of State, in November and December last, and which were transmitted to the late Council, by Mr. Bollan, and at the desire of the House, have been communicated by the present Council; in which letters, his Majesty's loyal subjects of this colony, in general, as well as his Majesty's Council, are traduced, and represented in a most odious and unjust light to his Majesty's ministers: The House, having also, carefully read and considered the remarks which the Council has made thereon, in their letters to his Lordship, copies of which have also been communicated at the desire of the House:

Resolved, That the House do highly approve of, and have an entire satisfaction in the zeal and attention of the late Council to the public interest, not only in thus vindicating their own character, but guarding their country from meditated ruin, by truly stating facts, and justly representing the duty and loyalty of this people, at that critical time, when the Governor of the province wantonly dissolved the General Assembly, and arbitrarily refused to call another, upon the repeated and dutiful petitions of the people.

LETTER

FROM D. DE BERDT, ESQ. AGENT FOR THE PROVINCE, IN ENGLAND, TO THE SPEAKER OF THE HOUSE OF REPRESENTATIVES.

London, July 29, 1768.

SIR,

SINCE my last, (May 14th.) I have received nothing from you; but several interesting affairs have arisen, of which I thought it my duty to acquaint the House, though of a disagreeable nature.

I have lately had a conference with Lord Hillsborough, relating to your circular letter to the other provinces, which greatly displeased the administration; some of whom, say it is little better than an incentive to rebellion. But they look on it as the sentiments of a party only, as it was rejected, in a full House, the beginning of the session, and taken up again at the end of it, when the House was thin.* Though I can see nothing unjust or unreasonable in it, yet if some healing measures are not pitched upon, consequences may be very serious. You have already, two regiments from New York, quartered upon you, and my Lord mentioned another to be embarked; and says, it has been resolved in Council, that Governor Bernard have strict orders to insist upon your revoking that letter; and, if refused by the House, he was immediately to dissolve them. Upon their next choice, he was again to insist on it; and, if then refused, he was to do the like; and as often as the case should happen. My Lord assured me of his great regard for America; nay, said if I did not represent it so, I should not do him justice. He wished nothing so much as a good understanding between the colonies and mother country; and assured me, that before the warm measures taken on your side, had come to their knowledge, he had settled the repeal of those acts, with Lord North, the Chancellor; but the opposition you had made, rendered it absolutely necessary to support the authority of Parliament, which the ministry, at all events, are determined to do. You may depend on my strictest attention to your interest and affairs, whenever you please to give me any fresh instructions: and if you think any thing further, necessary to be represented to that noble Lord, who declares himself averse to any severe measures, and thinks himself very unhappy that he has undertaken the American department, when the affairs are in such convulsions. He has condescended to assure me, that, whenever I have any thing further to urge, I should have free access to him.

With great respect, yours, &c.   D. DE BERDT.

LETTER

FROM D. DE BERDT, ESQ. AGENT IN ENGLAND, TO THE SPEAKER OF THE HOUSE OF REPRESENTATIVES.

London, August 29, 1768.

I DULY received yours of the 3d of June, accompanying a long letter from Lord Hillsborough, which I yesterday delivered him, and which his Lordship will answer very soon, to which I re-

* The circular was sent in February, 1768, and will be found above, in this volume. A committee was chosen, February 4th, to prepare the circular; and reported one on the 11th, which was then adopted.

fer you for his particular sentiments. I was with him a full hour, talking over American affairs, which now seem to be under the necessity of being regulated by Parliament, when they sit, it being neither in the minister's power, nor even the King himself, to dispense with the laws, or revoke them.

The whole ministry seem united in this one point; then when a law passes the legislature, it becomes part of the constitution; and therefore not to be dispensed with or opposed. I wish, in all your applications, you had left the matter of right out of question, and only applied for a repeal of the laws, as prejudicial to the colonies and mother country. And my Lord assured me, he would have used his interest for a repeal; and he believes he should have obtained it, which now with him is a matter of doubt.

His Lordship is fully sensible of the mischief which will arise from a breach with the colonies, and dreads the consequences. He says laws must be supported, or we sink into a state of anarchy, which he thinks must be avoided at all events.

I mentioned the measure of sending troops to America, which he said were about this time arrived. I expressed my fears that some arbitrary transactions of the military might be a means of inflaming the people. His Lordship assured me they had strict orders to preserve the peace, and act in concert with the civil magistrate; and I might depend, no measures would be taken, but what were entirely constitutional, and executed with as much lenity as the law would admit.

I have given you, out of a tender regard for your welfare, a summary of what passed with that minister, and doubt not your prudence will make a proper use of it.

With great respect, I am, &c.

D. DE BERDT.

═══

LETTER

OF THE COUNCIL TO LORD HILLSBOROUGH, JUNE 12, 1769.

My Lord,

THE President of the Council, (Mr. Danforth,) for the last and the present year, having communicated to this Board, a copy of a letter, dated April 15, 1769, sent to your Lordship, subscribed by eleven gentlemen, being the major part of the members of the Council, for the last year, in answer to six letters, wrote to your Lordship, by Governor Bernard, dated November 1, 5, 12, 14, 30, and December 5, 1768—They have unanimously resolved, that they approve of the measures, taken by the major part of the members of the last year's Council, &c.; a copy of which resolves, we have the honor to inclose to your Lordship. As the gentlemen, who wrote that letter, have been so full and explicit in defending themselves and the province against the Governor's groundless and injurious charges, we have the less reason to enlarge upon such a disagreeable subject. However, my Lord, if it appears to us, that there is any charge against the Council, in either of the aforementioned letters, to which there has either been no answer, or if mentioned, not so fully dilated upon, as the nature of the offence, with which the Board are charged, does require, your Lordship will indulge us the freedom, further to address you.

Permit us, then, my Lord, with all due deference to your Lordship's high rank and station, to animadvert with freedom, upon some part of the Governor's aforementioned letters.

The Governor says, in one of his letters, " the Council is under awe of their constituents, by the frequent removal of the friends of government, &c." Aspersions of the like nature, are several times cast upon the Council, in some of his other letters, which, for the sake of avoiding prolixity, we shall not repeat.

My Lord, if our fondness, for a seat at the Board, could possibly influence us to vote and advise contrary to the real sentiments of our hearts, the Governor's wanton exercise of power, in his frequent negatives, put upon Counsellors of the best abilities, either because they differed from him, in their political sentiments, in some instances, or from resentment to the House of Representatives, for dropping some of his friends, would have a much greater influence upon us, to fall in with his measures, than any risk we run from the honorable House, in what he calls supporting government. It being more in the power of a Governor to remove a Counsellor, than it is in the House ; consequently, if we had any great fondness for a seat at the Board, we should act inconsistently with our political interest, to oppose the Governor in his measures. But, my Lord, we can with great truth, say, that, while we have had the honor to be members of his Majesty's Council, we have endeavored to discharge a good conscience, and acted our part with uprightness and integrity ; having never been awed into undue conduct, either by the House or the Governor ; and the Governor's insinuations to the contrary, are unkind, and without foundation ; and unless we can act with the same freedom as usual, we cannot esteem it an honor to be of that body.

That the Council have appeared, of late, more engaged in defending the rights of the province, than formerly, may be a fact, which we have no disposition to controvert ; be that as it may, we beg leave to observe, that it never was so much the incumbent duty of the Council, as it was the last year, to defend the rights of the people. For upon the dissolution of the General Court, the Governor and Council are, by charter, to manage the affairs of the province ; so that the last year's Council had double duty devolved on them. Therefore, it was justly expected, that they should exert themselves in defence of the civil rights and liberties of the people, though, at the same time, they did, and we hope we ever shall, treat the Governor with that respect, that is due to the King's representative. And your Lordship may depend upon it, that the present Council will be as free to assert and maintain the just prerogatives of the Crown, as to defend the rights of the people.

We beg leave further to observe, my Lord, that the Governor, in his letter, dated November the 1st, speaking of the address to General Gage, says, " it was signed by fifteen of the Council, among whom, were five who knew not enough of the town to vote for the safety of the commissioners returning, but knew enough to join in an invective against them." This observation of the Governor's, was, no doubt, made with a design to ridicule the conduct of those gentlemen, and to represent their having acted an inconsistent part. But, we cannot conceive, by what rules of logic he can charge them with inconsistency. For, my Lord, may not the gentlemen say with great propriety, as they were not inhabitants of the town of Boston, but lived at a great distance from it, that they knew not enough of the temper and disposition of the town to say that it was safe for the commissioners to return ; and at the same time, from the evidence they had of the commissioners behaviour and conduct ever since they have been in office, join in what the Governor calls an invective against them. For our part, we can see no inconsistency in their conduct ; for certainly the commissioners haughty and insolent behavior may be such as to expose them to the resentment of the people ; and yet, it does not necessarily follow, that the people will offer the least insult or violence to them. They may, or they may not ; and therefore, as it was a matter of uncertainty, the five gentlemen might be well excused from voting in favor of the safety of the commissioners return. And the Governor's remark upon their conduct, shows rather the defect of his reasoning, than any inconsistency in them.

With a view to defeat the good ends proposed by the major part of the last year's Council, in their petitions to the two Houses of Parliament, and for other unjustifiable reasons, the Governor acquaints your Lordship, that he " cannot conceive, that all the persons who met at the several meetings, upon the occasion of preparing the petitions, put together, amount to the number of twelve ;" which he tells your Lordship made the majority of the whole. And after insinuating, that, by a majority, might only be meant four persons out of seven, who make a quorum of the Council, in his postscript, he gives your Lordship, what he calls a list of the names of those members who passed upon the petitions ; which, together, make no more than eight. We persuade ourselves, my Lord, that you will not imagine, that the Council of last year endeavored to impose on the two Houses of Parliament, by asserting their petitions to have been the doings of a major part, when in fact they were not. Who furnished the Governor with the list he mentions, we cannot say ; but we can take upon us to assure you, my Lord, that the names of Lincoln, Brattle, Gray and Russell, ought to have been inserted therein, they having also agreed to the petitions ; who, with the eight persons in the Governor's list, made the number twelve, being, as he mentions, a majority of the whole.

This information will, among a multitude of other things, serve to convince your Lordship, that Governor Bernard has spared no pains, to vilify the Council, and prevent the success of their applications for the redress of the grievances, which the colonies labor under ; and, that he never lost sight of his favorite object, *the obtaining of a Council by mandamus from the Crown.* And the Board are at a loss, how to reconcile his conduct with what he declares and promises to your Lordship, in his letter of the 30th of November last ; in which he says, " your Lordship may depend upon it, that my informations have been, and shall be, dictated by the spirit of truth and candor ;" when there is scarcely any thing in either of his letters, but what is in direct opposition to both.

It gives us the deepest concern, to find, by one of the resolutions, passed by the Lords, and afterwards agreed to by the Commons, that the Council of this province have been censured, as not exerting themselves, in suppressing riots. And, we are firmly persuaded, that the Council would have escaped the displeasure of the two Houses of Parliament, had it not been for the gross misrepresentations of Governor Bernard, transmitted to your Lordship ; which, we are constrained to say, we consider not only as extremely cruel, with respect to the Council, but as an high imposition on your Lordship, and even Majesty itself.

You will allow us to say, my Lord, that no Council on the continent, not even those appointed by the King, have a greater aversion to riots and disorders ; nor have any of them exerted themselves more to suppress them, than his Majesty's loyal subjects, the Council of Massachusetts Bay.

Had their conduct been truly represented, instead of censure, they would have met with the highest approbation. And if those, whose immediate business it is to suppress mobs and riots, (against whom, no complaint has been exhibited by the Governor,) had done their duty, some of the disorders might have been prevented. The Council, my Lord, have now done with their observations on Governor Bernard's letters, and they doubt not, your Lordship will consider what they have written, in answer to his charge, against the Council, as equally applicable to what has been objected against them, of the same nature, by his Excellency General Gage, in his letter to your Lordship, of the 31st of October last ; on which we shall only make this further remark, that the General being a stranger in the province, and but just arrived, could not possibly speak from his own knowledge ; but must have received his account of the people, and of the Council, in particular, from a quarter, which it is needless to point out to your Lordship.

We will not further trespass on your Lordship's patience.   In truth, my Lord, our own is almost exhausted.   The Council have had such repeated occasions to observe upon, and lament the unkind treatment of Governor Bernard towards the people, that the subject has become extremely disagreeable to us.

We have only to add, that we apprehend it needful to acquaint your Lordship that Samuel White, Esquire, one of the last year's Council, dying between the passing of the petitions above referred to, and the time of writing the letter to your Lordship, of the 15th of April last, eleven, at the last mentioned time, made a majority of the whole.

We have the honor to be, with great truth and regard, my Lord, your Lordship's most obedient, and most humble servants,

S. DANFORTH,
President of the Council, and in their behalf.

MESSAGE

FROM THE HOUSE OF REPRESENTATIVES, TO THE GOVERNOR,
MAY 31, 1769, THE DAY OF GENERAL ELECTION.

May it please your Excellency,

THE great General Court, or Assembly of this province, being once more convened by virtue of the authority with which you are invested by the royal charter ; the House of Representatives think it their indispensable duty, under the present aspect of affairs in the province, on their part, to claim that constitutional freedom which is the right of this Assembly, and is of equal importance with its existence.

We take this opportunity to assure your Excellency, that it is the firm resolution of this House, to promote, to the utmost of their power, the welfare of the subject, and support his Majesty's authority within this jurisdiction ; to make a thorough inquiry into the grievances of the people, and have them redressed ; to amend, strengthen, and preserve the laws of the land ; to reform illegal proceedings in administration, and support the public liberty. These are the great ends for which this Court is assembled.

A resolution so important, demands a parliamentary freedom in the debates of this Assembly.   We are therefore constrained, thus early, to remonstrate to your Excellency, that an armament by sea and land, investing this metropolis, and a military guard, with cannon pointed at the very door of the state house, where this Assembly is held, is inconsistent with that dignity, as well as that freedom, with which we have a right to deliberate, consult and determine.

The experience of ages is sufficient to convince, that the military power is ever dangerous, and subversive of free constitutions.

The history of our own nation affords instances of Parliaments, which have been led into mean and destructive compliances, even to the surrendering their share in the supreme legislative, through the awe of standing armies.

His Majesty's Council of this province, have publicly declared, that the military aid is unnecessary for the support of civil authority in the colony. Nor can we conceive that his Majesty's service requires a fleet and army here, in this time of the most profound peace.

We have a right to expect, that your Excellency will, as his Majesty's representative, give the necessary and effectual orders, for the removal of the above mentioned forces, by sea and land, out of this port and the gates of this city, during the session of the said Assembly.

[The committee who prepared this message, were J. Otis, Capt. Sheafe, S. Adams, Major Hawley, and T. Cushing.]

———

PROTEST AND RESOLUTIONS

OF THE HOUSE OF REPRESENTATIVES, MAY 31, 1769, PREVIOUSLY TO THEIR ENTERING ON THE BUSINESS OF THE ELECTIONS, REPORTED BY THE COMMITTEE WHO PREPARED THE FOREGOING MESSAGE.

WHEREAS their late Majesties, King William and Queen Mary, in the third year of their reign, did, by their royal charter, ordain and grant for themselves, their heirs and successors, that on the last Wednesday, in the month of May, every year, there should be convened, held and kept by the Governor of this province, for the time being, a great and General Court or Assembly, for such important purposes as in the royal charter are expressly mentioned.

And in the said charter it is particularly established and ordained, that yearly, once in every year, forever thereafter, the number of eight and twenty Counsellors or Assistants shall be, by the General Court, newly chosen; which election of Counsellors or Assistants by the General Assembly, as well as the election of a Speaker and Clerk of the House of Representatives, by said House, have been always made, on the said last Wednesday in May, annually.

And whereas the said great and General Court or Assembly is now convened by the authority of his Majesty, according to the said royal charter :

Resolved, That this House, as one branch of the same, in duty and loyalty to his Majesty, as well as in regard to their own just rights and privileges, will, to the utmost of their power, support and maintain a constitutional freedom in their elections, debates and determinations.

Resolved, As the opinion of this House, that the keeping an armed force by sea and land in this metropolis, and in the port of the same, while the General Assembly by his Majesty's command is here convened, is a breach of privilege ; and inconsistent with that dignity and freedom with which they have a right to deliberate, consult and determine.

Resolved, That this House proceed to take their part in the elections of the day, from necessity, and in strict conformity to the royal charter ; having before claimed their constitutional freedom, and now protesting, that their thus proceeding, while the above mentioned forces are suffered to remain in the metropolis where this Court is convened, is to be considered as a precedent in any time hereafter, or construed as a voluntary receding of this House from their constitutional claim.

====

MESSAGE

FROM THE GOVERNOR TO THE HOUSE OF REPRESENTATIVES, MAY 31, 1769.

Gentlemen,

I HAVE no authority over his Majesty's ships in this port, or his troops in this town ; nor can I give any orders for the removal of the same.   FRA. BERNARD.

====

SPEECH

OF GOVERNOR BERNARD, TO THE COUNCIL AND HOUSE OF REPRESENTATIVES, JUNE 1, 1769.

Gentlemen of the Council, and
        Gentlemen of the House of Representatives,

As I have nothing in immediate command from his Majesty to lay before you, I shall at present only recommend to you to give your earliest attention to the business of the province.   This is got into such an arrear, that it will require the utmost diligence to get it done within the usual time generally allotted to this session. What I shall have to point out to you, will be communicated by separate messages.

I shall be ready to concur with you, in all measures proposed for the good of the people, that are consistent with the invariable rule I have laid down, of not departing from the duty I owe to the King. The service of the Crown and the interest of the people are objects very compatible with each other ; they must be so under a Monarch, who makes the general welfare of all his subjects the sole end of his government. It shall not be my fault, if this coalition of duties is not as apparent as it is real.   FRA. BERNARD.

[The Governor objected to the following gentlemen, chosen Counsellors, viz. T. Brattle, J. Bowdoin, J. Gerrish, T. Saunders, J. Hancock, A. Ward, B. Greenleaf, Col. Otis, J. Bowers, J. Henshaw, and W. Spooner.]

———

ANSWER

OF THE HOUSE OF REPRESENTATIVES TO THE GOVERNOR'S MESSAGE,
MAY 31, 1769....JUNE 13.

May it please your Excellency,

THE House of Representatives have duly considered your message of the 31st of May, and are sorry to find your Excellency declaring, that you " have no authority over his Majesty's ships in this port, or his troops within this town ; and that you can give no orders for the removal of the same."

We clearly hold, that the King's most excellent Majesty, to whom we have, and ever shall bear, and, since the convening of this present Assembly, we have sworn true and faithful allegiance, is the supreme executive power through all the parts of the British empire ; and we are humbly of opinion, that, within the limits of this colony and jurisdiction, your Excellency is the King's Lieutenant and Captain General and Commander in Chief, in as full and ample a manner, as is the Lord Lieutenant of Ireland, or any other his Majesty's Lieutenants, in the dominions to the realm of Great Britain appertaining.

From thence, we think, it indubitably follows, that all officers, civil and military, within this colony, are subject to the order, direction and control of your Excellency, so far at least, as is necessary for the safety of the people and the security of the privilege of this House, as they are to the King's Majesty within the realm. And though we admit, that peace and war are in the King's hand, and that it is an indisputable part of the royal prerogative, neces-

22

sary for the preservation of the Commonwealth, as all other well grounded prerogative powers are—That to destine the fleets, and march the armies of the state to any part of the world, where they may be necessary for the defence and preservation of the society, belongs to the Crown ; yet it is impossible to believe, that a military power, or a standing army, procured and stationed here, in consequence of misrepresentations of the duty and loyalty of his Majesty's subjects of the province, and suddenly quartered, not only contrary to act of Parliament, and to every principle of reason, justice and equity, but accompanied with every mark of contempt, reproach and insult, to as brave and loyal a people as ever served a Prince, can be uncontrolable by the Supreme Executive of the province ; which, within the limits of the same, is the just and full representative of the Supreme Executive of the whole empire.

It is well known, that it is no uncommon thing for disturbances to happen in populous cities ; and such as have unfortunately taken place in this province, have been greatly misrepresented. We have not only been told of, but all parts of the empire have been alarmed with apprehensions of danger to his Majesty's government, in North America, in general, and this province in particular, by reason of the most exaggerated accounts of certain disturbances, which, however, have, in every instance, been far, very far, from being carried to that atrocious and alarming length, to which many have been in Britain, at the very gates of the palace, and even in the royal presence.

It is most certain, that every subject has a right to have the rules of his duty, obedience and allegiance, clearly defined and determined. Hence it may be inferred, that very miserable is the servitude of those, who know not whether they are subject to an absolute power, civil or military, or both ; as may most effectually prosper the machinations and fulfil the purposes of despotism. It must be obvious to all jurists, and to every man endued with an ordinary understanding, that the doctrine your Excellency has been pleased to advance, in your answer to the message of the House, involves us in that state, which is called, by the learned, *imperium in imperio,* or at least establishes a military power here, uncontrolable by any civil authority in the province.

It has been publicly said, that the military power is become necessary in this colony, to aid and support civil government, for which we have no less authority than the resolutions of the two Houses of Parliament, and the declaration of one of his Majesty's principal Secretaries of State. The use of the military power to enforce the execution of the laws, is, in the opinion of this House, inconsistent with the spirit of a free constitution, and the very nature of government. Nor can there be any necessity for it ; for the body of the people, the *posse comitatus,* will always aid the magistrate in the execution of such laws as ought to be executed. The very supposition of an unwillingness in the people in general, that a law should be executed, carries with it the strongest presumption, that it is an unjust law ; at least, that it is unsalutary. It cannot be their law ; for, by the nature of a free constitution, the people must consent to laws, before they can be obliged, in conscience, to obey them. In truth, no law, however grievous, has been opposed in the execution of it, in this province ; and yet, a military power is sent here, purposely to aid in the execution of the laws. And what adds to the injustice of those who procured this armament, is, that it was procured at the very time when the people were dutifully supplicating the throne for redress of grievances, occasioned by acts of Parliament, for the purpose of raising a revenue in America. We think we can infer, from your Excellency's declaration, that this military force is uncontrolable by any authority in the province. It is, then, a power without any check here ; and therefore so far absolute. An absolute power, which has the sword constantly in its hand, may exercise a vigorous severity whenever it pleases. What privilege, what security, is then left to this House, whose very existence, to any purpose, depends upon its privilege and security. Nothing remains in such a state, if no redress can be had from the King's Lieutenant in the province, but that the oppressed people unite in laying their fervent and humble petition before their gracious Sovereign.

[The committee appointed to reply to the Governor's Message of May 31, were Col. Otis, Mr. J. Otis, Mr. Adams, Gen. Prebble, Maj. Hanley, Mr. Hancock, and Col. Warren.]

═══

MESSAGE

FROM GOVERNOR BERNARD, TO THE HOUSE OF REPRESENTATIVES, IN REPLY TO THE FOREGOING, JUNE 15, 1769.

Gentlemen of the House of Representatives,

NOTWITHSTANDING the doubts and difficulties which you have expressed to me in your message of yesterday, it is certain that I have no authority to give orders for the removal of the King's ships out of the harbor, or his troops out of the town. Whoever is acquainted with the arrangement of the commands in America, which are all derived from the same King, knows that it is so.

I am sorry that this question should cause the non activity of the Assembly for an entire fortnight ; the expense of which has already cost the province upwards of five hundred pounds lawful ; and is, for what I can see, still increasing ; besides, the inconvenience accruing to persons attending the General Court for business, which falls harder upon them as individuals, than expenses generally dispersed among the people.

I cannot sit still and see such a waste of time and treasure to no purpose. If, therefore, you still continue of the opinion, "that the keeping an armed force in this town, and within its harbor, is a breach of privilege, and inconsistent with that freedom with which you have a right to deliberate, consult and determine," I must ap ply such remedy as is in my power to remove this difficulty ; and the only means I have, are to move the General Court to a place where it cannot operate.

It is an indifferent thing to me where the General Court is held. I know not that it is necessarily confined to any town ; that town seems to me to be the most proper for it, where the business can be most conveniently, easily and readily done. And as it is apparent, from your resolutions, and a fortnight's experience, that you do not think that this is, at this time, a proper town for the General Court to sit in, I shall remove it to Cambridge, against which place, no objection, that I know of, can be formed.

FRA. BERNARD.

[The General Court was adjourned to Cambridge.]

═══

MESSAGE

FROM THE HOUSE OF REPRESENTATIVES, TO THE GOVERNOR,
JUNE 19, 1769.

May it please your Excellency,

As you have not thought proper, in your reply to the message of this House, of the 13th instant, to throw any light on the subject, or invalidate the principles we therein advanced, your Excellency will allow us to conclude, that those principles were well grounded, and that there is no reason for us to alter our sentiments on this interesting point.

You are pleased to intimate, that much time and treasure has been spent in determining a merely speculative question. The House regard a standing army, posted within the province, in a time of the most profound peace, and uncontrolable by any authority in it, as a dangerous innovation ; and a guard of soldiers, with cannon planted at the doors of the State House, while the General Assembly was there held, as the most pointed insult ever offered to a free people, and its whole Legislative. This, sir, and not the question of your Excellency's authority to remove his Majesty's ships out of the harbor, or his troops out of the town of Boston, was the principal cause of the " non activity of the

Assembly." Had your Excellency felt for the Assembly, and the people over whom you preside, even though you had supposed yourself not properly authorized, you would have employed your influence, at least, for the removal of this grievance ; especially as his Majesty's Council, as well as this House, had before expressed to your Excellency their just indignation at so unprecedented an affront. But, instead of the least abatement of this military parade, the General Assembly has been made to give way to an armed force, as the only means in your power to remove the difficulty we justly complained of. Your Excellency has ordered a removal of the General Assembly itself, from its ancient seat and place, where the public business has generally been done with the greatest convenience, ease and despatch. It is with pain, that we are obliged here to observe, that the very night after this adjournment was made, the cannon were removed from the Court House, as though it had been designed, that so small a circumstance of regard should not be paid to the Assembly, when convened by the royal authority, and for his Majesty's service in the colony.

You are pleased to pass a censure upon this House, in saying, that " you cannot sit still and see such a waste of time and treasure to no purpose." Those alone are answerable for any expense of time and treasure on this occasion, who have brought us into such a situation, as has hitherto rendered our proceeding to business incompatible with the dignity, as well as the freedom of this House. No time can better be employed, than in the preservation of the rights derived from the British constitution, and insisting upon points, which, though your Excellency may consider them as non essential, we esteem its best bulwarks. No treasure can be better expended, than in securing that true old English liberty, which gives a relish to every other enjoyment. These, we have the satisfaction to believe, are the sentiments of our constituents, to whom alone we are accountable how we apply their treasure ; and we are fully persuaded, from what we have already heard, that, notwithstanding the apparent design of your message to prejudice their minds against us, what your Excellency is pleased to call our " non activity," will receive their approbation, rather than their censure ; for an entire fortnight, spent in silence, or a much longer time, cannot be displeasing to them, when business could not be entered upon, but at the expense of *their* rights and liberties, and the privilege of this House.

[The committee who reported the above, were the Speaker, Mr. Adams, Capt. Sheaffe, Col. Otis, Mr. Hancock, Capt. Fuller, and Mr. Porter.]

RESOLUTIONS

OF THE HOUSE OF REPRESENTATIVES, JUNE 21, 1769.

WHEREAS this House did, on the first day of the present session of the General Assembly, take into serious consideration the unhappy situation of this colony, by reason of a military force, procured and stationed here, in consequence of gross misrepresentations of his Majesty's loyal subjects of this colony ; and did then remonstrate to his Excellency the Governor, "that an armament by sea and land, investing the metropolis where this Court was convened and held, and a main guard kept, with cannon pointed at the very doors of the State House, was inconsistent with the dignity and freedom of this House :" And whereas his Excellency was pleased, in answer, to declare, "that he had no authority over his Majesty's ships in the harbor, and the troops in the town of Boston, and could give no orders for the removal of the same :" And instead of the grievance being redressed, this Assembly, itself, has been made to give way to the said armed forces, by his Excellency's adjournment of the said Assembly, from its usual and ancient place, to Harvard College, in Cambridge : And whereas this House has reason to apprehend that it has been, and still is, the endeavor of persons, inimical to our happy constitution, to have a military power, independent of, and uncontrolable by, any civil authority within this colony, established here :

Resolved, That this House will, at all times, to the utmost of their power, maintain the honor and dignity of our rightful and gracious Sovereign, and promote his Majesty's service in this jurisdiction, as well as support the just rights and liberties of the people, their own dignity, and the constitutional freedom of their debates and consultations.

Resolved, As the opinion of this House, that the British constitution admits of no military force within the realm, but for the purposes of offensive and defensive war ; and, therefore, that the sending and continuing a military force within this colony, for the express purpose of aiding and assisting the civil government, is an infraction of the natural and constitutional rights of the people, a breach of the privilege of the General Assembly, inconsistent with that freedom with which this House, as one branch of the same, hath a right, and ought to debate, consult and determine, and manifestly tends to the subversion of that happy form of government, which we have hitherto enjoyed.

Resolved, That the proceeding of this House to the public business of the colony, while a military force, for the purpose of aiding the civil authority, is quartered within the same, and declared to be uncontrolable by his Majesty's Lieutenant in this colony, is from *necessity ;* and is not to be considered as a precedent, at any time hereafter, or construed as a voluntary receding of this House, from any of those constitutional rights, liberties and privileges, which the people of this colony, and their representatives, in General Court assembled, do hold, and of right ought to enjoy.

MESSAGE

OF GOVERNOR BERNARD, TO THE HOUSE OF REPRESENTATIVES,
JUNE 21, 1769.

Gentlemen of the House of Representatives,

When, at the opening of the session, I recommended to you to give your earliest attention to the business of the province, I did not think that there was any occasion to specify the particulars of such business, as they must occur to you as readily as to me.

However, lest this omission should be made use of as an excuse for your inactivity, and as you have now entered into your fourth week, without having done any thing at all, I shall now capitulate the principal articles of the public business, which have hitherto waited for your notice.

They are, 1st, the support of the government ; 2d, the supply of the treasury ; 3d, the providing for the payment of the provincial debt, which now amounts to one hundred and five thousand pounds ; 4th, the tax bill ; 5th, the impost bill ; 6th, the excise bill, if thought proper ; 7th, the establishment for forts and garrisons ; 8th, the continuation of the truck trade ; 9th, the continuation or revival of expiring or expired laws, &c.

All these several matters, and such others of the ordinary business as I may have omitted, I now recommend to your immediate consideration. Such assistance as I can give you, especially in removing doubts or difficulties which may attend any of the said business, I shall be ready to afford you, so far as is consistent with my duty.   FRA. BERNARD.

MESSAGE

FROM GOVERNOR BERNARD, TO THE HOUSE OF REPRESENTATIVES,
JUNE 28, 1769.

Gentlemen of the House of Representatives,

I think it proper to inform you, that his Majesty has been pleased, by his sign manual, to signify to me his will and pleasure, that I repair to Great Britain, to lay before him the state of this province ; and has also, by his Secretary of State, given directions for the administration of this government, during my absence.

Upon this occasion, I think it necessary to communicate to you the 53d of his Majesty's instructions, whereby he orders, that when the Governor shall be absent from the province, one moiety of the salary, and the perquisites and emoluments, which would otherwise be due to the Governor, shall, during his absence, be paid to the Lieutenant Governor, for his maintenance, and for the support of the dignity of the government.

I have always considered the grant of the salary appointed to me, to be subject to this instruction, although it was not so expressed in the act ; and I have no objection at the present time, when the absence of the Governor is foreseen, that the grant of the salary shall be expressed to be subject to this instruction.

And I must, at the same time, observe to you, that as I am ordered to attend his Majesty, as Governor of this province, and am made to understand that I am to be continued in that office, and am instructed for the appropriation of the salary, whilst I am absent from the province, there is the same reason for the grant of the salary now, as there has been at any other time. I must, therefore, desire that, according to his Majesty's 49th instruction, such grant may be made to precede the other business of the session. FRA. BERNARD.

RESOLVES

OF THE HOUSE OF REPRESENTATIVES, JUNE 29, 1769:

The General Assembly of this, his Majesty's colony of the Massachusetts Bay, convened by his Majesty's authority, and by virtue of his writ issued by his Excellency the Governor, under the great seal of the province ; and this House, thinking it their duty, at all times, to testify their loyalty to his Majesty, as well as their inviolable regard to their own and their constituents rights, liberties and privileges, do pass the following resolutions, to be entered on their journal.

Resolved, That this House do, and ever will bear the firmest allegiance to our rightful Sovereign, King George the Third ; and are ever ready, with their lives and fortunes, to defend his Majesty's person, family, crown and dignity.

Resolved, As the opinion of this House, " that the sole right of imposing taxes on the inhabitants of this, his Majesty's colony of the Massachusetts Bay, is now, and ever hath been, legally and constitutionally vested in the House of Representatives, lawfully convened, according to the ancient and established practice, with the consent of the Council, and of his Majesty, the King of Great Britain, or his Governor for the time being."

Resolved, As the opinion of this House, that it is the indubitable right of the subjects in general, and consequently of the colonists, jointly or severally to petition the King for redress of grievances ; and that it is lawful, whenever they think it expedient, to confer with each other, in order to procure a joint concurrence, in dutiful addresses, for relief from common burthens.

Resolved, That Governor Bernard, by a wanton and precipitate dissolution of the last year's Assembly, and refusing to call another, though repeatedly requested by the people, acted against the spirit of a free constitution ; and if such procedure be lawful, it may be in his power, whenever he pleases, to render himself absolute.

Resolved, That a general discontent, on account of the revenue acts, an expectation of the sudden arrival of a military power, to enforce the execution of those acts, an apprehension of the troops being quartered upon the inhabitants, when our petitions were not permitted to reach the royal ear, the General Court, at such a juncture, dissolved, the Governor refusing to call a new one, and the people, reduced almost to a state of despair, rendered it highly expedient and necessary for the people to convene by their committees, associate, consult and advise the best means to promote peace and good order ; to present their united complaints to the throne, and jointly to pray for the royal interposition in favor of their violated rights. Nor can this procedure possibly be illegal, as they expressly disclaimed all governmental acts.

Resolved, As the opinion of this House, that Governor Bernard, in his letters to Lord Hillsborough, his Majesty's Secretary of State, has given a false and highly injurious representation of the conduct of his Majesty's truly loyal and faithful Council of this colony, and of the magistrates, overseers of the poor, and inhabitants of the town of Boston, tending to bring on those respectable bodies of men, particularly on some individuals, the unmerited displeasure of our gracious Sovereign ; to introduce a military government, and to mislead both Houses of Parliament into such severe resolutions, as a true, just and candid state of facts must have prevented.

Resolved, That Governor Bernard, in the letters before mentioned, by falsely representing that it was become " necessary the King should have the Council Chamber in his own hands, and should be enabled, by Parliament, to supersede by order, in his Privy Council, commissions granted in his name, and under his seal, throughout the colonies," has discovered his enmity to the true spirit of the British constitution, to the liberties of the colonies ; and has struck at the root of some of the most invaluable constitutional and charter rights of this province ; the perfidy of which, at the very time he professed himself a warm friend to the charter, is altogether unparalleled by any in his station, and ought never to be forgotten.

Resolved, That the establishment of a standing army, in this colony, in a time of peace, without the consent of the General Assembly of the same, is an invasion of the natural rights of the people, as well as of those which they claim as free born Englishmen, confirmed by magna charta, the bill of rights, as settled at the revolution, and by the charter of this province.

Resolved, That a standing army is not known as a part of the British constitution, in any of the King's dominions; and every attempt to establish it has been esteemed a dangerous innovation, manifestly tending to enslave the people.

Resolved, That the sending an armed force into this colony, under a pretence of aiding and assisting the civil authority, is an attempt to establish a standing army here, without our consent; is highly dangerous to this people; is unprecedented, and unconstitutional.

Resolved, That whoever has represented to his Majesty's ministers, that the people of this colony, in general, or the town of Boston, in particular, were in such a state of disobedience and disorder, as to require a fleet and army to be sent here, to aid the civil magistrate, is an avowed enemy to this colony, and to the nation in general; and has, by such misrepresentation, endeavored to destroy the liberty of the subject here, and that mutual union and harmony between Great Britain and the colonies, so necessary for the welfare of both.

Resolved, As the opinion of this House, that the misrepresentations of the state of this colony, transmitted by Governor Bernard to his Majesty's ministers, have been the means of procuring the military force, now quartered in the town of Boston.

Resolved, That whoever gave order for quartering even common soldiers and camp women in the court house, in Boston, and in the representatives' chamber, where some of the principal archives of the government had been usually deposited; making a barrack of the same, placing a main guard, with cannon pointed near the said house, and sentinels at the door, designed a high insult, and a triumphant indication that the military power was master of the whole legislative.

Whereas, his Excellency General Gage, in his letter to Lord Hillsborough, dated October 31st, among other exceptionable things, expressed himself in the following words : "From what has been said, your Lordship will conclude that there is no government in Boston ; in truth there is very little at present, and the constitution of this province leans so much to the side of democracy, that the Governor has not the power to remedy the disorders that happen in it :"

Resolved, As the opinion of this House, that his Excellency General Gage, in this and other assertions, has rashly and impertinently intermeddled in the civil affairs of this province, which are altogether out of his department ; and of the internal police of which, by his letter, if not altogether his own, he has yet betrayed a degree of ignorance, equal to the malice of the author.

With respect to the nature of our government, this House is of opinion, that the wisdom of that great Prince, William the Third, who gave the charter, aided by an able ministry, and men thoroughly versed in the English constitution and law ; and the happy effects derived from it to the nation, as well as this colony, should have placed it above the reprehension of the General, and led him to inquire, whether the disorders complained of, have not arisen from an arbitrary disposition in the Governor, rather than from too great a spirit of democracy in the constitution. And this House cannot but express their deep concern, that too many in power, at home and abroad, so clearly avow, not only in private conversation, but in their public conduct, the most rancorous enmity against the *free* part of the British constitution, and are indefatigable in their endeavors to render the monarchy absolute, and the administration arbitrary, in every part of the British empire.

Resolved, That this House, after the most careful inquiry, have not found an instance of the course of justice being interrupted by violence, except by a rescue committed by Samuel Fellows, an officer in the navy, and by the appointment of the commissioners, an officer, also, in the customs ; nor of a magistrate's refusing to inquire into, or redress any injury complained of ; while it is notorious to all the world, that even such acts of Parliament, as, by the whole continent, are deemed highly oppressive, have never been opposed with violence, and the duties imposed, and rigorously exacted, have been punctually paid.

Resolved, That the frequent entries of *nolle prosequi*, by the Attorney and Advocate General, in cases favorable to the liberty of the subject ; and rigorous prosecutions by information and otherwise, in those in favor of power, are daring breaches of trust, and insupportable grievances on the people.

Resolved, As the opinion of this House, that the late extension of the power of courts of admiralty in America, is highly dangerous and alarming; especially as the judges of the courts of common law, the alone check upon their inordinate power, do not hold their places during good behavior ; and those who have falsely represented to his Majesty's ministers, that no dependance could be had on juries in America, and that there was a necessity of extending the power of the courts of admiralty there, so far as to deprive the subject of the inestimable privilege of a trial by a jury, and to render the said courts of admiralty uncontrolable by the ancient common law of the land, are avowed enemies to the constitution, and manifestly intended to introduce and establish a system of insupportable tyranny in America.

Resolved, As the opinion of this House, that the constituting a board of commissioners of customs in America, is an unnecessary burthen upon the trade of these colonies, and that the unlimited power the said commissioners are invested with, of making appointments, and paying the appointees what sums they please, unavoidably tends so enormously to increase the number of placemen and pensioners, as to become justly alarming, and formidable to the liberties of the people.

Resolved, That it is the opinion of this House, " that all trials for treason, misprison of treason, or for any felony or crime, whatsoever, committed or done, in this, his Majesty's colony, by any person or persons residing therein, ought, of right, to be had and conducted in and before his Majesty's courts, held within the said colony, according to the fixed and known course of proceedings ; and that the seizing any person or persons, residing in this colony, suspected of any crime, whatsoever, committed therein, and sending such person or persons, to places beyond the sea, to be tried, is highly derogatory of the rights of British subjects ; as thereby the inestimable privilege of being tried by a jury from the vicinage, as well as the liberty of summoning and producing witnesses on such trial, will be taken away from the party accused."

[The committee who prepared the above, and those of the 21st of said month, were the Speaker, (Mr. Cushing) Col. Otis, Capt. Sheaffe, Gen. Preble, Mr. Adams, Mr. Hancock, Mr. Spooner, Mr. Otis, and Mr. Porter.]

═══

ANSWER

OF BOTH HOUSES, TO THE GOVERNOR'S SPEECH, AT THE OPENING OF THE SESSION, JUNE 29, 1769.

May it please your Excellency,

As your Excellency, in your speech to both Houses, at the opening of the present session, has recommended to us, " to give our earliest attention to the business of the province ;" we should have been glad if your Excellency had pointed out what was expected from us.

We agree with you, sir, that the business of the province is got into such an arrear, that it will require the utmost diligence to get it done within the usual time generally allotted to this session." Who brought the province under this difficulty, your Excellency can be at no loss to determine. Had the Assembly been called in the fall of the year past, there would have been no cause of such complaint.

Your Excellency has been pleased to tell us, " that you shall be ready to concur with us, in all measures proposed for the good of the people, that are consistent with the invariable rule you have

laid down, of not departing from the duty you owe to the King."
It is surprising, sir, that so soon after such a declaration, your
Excellency should suspend your assent to a resolve for an establishment for forts and garrisons, even for a single moment; especially as such an establishment was always a favorite object with
your Excellency. Does the "duty you owe to the King, or the
regard you have for the good of the people," forbid your signing
it? If so, how could your Excellency recommend this business
to the House, in your message of the twenty-first instant, as what
was necessary to be immediately done? We are sensible, may
it please your Excellency, that the service of the Crown, and the
interest of the people, are objects very compatible with each other;
and that they must be so, "under a monarch, who makes the general welfare of all his subjects, the sole end of his government."
This sentiment is what the two Houses have adopted, and have
always made their object. And had your Excellency, in humble
imitation of your royal master, during your administration, acted
from such noble principles, many of the disputes between your
Excellency and former Assemblies, would have had no existence.
We shall, with all convenient despatch, finish the business of the
present session, and we have a just right to expect that your Excellency will give your assent to all such resolves and acts, that
may be laid before you, as will be for the interest of the people,
and the real service of the Crown.

[The committee who reported the above, were B. Lincoln and
H. Gray, of the Council, and G. Leonard, Capt. Reed, and S. Hall,
of the House.]

ANSWER

OF THE HOUSE OF REPRESENTATIVES TO THE GOVERNOR'S MESSAGE, OF JUNE 28......JULY 4, 1769.

May it please your Excellency,

By your message to this House, of the 28th of June, we are
informed, that his Majesty has been pleased, by his sign manuel, to
signify to you his will and pleasure, that you repair to Great Britain,
to lay before him the state of this province. We are bound in duty
at all times; and we do, more especially at this time, cheerfully
acquiesce in the lawful command of our Sovereign. It is a particular satisfaction to us, that his Majesty has been pleased to order a
true state of this province to be laid before him; for we have abundant reason to be assured, that when his Majesty shall be fully acquainted with the great and alarming grievances which his truly

loyal subjects here have suffered, through your administration, and the injury they have sustained in their reputation, he will, in his great clemency and justice, frown upon, and forever remove from his trust, all those, who, by wickedly informing his ministers, have attempted to deceive even his Majesty himself.   Your Excellency is best acquainted with the part you have acted : your letters have enabled this House, and the public, in some measure, to form a judgment.   And while you will necessarily be employed, as this House conceives, in setting your own conduct in the most favorable light before his Majesty, we are persuaded we shall be able to answer for ourselves and our constituents, to the satisfaction of our Sovereign, whenever we shall be called to it.

You are pleased to communicate to this House, an instruction for the appropriation of the salary granted to his Majesty's Governor, during such time as he may be absent from the colony.   But as we are not made to understand, that your Excellency will be continued in your office, as Governor of this province, after your expected departure from it, the House cannot, in faithfulness to their constituents, make an unprecedented grant of their money for services which we have no reason to expect will ever be performed.

Your Excellency must be fully sensible, that the people of this province have never failed, in duty to his Majesty, to make ample provision for the support of his government.   You will be pleased to remember, that you are fully paid to the 2d of August next; before the expiration of which time you will embark for Great Britain. We shall then make the necessary provision " for the support of the dignity of government;" and when his Majesty shall be pleased to appoint another Governor, we trust this people will be ready, as they ever have been, to grant him an ample salary, proportional to their abilities, and suitable to his station and merit.   These are the only considerations which ought to have any weight with this House, in granting the people's money, for the support of a Governor.   His Majesty's 49th instruction, now before the House, and to which you refer us, is a rule for your Excellency ;   but we conceive it was never intended for the House of Representatives.   We have, however, the pleasure of observing, that your Excellency is not at all restrained by it, from signing any bills, or other matters, that may be laid before you, at any time preceding the grant of a salary for the support of government ; and, therefore, we have a just right to expect that you will not, on that account, retard such public business before you, as his Majesty's service, and the welfare of the people, indispensably requires.

[The committee which reported this answer, consisted of Mr. Otis, Col. Warren, Mr. Hancock, Capt. Sheaffe, and Gen. Preble.]

MESSAGE

Gentlemen of the House of Representatives,

I HEREBY communicate to you an extract of a letter I received some time ago from General Gage, desiring that I would lay before you the accounts of the expenditures incurred by quartering his Majesty's troops in Boston, that funds may be provided for discharging the same. I accordingly lay before you the said accounts, as communicated to me by Colonel Robertson, with a copy of a letter from him, on the subject. The vouchers, referred to in the said letter, are in the hands of Colonel Joseph Goldthwait, who will produce the same to your order. I desire that you will take these accounts into your consideration, and provide proper funds for discharging the same, so far, at least, as you are required by law.

I am also desired by the General, to make a requisition to you, that provision may be made for the further quartering his Majesty's forces in the town of Boston, and Castle Island, according to act of Parliament. This provision was made for the 65th regiment, whilst it was quartered at Castle Island by my order, with the advice of Council. But, now the General Court is sitting, it is proper that you should take order in this business, and especially in providing funds for that purpose, without which, further provision cannot be made. I desire you would act thereon as soon as you can, as I understand that the quartering the 29th regiment in the Castle barracks, is delayed for want of it. FRA. BERNARD.

MESSAGE

Gentlemen of the House of Representatives,

As the session is drawing to a conclusion, I must desire that you will give an answer to my message of the 6th instant, and that you will distinguish between the charges arising from the hiring of barracks, and furnishing them, and the charges of purchasing provisions, as are directed by act of Parliament to be provided by this province ; and that you will also give an answer, whether you will establish funds for the future supply of provisions, according to act of

Parliament, to the troops quartered in barracks, in Boston, or which may be quartered in the provincial barracks, on Castle Island, or either of them. And I desire that you will be explicit and distinct in those particulars, that there may be no mistake in the report of your resolutions on these heads.

In my former message, I omitted to inform you that the barracks on Castle Island will not conveniently hold a regiment without an additional building for officers' rooms. The want of such a building has been inquired into by the Commissioners, and found to be real; and an estimate of the expense has been made, which, I understand, amounts to two hundred and fifty pounds. I desire that you will take this also into consideration, and let me know your resolution thereon.   FRA. BERNARD.

——

ANSWER

OF THE HOUSE OF REPRESENTATIVES, TO THE GOVERNOR'S MESSAGES, OF JULY 6 AND 12....JULY 15, 1769.

May it please your Excellency,

THE House of Representatives have contemplated your several messages of the 6th and 12th instant, as fully as the time, to which you were pleased to limit them, would admit. And as General Gage's letter on this subject, dated 15th of May, of which we were favored with an extract only, must have been received before the meeting of the General Assembly, we think it very extraordinary that your Excellency should suffer five or six weeks to elapse, before you thought proper to give us the least intimation of this matter. It is also surprizing, that, as the Barrack Master General, Colonel Robinson, was in Boston near a month, the greater part of which time, the General Assembly was sitting, we never before heard of the " demand" which he had " the honor to make," as he is pleased to express himself, in his letter to your Excellency, of the 18th of June. It is wonderful indeed, that this House should have no notice of that demand, till the 6th instant, and that a quickening message should so soon follow. Between these messages, Lord's day intervening, the House had adjourned, as usual, from Saturday to Monday. But it is truly astonishing, that when the gracious desires of majesty itself, of aids in men and money in the late war, in which we freely bled with our fellow subjects and brethren of Great Britain, as well as of America; and on less arduous occasions have, with royal clemency and great condescension, ever been intimated in the form only of a requisition, the Barrack Master General should hold so high and peremptory a tone as the word *demand*, must necessarily imply. The indignity, thus offered to your Excellency's commission, would have been an affair entirely between your Excellency and the Barrack Master General, had it not been communicated to us as an appendage, nor accompanied your message of the 6th instant, the subject of which, we shall now, more immediately consider.

The public proceedings of this House, we trust, will sufficiently evince to the whole world, and to all posterity, the idea we entertain of the sudden introduction of a fleet and army here; of the unparalleled methods used to procure this armament; and of the indefatigable pains of your Excellency, and a few interested persons, to keep up a standing force here, by sea and land, in a time of profound peace, under the mere pretence, of the necessity of such a force, to aid the civil authority. But were it a time of war, and the necessity of such a force ever so great, of which it is admitted, the King, by virtue of his undoubted prerogative of marching his armies, and directing his fleets to any part of his realms or dominions, is the sole judge; yet, sir, it should be remembered, that the very nature of a free constitution, requires that those fleets and those armies should be supported only by the aids voluntarily granted by the Commons. Thus, till very lately, they have been supported, not only in Great Britain and Ireland, but in all the British dominions.

May it please your Excellency, we are constrained to be very explicit upon the funds proposed, and the law alluded to, both in your message of the 6th instant, and in the extract of General Gage's letter before us. By funds, we presume, is meant a provision for the reimbursement of such expenses as have been occasioned, or may accrue, in consequence of quartering the troops here; and by law, is meant the mutiny act, so commonly called, which was passed in the 6th year of the reign of our most gracious Sovereign. By this act, it is declared, " the officers and soldiers quartered, as therein more particularly expressed, shall, from time to time, be furnished and supplied by a person or persons, to be authorized or appointed for that purpose by the Governor and Council of each respective province; or upon the neglect or refusal of such Governor and Council, in any province, then by two or more Justices of the Peace, residing in or near the place" of quartering, with " fire," and other enumerated articles. And that the respective provinces shall " repay such person or persons, all such sum or sums of money, by him or them paid, for the taking, hiring, and fitting up uninhabited houses, and for furnishing the officers and soldiers therein, and in the barracks," with " fire," and the other enumerated articles. And such sum or sums are, by said act, required to be "raised in such manner as the public charges for the provinces respectively are raised." And it is also further declared by said act, that " the extraordinary expense of

24

carriages to be paid by the province or colony where the same shall arise."

From hence it is obvious, that a Governor and Council have no more right, by this act, to draw money out of a colony treasury, than the two justices mentioned therein. The duty prescribed, is entirely confined to the appointment of a person or persons, to furnish and supply the articles in said act mentioned. Such is the unreasonableness and severity of this act, that it leaves to the Assemblies not the least color of a privilege, but only the pitiful power to raise the sums in such manner as the public charges of the provinces are respectively raised. Hence it is manifest, how unwarrantably the Governor and Council have acted, in the payments they have ordered between the dissolution of the last year's Assembly and the convening of this, for articles furnished his Majesty's 65th regiment, lately quartered in the barracks, at Castle William; for it is known, there was no fund provided, consequently, there could be no appropriation made by the General Court for that purpose.

We shall now, with your Excellency's leave, take a nearer view of the act of Parliament above mentioned. The whole continent has, for some years past, been distressed with what are called acts for imposing taxes on the colonists, for the express purpose of raising a revenue; and that, without their consent in person, or by representative. This subject has been so fully handled by the several Assemblies, and in the publications that have been made, that we shall be as brief as possible upon that head; but we take leave to observe, that in strictness, all those acts may be rather called acts for raising a tribute in America, for the further purposes of dissipation among placemen and pensioners. And, if the present system of measures should be much further pursued, it will soon be very difficult, if possible, to distinguish the case of widows and orphans in America, plundered by infamous informers, from those who suffered under the administration of the most oppressive of the Governors of the Roman provinces, at a period, when that once proud and haughty republic, after having subjugated the finest kingdoms in the world, and drawn all the treasures of the east to imperial Rome, fell a sacrifice to the unbounded corruption and venality of its grandees. But of all the new regulations, the stamp act not excepted, this under consideration, is the most excessively unreasonable. For, in effect, the yet free Representatives of the free Assemblies of North America, are called upon to repay, of their own and their constituents money, such sum or sums, as persons over whom they can have no check or control, may be pleased to expend! As Representatives, we are deputed by the people, agreeable to the royal charter and laws of this province. By that charter and the nature of our trust, we are only empowered to "grant such aids," and "levy such taxes for his Majesty's service, as are reasonable;" of which, if we are not free and independent judges, we can no longer be free Representatives, nor our constituents free subjects. If we are free judges, we are at liberty to follow the dictates of our own understanding, without regard to the mandates of another; much less can we be free judges, if we are but blindly to give as much of our own and of our constituents substance, as may be commanded, or thought fit to be expended, by those we know not.

Your Excellency must, therefore, excuse us, in this express declaration, that as we cannot, consistently with our honor, or interest, and much less with the duty we owe our constituents, so we shall never make provision for the purposes in your several messages above mentioned.

[The Committee who prepared this answer, were, Col. Otis, Major Hawley, Col. Williams, Mr. Adams, Mr. Otis, Col. Ward, and Mr. Hancock.]

SPEECH

OF GOVERNOR BERNARD, TO THE HOUSE OF REPRESENTATIVES,
JULY 15, 1769.

Gentlemen of the House of Representatives,

At the opening of this session, I had in contemplation the expediency of passing the public bills which were necessary to the government, with all due expedition, and particularly the supply bill, without which, the whole provincial debt, by a law then subsisting, would have been levied in one year, which would have been a great burthen upon the people. And I had resolved with myself to promote the expediting such necessary bills, and to avoid and remove, as far as I could, all difficulties which might obstruct the same. But you, gentlemen, had not the same disposition; you not only put a stop to all business, with the most trifling pretences, for some weeks together, but you endeavored, by all means you could, to oblige me, in the course of my duty, to put an abrupt end to the session, before you would permit the necessary business of the province even to be brought before you.

In this, you had some success; you put me under the difficulty of either not making proper provision for the necessary service of the government, which could not be done without continuing the session, or by a continuation of it, showing a want of regard to the dignity of the Crown. The assertions, declarations and resolutions which you have, from the beginning of the session to this time, continued to issue, in direct opposition to the sense of the sovereign legislature, as it has been lately declared, and in terms entirely inconsistent with the idea of this province being a part of the British empire, would have demanded of me an immediate vindication of the honor of the Crown, by putting an early end to this session, if I had not been restrained by my concern for the exigency of the state.   And I must rely upon his Majesty's favorable indulgence in accepting my attention to the necessities of the people, in lieu of the resentment which was due to the misbehavior of their Representatives.

To his Majesty, therefore, and, if he pleases, to his Parliament, must be referred your invasion of the rights of the imperial sovereignty.   By your own acts you will be judged.   You need not be apprehensive of any misrepresentations ; as it is not in the power of your enemies, if you have any, to add to your publications ; they are plain and explicit, and need no comment.

It is my duty, and I shall do it with regret, to transmit to the King, true copies of your proceedings ; and, that his Majesty may have an opportunity to signify his pleasure thereon, before you meet again, I think it necessary to prorogue this General Court, immediately, to the usual time of its meeting for the winter session.   FRA. BERNARD.

PETITION

OF THE HOUSE OF REPRESENTATIVES TO THE KING, TO REMOVE SIR FRANCIS BERNARD FOREVER FROM THIS GOVERNMENT, AGREEBLE TO THE UNANIMOUS VOTE OF THE HOUSE. JUNE 27, 1769.

Most Gracious Sovereign,

We, your Majesty's most dutiful and faithful subjects, the Representatives of your ancient and loyal colony of the Massachusetts Bay, impressed with the deepest gratitude to Almighty God, for calling to the British succession your illustrious family; and so firmly establishing your Majesty on the throne of your royal progenitors : And being abundantly convinced of your Majesty's grace and clemency, most humbly implore the royal favor, while we briefly represent our grievances, which your Majesty alone, under God, can redress.

We are constrained, in duty to your Majesty, and in faithfulness to our constituents, to lay before your Majesty our complaints of his Excellency Sir Francis Bernard, Baronet, your Majesty's Governor of this colony, whose whole administration appears to have been repugnant, not only to your Majesty's service, and the welfare of your subjects in the colony, but even to the first principles of the British constitution.

From his first arrival here, he has, in his speeches and other public acts, treated the Representative body with contempt.

He has, in his public speeches, charged both Houses of the General Assembly expressly, with oppugnation against the royal authority; declaring that they had left gentlemen out of the Council, only for their fidelity to the Crown.

He has, from time to time, indiscreetly and wantonly exercised the prerogative of the Crown, in the repeated negative of Counsellors of an unblemished reputation, and duly elected by a great majority, some of them by the unanimous suffrage of both Houses of Assembly.

He has declared, that certain seats at the Council Board shall be kept vacant, till certain gentlemen, who are his favorites, shall be reelected.

He has, unconstitutionally, interfered with, and unduly influenced elections, particularly in the choice of an agent for the colony.

He has very abruptly displaced divers gentlemen of worth, for no apparent reason, but because they voted in the General Assembly with freedom, and against his measures.

He has, in an unwarrantable manner, taken upon himself the exercise of your Majesty's royal prerogative, in granting a charter for a college, contrary to an express vote of the House of Representatives, and without even asking the advice of your Majesty's Council.

He has practiced the sending over depositions to the ministry, privately taken, against gentlemen of character here, without giving the persons accused, the least notice of his purposes and proceedings.

He has very injuriously represented your Majesty's loving subjects of this colony in general; as having an ill temper prevailing among them; as disaffected to your Majesty's government, and intending to bring the authority of Parliament into contempt. And, by such false representations, he has been greatly instrumental, as this House humbly conceive, in exciting jealousies, and disturbing the harmony and mutual affection which before happily subsisted, and we pray God, may again subsist between your Majesty's subjects in Great Britain and America.

He has, in his letters to one of your Majesty's ministers, unjustly charged the majority of your Majesty's faithful Council in the colony, with having avowed the principles of opposition to the authority of Parliament, and acted in concert with a party, from whence such opposition originated.

He has, also, in his letter to another of your Majesty's ministers, falsely declared, that a plan was laid, and a number of men actually enrolled, in the town of Boston, to seize your Majesty's Castle William, in the harbor of the same, out of your Majesty's hands.

Such representations of the state and circumstances of this

colony, from a gentleman of the highest trust in it, will, of necessity, be received with full credit, till they are made to appear false. And, in consequence thereof, your Majesty's true and loyal subjects have suffered the reproach, as well as other hardships, of having a military force stationed here, to support your Majesty's authority, and the execution of the laws; which measure has been approved by your Majesty's two Houses of Parliament, as appears in their resolutions, that the town of Boston had been in a state of disorder and confusion, and that the circumstances of the colony were such as required a military force, for the purposes above mentioned.

Having been a principal intrument, as we apprehend, in procuring this military force, your Majesty's said Governor, in an unprecedented manner, and as though he had designed to irritate to the highest degree, ordered the very room which is appropriated for the meeting of the Representatives of the General Assembly, and was never used for any other purpose, and where their records are kept, to be employed as a barrack for the common soldiers. And the sentinels were so posted, as that your Majesty's Council, and the Justices of the Courts of Common Law, were daily interrupted, and even challenged, in their proceeding to the business of their several departments.

He endeavored, contrary to the express design of an act of Parliament, to quarter your Majesty's troops in the body of the town of Boston, while the barracks, provided by the government at the Castle, within the town, remained useless. And, for purposes manifestly evasive of said act, he unwarrantably appointed an officer to provide quarters for the troops, otherwise than is therein prescribed.

After having dissolved the General Assembly, at a most critical season, and while they were employed in the most necessary and important business of the colony, he arbitrarily refused to call another, for the space of ten months, and until the time appointed, in the royal charter, for the calling a General Assembly, against the repeated dutiful petitions of the people.

It appears, by his letters to the Earl of Hillsborough, your Majesty's Secretary of State, that he has endeavored to overthrow the present constitution of government in this colony, and to have the people deprived of their invaluable charter rights, which they and their ancestors have happily enjoyed, under your Majesty's administration, and those of your royal predecessors.

By the means aforesaid, and many others that might be enumerated, he has rendered his administration odious to the whole body of the people ; and has entirely alienated their affections from him, and thereby wholly destroyed that confidence in a Governor, which your Majesty's service indispensibly requires.

Wherefore, we most humbly entreat your Majesty, that his Excellency Sir Francis Bernard, Baronet, may be *forever* removed from the government of this province. And, that your Majesty would be graciously pleased, to place one in his stead, worthy to serve the greatest and best Monarch on earth.

[The committee, who reported this petition, were, the Speaker, (Mr. Cushing,) Col. Otis, Capt. Sheaffe, Gen. Preble, Mr, Adams, Mr. Hancock, Mr. Spooner, Mr. Otis, and Mr. Porter.]

====

LETTER

FROM THE COUNCIL AND HOUSE OF REPRESENTATIVES, TO W. BOLLAN, ESQ. AGENT IN ENGLAND, ON APPEALS, JULY 16, 1769.

THIS colony has lately been very much alarmed, by an order's being obtained from his Majesty, in Council, granting an appeal to them from a final judgment of the Supreme Court of Judicature, &c. in this colony, in an action of ejectment, wherein one David Jeffries was demandant, and Nathaniel Donnell, Esq. defendant.

Although this action is a dispute about private property, between individuals, yet as the establishing such a precedent, would be fatal in its consequences to the American colonies, it demands the attention of the General Assembly.

This colony was settled by private adventurers, at their own expense, and thereby an extensive country added to the dominion of Great Britain. The lands were purchased of natives, by those adventurers, and their successors, who thereby acquired as absolute a property in the soil, as a British subject can attain. The right to the soil hath been confirmed and established by royal charters, and is expressly confirmed and established, by the charter granted to this province, by their late Majesties, King WIlliam and Queen Mary, of glorious memory, which has never been forfeited, or any way vacated, wherein their said Majesties, for themselves, their heirs and successors, granted to the inhabitants of the province or territory of the Massachusetts Bay, all the lands and hereditaments, whatsoever, lying within the limits of said province ; to have and to hold the same, with their appurtenances, to the said inhabitants and their successors, to their only proper use and behoof forever, to be holden of their said Majesties, their heirs and successors, as of the Manor of East Greenwich, in the county of Kent, by fealty only, in free and common sockage, yielding and paying therefor, to their said Majesties, their heirs and successors, the fifth part of all gold and silver ore, and precious stones, which may, from time to time, and at all times, be found and obtained, in any of the said lands or premises.

In and by the same charter, their said late Majesties did, for themselves, their heirs and successors, give and grant, that the General Court of the same province, should forever have full power and authority to erect and constitute Judicatories, and Courts of Record, or other Courts, to be held in the name of their said late Majesties, their heirs and successors, for the hearing, trying and determining of all manner of crimes, offences, pleas, processes, plaints, actions, matters, causes and things, whatsoever, arising or happening within the same province, or territory, or between persons happening or residing there, whether the same be criminal or civil ; whether the said crimes be capital or not capital ; and whether the said pleas be real, personal or mixed ; and for the awarding execution thereupon, saving only an appeal to his Majesty, in Council, in personal actions, wherein the matter in difference exceeds the value of 300*l.* sterling : Provided always, that nothing therein, should extend or be taken to erect, grant, or allow the exercise of any Admiralty Court, jurisdiction, or power, but that the same should be, and thereby was reserved to their said late Majesties and their successors. From which it follows, according to the ancient maxim, *exceptio probat regulam*, that the Judicatories and Courts, erected and constituted in this colony, in consequence, and by virtue of the same charter, have cognizance of, and full power and authority of finally judging and determining all actions, arising or happening within the province, excepting matters properly cognizable in the Admiralty Court, and that no appeal lieth from such determinations and judgments, to any court or jurisdiction, whatever, excepting only, the above mentioned instance in personal actions, where the matter in difference exceeds the value of 300*l.* sterling.

We also clearly hold, that, of common right, actions of ejectment, and all real actions, are local, and triable only in the respective counties where the lands or tenements, in question, be. This principle of law is so fully established, that whenever attempts have been made to draw into question titles of law, in other counties, (though in actions in their own nature transitory,) such attempts have ever been suppressed by the wisdom of the judges and sages of the law, as subtle and dangerous innovations in derogation of the common law. Therefore, the establishing a precedent for granting appeals to his Majesty in Council, from the final judgment and determinations of the proper courts in this colony, in real, or any other actions, that draw the title of freeholders, in question, would be the subverting of an ancient principle of the common law, as well as contrary to the great charter, which ordains that no freeman shall be disseized of his freehold, or any otherwise destroyed, but by lawful judgment of his peers, by the law of the land, would be in direct violation of the royal charter, granted to this colony, and pregnant with every mischief that can possibly arise to its inhabitants.

Without mentioning the parties being deprived of a trial by a jury from the vicinity. who must be supposed to be the most competent judges of the facts, views. and all circumstances of local evidence, it will be impossible for the inhabitants of this colony, in general, to defend their titles at the distance of three thousand miles, against claims, however groundless and unjust. The greater part of the estates in this colony are so small, that it is with difficulty that the freeholder, however industrious or frugal, supplies his family with the necessaries of life, and pays his proportion of taxes for the ordinary support of government. His whole estate, converted into money, would be insufficient to defray the ordinary expense and charges of defending a suit in Great Britain. In every such appeal, judgment must, therefore, of course, be obtained against him by default, and he subjected to perpetual imprisonment, for cost. This is the case of by much the greater part of the landholders in this colony, and, indeed, there are but few that would not be within the same mischief. Therefore, the establishing such a precedent, would infallibly enable a few wealthy men, whether resident in the colonies, or elsewhere, by setting up groundless and unjust complaints, to possess themselves, under color of law, of the greatest part of the lands and hereditaments of his Majesty's faithful subjects in this colony, and would actually reduce them to as abject and miserable situation and condition, as that of ancient Villenage, where, although the villain might purchase lands in fee, yet he held them only at the will of his lord.

The train of evils, consequent upon this, is obvious ; agriculture, the natural livelihood of this infant colony, will be discouraged, and the settling and peopling this extensive continent, prevented. The trade of the colonies is already unhappily expiring, and should agriculture meet with the same fate, the very sinews of the Commonwealth will be destroyed, and his Majesty's subjects, in this colony, reduced to a state of desperation.

You are, therefore, strictly enjoined, to use your utmost endeavor to prevent so fatal a precedent's being established. And we would inform you, for your assistance herein, that an appeal, claimed to his Majesty in Council, from a judgment of the Supreme Court, in the province of New York, in the case of Forsey vs. Cunningham, even in a personal action, has lately been dismissed, as not warranted by law.

25

LETTER

FROM D. DE BERDT, ESQ. AGENT IN ENGLAND, TO THE SPEAKER OF THE
HOUSE OF REPRESENTATIVES.

London, February 11, 1769.

SIR,

You are not without warm and steady friends, in both Houses of Parliament, who are grieved at the hardships you are under. I waited, yesterday, on Lord Shelburne, who is deeply impressed with a sense of your difficulties; and says, if he had been still in the Ministry, he should have composed all your difficulties, without any military force: for, when he was in the administration, your colony paid him the most respectful and obliging conduct of any of the colonies; and he will endeavor to serve you, in any particular, wherein he thinks it just to do it.

The Ministry seem confused and perplexed, and intoxicated with high notions of power, which gives great uneasiness here, as well as the affairs of America.

Yesterday, the livery of London met, to give instructions to their Representatives, which were of a very spirited nature; in which, they recommend their care to encourage and promote our trade to all the British colonies. The whole of such instructions must be displeasing to the Ministry. And, now London has begun, it is more than probable, this method of instruction will run through the greatest part of the kingdom; and, I hope, will have a good effect; at least, that it will shew the general temper of the people, to cultivate a good understanding and trade with America.

I was, also, since my last, with Colonel Barre, who is a hearty and zealous friend to America, and to your colony in particular. He is very sensible of the difficulties you are under; and is ready, at all times, to exert himself in your favor.

D. DE BERDT.

SPEECH

OF THE LIEUTENANT GOVERNOR, TO THE COUNCIL AND HOUSE OF REPRE-
SENTATIVES, MARCH 15, 1770, AT THE OPENING OF THE SESSION.

Gentlemen of the Council, and
Gentlemen of the House of Representatives,

I INTENDED to have met the Court, on the 10th of January, at Boston, being the time and place to which it stood prorogued, when the Governor left the province; but, by the two last packets from

England, I have received such instructions, as made it necessary for me further to prorogue it to this time and place ; and, I am informed, that, before the session is ended, I may expect to have something, in special command from his Majesty, relative to the state and circumstances of the province, to lay before you. In the mean time, I shall be ready to join with you, in such of our interior business, as shall be thought necessary, or expedient. The state of this business, I am not able, particularly, to point out to you, having had but little knowledge of the affairs of the General Court, for several years past. There are amendments or alterations, absolutely necessary to be made, in some of our laws, the defects of which have, of late, been a subject of general complaint; I shall, hereafter, propose them to you by messages. I have another matter, also, of general utility, which I shall lay before you in the same way.

You cannot oblige me more, than by putting it in my power to concur with you in measures for promoting the peace, good order, and lasting tranquillity of the province.

I am sensible the season of the year is approaching, when you cannot be absent from your several homes, without peculiar prejudice to your private affairs. I shall, therefore, do all that is necessary, on my part, to give the greatest despatch to the business of the session ; at the same time, I am willing to give attendance upon it, as long as we can employ ourselves for the benefit of the province.   T. HUTCHINSON.

===

REMONSTRANCE

OF THE HOUSE OF REPRESENTATIVES, AGAINST THE PROROGATION OF THE
GENERAL COURT, BY THE MANDATE OF THE MINISTER, &c. ADDRESSED
TO THE LIEUTENANT GOVERNOR, MARCH 15, 1770.

May it please your Honor,

' THE House of Representatives of this, his Majesty's colony, observing in your proclamation for proroguing the General Assembly, that you were pleased to assign as the *only* reason, " that you had received instructions to meet the said Assembly, at Cambridge," think it their indispensable duty to remonstrate to your Honor, against any such reason, for proroguing this Court, as being an infraction of our essential rights, as men and citizens, as well as those derived to us by the British constitution, and the charter of this colony.

We would further beg leave to remonstrate to your Honor, that the holding a General Assembly in Harvard College, is utterly repugnant to the interest of that seminary of learning, and, consequently, to the designs of the Representatives of this people, in so liberally granting the monies of their constituents, for its emolument and support.

For these reasons, the House of Representatives are indispensably obliged to pray your Honor to exert the authority derived to you from his Majesty's royal commission, agreeable to the charter of this colony, and vested in you alone, in adjourning this great and General Assembly, to its ancient place, the Court House, in Boston.

We forbear to mention, particularly to your Honor, the great inconveniences which attend the sitting of the Assembly, in Cambridge, where the Members cannot be accommodated ; but more especially, as they are at a distance from the place where the records of the Assembly are kept.

[This remonstrance was prepared by the Speaker, Mr. Adams, Mr. Otis, Capt. Sheaffe, Mr. Hancock, Col. Bowers, and Mr. Hall.]

===

MESSAGE

FROM THE LIEUTENANT GOVERNOR, TO THE HOUSE OF REPRESENTATIVES,

MARCH 16, 1770.

Gentlemen of the House of Representatives,

THERE being reserved, by the royal charter, to this province, certain powers to the Governor, whensoever his Majesty's pleasure is signified to me, whilst I am Commander in Chief, in what manner those powers shall be exercised, I think myself bound to conform to it.

I wish that every part of my administration, whether by force of instructions, or otherwise, might be satisfactory to the Members of the House ; but I must not depart from my duty to the King. If I should comply with the desire of the House, in adjourning or proroguing the Court, to Boston, I apprehend I should incur his Majesty's displeasure ; and I the rather hope it will not be expected from me, because I shall never take exception to the exercise of any powers, which are constitutionally in the House, although such powers should be exercised, in consequence of instructions given to the Members of the House, by their constituents.

T. HUTCHINSON.

[The House sent a message to the Council, requesting them to take such measures as they shall think proper for the removal of the Court, to Boston. The Council sent a message to the Lieutenant Governor on the subject, and he replied to the Council, by message ; both of which follow.]

ADDRESS

OF THE COUNCIL TO THE LIEUTENANT GOVERNOR, IN REPLY TO HIS
SPEECH, AT THE OPENING OF THE SESSION, MARCH 20, 1770.

THE Board have given all due attention to your speech at the opening of the present session. Your Honor is pleased to say, that your intention was to have met the Court, at Boston, on the 10th of January, judging, we humbly presume, that it was most for the public benefit, as well as the particular convenience of the Members, that the Court should convene at that time, and that the business of the province should be then transacted. It gives us, therefore, sensible concern, to find your Honor, immediately after declaring, that "instructions received from England, made it necessary for you further to prorogue it to another time and place." Solicitous, as we always are, for the preservation of the royal prerogative, we are equally anxious for the good of the people. We cannot excuse ourselves, therefore, from observing to your Honor, that if his Majesty's Representatives should, from time to time, receive directions respecting such matters, as, from the local circumstances of the province, he must have greater advantages to judge of himself, we fear many inconveniences may arise.

If your Honor should, upon thoroughly revolving the matter again in your mind, be convinced, that though you were instructed to meet the Assembly, in Cambridge, yet his Majesty's service, and the interest of the province, conspire to render it fit that the remaining part of the session should be at the usual place for holding the General Court; or should think that the reason for its sitting in this place has now ceased, the Board presume to hope, that your Honor will adjourn it to the Court House, in Boston.

The Board, moreover, beg leave to suggest to your Honor, that Governor Bernard's wanton exercise of power, in rejecting so great a number of the gentlemen who were elected Counsellors in May last, has rendered a very general attendance of the present Council necessary. And as a number of Members are prevented, by bodily indisposition, from giving their presence, who could attend if the Court was removed to its former place, there is danger, from the great number of committees, which will be wanted in the course of the session, that if it should continue here, the business of the province may be greatly retarded.

The Board are humbly of opinion, considering the present state of the province, that your Honor will run no risk of incurring his Majesty's displeasure, by complying with the request of both Houses.

When your Honor shall "lay any matter before the Court, which you may receive in special command from his Majesty, relative to the state and circumstances of the province," the Board will not fail to pay that regard to it, which every thing coming from our gracious Sovereign, justly demands.

The disadvantages arising from the prorogation of the Court at this time, when the season of the year is approaching, that the Members cannot be absent from their several homes, without peculiar prejudice to their private affairs, is sensibly felt by us.   So great despatch cannot be given to the business of the session, if the Court should continue here, as if removed to its ancient seat. We are, however, obliged to your Honor, for assuring us that you shall do all which is necessary to that end, on your part; and that you are willing, at the same time, to give attendance upon it, as long as the Court can be employed for the benefit of the province; which, we assure your Honor, this Board will ever make the great object of their pursuit.

MESSAGE

FROM THE LIEUTENANT GOVERNOR TO THE COUNCIL, IN REPLY TO THE FOREGOING, MARCH 21, 1770.

Gentlemen of the Council,

I THANK you for your address.   Had my removal of the Court from Boston to Cambridge, been founded merely upon my own opinion of the expediency of the measure; or if I knew that the motives, which caused my order to prorogue the Court were ceased, the reasons urged by the Council, and the House, would have their due weight and influence over me; but I neither prorogued the Court here, from my own motives, nor have I reason to think that the motives for ordering it to be done, now cease. However it may seem to others, I must consider myself as a servant of the King, to be governed by what appears to me to be his Majesty's pleasure in those things, which otherwise I might have a right to do, or not to do, according to my discretion.

T. HUTCHINSON.

ANSWER

OF THE HOUSE OF REPRESENTATIVES, TO THE SPEECH OF THE LIEUTEN-
ANT GOVERNOR, DELIVERED TO BOTH HOUSES, AT THE OPENING OF THE
SESSION, MARCH 27, 1770.

May it please your Honor,

THE House have taken your speech, at the opening of this session, into their consideration, and cannot but express their concern, at your Honor's supposing yourself to have been necessitated, by the instructions you have received, to prorogue the General Court to this time and place ; and are constrained to say, that if your Honor's principles, in that respect, are hereafter to be adopted by the Commanders in Chief, of this province, we hope his Majesty's Ministers will pay more regard to the charter and constitution of this province, than they seem to have done in this instance, before they again advise our most gracious Sovereign to give such instructions.

We shall cheerfully attend to your Honor's message, respecting any necessary amendments or alterations in our laws, or any other matter of common utility, and are very desirous of transacting the business of this province, which is now greatly in arrear, with despatch ; but the many inconveniences attending the holding of the General Court, at Cambridge, will, of necessity, greatly retard it.

However, your Honor may rely upon it, that this House will do every thing in their power for promoting the peace, good order, and lasting tranquillity of this province.

[The committee who prepared the above, consisted of the Speaker, Mr. Adams, Mr. Leonard, Col. Otis, and Major Hawley.]

====

MESSAGE

FROM THE LIEUTENANT GOVERNOR TO THE HOUSE OF REPRESENTA-
TIVES, IN ANSWER TO THEIR VERBAL MESSAGE, MARCH 22, 1770.

Gentlemen of the House of Representatives,

YOUR committee, by a verbal message, have desired me to communicate to the House, a copy of the instructions, which I have received, for meeting the Court, at Cambridge. I shall always be sorry when it is not in my power to comply with the desire of the House. I am not at liberty to do it now, because the King has been pleased to order that no letters nor instructions to his Governor, shall be communicated, without his Majesty's special leave.

T. HUTCHINSON.

====

MESSAGE

FROM THE HOUSE OF REPRESENTATIVES, TO THE LIEUTENANT
GOVERNOR, MARCH 23, 1770.

May it please your Honor,

THE House of Representatives beg leave still to remonstrate to your Honor, against the holding this General Assembly in Cambridge, as being repugnant to the constitution, and the law of this Commonwealth.

By an act, passed in the tenth year of his late Majesty, King William, of glorious memory, which received his royal approbation, and is now in force. the form of a writ for calling the General Assembly, is established ; wherein it is ordered, that the General Assembly be convened, held and kept in the Town House, in Boston. Hence it appears, that the Town House, in Boston, is, by law, established, as the only place for holding the Assembly; and we take the liberty to express our sentiments, that no instruction ought to be deemed of sufficient force, to invalidate the law.

With regard to the instruction, which seems to lie with so much weight on your Honor's mind, we would observe, that when a bill was brought into the British Parliament, to give the royal instructions in the colonies, the force of law, the Commons then asserted the rights of the people, and rejected it with disdain.

We, therefore, again intreat your Honor, further to take this matter under your consideration, and, agreeable to the request of both Houses, to order the removal of this General Assembly, to its ancient and legal place, the Court House, in Boston.

[The committee, by whom this message was reported, was Col. Otis, Mr. Hancock, Capt. Sheaffe, Mr. Adams, and Mr. Leonard.]

=====

MESSAGE

FROM THE LIEUTENANT GOVERNOR TO THE HOUSE OF REPRESENTA-
TIVES, IN REPLY TO THE FOREGOING, MARCH 23, 1770.

Gentlemen of the House of Representatives,

Your observation upon the form of the writ for calling the General Assembly, has been made in former controversies, so long ago as in Governor Burnet's administration, but it did not then prevail. The words, " the town of Boston," in the writ, like the words " William the Third," were understood to be mere matter of form ; the one adapted to the place where the Court had usually been held ; the other, to the Prince then on the throne.

I have never attempted to give the King's instructions the force of laws. If I was convinced, that, by any law, the Court must be held at Boston, I should not very easily be induced to prorogue it to any other place, until such law should be repealed.

T. HUTCHINSON.

REPORT AND RESOLUTIONS,

ADOPTED MARCH 24, 1770, IN THE HOUSE OF REPRESENTATIVES; PREPARED BY A COMMITTEE, APPOINTED TO CONSIDER THE STATE OF THE PROVINCE, AND TO INQUIRE INTO PUBLIC GRIEVANCES.

[The committee were. Mr. Cushing, (the Speaker,) Mr. Adams, Maj. Hawley, Col. Otis, Mr. Leonard, Mr. Hancock, Capt. Sheaffe, Mr. Spooner, and Capt. Derby.]

WHEREAS, in and by an act of this province, made and passed in the tenth year of his late Majesty, King William the Third, it is enacted and ordained, that the writ, to be at any time thereafter issued by the Governor of the said province, shall be in the form following: [Here the form of the writ is given; which requires that the great and General Court or Assembly of the province, should be holden " *at the Town House, in Boston,*" &c.] which said act was, in due season, laid before his said Majesty, King William the Third, of glorious memory; and did then receive his royal approbation; and therefore, being a perpetual act, and not repealed, is now in full force, and cannot be repealed by any authority, but that of the legislative body of this province. This being the form of the writ prescribed in the said act, *the Town House, in Boston*, is the place thereby established, for the holding and keeping, as well as the convening the great and General Assembly of this province.

And whereas this province, by a perpetual act of the fifth of William and Mary, both made provision for upholding and repairing the said Town House, in Boston, for the holding of the said Assembly, which amounts to an establishment of the seat of government in that place; and seems to be the foundation and reason of expressly inserting the name of the place, in the form of the writ aforesaid: And also, in providing them an elegant mansion house, for the residence of the Governor: And the said General Assembly hath constantly been convened, held and kept, at the said town house, in Boston, agreeably to the act aforesaid; pestilential sickness in said town, and other extraordinary cases, necessarily preventing it, excepted:

Resolved, That the holding and keeping, as well as the convening the said great and General Assembly, by force of instruction, or otherwise, at any *other* place, than in Boston aforesaid, is attended with very great inconveniences; is contrary to the ancient custom and usage of the said Assembly; in direct repugnance of the constitution and the establishment aforesaid; and therefore a grievance.

And whereas both Houses of this Assembly, have remonstrated to his Honor the Lieutenant Governor, and present Commander in Chief of this colony, against the holding this General Assembly,

26

in Cambridge ; and have prayed his Honor to remove the same to its ancient seat, the Court House, in Boston ; but his Honor hath repeatedly refused to comply with their request :

Therefore, resolved, That this House do now proceed to business, under this grievance, *only from absolute necessity ;* hereby protesting against the illegality of holding the Assembly as aforesaid ; and ordering this, their protest, to be entered on their journals, to the end, that the same may not be drawn into precedent at any time hereafter.

And whereas his Honor, the Lieutenant Governor, hath been pleased, in his answer of yesterday, to a message of this House, to intimate, that the aforesaid act of this province, of the tenth of William the Third, in no wise establishes the Town House, in Boston, as the place for convening, holding and keeping the General Assembly ; expressly declaring, that " the words *the town of Boston,* in the writ prescribed in said act, like the words *William the Third,* were understood to be mere matters of form."

Resolved, As the sense of this House, that his Honor's strictures thereon, are not satisfactory or conclusive. The name of the King, is of the substance of the writ ; but the words *William the Third,* as all other words, descriptive of things, in their own nature changeable, must, in all established forms, be equally changeable themselves ; and so far, may be considered as mere matter of form, or *gratia exempli.* Yet, that can by no means be the case, with respect to words, descriptive of things in their own nature, fixed and perpetual, as when a certain place is designated.

Therefore, resolved, That the determination of this House, to proceed to business, is by no means to be considered, at any time hereafter, as a renunciation of the claim of the House to the legal right of sitting in General Assembly, at its ancient place, the Court House, in Boston.

MESSAGE

FROM THE LIEUTENANT GOVERNOR, TO THE COUNCIL AND THE HOUSE OF
REPRESENTATIVES, APRIL 7, 1770.

Gentlemen of the Council, and
  Gentlemen of the House of Representatives,

THE Secretary will lay before you several papers, which I have received from one of his Majesty's Justices of the Peace, and divers other persons, inhabitants of the town of Gloucester, and which relate to a very disorderly and riotous transaction in said town. A person appears to have been most inhumanly treated, for seeking redress in the course of the law, for former injuries received.

As this information comes to me while the General Court is sitting, I have thought it proper to communicate it to the House of Representatives, as well as to his Majesty's Council, that if any act, or order of the whole Legislature, shall be judged necessary, for strengthening or encouraging the executive powers of government, there may be an opportunity for it. I must observe to you, that a number of persons, of the same town, were prosecuted and fined, at the Superior Court, for the county of Essex, in June last, for injuring the person and property of the present complainant, in a barbarous manner; and if it be truly represented, that the same persons have been concerned in this second offence, it is a great aggravation of their crime, and a defiance of the laws and authority of government.   T. HUTCHINSON.

ANSWER

OF THE HOUSE OF REPRESENTATIVES, TO THE FOREGOING,
APRIL 23, 1770.

May it please your Honor,

THE House of Representatives have taken into due consideration your message of the 7th instant, with the papers laid before them by the Secretary, agreeable to your direction.

We assure your Honor, that we have the utmost abhorrence of all disorderly and riotous transactions. It is the disposition, as well as the duty, of this House, to take the most effectual measures to discountenance them; and to strengthen and encourage the executive officers in the exercise of all their lawful powers of government. Nothing, therefore, shall be wanting on our part, for the promoting of these purposes, whenever any further steps shall appear to us to be necessary. At present, it is the opinion of the House, that the laws now in being, duly executed, would be fully sufficient; and, to add to the severity of the provision made by them, without an apparent and very urgent necessity, might put into the hands of the civil magistrate, a power that would be dangerous to the rights and liberties of the people.

When complaints are made of riots and tumults, it is the wisdom of government, and it becomes the Representatives of the people, especially, to inquire into the real causes of them. If they arise from oppression, as is frequently the case, a thorough redress of grievances will remove the cause, and, probably, put an end to the complaint. It may justly be said, of the people of this province, that they seldom, if ever, have assembled in a tumultuous manner, unless they have been oppressed. It cannot be expected, that a people, accustomed to the freedom of the English constitution,

will be patient, while they are under the hand of tyranny and
arbitrary power. They will discover their resentment in a manner,
which will naturally displease their oppressors ; and, in such a
case, the severest laws, and the most rigorous execution, will be to
little purpose. The most effectual method to restore tranquillity,
would be to remove their burthens, and to punish all those who
have been the procurers of their oppression.

Your Honor, in your message, has pointed us to an instance,
which you are pleased to call "a very disorderly and riotous
transaction, in the town of Gloucester ;" but, we cannot think it
consistent with the justice of this House, to come into measures,
which may imply a censure upon individuals, much less upon a
community hitherto unimpeached in point of good order ; or even
to form any judgment upon the matter, until more light shall appear, than the papers, accompanying your message, afford. The
House cannot easily conceive, what should determine your Honor
so particularly to recommend this instance to the consideration of
the Assembly, while others of a much more heinous nature, and
dangerous tendency, have passed altogether unnoticed in your
message. Your having received the information, while the General Court is sitting, cannot alter its nature and importance, or
render it more or less necessary to be considered by the Legislature. The instance, admitting it to be truly represented, in all
its aggravating circumstances, certainly cannot be more threatening
to government, than those enormities which have been notoriously
committed by the soldiery of late ; and, in many instances, have
strangely escaped punishment, though repeated more than a second
time, and in defiance of the laws and authority of government.

A military force, if posted among the people, without their express consent, is itself one of the greatest grievances, and threatens
the total subversion of a free constitution ; much more, if designed
to execute a system of corrupt and arbitrary power, and even to
exterminate the liberties of the country. The bill of rights, passed
immediately after the revolution, expressly declares, that "the
raising and keeping a standing army within the kingdom, in a time
of peace, without the consent of Parliament, is against law." And
we take this occasion to say, with freedom, that the raising and
keeping a standing army within this province, in a time of peace,
without the consent of the General Assembly, is equally against
law. Yet we have seen a standing army procured, posted and
kept within this province, in a time of profound peace, not only
without the consent of the people, but against the remonstrance of
both Houses of Assembly. Such a standing army must be designed
to subjugate the people to arbitrary measures. It is a most violent
infraction of their natural and constitutional rights. It is an unlawful assembly, of all others the most dangerous and alarming ;
and every instance of its actually restraining the liberty of any
individual, is a crime, which infinitely exceeds what the law in-

tends by a riot. Surely then, your Honor cannot think this House can descend to the consideration of matters, comparatively trifling, while the capital of the province has so lately been in a state of actual imprisonment, and the government itself is under duress.

The fatal effects, which will forever attend the keeping a standing army within a civil government, have been severely felt in this province. They landed in a hostile manner, and with all the ensigns of triumph ; and your Honor must well remember, that they early invested the Manufactory House, in Boston ; a capacious building, occupied by a number of families, whom they besieged and imprisoned. The extraordinary endeavors of the Chief Justice of the province, to procure the admission of troops into that house, in a manner plainly against law, will not easily be erased from the minds of this people. Surely your Honor could not be so fond of military establishments, as willingly to interpose in a matter which might possibly come before you as a judge. To what else can such astonishing conduct be imputed, unless to a sudden surprize, and the terror of military power in the Chief Justice of the province, which evidently appeared to have also arrested the inferior magistrates.

We shall not enlarge on the multiplied outrages committed by this unlawful assembly; in frequently assaulting his Majesty's peaceable and loyal subjects; in beating and wounding the magistrate, when in the execution of his office; in rescuing prisoners out of the hands of justice; and finally, in perpetrating the most horrid slaughter of a number of inhabitants,* but a few days before the sitting of this Assembly, which your Honor must undoubtedly have heard of. But not the least notice of these outrageous offences has been taken ; nor can we find the most distant hint of the late inhuman and barbarous action, either in your speech, at the opening of the session, or even in this message to both Houses. These violences, so frequently committed, added to the most rigorous and oppressive prosecutions, carried on by the Crown against the subjects, grounded upon unconstitutional acts ; and in the Court of Admiralty, uncontroled by the Courts of Common Law, have been justly alarming to the people. The disorder, which your Honor so earnestly recommends to the consideration of the Assembly, very probably took its rise from such provocations. The use, therefore, which we shall make of the information in your message, shall be to inquire into the grounds of the people's uneasiness, and to seek a radical redress of their grievances. Indeed, it is natural to expect, that while the terror of arms continues in the province, the laws will be in some degree silent. But when the channels of justice shall be again opened, and the law can be heard. the person who has complained to your Honor, if he has truly represented his case, will have his remedy. We yet entertain hopes, that the military pow-

* The massacre of March 5, 1770.

er, so grievous to the people, will be removed from the province, to stations where it may better answer the design, for which it was originally raised. Till then, we have nothing to expect, but that tyranny and confusion will prevail in defiance of the laws of the land, and the just and constitutional authority of government.

We cannot avoid, before we conclude, to express the deepest concern, that while the people are loudly complaining of intolerable grievances, the General Assembly, itself, has just reason to remonstrate against a violent and repeated infringement of their constitutional right. In order to avoid the most flagrant impropriety of its being kept in a garrisoned town, it was the last session, as it were, driven from its ancient and legal seat ; and even now, it is held in this place, at a distance from its offices and records, and subject to the greatest inconveniences, without any necessity, which we can conceive, or the least apparent reason. These alarming considerations have awakened and fixed our attention ; and your Honor cannot think, we can very particularly attend to things of less moment, within the jurisdiction of the Executive Courts, at a time, when, in faithfulness to our constituents, our minds are necessarily employed in matters which concern the very being of the constitution.

[The committee were, Col. Otis, Mr. Williams, of Taunton, Maj. Hawley, Mr. Adams, Mr. Otis, Mr. Hancock, and Mr. Sanders, of Gloucester.]

NOTE.

At the session in April, 1770, T. Cushing, the Speaker, being unable to attend, by reason of sickness, John Hancock was chosen Speaker, pro tem. ; but the Lieutenant Governor did not approve of him, and Col. J. Warren was then chosen.

MESSAGE

FROM THE HOUSE OF REPRESENTATIVES TO THE LIEUTENANT GOVERNOR, MAY 31, 1770.

May it please your Honor,

BEING returned, by our respective towns, to represent them in the great and General Court or Assembly of this province, directed by his Majesty's writ, under your hand and seal, to be convened at Harvard College, in Cambridge, we beg leave to represent to your Honor, our opinion, that the only writ, established by law, for convening a General Assembly, is apparently formed upon a supposition. that the Town House, in Boston, is the *only* place, where the said Assembly is to be convened, held and kept.

Our fathers, in 1721, were evidently of opinion, that the convening, holding and keeping the Assembly at any other place, was contrary to the act of this province, of the 10th of William the Third, which establishes the form of the writ. Accordingly, when the Assembly was then adjourned to this place, though the Providence of God had rendered it impossible for them, consistent with safety to their lives, to meet in Boston, by reason of a contagious distemper, which raged there, Governor Shute declared, that he did not mean the adjournment should ever after be drawn into precedent ; and the three branches of the Legislature passed a resolve, to make valid their proceedings ; which they would not have done, if they had thought the adjournment from the Town House, in Boston, however necessary, had been consistent with the before mentioned legal establishment.

Indeed, in 1729, Governor Burnet, without any such necessity, ordered the Assembly to be convened at Salem ; but the Representatives of the people then remonstrated to the Governor against the illegality of the measure ; and although he insisted upon it, they never yielded the point. We do not recollect any other instance of the removal of the Assembly from Boston, except in cases of the same necessity with that in 1721. But, in the present case, not the least shadow of necessity appears ; for no instructions, or orders, from any authority, inferior to that of the whole Legislature, can avail with your Honor, to set aside a legal establishment. How far you may be bound, by the instructions you may have received, is not for us to determine ; but when such instructions shall, in their operation, infringe on the legal and essential rights of this Assembly, you cannot but expect they will awaken our attention, and alarm our jealousy.

If we could possibly admit, that the law above mentioned, did not absolutely determine the Town House, in Boston, to be the established seat of this Assembly, and that it, therefore, remained a prerogative of the Crown, in your Honor's discretion, to remove it to this, or any other place, it ought always to be remembered, that the prerogative is a discretionary power, in some instances, vested in the King only, for the good of the subject. We cannot presume, that his Majesty would exercise that power, or suffer any servant of his to exercise it to a different end. " The prerogative of the Crown extends not to do any injury ; for being created for the benefit of the people, it cannot be exerted to their prejudice." But the continuance of the Assembly in this place is not only attended with very great inconvenience to us, being at a distance from our offices and records ; is not only contrary to the ancient custom and usage of the Assembly ; in direct repugnance to the constitution and establishment aforesaid ; but is also, in many respects, so far from tending to the good of the subjects, that it extends to their injury and prejudice. And we would particularly observe upon the great impropriety of the Assembly being held in this place, as it is an invasion of private property, and a perversion of the true design of our forefathers, in planting this seminary of learning ; and it may also hereafter be made a precedent for establishing the authority of the College in very different hands from those in which its happy constitution has placed it.

For the above mentioned reasons, we think it our indispensable duty, before we proceed upon the business of the Assembly, to remonstrate to your Honor, against its being held in this or any place, other than the Town House, in Boston.

[The remonstrance above, passed the House the 30th, being the first day of the session ; but the Lieutenant Governor, not being in the chair, it could not be presented that day. The House, therefore, ordered the following protest to be entered on their journal.]

===

PROTEST

OF THE HOUSE OF REPRESENTATIVES, ADOPTED AND ENTERED ON THEIR JOURNAL, MAY 30, 1770.

WHEREAS, this House hath passed a remonstrance to his Honor the Lieutenant Governor, against holding the General Court in this place, or any other, than in the Town House, in Boston ; which remonstrance cannot now be presented, his Honor not being in the chair ; and whereas, according to the royal charter of this province, it is necessary that this Court proceed to the choice of Counsellors, for the year ensuing, on this day, being the last Wednesday of May : Therefore, resolved, that this House do proceed to the said election of Counsellors, at this time, only from necessity ; protesting against its being drawn into precedent at any time hereafter, or considered as a voluntary receding of the House from their constitutional claim.

===

SPEECH

OF THE LIEUTENANT GOVERNOR, TO BOTH HOUSES, MAY 31, 1770.

Gentlemen of the Council, and
       Gentlemen of the House of Representatives,

NOT having received any special commands from his Majesty, to be communicated to you, I have only to recommend to your consideration, the public business of the province, which it has been usual for the General Court to act upon, at this season of the year.

Analagous to the constitution of the Supreme Legislature, it is with you, gentlemen of the House of Representatives, to originate a bill for supplying the treasury with a sum sufficient to defray the necessary charges of government; an estimate of which, the Treasurer will lay before you. The consideration of the tax for the present year, comes also within the same rule. For several years past, the taxes have been much reduced, and in one year, there was no provincial tax; a large public debt, therefore, still remains, with which the present year is burdened; and you will, I doubt not, think it greater than your constituents can conveniently discharge at once. I am ready to give my consent to a bill for reducing this sum, and charging a part of it upon a future year; but, out of regard to the public interest, I cannot help putting you in mind, that, although we are now in a state of peace, yet, from the vicissitudes to which all human affairs are liable, and from the present commotions in Europe, the time of our continuance in this state, is very uncertain; and his Majesty's British dominions may, ere long, be again involved in war. If we shall have then a large public debt remaining, it will be a heavy clog upon us, and we may see, too late, that it is good policy, in times of peace, to discharge the debts incurred in times of war. If I am rightly informed, some of the other colonies are entirely free from their debts, contracted in the last war; and all of them are more so, in proportion, than we are.

I will not determine, gentlemen, but I pray you to consider, whether the discontinuing the excise upon spiritous liquors, which used to ease the tax upon polls and estates, has been of advantage to the province, or whether it is not probable that it has only caused a proportionably greater unnecessary consumption of such liquors, to the detriment of the health and morals of the people.

Gentlemen,

A multitude of petitions came before the General Court the last year, some of which, seemed to be of very small importance, and I thought it hardly consistent with the dignity of the Court, to take cognizance of them. The Assembly then passed one act, which had a tendency to lessen the number of private petitions; and I should be glad if further expedients could be agreed upon to the like purpose.

I wish for a happy harmony in the Legislature, and I will most readily concur with you, in every measure you shall propose, as far as can consist with my duty to the King, and the regard I bear to the interest of the province.   T. HUTCHINSON.

MESSAGE

Gentlemen of the House of Representatives,

By the charter, the Governor has the power of adjourning and proroguing the General Assembly. There is no limitation of time or place. Can it be supposed, that, merely by force of the form of a writ, for calling the General Assembly, this power is taken away or abridged ? Will it not rather be supposed, that the word·"*Boston*," in this writ, is mere matter of form ; especially when it is considered, that it will be equally necessary for the writ to be dated at Boston ; for that is a part of the form, as it is for the Court to be convened there ? Now it must, in the very nature of the thing, be perfectly indifferent in what place the writ is dated.

I am sensible there have been disputes upon this point, both in Governor Shute's and Governor Burnet's administration. But in Governor Burnet's time, the dispute, as I apprehend, was settled ; and I cannot help being of opinion, that you are moving a matter which has been more than forty years at rest ; and I must put you in mind, that in 1737, the King, for the more convenient carrying into execution a commission for settling the line between this province and New Hampshire, instructed the Governor to remove the General Court to Salisbury, where more than one session was held. Whether this was necessary, I will not determine. But if it was necessary, I know that his Majesty was the sole judge of the necessity. I was then a Member of the House ; and do not remember a word to have been said of the illegality of holding the Court in any other town than Boston. The point had been settled a few years before, and was fresh in the memory of the House.

If the removal of the Court to Cambridge, had been illegal, I do not think I could have justified myself in such removal. I am sure his Majesty never intended that his instructions should supersede or control the law.

I agree with you, that the prerogative of the Crown does not extend to do any injury ; but I cannot admit, that the exercise of the prerogative, in this particular instance, is an injury. I persuade myself, you intend no more than to represent to me your opinion, that though it should be admitted to be legal, yet it is inconvenient to you, and to the College.

If you desire me to adjourn or prorogue the Court to any other place in Cambridge, than the College, I will immediately do it ; and to such place, where you may be best accommodated ; but I cannot remove the Court from Cambridge, until I know more of his Majesty's pleasure, than I do at present ; for, as I had occasion to observe to the last Assembly, I must govern myself by his

Majesty's pleasure, as it shall be signified to me, in all cases ; in which, otherwise, I might have a right to act, or not to act, according to my own discretion.   For it appears to me to be preposterous to suppose, that the sole power, given to the Governor, of proroguing or dissolving the Court, was intended, as some would have it, to exclude the King from his right of controling the Governor. Nothing can be more manifest, than that it is intended for no other purpose, than to exclude both the other branches of the Court from any share in this power.

I have transmitted every thing which passed the last session of the Court, on this subject, to be laid before his Majesty.   I shall do the same with the message you have sent me, and this, my answer to it ; and, I have no doubt, the royal determination will be such as to give no just cause of complaint.

T. HUTCHINSON.

═══

MESSAGE

FROM THE LIEUTENANT GOVERNOR TO THE HOUSE OF REPRESENTATIVES,

JUNE 5, 1770.

Gentlemen of the House of Representatives,

You have sent to me a verbal message, by a committee, who have desired a copy of my instruction, or instructions, relative to my convening the General Court at Harvard College.   I have no instruction for convening the Court at Harvard College, and I am willing to adjourn or prorogue it, to any part of the town of Cambridge, where it can be accommodated.

My orders are sufficient to convince me, that it is his Majesty's pleasure the Court should be held in Cambridge ; but I am not at liberty to lay a copy of those orders before the House, being restrained by a general instruction, which requires me to make no copies of letters, or papers, from the Secretary of State, public, without special leave first given me so to do.   I take no pleasure in refusing to comply with the request of the House, but you will not expect me to do any thing inconsistent with my duty to the King.   T. HUTCHINSON.

REPORT AND RESOLUTIONS.

[After the above message was read, a committee was appointed, composed of the Members following, viz. T. Cushing, (the Speaker,) Mr. Adams, Mr. Leonard, Maj. Hawley, Mr. Hancock, Mr. Porter, Col. Worthington, Capt. Sheaffe, and Col. Warren, to consider what may be further proper to be done, while the General Assembly is held out of the Town House, in Boston. The 6th of June they made report, which was accepted, ninety-six to six. The report was as follows :]

In and by an act of this province, made and passed in the tenth year of his late Majesty, King William the Third, it is enacted, that the writ, to be at any time thereafter issued by the Governor, or Commander in Chief of the said province, shall be in the form following, viz. [Here the form of the writ was recited, and it required that the persons chosen to be Representatives of the people, should convene at the *Town House, in Boston*, where the General Assembly was to be held and kept.] Wherefore, inasmuch as no other writ could be issued for convening a General Assembly, and the place where it should be convened, held and kept, was expressly declared, in and by said writ, to be the *Town House, in Boston*, it was the opinion of the House of Representatives, in the last year, that the above mentioned act, by establishing that to be the form of said writ, had established the Town House, in Boston, as the only legal place for convening, holding and keeping the General Assembly.

Nor was that a novel construction of said act ; for in the year 1721, under the administration of Governor Shute, when the small pox raged in the town of Boston to such a degree, as that the General Assembly could not be held there, without endangering the lives of the Members, (for which reason the three branches of the Court were desirous of its being removed,) the two Houses refused to pass one governmental act, out of the town of Boston, until they had passed a resolve to make such acts valid. To which resolve, his Majesty's Representative gave his assent ; and engaged on his part, that the removing of the Court there, should not be drawn into precedent for the removing of the Court from Boston, for the future.

It must be absurd to suppose that the words, " Town House, in Boston," were inserted in the writ, through inadvertence ; and thus much, at least, may certainly be inferred, from their being inserted ; that at the time of enacting said law, it was the common understanding and consent of all the branches of the Court, that the Town House, in Boston, was the most proper and convenient place for holding the General Assembly ; and that it would always be held there, extraordinary cases excepted.

Especially, considering that the General Court had, before, by a perpetual act of the 5th of William and Mary, made provision for upholding and repairing the Town House, in Boston, for the holding of the General Assembly; and that it hath generally been the understanding and sense of the three branches of the General Assembly ever since, that the Town House, in Boston, was the established place for holding the General Court, appears by their rebuilding, with the province monies, the Town House, in Boston, when it was consumed by fire ; and their procuring at Boston, an elegant mansion house, for the residence of the Governor ; and also by their repairing and upholding them, for the same purpose, to this day.

But if it could be admitted that the above mentioned act, of the 10th of William, is not conceived, in such express terms, as to abridge the King's prerogative, and that the right of assigning the place for the sitting of the General Assembly, still remains a prerogative of the Crown, at the discretion of the Governor of this province; yet he can by no means be justified, or excused, in holding the General Assembly out of the town of Boston, contrary to their entreaties and remonstrances, to their manifest injury, and when no one good purpose can be served hereby.

The prerogative is a discretionary power, in some instances, vested in the King, for the good of the subject. " It extends not to do an injury ; for being created for the benefit of the people, it cannot be exerted to their prejudice." But the holding the General Assembly at Cambridge, is greatly prejudicial to the whole province, as well as to the Members of the Court. It deprives the General Assembly of the house provided for their accommodation ; and, at the same time, obliges us to be dependant on the owners of private property, for the place of holding the Assembly.

It, in a great measure, deprives the Assembly of the benefit of the public offices, and records of the province ; and thereby very much obstructs and retards the public business.

It also, in a great degree, prevents a communication between the Members of the House of Representatives and their constituents ; and in many cases, at this critical time, renders them unable to guide their measures by the sentiments of their principals ; and it is inconvenient to the Members, as they cannot be so well accommodated, as in the place where the Assembly has been wont to be held.

There have been some few instances of the General Court's being held out of the town of Boston ; but they were all in extraordinary cases, when the necessity of the removal of the Court was notorious, or when, from some special emergency, all were convinced of the expediency of the measure, and tacitly consenting to it, as in the instance under the administration of Governor Belcher. Excepting one instance, in the year 1729, when Governor Burnet, in a wanton and arbitrary manner, removed the

Court to Salem ; evidently designed, by that constraint, to force them to make a perpetual establishment of the Governor's salary, and thereby to relinquish an essential right of the Commons of this province ; and he gave it, as one reason for his extraordinary conduct, that " the inhabitants of Boston used endeavors to work on the minds of the Representatives, to bring them to their way of thinking ;" thereby insinuating, that the Representatives of the people ought not to be influenced by the reasonings and arguments of the people without doors. But that arbitrary and injurious removal of the General Assembly from its ancient seat, favoring more of despotism than a due exertion of the prerogative of a British Prince, will never be mentioned as a constitutional precedent, by any friend to the British constitution, especially as the House of Representatives did then, to their great honor, remonstrate and protest against it.

Wherefore, inasmuch as the General Assembly of this province, notwithstanding the entreaties, remonstrances and protest of the House of Representatives, to the contrary, was the last year continued at Cambridge ; and now, a new Assembly is convened ; and against the remonstrance of this House, to the great inconvenience of its Members, and the injury of the province, without any necessity, or the least probability of serving one good purpose, is constrained to hold the session at Cambridge :

Resolved, As the opinion of this House, that upon a supposition, that it still remains a prerogative of the Crown, in the discretion of the Commander in Chief of this province, in any case of necessity or special emergency, to remove the General Assembly out of the Town House, in Boston, yet the convening and holding the Assembly, in Cambridge, is, in this instance, a very great grievance.

And, as his Honor the Commander in Chief, has not thought fit to communicate any reason for the convening and holding this Assembly, in Cambridge ; but that he has been instructed by his Majesty, so to do ; and being requested to lay before this House a copy of such instructions, he has declined : The House are utterly at a loss to conceive any good reason, for thus convening and holding the Assembly here.

And as the prerogatives of the Crown, however salutary, when they are exerted for the good of the people, have the most pernicious tendency, when exerted to their prejudice ; and such exertions, unchecked, may overthrow the constitution itself ; we cannot view the present situation of the General Assembly, in any other light, than as truly alarming. And it is become our indispensable duty, as the guardians of the people's rights, now to make a constitutional stand.

And, as the former House of Assembly, rather than maintain any controversy with the Lieutenant Governor, submitted to the grievance, in hopes that it would not be continued, but be speedily redressed : yet, inasmuch as the prayers, entreaties, remonstrances, and protests of this, and the former House, have, hitherto, effected no relief; and the proceeding to public business, at Cambridge, may be construed as a tacit submission, and may render abortive all future measures to obtain a redress of this grievance :

Resolved, That, notwithstanding there are matters now lying before the Assembly, of very great importance, and which we are desirous of entering upon and completing ; nevertheless, it is by no means expedient to proceed to business, while the General Assembly is thus constrained to hold their session out of the town of Boston.

Resolved, That his Honor the Lieutenant Governor be addressed, to remove the General Assembly to its ancient and usual seat, the Town House, in Boston.

MESSAGE

FROM THE HOUSE OF REPRESENTATIVES TO THE LIEUTENANT GOVERNOR, JUNE 7, 1770.

May it please your Honor,

THE House of Representatives have taken into consideration the state of the province, with regard to the moving the General Assembly out of the town of Boston ; and, by a majority of 96, out of 102 Members present, have resolved, that the convening, holding, and keeping the great and General Court out of the said town of Boston, to the manifest injury of the province, and the great inconvenience of the Members of both Houses, without any necessity, or the least probability of serving any one good purpose, notwithstanding the prayers, entreaties, remonstrances, and protestations of this and the former House to the contrary, is a very great grievance ; and that it is by no means expedient to proceed to business, while the General Assembly is thus constrained to hold their session out of the town of Boston. And as there are matters now lying before the Assembly, of very great importance, which they are very desirous of entering upon, and completing, they humbly pray that your Honor would be pleased to remove the great and General Court to its ancient, usual, and only convenient seat, the Town House, in Boston.

[The committee who prepared the above, were, S. Adams, J. Adams, J. Hancock, Col. Warren, and S. Leonard.—J. Adams, Esq. was this year elected a Member from Boston, in the room of J. Bowdoin, Esq. chosen into the Council.]

MESSAGE

FROM THE LIEUTÉNANT GOVERNOR TO THE HOUSE OF REPRESENTA-
TIVES, JUNE 7, 1770.

Gentlemen of the House of Representatives,

I THINK it my misfortune, that so great a majority of your
House, as 96 in 102, should appear to differ from me, in sentiment,
upon any public measure. I have told you, that I have not the
least doubt of the legality of my adjourning or proroguing the
Court to any town in the province. The place, as well as time of
its meeting, is left to the Governor. The Governor is the servant
of the King, and by his commission, is to govern the province, according to the charter, and according to such instructions, as he
shall, from time to time, receive from the King. Without a violation of my instructions, I cannot now remove the Court from
Cambridge to Boston ; I am afraid of incurring his Majesty's displeasure, if I should do it. I am as sensible, as you can be, that
there are many important matters lying before the Court. I am
also sensible, that the necessity of their being acted upon, is so
great, that, even on your own principles, you may be as fully justified, in proceeding to act upon them, as the House of the last
year could be justified for the business they did, or as you will be
able to justify yourselves, for what you have already done, the present session.

Does it not appear to you, of necessity, that the act of the province, which requires the Treasurer to issue his warrant for levying a tax of more than eighty thousand pounds, should be repealed
in part ? Will it be safe for you to leave Castle William and Fort
Pownal without any establishment ? Are you willing, the act for
limitation of suits at law, which has been often suspended, should
now take place ? To omit the mention of many other laws, which
I believe you judge necessary to be continued or revived. Would
you be willing, the enemies of our happy constitution should have
it in their power to say, that when the Governor had caused the
General Court to be convened, pursuant to the powers reserved to
him by the charter, the House of Representatives refused to do
business, because he had convened it at Cambridge ; and, in their
opinion, without any necessity, or the least probability of serving
any good purpose ? Would not the construction of my conduct be,
if I should carry you to Boston, after this message to me, that I
had given up, to the House of Representatives, the power reserved
by the charter to the Crown.

In 1747, or 1748, when the Court House, in Boston, had been
consumed by fire, the major part of the then House of Representatives was averse to rebuilding it, and disposed to build a house for

the General Court, in some town in the country. Being then one of the Representatives of Boston, I used my influence, in every way I could, with propriety, in favor of rebuilding the Court House, in Boston ; but finally could prevail thus far, and no farther. The House, upon the question whether a grant should be made, for rebuilding the Court House, was equally divided ; and I, being then Speaker of the House, gave my casting vote in favor of the town. I have still a very good affection for the town of Boston. I was then the servant of the town, and know I was acting the mind of my constituents. I am still satisfied I did my duty. I now consider myself as the servant of the Crown. I know his Majesty's pleasure, and I am doing my duty in acting according to it ; and, if you should finally refuse to do business at Cambridge, which I hope you will not, all the ill consequences will be attributed to you, and not to me.   **T. HUTCHINSON.**

REASONS

OF THE HOUSE OF REPRESENTATIVES, FOR ADHERING TO THEIR RESOLU-
TIONS OF THE SIXTH, THAT IT WAS NOT EXPEDIENT TO PROCEED TO
BUSINESS, WHILE THE GENERAL ASSEMBLY WAS HELD OUT OF THE
TOWN HOUSE, IN BOSTON, ADOPTED JUNE 12, 1770.

At present, the House waive any further observations on the legality of convening, holding, and keeping the General Assembly out of the Town House, in Boston. The " power of calling Parliaments in England, as to precise time, place, and duration, is an acknowledged prerogative of the King; but still it is with this trust, that it shall be made use of for the good of the nation, as the exigency of the times, and variety of occasion, shall require." Wisdom and goodness will always direct to such places for them to assemble in, as shall be most subservient to the public good, and best suit the ends of Parliament. " Prerogative is a power to act according to discretion, for the public good :" but when mistake or flattery have prevailed with weak princes, to make use of this power for private ends of their own, and not for the public good, the people have, sometimes, by express laws, got the prerogative determined, in those points wherein they found a disadvantage from it.

It has been found, by long experience, that the Town House, in Boston, is the only convenient place for holding the General Assembly of the province. No alteration can, therefore, be made, unless some occurrence of times, or change of affairs, shall require it. Without those, the convening and holding the Assembly in any other place, is a wanton exercise of power, which ought to be withstood; a grievance which ought to be redressed. While Parliaments are duly cautious, they will forever be watchful, lest a power be exerted to the injury of the public, under the pretext of prerogative. Such is the imperfection of human nature, as to render discretionary power, however necessary, always in a greater or less degree dangerous; and the wickedness of men has very often prompted them to make an ill use of it. If it should be admitted that the Governor of this province has still, by law, the power of convening, holding and keeping the General Court in any town, out of Boston, yet the House have as clear a right, by law, to inquire into the exercise of this power, and to judge for themselves, whether it be wisely and beneficially, or imprudently and arbitrarily, exercised. And it is their duty, as well as their right, to remonstrate against all undue and oppressive exertions of a legal, as much as against a claim and exercise of an usurped prerogative. There are prerogatives in the Crown, which may be exercised to the destruction of the constitution, and the ruin of the people.

To consider more closely the prerogative now claimed and exercised by the Lieutenant Governor. In one of his messages to the House, he says, " by the charter, the Governor has the sole power of adjourning and proroguing the General Assembly; there is no limitation of time or place." And in another, " I have not the least doubt of the legality of my adjourning and proroguing the Court to any town in the province. The place, as well as time of meeting, is left to the Governor." Admitting this to be true, it is in the power of the Governor to carry the Assembly from one extreme part of the province to another, adjourning them from place to place, till the year expires, or perhaps till he shall have worried them into a compliance with some arbitrary mandate, to the ruin of their own and their constituents liberties. If this would be legal, it would be attended with consequences as fatal, as if it were illegal. None, therefore, can doubt, but it would be the duty of the two Houses, firmly and earnestly to remonstrate against it; to make a stand, if their remonstrances should prove ineffectual, and refuse to attend him, in his absurd career. The supposition now made, is only carrying the doctrine to its just and necessary consequences. The present case is the same in kind, though not in degree. The Assembly is removed from its ancient, usual, and only convenient place. This may be the first stage in an intended circuit; without one reason assigned, or any good one conceivable by this House. Indeed, we are told, it is in obedience to instructions; but we are not to be indulged with a sight of such instructions. The Lieutenant Governor has expressly said, that he is restrained from making a copy of them public. Such a severity has awakened and fixed our attention. It is, indeed, alarming; for it is not usual for a well advised prince to withhold from his subjects the grounds he may have for the exercise of a prerogative, which regards only the administration of the civil government.

His Honor is pleased to say, that he cannot remove the Court to Boston, without a violation of those instructions: but as it is impossible for any man, more especially at the distance of three thousand miles, to foresee the fittest place for holding the Assembly, or the emergencies which may render it impracticable for it to be held in any particular place, it is rather to be supposed he is mistaken, when he apprehends such instructions to be indispensable. And he further says, that as, by his commission, he is to govern the province according to the charter, as well as according to such instructions as he shall, from time to time, receive, it is natural to conclude that he is still left to act with his own discretion; and that, when circumstances take place to render it impossible, consistent with the public good, that the Assembly should meet at one certain place, or more eligible for it to be held in any other, he may act his own judgment therein, especially considering, that, by the charter, he is expressly vested with the power of adjourning and proroguing the General Assembly, as he shall, from time to time, judge necessary. But if there be such peremptory and absolute instructions, we have reason to conclude, that the ministry thereby intended to insult the General Assembly, and make them meanly compliant for time to come. Past experience serves to increase this apprehension. The Assembly, the last year, suffered the greatest indignity; surrounded, while sitting, by a military guard, with cannon at their doors, to affront or awe them; and when they remonstrated against the high breach of their privilege, they, and not the soldiers, were made to give way. Can freedom and dignity, then, exist in an Assembly, that can tamely brook such usage ? Would it not be betraying the constitution, and the rights of this Assembly, to proceed to business, while we are thus constrained to hold the session here ? Besides, is there nothing further to apprehend ? If the Assembly should, in this situation, proceed to do business, act uprightly, and according to their consciences, and thereby give further umbrage to a despotic Minister; may they not expect to be convened, held and kept in a state still more humiliating and disgraceful, until they shall become sufficiently ductile and obsequious ? Indeed, we cannot find that ever a Parliament was prorogued in England, or summoned to any place, for the sake of punishing the Members, or putting them to any inconvenience. This is not the method of managing an English Parliament. They have, sometimes, even refused to be dissolved, till they have done the business of the nation; and, at other times, they have declined to obey the summons of the King, by his writ, to attend, when called for a purpose they disliked, and to a place where they thought they should be under any awe or restraint. As particularly, in the 28th of Henry VI.

when it was resolved, that the conduct of the Duke of Suffolk should undergo a national inquiry. "The Queen, apprehensive of the danger her favorite was in, from such a procedure, did all she could to prevent it ; first, by endeavoring to hinder a Parliament from being called ; and next, when she could not avoid that, by having it summoned to meet at Leicester ; where, in a country town, she imagined her numerous attendants might overawe the Members. But the Lords and Commons, who knew they were safe, under the protection of the city of London, positively refused to meet at all, unless they were appointed to come to Westminster."

His Honor mentions, as the House had done before, the important matters lying before the Court, and the necessity of their being acted upon. But these important matters may, to much better purpose, as well as with greater convenience, be acted upon in the Town House, in Boston, where the records of the province are kept ; and besides, the greater the importance of the business is, the stronger is the reason why the Assembly should act upon it in the metropolis, where there is usually a concourse of the people from all parts of the province, whose reasonings and arguments, upon matters of public importance, ought forever to be regarded. Wise Parliaments have always reaped great advantage from the wisdom of the people, without doors ; and have frequently been adjourned to a distant time, when such matters have been brought on, that they might have the opportunity of consulting their constituents.

His Honor, in his message, has introduced an anecdote, concerning his own conduct, when Speaker of the House, in 1747 or 1748 ; but to what purpose, is not easy to discover, or conceive. He seems to insinuate, without affirming, that his own judgment then was, and still is, in favor of the sentiments of the present House, that the Town House, in Boston, is the most convenient seat of government. But if this was not his meaning, his conduct at that time, whether it proceeded from his own opinion, or was merely in compliance with the minds of his constituents, which he has been pleased to leave ambiguous, (as he has, whether his present conduct is merely in obedience to instructions, against his own judgment, or whether his own judgment is conformable to his instructions,) is a full justification of the House, as far as his Honor's example can justify them ; for the House are well assured, that the minds of their constituents, at this day, are, that the seat of government should be in Boston, and not elsewhere.

Another insinuation in his Honor's message, is, that heretofore the province has been doubtful whether Boston was the most convenient seat of government, or not.

But we have great reason to question, whether one half, or one quarter of the province, ever thought, in earnest, of building a State House, out of Boston, notwithstanding the division of the House, in 1747 or 1748, upon the question, whether a grant should be made for rebuilding the Town House, in Boston, or not. The diversity of opinions upon the question in the House, at that time, arose, as we conceive, from a concurrence of many other causes, which we have not time now to enumerate, and the party who were against the grant, were, most of them, as we have reason to believe, against it from other particular views, motives and designs, not from any opinion that Boston was not the best seat of government. But, had the House then been fully for removing the seat of government into the country, we are convinced that many alarming events and occurrences have happened, since that time, which have placed the expediency, if not the necessity, of holding the General Court in Boston, beyond all dispute.

We are also told, that " we may be as fully justified, even on our own principles, in proceeding to act upon these matters of public importance, as the House of the last year could be justified for the business they did, or, as we shall be able to justify ourselves, by what we have already done the present session." Thus we find one instance of a compliance of a former House, makes way for a new demand. ' The last House submitted to all the inconvenience and hardships to themselves, and injuries to the province, which arose by their sitting at Cambridge ; and their condescension is now quoted as a precedent, and an argument for our submitting to the grievance, also. This certainly affords a good reason for the House to adhere to their resolution, to prevent the establishment of such a precedent. Besides, the former House yielded to it, conceiving it as only a temporary evil ; but now there is great reason to apprehend a fixed design, either entirely to change the seat of government, or, by moving the Assembly from place to place, to harass, and bring them into a compliance with arbitrary and despotic purposes. With regard to the business we have already done, " the present session," namely, the election of Counsellors, the House are of opinion, that they can fully justify themselves therein, consistent with this resolution. The Counsellors are to be elected according to the terms of the charter, " yearly, once in every year ;" and it has been the invariable usage, as it has been thought to be agreeable to the spirit of the charter, to proceed to that business on the last Wednesday in May. The House, therefore, proceeded to it on that day, though with great precaution, that " the enemies of our constitution," who are sedulous to take all advantages against it, might not " have it in their power to say," that by an omission, we had forfeited our invaluable charter. It was, therefore, viewed as of absolute necessity, to enter upon that business, at that time ; though it could not be done in the ancient and proper place of holding the General Assembly. But no business, now before us, can be of such absolute necessity, as that the omitting it, will endanger the constitution. On the contrary, the danger to the constitution now lies in proceeding to business, under the present grievance ; and, therefore, we do our duty, finally to refuse to proceed to business in Cambridge; as judging it the least likely to be attended with ill consequences to ourselves, our constituents and posterity.

It is further to be observed, that the House have no other power, or check, whereby to restrain the undue exercise or abuse of the prerogative. It is presumed that the Commons ought to be as free and independent as any other part of the Legislature; because the democratical branch is, at least, as important to the people and the constitution, as the monarchical or aristocratical; and they have, at least, as clear a right to judge of the proper time for them to do their part of the business of the province, as the Governor has to judge of his. The Governors of the province have, of late years, refused to consent to any act, or business, whatever, until they have had a grant for their support; and for this, they have pleaded an instruction. Here, therefore, is an example of a resolution, in the King's Ministers and servants, that no business shall be done, until the people shall exert their prerogative, in a manner agreeable to the Crown : and the prerogative of the people to grant money, in their own time, to raise it in their own way, and by their own means, and to appropriate it for such purposes as they shall judge proper, is surely much clearer and more indisputable, than that of the Governor of the province to convene and hold the General Assembly in any other place beside the Town House, in Boston.

His Honor has been pleased to mention divers matters to be acted upon, which, we readily acknowledge, are necessary and important; and it is still our earnest desire to proceed to the consideration of them without any unnecessary delay. The further suspension of the act for limitation of law suits, and a proper establishment for Castle William and Fort Pownal, demand our attention; and the repealing, in part, the act which requires the Treasurer to issue his warrants for levying a tax of more than eighty thousand pounds, is of particular importance at this time, when the embarrassments of the trade, and other grievous hardships the people are made to suffer, would render it difficult for them to bear so great a burden; but we have, notwithstanding, reason to believe, that they had much rather be subject even to the immediate payment of that whole sum, distressing as it would be, than to concede to so pernicious a precedent; and to have the General Assembly hereafter controlled by the mandates of a Minister, and made to submit to measures, which will be much more injurious to them, and dangerous to posterity. If, therefore, his Honor should finally refuse to remove the Assembly to the Town House, in Boston, (which we hope he will not,) while there can be no necessity for holding us here, the world will judge to whom the ill consequences of it must be attributable.

[The above reasons were ordered to be laid before the Council.]

ADDRESS

OF THE COUNCIL TO HIS HONOR THE LIEUTENANT GOVERNOR,
JUNE 12, 1770.

May it please your Honor,

It would give us great pleasure to proceed upon the public business, agreeable to the recommendation in your Honor's speech, at the opening of the present session. But, as in consequence of a motion, made in Council, that your Honor should be requested to adjourn the General Court to Boston, you informed the Board you could not do it consistently with your instructions, it is first incumbent on us to observe that the province charter ordains, " that the Governor, for the time being, shall have full power and authority, from time to time, as he shall judge necessary, to adjourn, prorogue and dissolve the great and General Court." This power is a full power. It is wholly in the Governor, and to be exercised as he shall judge necessary. It cannot, therefore, be subject to the control of instructions. Such a power, and such a subjection of it, are incompatible. The moment it is subjected, it ceases to be a full power ; and the Governor is no longer the judge, with regard to the exercise of it. It is, therefore, a palpable contradiction, to suppose it under such control ; and, in fact, judging of it by the charter only, it is controlable by nothing but the convenience and safety of the General Court, and the general utility of the province. For those ends, that power was lodged by the Crown, exclusive of itself, in the Governor solely. True it is, that no mention is made of the place of such adjournment or prorogation. The same is also true, as to the time ; but they are both necessarily included in the idea of adjourning and proroguing. And if these last be wholly and exclusively in the Governor, which is very evident, the time and place must be also.

There is nothing absurd or unreasonable in this construction of the above cited clause of the charter. For it is impossible, in the nature of things, that the Crown, at the distance of a thousand leagues, should be able, understandingly, and with a knowledge of present circumstances, upon which the fitness of such a measure depends, to exert that power. It is, therefore, fit and necessary, that such exclusive power should be vested in its Representative here ; and the said clause does, in fact, make such an investiture.

It cannot be said, " that this sole power is intended for no other purpose, than to exclude both the other branches of the Court from any share in it ;" because there is not a word in the charter, that even intimates such an intention ; and because the clause, giving the power, is expressed in terms, vesting that power solely and exclusively in the Governor.

With regard to the convening the General Court, the charter ordains and grants, "that there shall, and may be convened, held and kept by the Governor, for the time being, upon every last Wednesday in the month of May, of every year forever, and at all such other times, as the Governor shall think fit and appoint, a great and General Court."

The time of convening in May, is fixed ; and, therefore, not alterable by instructions. Other times of convening, are to be such as the Governor shall think fit. He is made the judge of the fitness of such other times, which, therefore, in regard to time, excludes the control of instructions ; as to place, although the charter be silent, the convening must have relation to place, as well as time. The right of judging of the latter, implies the same right in respect to the former ; and the reasons for both are the same, as well as for adjourning, proroguing and dissolving the Court, which, it is evident, are exclusively in the Governor. The power is the same, as to all those particulars ; and it is fit it should be so ; for the Governor, being in the province, must have the best opportunities of knowing what the general convenience, safety and utility require. It must be reasonable, therefore, to suppose, that such an exclusive power was intended by the charter to be lodged in him ; and in fact it is, by the said clauses, very perspicuously so lodged. Hence it is, (admitting the act, for establishing the form of the writ for calling a General Court, to be out of the question,) that after long experience had determined Boston to be the most convenient and fit place for the meeting of the General Court, all the Governors of the province, except Mr. Burnet, from the date of the charter, to the last year, have convened the General Court at Boston ; excepting in a few cases, wherein the safety of the General Court, or the public utility, made it proper to convene the Court elsewhere. And in those cases, the removal of the General Court were justified, by the respective reasons for them. "The power of calling Parliaments, in England, as to precise time, place, and duration, is certainly a prerogative of the King ; but still with this trust, that it shall be used for the good of the nation, as the exigencies of the times, and variety of occasions, shall require." The power of calling the General Court, in like manner, for the good of the province, is, by the charter, vested in the Governor, for the time being. But, considering the several acts of the General Court, whereby a Court House, which has been several times rebuilt, for accommodating the General Court, and a commodious and elegant dwelling house, and other accommodations for the residence of the King's Governor, have been provided at Boston, at a great public expense. Considering, also, "the act for establishing the form of the writ, and precept for calling a great and General Court," whereby it appears, that in the writ, precept and return, the Town House, in Boston, is mentioned to be the place where the General Court is appointed to be convened, held and kept. The proceedings also of Governor Shute and the Assembly, in 1721, whereby it appears the Governor declared, that the adjournment from Boston should not be drawn into precedent; and a resolve was passed by the whole Court, validating and confirming the acts of the Court; which proceeding clearly manifest their apprehensions that Boston was the place established by law, for the Governor's convening and holding the General Court: When these acts are considered, if they do not amount to a strictly legal establishment of the place of convening and holding the General Court, they at least furnish, in our humble opinion, a rule, by which the Governor ought to conduct himself in that regard; and from which he may not depart, but in cases of exigency.

When exigencies happen, of which every one can judge, they afford a sufficient reason for deviating from the rule; and the deviation will not, nor can be, complained of.

Governor Burnet's conduct, in convening the General Court out of Boston, cannot be deemed an acknowledged or constitutional precedent to justify a similar conduct; because it was not acquiesced in, but remonstrated against by the House of Representatives; and because it was not founded on the only reason, on which the prerogative of the Crown can be justly founded, the good of the community.

In Governor Belcher's time, when in consequence of the instructions, he removed the General Court to Salisbury, the removal was for " the more convenient carrying into execution a commission for settling the line between this province and New Hampshire."

Here convenience was the reason for the removal. It was convenient, that the Assemblies of both provinces, which were then under the administration of the same Governor, should be as near each other, as might be, for the settlement of the line between the two provinces; and it was not only convenient, but the general good of both, required such a settlement.

As long as prerogative is exercised for the real good of the community, which the community must feel and will always acknowledge, it is seldom examined whether that exercise be strictly legal, or not; but that omission does not take away the right of examining, whenever prerogative is exercised for a different purpose.

In the present case, when every reason arising from convenience, safety and utility, remonstrates and urges the fitness of the Courts' sitting in Boston, the convening and keeping it elsewhere, contrary to the mind of the two Houses, and the province in general, we humbly apprehend is an exercise of the prerogative, if not against law, yet certainly against ancient usage, and unwarranted by the reason, which supports all prerogative, namely, the public good.

We are sensible " the Governor is the servant of the King, and by his commission, is to govern the province according to charter, and according to such instructions as he shall, from time to time, re-

29

ceive from the King." Those instructions, however, must be understood to be such as do not militate with, or in any degree vacate the charter : otherwise the charter would be annihilable at pleasure : from whence it would follow, that it neither was, nor is, in the power of the Crown to grant any charter whatever, vesting in the grantees any durable privileges, much less, such as are granted of this province, which are perpetual. But we hold it to be clear law, that the Crown had, and hath, such a power ; and it is equally clear, that their late Majesties, King William and Queen Mary, for themselves, their heirs and successors, did, by their charter, in the third year of their reign, grant to the inhabitants of this province, and to their successors thenceforth forever, all the powers and privileges in the said charter mentioned ; one of which is, that the Governor, for the time being, shall convene, adjourn, prorogue and dissolve the General Court, as in the two clauses above quoted ; which clauses, for the reasons aforesaid, we humbly apprehend, vest in the Governor, for the benefit of said inhabitants, an exclusive right for those purposes ; and therefore, that no instructions can supersede or control that right, which is a beneficiary grant to the people, without injuring them, and so far vacating the charter. Your Honor has observed very justly, "that his Majesty never intended his instructions should supersede or control the law." This is and must be true also, with respect to the charter ; because it is the great law of the constitution ; and is the foundation of the laws of the province ; and because his Majesty is just ; has a paternal affection for his people ; and never intended his instructions should subject them to any unnecessary inconvenience, much less, infringe their rights.

We, therefore, earnestly request, that for his Majesty's service, the ease and happiness of your Honor's administration, the convenience of the General Court, the utility and satisfaction of the province in general, in pursuance of the intention and spirit of diverse acts and laws of the province, pursuant to the usage (under both charters,) of more than a hundred years standing ; but more especially, pursuant to the full and exclusive powers vested in the Governor by the present charter, your Honor will please to adjourn or prorogue the great and General Court to its ancient and constitutional place, the Town House, in Boston.

[The committee of Council, who reported this address, were, W. Brattle, J. Bowdoin, Col. Otis, R. Tyler, and S. Dexter.]

MESSAGE

Gentlemen of the Council,

You seem, as far as I can collect from your address, to decline proceeding in your Legislative capacity, upon public business. You have expressed your sense, in very strong terms, that I ought not to have caused the General Court to convene at Cambridge, in consequence of instructions; and that it is necessary to the public good, that it should be convened at Boston.

I have "thought fit, and have appointed," that the General Court should convene at Cambridge. I have done no more than what the charter authorizes me to do. If I have done it merely in consequence of instructions, and from a sense of my obligations to conform to what appears to me to be his Majesty's pleasure, I shall, notwithstanding, be justified; for the Crown, neither by the charter, nor in any other way, hath ever divested itself of the right of instructing the Governor in what manner this power, delegated to him, shall be exercised. The practice of giving instructions, which began with the charter, and which has continued four score years, I think should have been sufficient to prevent the Council from taking exception to them.

If, without regard to any signification of his Majesty's pleasure, I had, in my own judgment, thought fit and necessary that the Court should be convened at Cambridge, it would now be to no purpose for me to tell you so; for although you admit it to be a part of the prerogative, that I should convene the Court at such time and place as I judge to be most fit, yet you have a reserve; for you have explained away all the prerogative, and removed it from the King and his representative, and made yourselves and the people the judges, when it shall be exercised; and, in the present case, have determined that it is not fit it should be exercised.

I will not engage in a dispute with you upon these points. I think it enough for me to tell you, that I have not the least doubt of the right of the Crown to control the Governor, by instructions, or other signification of the royal pleasure; that I believe it to be for the benefit of the people, that a Governor should be under this control; that the present set of instructions, for the Governors of this province, are wisely framed for the advantage of the province; that I have no instructions at present, nor have I reason to expect any, militating with the charter, nor with any law of the province: I must, therefore, adhere to them.

As his Majesty's Council for the province, I shall consult you upon every occasion; and your advice will have great weight with me. But I must finally judge for myself of the fitness and expediency of exercising the powers devolved upon me, by virtue of my commission.

I am not able to comply with your request, to adjourn or prorogue the Court to Boston. I therefore earnestly recommend to you to proceed, without further delay, upon the public business of the province.   T. HUTCHINSON.

———

MESSAGE

FROM THE HOUSE OF REPRESENTATIVES TO THE LIEUTENANT
GOVERNOR, JUNE 15, 1770.

May it please your Honor,

THE House of Representatives beg leave to remind your Honor, that, by their message of the 7th instant, they made known to you their resolution, that it was not expedient for them to proceed to business, out of their ancient, usual, and only convenient place, the Town House, in Boston ; and prayed your Honor would be pleased to remove this General Assembly to that place. Your Honor, in answer, was pleased to express your hopes, that we would not finally refuse to do business in Cambridge. We, therefore, take this opportunity to assure you, that having had further time maturely to consider the matter, we are still determined to abide by the resolution, and are ready to answer for all the ill consequences that can be attributed to us. Surely you cannot think it for the honor of the House, without any declared or conceivable reason, to be kept here, dependant upon private persons even for shelter, in a manner deforced from the House, provided and established for the Assembly, at a great expense to the people, which now stands entirely useless and solitary.

We again, in duty to his Majesty, and in faithfulness to our constituents, make a tender of ourselves, as ready to transact the public business; provided your Honor will remove us to the aforesaid ancient and established seat of government.

If you are still determined not to gratify the request of the two Houses, in removing the Assembly there, you will please to consider, whether it will tend to the cultivation of that harmony in the Legislature, which all good men desire, to continue us sitting. The Members of this House, unwilling that their constituents should be put to an unnecessary expense, are desirous of leave to retire to their several homes.

[The committee who prepared the message of June 15, were, Mr. Cushing, (the Speaker,) Maj. Hawley, Mr. S. Adams, Capt. Sheaffe, and Mr. J. Adams.]

MESSAGE

Gentlemen of the House of Representatives,

I HAVE reason to expect, every day, letters from his Majesty's Secretary of State, and it appears to me probable that they may contain matters of importance to the government. I, therefore, think it necessary the Court should continue sitting some time longer, that I may have an opportunity of communicating them, so far as I may be required or allowed to do it.

T. HUTCHINSON.

MESSAGE

May it please your Honor,

WE have attentively considered your Honor's message in answer to our address, and we beg leave to make a few observations upon it.

The charter of the province, as it creates and defines the powers of its Governor, is the only rule (where the province law is silent) by which to judge of those powers. It is a compact between the Crown and this people, to be mutually observed and kept. There is no reservation in it that instructions shall be a rule of government to the Governor. No such instructions, therefore, can be a rule to him in cases wherein they alter those powers, or in any other way affect the charter. This inference, we apprehend, your Honor will allow to be just in general ; and we think you will allow it to be just also with regard to the Governor's power of adjourning, proroguing and dissolving the General Court. For, although we particularly quoted the clause of the charter, which relates to that power, and have delivered our sentiments pretty fully upon it; and it appears clearly, that it vests in the Governor an exclusive right to exercise that power, yet your Honor wholly confines your observations to the power of convening the General Court; which induces us to think you are satisfied the Governor has an exclusive right, relative to the adjourning and proroguing; and, consequently, that it is not controlable by the instructions. It is, therefore, needless, with regard to the power of convening the

Court, to say any thing concerning it, in addition to what we have said in our address, as the object of our present desire is, that you would please to adjourn or prorogue the Court to Boston.

Your Honor is pleased to tell us, that "the practice of giving instructions, which began with the charter, and has continued near four score years, should have been sufficient to prevent the Council from taking exceptions to them." Our address furnished no occasion for this observation; for the instructions, therein referred to, were not instructions in general; but such only, as we apprehend, militated with the charter. On such instructions, when made the rule of government, it is the duty of the Council, in a becoming manner, to signify their mind, even though such instructions had begun with the charter, and continued to the present time. And such a signification of their mind, we humbly apprehend, can never subject the Council to his Majesty's displeasure.

Your Honor informs us, that, "although we admit it to be a part of the prerogative, that you should convene the Court at such time and place as you judge fit, yet we have a reserve; for we have explained away all the prerogative, removed it from the King and his Representative, and made ourselves and the people the judges, when it shall be exercised; and, in the present case, have determined that it is not fit it should be exercised."

We wish your Honor had quoted the clauses on which you ground the several declarations contained in the foregoing paragraph. Had this been done, you would not have found, that they justified all of them. We do not admit the convening of the Court on the last Wednesday of May, yearly, to be a part of the prerogative, in such a sense as to make the convening of it, on that day, doubtful. We have made no reserve, but what is warranted by the charter; by several laws of the province; by ancient usage; and by the nature and design of the institution. We have not explained away all the prerogative, or any part of it; but shewn, in the first place, what it is, according to the charter; and, in the next, that those laws, with certain proceedings of the General Court, if they do not amount to a strictly legal establishment of the place of convening and holding the General Court, at least furnish, in our humble opinion, a rule, by which the Governor ought to conduct himself; and from which he may not depart, but in cases of emergency. We have not removed the prerogative from the King and his Representative; but, on the contrary, shewn, that it has been vested by the King, in his Representative, to be exercised for the good of the people, which is the great end of prerogative. We have not made ourselves and the people, either jointly, or severally, the judges when it shall be exercised; but, on the contrary, in the fullest and most express manner, have declared it to be exercised as the King's Representative shall judge it fit, consistent with the rule aforesaid. But, if there were no such rule to guide his judgment, he would not be lawless in this case; nor could make mere will and pleasure, the rule, (if they can be called a rule) of his judging. For, by the very terms, and by the reason which ought to influence all his determinations, there is to be a fitness in his judging; a fitness arising from convenience, safety, and utility ; agreeable to which, it would be his duty to act : and, therefore, although we have given our opinion what the general convenience require ; and that, in the present case, they require the removal of the General Court to Boston ; yet, we have not made ourselves, nor the people, the judges in this matter; but, on the contrary, have declared in the address, to which your message is an answer, that the Governor of the province is the sole judge. And, therefore, as we could not suppose your Honor has designedly misrepresented our address, you will give us leave to say, you have greatly mistaken it.

We are sorry to have reason to say, that in this clause of the message, there is discoverable, not only a disposition unkind and unfriendly to the Council, but a want of candor and justice.

Is it kind or friendly—does it consist with candor and justice to represent, that we first admit the convening of the Court to be part of the prerogative fully vested in the Governor ; that we then make reserves concerning it; that we explain it wholly away; that we remove it from the King and his Representative ; and that we make ourselves and the people the judges, when it ahall be exercised ?

If your Honor intended to bring upon the Council the displeasure of his Majesty, and, in consequence of it, procure an alteration of its constitution, you could not do it more effectually, than by such a representation. But, on examining, it will be evident, that there is no foundation for it ; either in the address, or in any other act of the Council. And, therefore, such a representation is not only unkind and unjust to the Council ; but, if we had let it pass unnoticed, might have proved injurious to the charter rights of the province.

It is with regret we make these observations; but we are constrained to it by the justice due to ourselves, and by the claim the province has upon us to defend the constitution of its government. We have the warmest sentiments of duty and loyalty to his Majesty, which will stimulate us, on the one hand, to defend the just prerogative of the Crown; and, on the other, to promote, as far as we can, the end and design of such prerogative, the good of the people.

As your Honor has not condescended to give the Board the reasons on which you ground your opinion, concerning the efficacy of instructions to control the Governor's power of convening the General Court; as you are wholly silent about his power of adjourning and proroguing the Court, and have not pointed out the insufficiency of the reasons by which we have endeavored to support our own opinion on those points, we are under a necessity, till we have further light, to continue in the same opinion.

In the mean time, we beg leave to offer a few observations on the remaining part of your Honor's message. It informs us you " will not engage in a dispute with us upon these points; that you think it *enough for you to tell us* that you have not the least doubt of the right of the Crown to control the Governor by instructions, or other signification of the royal pleasure; and, that you believe it to be for the benefit of the people, that the Governor should be under this control." As we are not inclined to be captious, we will not suppose your Honor intended to intimate your own superiority, or that it would be too great condescension in you, and below your dignity, to discuss this subject with the Council. We shall, therefore, only observe, that if you have no doubt of the right of the Crown to control the Governor by instructions, you can have no doubt of your own right, not only of convening the Court at Cambridge, and holding it here, contrary to the prayers of both Houses, and all the reasons offered by them; but (in case you had been so instructed,) of refusing to convene it at all, either on the last Wednesday of May, yearly, as required by the charter, or at any other time; nor can you, in the same case, doubt of your right to dissolve the charter wholly, and with it the present form of government, and to introduce another. These are necessary consequences of the doctrine delivered in your Honor's message. It is, therefore, a doctrine inconsistent with every idea of English government, and utterly subversive of the ends of all government; and it puts the property, liberties, and rights of the people of this province on a very precarious foundation, or rather destroys the foundation entirely. We cannot see how it can be " for the benefit of the people, that a Governor should be under this control;" the control of instructions, that, in their nature and consequences, may prove ruinous to the people. But as we hope your Honor does not entertain principles of such a tendency, we suppose you must have meant such instructions only, as were consistent with the charter, and the rights and privileges of Englishmen.

Your message further declares, " that the present set of instructions, for the Governors of this province, are wisely framed for the advantage of the province." You are pleased here to express your entire approbation of the instructions you have received, one of which, we have been made to understand, is, that the General Court shall be held in the town of Cambridge. Till this declaration, we had pleased ourselves with the thought that you were sincerely desirous, (had it consisted with your instructions,) that the Court should be removed to Boston. But how can it be supposed your Honor can desire that this removal should take place, the direct contrary to which you have, by fair implication, declared is for the advantage of the province? That advantage, however, can never appear, if the instructions, which are the only evidence of it, be kept secret.

If instructions are to be the law and rule of government, is it not fit and proper that they should be known ? Are we not, otherwise, not only in a state of vassalage, but distinguished from others in that state, in this essential circumstance, that they have a known law, which they might obey; and we an unknown one, which, for that reason, we can neither obey or disobey; and yet may possibly be punished for not obeying?

Your Honor tells us, " you have no instructions militating with the charter." If there be an instruction, forbidding the adjourning or proroguing the General Court to Boston, we apprehend it does militate against the charter; and we think we have, in our address, clearly proved, from the charter, that it does militate. In which case, we submit it to your Honor's consideration, whether you can be held to observe it ?

Whenever your Honor shall think proper to consult the Council, upon any occasion, you may depend on our best advice for his Majesty's service, and the good of the province. These necessarily include each other; and are, in fact, but different names for the same thing, there being no room for distinction or separation between them. Whoever attempts, therefore, to make a separation, is an enemy to both.

As his Majesty is the wise and tender father of his people, he will always look upon those as the best promoters of his service, who, in the best manner, promote their interest and happiness. And we are still of opinion, that, with that interest and happiness, is connected the removal of the General Court to Boston.

——

LETTER

FROM THE COUNCIL TO WILLIAM BOLLAN, ESQ. AGENT FOR THE PROVINCE, IN ENGLAND, MARCH, 1770, GIVING AN ACCOUNT OF THE MASSACRE OF THE FIFTH OF THAT MONTH.

Sir,

THE last letter sent you in the name, and in consequence of the appointment of the Council, was dated in January last ; since which, the General Court, pursuant to the ministerial mandate, has been prorogued by the Lieutenant Governor, to Cambridge, where it has been sitting from the 15th instant. This the two Houses, (to say nothing of the great inconveniences to which they are thereby subjected,) deem an infringement upon one of the rights of the charter ; which, after ordaining that there shall be held and kept a General Court, every year, in May, vests the Governor of the time being, with the sole power of convening, proroguing and dissolving the said Court, without any reserve whatever.

30

What has passed between the Lieutenant Governor and the two Houses, on this subject, will be sent you herewith.

The principal thing, which we think it necessary you should be informed of, at this time, is the *horrid massacre*, which happened in Boston, on the evening of the 5th instant, when eleven of his Majesty's subjects were killed and wounded by a party of soldiers, of the 29th regiment, their leader being Capt. Preston.

The soldiers in general, and particularly of that regiment, have behaved with great insolence, and have committed many abuses upon the inhabitants of the town ; for which it were to be wished, their punishment had been adequate to their deserts. But the affair, which was more immediately introductory to the said massacre, was a quarrel between some soldiers of the 29th regiment and certain rope-makers at the rope-walk of one Mr. Gray. In the contest, the soldiers were worsted ; and this reflecting, as they thought, on the honor of the regiment, there was a combination among them to take vengeance on the town, indiscriminately. Of such a combination there is satisfactory proof ; and in consequence thereof, there was, on the evening of the 5th, a great number of abuses committed by the soldiers on the inhabitants, in various parts of the town ; and being carried to such excess by one party, a bell at the head of King Street was rung, as for fire, which brought the neighboring inhabitants into the street ; and as King Street was the last scene of that party's exploits, a number of people collected there ; about which time the centry, at the custom house, on pretence of having been insulted, knocked at the door of said house ; and speaking with somebody who came out, there went from thence two persons to the main guard, opposite the court house, and procured Capt. Preston, with a party of soldiers, to go to the centry. Capt. Preston, therefore, went from the guard house with a party of seven or eight men, who passed roughly through the people, and pushed some with their bayonets, till they were posted near the custom house. This was resented by some of the people, by throwing snow balls. Soon after which, the said party fired, not all together, but in succession ; by which means eleven persons were killed and wounded, as above mentioned.

There are depositions which mention, that several guns were fired from the custom house ; and this matter is now inquiring into. Soon after the firing, the main body of the 29th regiment appeared in arms, in King Street, and were drawn up between the court house and the main guard, and in such a posture, as put the inhabitants in fear of a further massacre ; but, by the good hand of Providence, it was prevented.

The foregoing is a short and general account of this unhappy affair, according to the best intelligence we have hitherto been able to obtain. The particulars of it, are contained in a narrative just printed, with depositions annexed to it ; one of which will be sent to you by a committee of the town.

There is great reason to apprehend, that depositions have been taken in this affair, by the procurement of the *disturbers* of the peace and union, which ought to subsist between Great Britain and the colonies; depositions, intended to make the town the *faulty* cause of that massacre; and to make it believed, that the custom house was then in danger of being pillaged. But if any such depositions have been sent home, they are altogether without foundation; there not being the least ground, so far as we can learn, even to suspect that any such design has been formed. The Council desire you, and you are hereby instructed, to use your best endeavors to procure copies of such depositions, (if such there be,) and to transmit them as soon as may be; and, in the mean time, to ward off any ill impressions, which otherwise may be thereby made, to the disadvantage of the town in particular, and of the province in general.

The longer continuance of the troops in town, being, in the unanimous opinion of the Council, absolutely inconsistent with the safety of the inhabitants, they advised the Lieutenant Governor to request Col. Dalrymple to order the troops to the barracks, at Castle Island; and, in consequence of that advice, the commanding officer has removed them all thither. You will use your utmost endeavors, that those troops be ordered by his Majesty to be removed out of the province, and that no more be sent hither, to be quartered in the province.

By order of the Council,

S. DANFORTH, *President.*

MESSAGE

FROM THE HOUSE OF REPRESENTATIVES TO THE LIEUTENANT GOVERNOR, JUNE 21, 1770, BEING IN REPLY TO HIS MESSAGE OF JUNE 15.

May it please your Honor,

In your last message to this House, you was pleased to say, that you were in daily expectation of a letter from his Majesty's Secretary of State, which it was probable would contain matters of importance to the government; and that, therefore, you then thought it necessary that the Court should continue sitting some time longer.

The House would be glad to be informed, whether, in consequence of any letters you have received by the packet, now arrived, your Honor has any matters to lay before the Assembly. If so, the House is ready to attend to their duty, provided you will be pleased to remove the Assembly to its constitutional place, the

Town House, in Boston ; but if your Honor is yet determined against such removal, the Members of the House are very desirous of returning to their respective homes.

MESSAGE

Gentlemen of the Council, and
    Gentlemen of the House of Representatives,

I CANNOT remove the Court to Boston. I am so sensible of the mischief which must be the consequence of your final refusal to proceed in the public business, that I must earnestly recommend to you a reconsideration of your votes or resolves to the contrary. I am still in expectation of important advices. If I should not receive any before Monday, and you shall persist in your refusal, it is my intention then to give you a short recess.

T. HUTCHINSON.

[On receiving the foregoing message from the Lieutenant Governor, it was therefore moved and voted, *unanimously*, that the House adhere to their resolution, " that it is by no means expedient to proceed to business, while the General Assembly is thus constrained to hold its session out of the town of Boston."]

MESSAGE

May it please your Honor,

YOUR message, of the 21st instant, has been read and considered in this House ; in answer to which, we beg leave to say, that the mischiefs which must be the consequence of our receding from the votes and resolutions to which you refer, are so obvious, that the House have now unanimously resolved to adhere to the same ; therefore, if your Honor is yet determined not to remove the Assembly to Boston, we are very desirous of leave to return to our respective homes.

[The Lieutenant Governor then directed the Secretary to prorogue the Court to July 25th.]

SPEECH

OF THE LIEUTENANT GOVERNOR TO THE COUNCIL AND HOUSE OF REPRE-
SENTATIVES, JULY 25, 1770.*

Gentlemen of the Council, and
     Gentlemen of the House of Representatives,

PURSUANT to the direction in the royal charter, I caused writs
to be issued, for convening a great and General Court or Assembly,
the last Wednesday in May.   You met together, at the time and
place, and the House of Representatives proceeded to the choice
of their Speaker and Clerk ; and the Council and House, by joint
ballot, proceeded to the choice of Counsellors, for the year ensuing ;
but the Council and House requested me to adjourn or prorogue
the Court to Boston, and gave several reasons against sitting in any
other place.   The House expressly refused to proceed upon any
further business, and repeatedly desired, that, unless I would remove the Court to Boston, they might be allowed to return to their
respective homes.   I could not, consistently with my duty to the
King, remove you to Boston.   To continue you sitting, was continuing a burden upon the people, without any benefit ; for their
ease, I prorogued the Court for four weeks.   From a regard to their
interest; and because the public business will not admit of further
delay, I meet you at the time to which you stood prorogued : I
meet you at Cambridge, because I have no reason to think there
has been any alteration in his Majesty's pleasure, which, I doubt
not, was determined by wise motives, and with a gracious purpose,
to promote the good of the province ; and I must renew my earnest
recommendation to you, to proceed, without delay, upon such affairs
as lie before you.

The illegality of holding the Court any where, except in the town
of Boston, I think, you will no longer insist upon.   I know of
nothing to support you, except the form of a writ, for calling the
Assembly ; and, upon the force of this, you have the opinion of the
Attorney and Solicitor General, in the following words : That the
sole power of dissolving, proroguing or adjourning the General
Court or Assembly, either as to time or place, is in his Majesty's
Governor ; and, that the reasons against it, from the act of the
tenth of King William, have no real foundation, there being no
clause in that act, laying any such restraint upon the Governor ;
but, in the form of the writ, the word Boston is mentioned, which
must be understood, by way of instance or example only, and not

* Before the Lieutenant Governor delivered this Speech, and immediately after the Members of the Court had convened, Mr. Hancock and others, were appointed a committee of
the House of Representatives, to wait on the Lieutenant Governor, and acquaint him that a
quorum was present, (in the College Chapel,) and that they were very desirous his Honor
would be pleased to remove the General Assembly to its ancient and legal place, the town of
Boston.

to limit the power the Crown has, of summoning or holding General Courts or Assemblies at any place, much less of adjourning them from one place to another after they were summoned ; which report was accepted by the King in Council. And although this form of a writ was afterwards brought, by the House of Representatives, as an objection against holding the Court in Salem, in the year 1728, yet they did not think it sufficient to justify them in refusing to do business ; and the Council for that year, who are allowed to have been men of integrity and superior understanding, as well as of the first families and estates in the province, in a message to the House, express their sense in the following words, viz. : " touching the adjournment, they apprehend it improper and inconvenient to make any doubt of the validity thereof ; and they are ready to join with the Honorable House, in proceeding to do the proper and necessary business of the province." From that time, I have never known it suggested, until the present day, that the General Court, by charter or by law, is confined to the town of Boston. I have given you one instance, in the year 1747, which makes it probable, that the House of Representatives rather chose the Court should sit elsewhere ; and I may add another, in the year 1754, when a committee of the House was appointed to consider of, and report a proper place for a Court House, at a distance from Boston.

Your next objection, that I act in consequence of instructions, has still less color. Instructions relative to any matter, not unconstitutional, must be obligatory upon me : my commission makes them so. I have no authority to act, but what I derive from this commission, and I must act in conformity to my instructions, or not at all ; and I think I may safely say, there is not one of you, who, if he was in my station, would venture to depart from them.

The only remaining exception is this, that admitting it to be legal and a part of the prerogative, the other branches have nevertheless a clear right to inquire into the exercise of this power, and to judge for themselves, whether it be wisely and beneficially, or imprudently and arbitrarily exercised—" to remonstrate"—to " make a stand"—and " finally to refuse to do business." The actual inconveniences which you have enumerated, from sitting at Cambridge, can easily be removed, or they are so inconsiderable, that a very small public benefit will outweigh them.

The House of Representatives mention an inconvenience, which may arise from the use of this part of the prerogative, because it gives power to the Governor " to carry the Assembly from one extreme part of the province to another, till he shall have worried them into a compliance with some arbitrary mandate, to the ruin of their own, and their constituents liberties." The same exception may be made to the use of every other part of the prerogative, for every part is capable of abuse, and so is every authority, or trust, whatsoever. I will, however, assure you, that I have never received any arbitrary mandates; I have no design myself; I know of no "fixed design to harass you, in order to bring you into a compliance with any arbitrary measures." I have nothing to lay before you, but the common business of the province, which is necessary for the general interest of the people. Consult this interest, in every constitutional way. Do it with as much deliberation as the importance of every case shall require; I will patiently wait the result of your debates. Do it with as much diligence and despatch as you please, and I will give you no interruption, nor occasion any delay.

But pray consider this last exception, and the effect of a concession to it.

You allow that the appointment of a place for holding the Court, is a part of the prerogative, but you refuse or neglect to do business any where, except in Boston; for this prerogative, you say, is to be exercised for the public good, and you do not think it for the public good, that the Court should sit any where, except in Boston; his Majesty thinks it for the public good, that the Court should sit in Cambridge. If your opinion is to prevail against his Majesty's opinion, to what purpose was this, or any other reserve in the charter, made to the Crown.

You consider the charter as a compact between the Crown and the people of the province. Shall one party to the compact be held, and not the other? The Crown, by charter, grants as a privilege to the people, that a great and General Court or Assembly, shall be held every last Wednesday in May, forever. You would have thought me culpable, and very justly, if I had deprived the people of this privilege, by refusing to issue writs, for convening the Court on the last Wednesday in May, or by refusing to do my part of the peculiar business, for which it is then convened. By the same charter, the Crown reserves, as part of the prerogative, the power of adjourning, proroguing, and dissolving the great and General Court or Assembly. Conformable to this reserve, I have prorogued you to this time and place. If you had refused to meet, or should refuse to do business, now you are met, would you not deprive the Crown of the exercise of the prerogative, and fail of performing your part of the compact? The House of Representatives say, they are ready to answer for the ill consequences which can be attributed to them; and yet they seem to have been sensible of the danger, from a failure of the same nature; for they acknowledge, "they proceeded to the election of Counsellors, that the enemies of our constitution might not have it in their power to say, that, by an omission, they had forfeited our invaluable charter." At the same time, they refused to do any other business, because "none lay before them of such necessity, as, that omitting it, would endanger the constitution." Let me observe to you, gentlemen, that it is not the importance of the business omitted, but it is the refusal of the two Houses to comply with what the charter requires of them, which our enemies will take the advantage of, and which will endanger the constitution; and your refusing, or neglecting, to do business now, will be as certain an instance of your non-compliance with what your charter requires of you, as if you had refused to proceed to the election of Counsellors in May last.

If you shall persist in your refusal, I must prorogue you to some future time. Without further signification of his Majesty's pleasure, it is not in my power to remove you to Boston. But, I flatter myself, you will not persist—you will not leave it in the power of your enemies to hurt you. I am sure, you have friends, who will think themselves happy, if you do not put it out of their power to serve you. Your compliance can be no benefit to our Sovereign, any further, than as he interests ·himself in the happiness of his subjects. I am not thus importunate with you, from any view to my private or personal advantage, for, if I am faithful in the discharge of my trust, I shall have the same approbation, whether I am successful or not. It is the interest of the people only, which is at stake. By persisting in your refusal, you are most effectually disserving this interest. You are even rendering more difficult the accomplishment of what you profess to desire and pursue.

T. HUTCHINSON.

MESSAGE

FROM THE HOUSE OF REPRESENTATIVES TO THE LIEUTENANT
GOVERNOR, AUGUST 1, 1770.

May it please your Honor,

The House of Representatives having duly attended to your speech to both Houses, at the opening of this session, and maturely considered the several parts of it, have unanimously, in a full House, determined to adhere to their former resolution, " that it is by no means expedient to proceed to business, while the General Assembly is thus constrained to hold the session out of the town of Boston." Upon a recollection of the reasons we have before given for this measure, we conceive it will appear to all the world, that neither the good people of this province, nor the House of Representatives, can be justly charged with any ill consequences that may follow it. After the most attentive and repeated examination of your speech, we find nothing to induce us to alter our opinion, and very little that is new and material in the controversy: but, as we perceive it is published, it may possibly be read by some who have never seen the reasons of the House;

and as there are specious things contained in it, which may have a tendency to make an unhappy impression on some minds, we have thought proper to make a few observations upon it.

You are pleased to say, " you meet us at Cambridge, because you have no reason to think there has been any alteration in his Majesty's pleasure, which, you doubt not, was determined by wise motives, and with a gracious purpose to promote the good of the province." We presume not to call in question the wisdom of our Sovereign, or the rectitude of his intentions : but there have been times, when a corrupt and profligate administration have ventured upon such measures, as have had a direct tendency to ruin the interest of the people, as well as that of their royal master.

This House have great reason to doubt, whether it is, or ever was, his Majesty's pleasure, that your Honor should meet the Assembly at Cambridge, or that he has ever taken the matter under his royal consideration : because the common, and the best evidence in such cases, is not communicated to us.

It is needless for us to add any thing to what has been heretofore said upon the illegality of holding the Court any where, except in the town of Boston : for, admitting the power to be in the Governor to hold the Court in any other place, when the public good *requires* it ; yet, it by no means follows, that he has a right to call it in any other place, when it is to the manifest injury and detriment of the public.

The opinion of the Attorney and Solicitor General has very little weight with this House in any case, any further, than the reasons which they expressly give, are convincing. This province has suffered so much by unjust, groundless, and illegal opinions of those officers of the Crown, that our veneration, or reverence for their opinions, is much abated. We utterly deny, that the Attorney and Solicitor General have any authority or jurisdiction over us ; any right to decide questions in controversy between the several branches of the Legislature here : nor do we concede, that even his Majesty in Council, has any constitutional authority to decide such questions, or any controversy whatever, that arises in this province, excepting only such matters as are reserved in the charter. It seems a great absurdity, that when a dispute arises between the Governor and the House, the Governor should appeal to his Majesty in Council to decide it. Would it not be as reasonable for the House to appeal to the body of their constituents to decide it ? Whenever a dispute has arisen within the realm, between the Crown and the two Houses of Parliament, or either of them, was it ever imagined that the King, in his Privy Council, had authority to decide it ? However, there is a test, a standard common to all ; we mean the public good. But your Honor must be very sensible, that the illegality of holding the Court in any other place beside the town of Boston, is far from being the only dispute between your Honor and this House. We contend, that the people and their Representatives, have a right to withstand the abusive exercise of a legal and constitutional prerogative of the Crown. We beg leave to recite to your Honor, what the great Mr. Locke has advanced in his Treatise of Civil Government, upon the like prerogative of the Crown. " The old question, says he, will be asked in this matter of prerogative, who shall be judge when this power is made a right use of ?" And he answers, " between an executive power in being with such a prerogative, and a legislative that depends upon his will for their convening, there can be no judge upon earth, as there can be none between the legislative and the people, should either the executive or legislative. when they have got the power in their hands, design or go about to enslave or destroy them. The people have no other remedy in this, as in all other cases, where they have no judge on earth, but to appeal to Heaven. For the rulers, in such attempts, exercising a power the people never put into their hands, (who can never be supposed to consent, that any body should rule over them for their harm,) do that which they have not a right to do. And, when the body of the people, or any single man, is deprived of their right, or under the exercise of a power without right, and have no appeal on earth, then they have a liberty to appeal to Heaven, whenever they judge the cause of sufficient moment. And, therefore, though the people cannot be judge, so as to have, by the constitution of that society, any superior power to determine and give effective sentence in the case ; yet they have, by a law, antecedent and paramount to all positive laws of men, reserved that ultimate determination to themselves, which belongs to all mankind, where there lies no appeal on earth, viz. : to judge whether they have just cause to make their appeal to Heaven." We would, however, by no means be understood to suggest, that this people have occasion at present to proceed to such extremity.

Your Honor is pleased to say, " that the House of Representatives, in the year 1728, did not think the form of the writ sufficient to justify them in refusing to do business at Salem." It is true they did not, by any vote or resolve, determine not to do business : yet the House, as we read in your Honor's history, " met, and adjourned from day to day, without doing business ;" and we find by the records, that from the 31st of October, 1728, to the 14th of December following, the House did meet and adjourn without doing business ; and then they voted to proceed to the public and necessary affairs of the province, " provided no advantage be had or made, for, and by reason of the aforesaid removal, (meaning the removal to Salem,) or pleaded as a precedent for the future." Yet, your Honor has been pleased to quote the conduct of that very House, as a precedent for *our* imitation. We apprehend their proceeding to business, and the consequences of it, viz. : the encouragement it gave to Governor Burnet to go on with his design of harassing them into unconstitutional compliances, and the use your Honor now makes of it as an authority and a precedent, ought to be a warning to this House, to make a determined and effectual stand. Their example, though respectable, is not obligatory upon this House. They lived in times, when the encroachments of despotism were in their infancy. They were carried to Salem by the mere caprice of Governor Burnet, who never pleaded an instruction for doing this—an instruction, from a Ministry, who had before treated them with unexampled indignity—an instruction, which they were not *permitted* to see. They had no reason to apprehend a fixed design to alter the seat of government, to their great inconvenience, and the manifest injury of the province.

We are not disposed to dispute the understanding, integrity, families, and estates of the Council, in 1728. We believe them to have been such, that if they were now upon the stage, they would see so many additional, and more weighty reasons, against proceeding to business, out of Boston, that they would fully approve of the resolution of this House ; as well as of what has been lately advanced by their successors, who are also gentlemen of understanding, integrity, fortune, and family, in the following words : " Governor Burnet's conduct in convening the General Court out of Boston, cannot be deemed an acknowledged or constitutional precedent, because, it was not founded on the only reason on which the prerogative of the Crown can be justly founded, the good of the community." We shall only add, that the rights of the province having been, of late years, most severely attacked, has induced gentlemen to examine the constitution more thoroughly, and has increased their zeal in its defence.

You are pleased to adduce an instance in 1754, in addition to that in 1747, which, you say, " makes it probable, that the House of Representatives rather chose that the Court should sit elsewhere, when a committee was chosen to consider of, and report a proper place for a Court House, at a distance from Boston." We beg leave here to observe, that both these are instances of the House's interesting themselves in this affair, which your Honor now claims as a prerogative. If the House were in no case to have a voice, or be regarded, in choosing a place to hold the Court, how could they think of holding a Court in a place, to which they never had been, and probably never would be called ?

While the House have been, from time to time, holding up to view, the great inconveniencies and manifest injuries resulting from the sitting of the Assembly at Cambridge, and praying a removal to Boston ; it is with pain that they have heard your Honor, instead of pointing out any one good purpose, which can be answered by it, replying, that your *instructions* will not permit you to remove the Court to Boston. By a royal grant in the charter, in favor of the Commons of this province, the Governor has the sole

power of adjourning, proroguing, and dissolving the General
Court: and the wisdom of that grant, appears in this, that a person residing in the province, must be a more competent judge of
the fitness of the time, and, we may add, the place of holding the
Court, than any person residing in Great Britain. We do not
deny, that there may be instances, when the Commander in Chief
ought to obey the royal instructions : and should we also admit,
that in ordinary cases he ought to obey them, respecting the convening, holding, proroguing, adjourning, and dissolving the General Court, notwithstanding that grant ; yet we clearly hold, that
whenever instructions cannot be complied with, without injuring
the people, they cease to be binding. Any other supposition would
involve this absurdity in it, that a substitute, by means of instructions from his principal, may have a greater power than the principal himself; or, in other words, that a Representative of a King,
who can do no wrong, by means of instructions, may obtain a right
to do wrong : for that the prerogative extends not to do any injury, never has been, and never can be denied. Therefore, this
House are clearly of opinion, that your Honor is under no obligation to hold the General Court at Cambridge, let your instructions
be conceived in terms ever so peremptory, inasmuch as it is inconvenient and injurious to the province. As to your commission, it is certain, that no clause contained in that, inconsistent
with the charter, can be binding. To suppose, that when a grant
is made by charter in favor of the people, instructions shall supersede that grant, and oblige the Governor to act repugnant to it, is
vacating the charter at once, by the breath of a Minister of State.
Your Honor thinks you may *safely* say, " there is not one of us,
who, if he was in your station, would venture to depart from the
instructions." As you had not the least shadow of evidence to
warrant this, we are sure you could not say it with *safety:* and
we leave it with your Honor to determine, how far it is reconcileable with *delicacy*, to suggest it. In what particulars, the holding
the General Court at Cambridge, is injurious to us and the province, has already been declared by the House, and must be too
obvious to escape your Honor's observation. Yet you are pleased
to tell us, that " the inconveniencies can easily be removed, or,
are so inconsiderable, that a very small public benefit will outweigh them." That they are not inconsiderable, every day's experience convinces us ; nor are our constituents insensible of them.
But how they can be easily removed, we cannot conceive, unless
by removing the Court to Boston. Can the public offices and records, to which we are under the necessity of recurring, almost
every hour, with any safety or convenience to the public, be removed to Cambridge ? Will our constituents consent to be at the
expense of erecting a proper house at Cambridge, for accommodating the General Court, especially, when they have no assurance
that the next freak of a capricious Minister will not remove the

Court to some other place ?   Is it possible to have that communication with our constituents, or to be benefitted by the reasonings
of the people without doors here, as at Boston ?   We cannot but
flatter ourselves, that every judicious and impartial person will
allow, that the holding the General Court at Cambridge, is inconvenient and hurtful to the province ; nor has your Honor ever yet
attempted to show a single instance, in which the province can be
benefitted by it ; no good purpose, which can be answered by it,
has ever yet been suggested by any one to this House.   And we
have the utmost confidence, that our most gracious Sovereign has
no desire to hold the General Court at any place inconvenient to
its Members, or injurious to the province ; but rather, that he
will frown upon those, who have procured its removal to such a
place, or persist in holding it there.

We are not indeed sure, that the Ministry caused the Assembly
to be removed to Cambridge, in order to worry them into a compliance with any arbitrary mandate to the ruin of our own, or
our constituents liberties ; but we know, that the General Assembly has in times past, been treated with such indignity and abuse,
by the servants of the Crown, and a wicked Ministry may attempt
it again.

Your Honor observes, that " the same exception may be made
to the use of every other part of the prerogative, for every part is
capable of abuse."   We shall never except to the proper use of
the prerogative—we hold it sacred as the liberty of the subject.
But every abuse of it will always be excepted to, so long as the
love of liberty, or any public virtue, remains.   And whenever any
other part of the prerogative shall be abused, the House will not
fail to judge for themselves, of the grievance, nor to exert every
power with which the constitution hath entrusted them, to check
the abuse of it, and redress the grievance.

The House had expressed to your Honor their apprehension of
a fixed design, either to change the seat of government, or to harass us, in order to bring us into a compliance with some arbitrary
mandate.   Your Honor says, you know of no fixed design to harass us, &c.   Upon which, we cannot but observe, that if you did
not know of a fixed design to change the seat of government, you
would not have omitted so fair an opportunity to satisfy the minds
of the House in a matter of such importance to the province.   As
to your very condescending and liberal professions, of exercising
patience or using despatch, as would be most agreeable to us, we
shall be very much obliged to your Honor, for the exercise of those
virtues, whenever you shall see cause to remove us to our ancient
and established seat ; but these professions can be no temptations
to us, to give up our privileges.

Your Honor is pleased to say, " we consider the charter as a
compact between the Crown and the people of this province."
And to ask a question, " shall one party to the compact be held,

and not the other ?" It is true, we consider the charter as such a compact, and agree that both parties are held. The Crown covenants, that a great and General Court shall be held every last Wednesday in May, forever; the Crown, therefore, doubtless is bound by this covenant. But we utterly deny, that the people have covenanted to grant money, or to do business, at least any other business, than choosing Officers and Counsellors to complete the General Court, on the last Wednesday in May, or any other day or year whatever; therefore, this House, by refusing to do business, do not deprive the Crown of the exercise of the prerogative, nor fail of performing their part of the compact.

Your Honor would, doubtless, have been culpable, had you refused to call a General Court on the last Wednesday in May; and the House might have been equally culpable, if they had refused to choose a Speaker and a Clerk, or, to elect Counsellors, whereby to complete the General Court; for, in case of omission in either part, a question might arise, whether the people would have a legislative. When the General Assembly is thus formed, they are empowered by the charter to make, ordain, and establish all manner of wholesome and reasonable orders, laws, statutes, or ordinances, directions and instructions, either with penalties or without. But the charter no where obliges the General Court to make any orders, laws, statutes, or ordinances, unless they, at that time, judge it conducive to the public good to make them; much less does it oblige them to make any laws, &c. in any particular session, year, or number of years, whenever they themselves shall judge them not to be for the public good. Such an obligation would not leave them the least color of freedom, but reduce them to a mere machine; to the state the Parliament would have been in, if the opinion of the two Chief Justices and the three Puisne Judges had prevailed, in the reign of Richard the Second, " that the King had the governance of Parliaments, and may appoint what shall be first handled, and so gradually what next, in all matters to be treated of in Parliament, even to the end of the Parliament; and if any persons shall act contrary to the King's pleasure made known therein, they are to be punished as traitors;" for which opinion, those five Judges had judgment, as in case of high treason. Your Honor will allow us to ask, whether the doctrine contained in your question, viz.: " if you should refuse to do business now you are met, would you not deprive the Crown of the exercise of the prerogative, and fail of performing your part of the compact?" which implies a strong affirmation, is not in a degree the very doctrine of Chief Justice Tresilian, and the four other Judges, just now mentioned? By convening, in obedience to his Majesty's writ, tested by your Honor, and again, at the time to which we are prorogued, we fully have submitted to the prerogative, and performed our part of the compact.

This House has the same inherent rights in this province, as the

House of Commons has in Great Britain. It is our duty to procure a redress of grievances; and we may constitutionally refuse to grant our constituents money to the Crown, or to do any other act of government, at any given time, that is not affixed by charter, to a certain day, until the grievances of the people are redressed. We do not pretend that our opinion is to prevail against his Majesty's opinion; we never shall attempt to adjourn, or prorogue, or dissolve the General Court; but, we do hope, that our opinion shall prevail against any opinion whatever, of the proper time, to make laws and to do business. And by exerting this power which the constitution has given us, we hope to convince your Honor and the Ministry, of the necessity of removing the Court to Boston.

All judicious men will allow, that the proper time for the House to do their part of the business of the province, is for the House to judge of and determine. The House think it is not, in the present circumstances of the province, a proper time to do the business, while the Court is constrained to hold their session out of Boston. Your Honor is of a different opinion. We have conformed to this opinion, as far as the constitution requires us, and now our right of judging commences. If your Honor's, or even his Majesty's opinion, concerning this point, is to prevail against the opinion of the House, why may not the Crown, according to the Tresilian doctrine, as well prescribe and require what business we shall do, and in what order.

The House are still ready to answer for the ill consequences which can be justly attributed to them; nor are they sensible of any danger, from exerting the power which the charter has given them, of doing their part of the business in their own time. That the province has enemies, who are continually defaming it and their charter, is certain; that there are persons who are endeavoring to intimidate the province, from asserting and vindicating their just rights and liberties, by insinuations of danger to the constitution, is also indisputable. But no instance happened, even in the execrable reign of the worst of the Stuart race, of a forfeiture of a charter, because any one branch of a legislative, or even because the whole government under that charter, refused to do business, at a particular time, under grievous circumstances of ignominy, disgrace, and insult; and when their charter had explicitly given to that government the sole power of judging of the proper season and occasion of doing business. We are obliged, at this time, to struggle with all the powers with which the constitution has furnished us, in defence of our rights; to prevent the most valuable of our liberties from being wrested from us, by the subtle machinations and daring encroachments of wicked Ministers. We have seen, of late, innumerable encroachments on our charter: Courts of Admiralty, extended from the high seas, where, by the compact in the charter, they are confined, to numberless important causes upon land; multitudes of civil officers, the appointment of all which, is, by charter, confined to the Governor and Council, sent here from abroad by the Ministry; a revenue, not granted by us, but torn from us; armies stationed here without our consent; and the streets of our metropolis *crimsoned* with the blood of our fellow-subjects. These, and other grievances and cruelties, too many to be here enumerated, and too melancholy to be much longer borne by this injured people, we have seen brought upon us, by the devices of Ministers of State; we have seen and heard of late, instructions to Governors, which threaten to destroy all the remaining privileges of our charter. In June, 1768, the House, by an instruction, were ordered to rescind an excellent resolution of a former House, on pain of dissolution; they refused to comply with so impudent a mandate, and were dissolved; and the Governor, though repeatedly requested, and although the exigencies of the province demanded a General Assembly, refused to call a new one, until the following May. In the last year, the General Court was forced to give way to regular troops, illegally quartered in the town of Boston, in consequence of instructions to Crown Officers; and whose main guard was most daringly and insultingly placed at the door of the State House; and afterwards they were constrained to hold their session at Cambridge; the present year, the Assembly is summoned to meet, and is still continued there in a kind of duress, without any reason, that can be given—any motive whatever, that is not as great an insult to them and breach of their privilege, as any of the foregoing. Are these things consistent with the freedom of the House; or, could the General Court's tamely submitting to such usage, be thought to promote his Majesty's service? Should these struggles of the House prove unfortunate and ineffectual, this province will submit, with pious resignation, to the will of Providence; but it will be a kind of suicide, of which we have the utmost horror, thus to be the instruments of our own servitude.

We beg leave, before we conclude, to make one remark on what you say, that " our compliance can be of no *benefit* to our Sovereign, any further, than as he interests himself in the happiness of his subjects."

We are apprehensive that the world may take this for an insinuation very much to our dishonor, as if the benefit of our Sovereign is a motive in our minds against a compliance. But as this imputation would be extremely unjust, so we hope, it was not intended by your Honor. We are obliged, however, in justice to ourselves and constituents, to declare, that, if we had reason to believe that a compliance would be any, the least benefit to our Sovereign, it would be a very powerful argument with us; but, we are, on the contrary, fully persuaded, that a compliance, at present, would be very injurious and detrimental to his Majesty's service.

[The committee who prepared the above, were, Mr. Hancock, Maj. Hawley, Mr. S. Adams, Mr. J. Adams, Capt. Denny, and Maj. Gallison.]

MESSAGE

Gentlemen of the House of Representatives,

You have sent me a message, in which you profess to make a few observations upon some " specious" things contained in my speech to the Council and House, which, you say, may have a tendency to make an unhappy impression upon some minds.

I shall make some general remarks upon your message, not from any expectation of prevailing with you, at this time, to alter resolutions which you have come into, but from a desire to convince the good people you represent, that your reasons for refusing to proceed to business, are very insufficient.

You make a doubt, whether it is, or ever was, his Majesty's pleasure, that the Court should meet at Cambridge. I have no doubt of it. You give this reason for your doubt, that my orders are not communicated to you. I know it to be his Majesty's pleasure, that I should not communicate them ; and the restraint I am under, appears to me to be founded in wise reasons. You speak of times, when there has been a corrupt and profligate administration—of daring encroachments of wicked Ministers—of devices of Ministers of State ; and you suppose instructions to Governors, to be acts of Ministers, and not of the King ; particularly, you call an instruction in June, 1768, an *impudent* mandate. It may not be presumed you would have done this, had you known it to be an order from his Majesty. I wish, however, that you had spared this coarse and indecent epithet.

I cannot help observing to you, that you have no sufficient grounds to suppose instructions to be the acts of the Minister, and not of the King. I know of no ministerial mandate, or instructions. The affairs of America, and of this province in particular, are become too serious to escape his Majesty's immediate attention ; and your message, which I am now answering, will be laid before his Majesty, immediately upon its being received by his Secretary of State ; who, by virtue of his office, has free access, and who receives the signification of his Majesty's pleasure, and will give no directions, but such as he knows to be agreeable thereto ; and every order from the Secretary of State, must be supposed to come immediately from the Crown, and ought not to be treated with indignity and contempt.

The freedom you have used with the characters of the Attorney and Solicitor General, will, I fear, likewise bring dishonor upon you. Those offices, for more than fifty years past, have been filled, in almost every instance, with persons of the highest respectabil-

32

ity for learning and integrity, and many of them have been advanced to the first stations in the courts of law and equity, which are, and have been, for years past, the ornament and glory of the English nation. Although you do not think the opinion of the Attorney and Solicitor General, in the case in dispute between us, nor the confirmation of such opinion by the King, in Council, to be any authority for you, yet I must govern myself thereby, until I have better reasons against it, than any you have given in your message.

Your quotation from Mr. Locke, detached as it is from the rest of the treatise, cannot be applied to your case. I know of no attempts to enslave or destroy you; and, as you very prudently would not be understood to suggest that this people have occasion, at present, to proceed to such extremities as to appeal to heaven, I am at a loss to conceive for what good purpose you adduce it.

You find nothing in your records, which does not agree with what I have said, of the proceedings of the House, at Salem, in Governor Burnet's administration, nor did I cite the instance for any other purpose, than to show, that they were very careful to avoid a resolution, which you, as I think, too suddenly came into; nor does my speaking respectfully of the Council of that day, lessen the Council of the present day, who, although they have discovered a desire in their messages to me, that the Court should be removed to Boston, yet, they declare, that they never refused to do business at Cambridge, and I have now no doubt, that if you had done your part of the public business, they would have joined and done their part also.

From the appointment of a committee by the House, in 1754, to consider of a proper place to build another Court House, you infer, that the House was to have a voice in determining the place where the Court should meet. You are very sensible, that a vote, for building a Court House, which incurs expense upon the people, must, by the constitution, originate with the House of Representatives. If one, or divers other Court Houses, besides that in Boston, had been built, the Governor's right to call the Court to which he pleased, or to any other place, remained inviolate; the votes of the Representatives, for building a Court House, notwithstanding.

You then proceed to call in question my obligation, or right, to observe my instructions. And you say, that by a royal grant in the charter, in favor of the Commons of the province, the Governor has the sole power of adjourning, proroguing, and dissolving the General Court; and you think it discovers the wisdom of the grant, because a person residing in the province, is a more competent judge of the fitness of the time and place of holding the Court, than any person residing in Great Britain, and a grant thus made in-favor of the people, cannot be superseded by instructions, without vacating the charter by the breath of a Minister of State.

Your making use of the word sole, instead of full; the word in the charter, must proceed from inattention.   I must observe to you, that many cases may happen, to make it necessary to alter the place of holding the Court, which a person in Great Britain may as well judge of, as one who is upon the spot, and, perhaps, the present case is such an one.   But, where you find that the power of adjourning, proroguing, and dissolving the Court, was granted to the Governor in favor of the Commons, I am utterly at a loss. The charter is, undoubtedly, a royal grant, in favor to the people of the province, of every order.   They were at the time of the grant, living in the colony, under a form of government, which would not admit of an adjournment, prorogation, or dissolution of the General Court, without the act or consent of the Council and Representatives.   They were soliciting, by their agents, a confirmation of their privileges.   The King determines, that, for the future, the Governor should have the full, or sole power, if you choose it, of adjourning, proroguing, and dissolving the General Court.   Is it not very extraordinary, that the Representatives should now assert, that depriving them of a share in this power, and confining it to the Governor alone, was a grant in favor of the Commons ?   The Governor, under the old form, had no negative in any case; but now, no acts of Council or Assembly are valid, to which he denies his consent.   May it not, with equal reason, be said, that this power was also reserved to the Governor in favor of the Commons ?   It is very certain, that unless it be so, there will be no supporting the doctrine, that the Crown has divested itself of its right of controling the Governor.

You are sensible that this can hardly be supported, for you allow that, in some cases, instructions may be binding, and you do not seem very averse from admitting that in ordinary cases, notwithstanding this singular grant in favor of the Commons, that the Commander in Chief ought to obey instructions respecting the convening and holding the Court, but you are clear that, when they cannot be complied with, without injuring the people, they cease to be binding, otherwise the Representative of a King, who can do no wrong, by means of instructions, may obtain a right to do wrong.

I am not contending, gentlemen, for a right to do wrong, and I am very willing to understand the maxim, that the King can do no wrong, in the commonly received sense of it, that his servants alone shall be punished for the wrong they do, and not avail themselves of a royal order, or instruction, for their justification ; and if I was convinced, that removing the Court from Boston, was an encroachment upon your natural or constitutional rights, I would not urge my commission or instructions, to justify the doing it; but I must make my own reason and judgment my rule, and not yours ; and until I am convinced of the encroachment, must conform to my instructions.

You think I ought not to have deemed the inconveniencies of your sitting out of Boston, inconsiderable : or, that they can easily be removed; and you ask me, if the public offices and records can, with safety or convenience, be removed to Cambridge? I think the expense of one or two days wages of the Members, would have removed all that are necessary, to Cambridge, and kept them there with safety and convenience, the whole session; and, if we may judge from the sessions at Concord, you would do your business with so much greater despatch at Cambridge, than at Boston, as to shorten the session more than two days. You ask, whether I think your constituents would be at the expense of building a Court House at Cambridge? I am not certain, what their present disposition is, but I know there is no necessity for it; you have the use of a very commodious room, without any inconvenience to the College, in this time of vacation; and, if you think the benefit which the students receive by attending your debates, is not equal to what they may gain in their studies, they may easily be restrained, and then your sitting in the College, will be little or no inconvenience at any other time. You add, is it possible to have that communication with our constituents, or to be benefitted by the reasoning of the people without doors, in Cambridge, as at Boston? In whatever town the Court shall sit, the Representatives of that town, must have opportunity beyond the rest of the House, for consulting their constituents; the consulting of a transient person passing through any town, cannot afford any great advantage, nor ought, constitutionally, the opinion of such persons to have any influence upon your votes and determinations; for, if I have any just idea of a House of Representatives, in the English constitution, you are sent by your constituents, to assemble together, that they may have the benefit of your reasoning within doors, and not the reasoning of any particular town or person, without doors.

Because, when I told you I knew of no fixed design to harass you, I did not add, nor to change the seat of government, you determine that I am privy to such a design; but I am not. If there be any such design, I think, your proceeding to business at this time, would have the best tendency of any thing in your power, to cause it to be laid aside.

You allow that the charter is a compact, and that both parties are held; but you say the people never covenanted to grant money, or to do any business, except choosing Officers and Counsellors, to complete the General Court, on any day or year whatsoever. I never said they did. I never had the least dispute with you, except upon the place of your meeting. The time, there has been no exception to. It has been a matter of indifference to me personally. I have endeavored to find out when it would be most convenient for you, that I might oblige you; and the business of the Court, I have left to you to arrange and act upon, when, and in what order, you thought proper.

In my speech to you, I ask you, if you had refused to meet, or should refuse to do business, now you are met, would you not deprive the Crown of the exercise of the prerogative, and fail of performing your part of the compact ?   Without the least color for it, you make a forced, unnatural construction of my words, and determine that I am directing the several parts of the business you shall do, and the time of doing them, and that I hold the doctrine of Tresilian in degree, " that the King hath the government of Parliament, and may appoint what shall be first handled, and so gradually, what next in all matters to be treated of in Parliament, even to the end of Parliament; and if any person shall act contrary to the King's pleasure, made known therein, they are to be punished as traitors." I have ever treated your messages with the utmost fairness.   I have passed over, in silence, many passages in them, extremely exceptionable, and, in return, you have wrested my expressions to a sense, in which no man alive, could suppose, I intended them.   Had Tresilian advanced no more than I have done, he would never have met with any blame.   Had he only asserted that the King, by virtue of his prerogative, had a right to assemble the Parliament, at such time and place, as he thought proper, and that if the Commons should refuse to assemble or to do the necessary business of the kingdom, when they were assembled, they would, upon the principles of the English constitution, fail of performing what was incumbent on them, he would never have been called in question for his doctrine ; and yet this is all I have said to you.   I am willing to attribute this injurious treatment to inadvertence in the body of the House, by their passing upon so long and important a message, and which the committee took so many days to prepare, with so little debate after it was reported.

After all your objections, you tell me that you did convene, in obedience to his Majesty's writ ; that you met again, at the time to which you stood prorogued; that you conformed to my opinion, so far as the constitution requires you ; and now your right of judging commences.   Consider, then, how the case now stands. You are held, by the constitution, to convene at a time and place appointed, but you are under no obligations to do any business, except at such times as you think proper ; and, if you do not like the place, you will exercise your right, and determine it is not a proper time.   Can any thing render the prerogative more futile ? Let me ask you, whether, if your agents, when they were soliciting the charter, had been held to say, how far they acknowledged his Majesty's prerogative to convene the Court, at such time and place as he thought proper ; and they had replied that they acknowledged it with this reserve, that the House of Representatives should be at liberty to refuse to do business, until the Court should be removed to such place as they thought proper, you imagine the charter would have passed the seals ?   Neither your more thorough examination of the constitution, nor your extraordinary zeal for its defence, of which you speak, can alter the original frame and intention.

Your main reserve, if it could be admitted, that whensoever the prerogative shall be exercised in a manner not for the public good, of which you are to be judges, it ceases to be a prerogative, is unanswerable. In all controversies, as soon as one party is allowed to be the sole judge, the knot is cut, and there must be an end of strife. But to this I spoke fully at opening the session.

You are still ready " to answer for all the ill consequences which can justly be attributed to you." The dangers may be irreparable, and it may be out of your power to compensate them. The people will then see what was their real interest; but they will see it too late.

I cannot omit taking notice of a remark, at the close of your message, upon an observation I made, that " your compliance could be no benefit to his Majesty." I had no other intention, than to express my sense, that the people solely can be affected by your refusal to do business. You had no room to suppose, that I intended by it, to set you in an unfavorable light, as disaffected to his Majesty, and so induced to a non-compliance with his royal pleasure.

The remaining parts of your message, having no immediate relation to this controversy, but respecting matters which concern the colonies in general, and the authority of the Supreme Legislature, upon which, in language very much the same, the House of Representatives have repeatedly enlarged, which has, from time to time, been transmitted to be laid before his Majesty, I will make no reply to them, for I have no inclination to multiply controversies with you; and those subjects have been so fully discussed, that it is not probable, you or I shall be able to cast any new light upon them.

I called you together, that you might further consider what, by the constitution, as appeared to me, it was your duty to do, and to give you an opportunity of doing it. You came, very soon, to a resolution to do no business. If you had stopped there, I should have prorogued you, without much delay; for I have no intention to compel you to any measure by duress, nor to cause any unnecessary charge upon the people; but you appointed a committee to answer my speech, which answer I did not receive until the eighth day after the meeting of the Court. I have taken one day only for my reply, and shall now order a further prorogation. It will be happy for the province, if, when you again assemble, you can join with me in what is necessary for its real interest. T. HUTCHINSON.

[The Court was then prorogued by the Secretary, to September 20th, to meet in the College Chapel, in Cambridge.—Some apology, perhaps, is necessary, for giving in this volume, all the speeches and messages of the Lieutenant Governor, and the messages and resolutions, &c. of the House of Representatives, and of the Council, respecting the convening and holding of the General Court at Cambridge. This has been done in conformity to the advice of the highly respectable personage, who was consulted on the subject, and who approved of this publication ; and the Editor feels a confidence, that the papers relating to this controversy, will be read with interest, by those who wish to know all the proceedings of the patriots of that eventful period. These documents are, likewise, such as were promised in the proposals for this volume, and serve to exhibit the characters and principles of the men, who stood forth in opposition to the arbitrary assumptions of the British Ministry.]

===

SPEECH

OF THE LIEUTENANT GOVERNOR TO THE COUNCIL AND HOUSE OF REPRE-
SENTATIVES, SEPTEMBER 27, 1770.[*]

Gentlemen of the Council, and
  Gentlemen of the House of Representatives,

It is now become, in several respects, more necessary for the General Court to proceed upon the business of the province, than it was when I met you in your two last sessions. Many of our laws, which have been of great utility, are expired ; some for the punishment of criminal offences ; others which affect the course of our judicial proceedings ; and the people call for the revival of them. There are other affairs depending, of a very interesting nature, which had not then come to our knowledge, and which may be determined, before we can have another opportunity of acting upon them. The Council thought it not advisable for me to prorogue the Court to a further time. Their opinion and advice, which always have weight with me, induced me to call you together rather sooner than I had before intended.

Pursuant to my instructions, and the established practice, I caused the acts and doings of the General Court, at the session in March last, to be transmitted to England, by the first opportunity. Particular notice has been taken of a grant, made in that session, to a number of persons, who had settled upon lands in the eastern part of the province ; and, it appearing that other persons had also began settlements eastward of Sagadahock, some under color of grants from the General Court, notwithstanding that, by the ex-

---

[*] A committee had waited on the Lieutenant Governor, to inform him, that a quorum of the House of Representatives had met, and were desirous he would remove the General Court to its ancient and legal seat, the Town House, in Boston.

press terms of the charter, such grants are of no force, validity, or effect, until approved by the Crown; others, without any color of grant or title whatsoever. These settlements are deemed of great importance in various lights, but in none more so, than in that of the encouragement they have given to the waste and destruction of the King's timber, which is a matter of the most serious consideration, in respect of the naval strength of the kingdom. It is made my duty to inform you, that, as the remedy for this great mischief, ought properly, and can only effectually come from the province within whose jurisdiction the lands lie, it is expected all trespassers should be prosecuted; and I am further to inform you, that the neglecting to exert every legal means to remove and prevent all unwarrantable intrusions, will be imputed as a default, for which the province will stand responsible. From a sense of my duty to the King, and from regard to the interest of the province, I must desire you to take this affair into your consideration, and do what is necessary on your part. I will assist and concur with you, to the utmost of my power.

Gentlemen of the House of Representatives,

In order to conform to the laws of the province, and to maintain the public faith, it was necessary the Treasurer should issue his warrants, for the assessment of the whole province debt, in the current year. If these warrants have not been so far executed as to render any alteration impracticable, and you shall be of opinion, that the burden will be too great for the people to bear, I am willing to consent to an act for affording the necessary relief, by easing the present year of part of this tax, and charging the same sum upon a future year.

A state of the treasury will be laid before you, by which it will appear, that a supply will be necessary. Some appropriations are quite exhausted.

His Majesty having thought fit to order that the garrison of Castle William, in the pay of the province, should be withdrawn, and that this fortress should be garrisoned by his Majesty's regular forces, I am prevented from desiring you to make the usual establishment. The last establishment expired the 20th day of June last. I know you did not expect I should then dismiss the officers and men. I must now desire you to continue their pay and subsistence from the expiration of the establishment; and, as they are discharged at a season of the year when it will be difficult for them to find employ, I could wish that the continuance might extend, at least, to the 20th of November, the usual time of making up the roll. It is no more than justice to the garrison to say, they have behaved well, and have some claim to favor.

The establishment for Fort Pownall being also expired, I must recommend to you to provide for the revival and continuance of it.

Gentlemen of the Council, and House of Representatives,

As the affairs which lie before you, are of great moment, and deserve your serious and mature deliberation, so they must take up much time. It is therefore more necessary, that you should begin, without delay, and should proceed with all diligence. I wish there may be a good harmony in the Legislature, and that we may unite in such measures as our common interest, and the interest of the province, requires of us. **T. HUTCHINSON.**

MESSAGE

FROM THE HOUSE OF REPRESENTATIVES TO THE LIEUTENANT GOVERNOR, OCTOBER 4, 1770.

May it please your Honor,

The House of Representatives having taken into consideration your speech to both Houses, at the opening of this session, beg leave to request your Honor to explain a part of it, which is expressed in such terms, as leave it uncertain in its true intent and meaning. The passage referred to, is that wherein you say, " there are other affairs, of a very interesting nature, which had not then come to our knowledge, and which may be determined before we can have an opportunity of acting upon them." No such matters have come to the knowledge of this House; if they have been communicated to your Honor from his Majesty, or his Ministers, we desire you would be pleased to lay them before us, that we may have a precise understanding of what your Honor intends; the want of which, prevents our coming at present to any determination on your speech.

The House are also very desirous your Honor would inform them, whether you have received any late instructions, agreeable to your expectation, expressed in your message to this House, of the first of June last, relating to the continuance of this Assembly out of its ancient, legal, and only convenient place, the Town House, in Boston.

33

MESSAGE

FROM THE LIEUTENANT GOVERNOR TO THE HOUSE OF REPRESENTATIVES,
OCTOBER 4, 1770.

Gentlemen of the House of Representatives,

I AM not at liberty to make public, or communicate to you, by speech or message, an order of his Majesty in Council, of the 6th of July last, but it appears to me, that in consequence thereof, the state of the province of Massachusetts Bay will, undoubtedly, be recommended to the consideration of Parliament in the approaching session. This is the principal matter of moment to which my speech, at the opening of the session of the General Court, had respect. Although I am not at liberty to lay this order before you, yet, I am very ready to give all the information, in my power, to any committee, you may think proper, of the facts and ground upon which this order is founded, so far as shall consist with my instructions.

His Majesty has been pleased to cause to be expressed his entire approbation of my summoning the Court to meet at Cambridge. I am restrained from removing it to Boston, but I am not confined to the town of Cambridge. I am willing to meet the Court at any town in the province, which shall appear to me to be most for the convenience of the members, and which shall not militate with the spirit of my instructions.

T. HUTCHINSON.

MESSAGE

FROM THE HOUSE OF REPRESENTATIVES TO THE LIEUTENANT GOVERNOR, OCTOBER 13, 1770.

May it please your Honor,

IN your speech to both Houses at the opening of the session, you was pleased to say, that his Majesty had thought fit to order the garrison of Castle William, in the pay of the province, to be withdrawn, and the fortress to be garrisoned by his regular forces.

Your Honor must be assured, from a thorough knowledge of this people, that they are inferior to none of his Majesty's subjects, in loyalty and warmth of affection to his Majesty's person, family, and government. We have reason, therefore, to believe, that very false representations have been made of them to our Sovereign, to induce him to pass an order, which implies a total want of confidence, and carries in it the evident marks of his royal displeasure.

If you are knowing to any such representations, we have a right to expect that you will communicate them to us; and thereby give us the opportunity of taking the most effectual measures, to clear up our own and our constituents innocence, and recover his Majesty's favor. This request must appear to your Honor so reasonable in itself, and so important to us, that it cannot be denied; for it is repugnant to the common principles of natural justice, that we should remain under such injurious representations, without being made acquainted with the crimes that are alleged against us.

By the royal charter, it is expressly granted, established, and ordained, that the Governor of the province, for the time being, " shall have full power, from time to time, to erect forts, and to fortify any place or places within the province, and the same to furnish with all necessary ammunition, provision, and stores of war, for offence or defence, and to commit, from time to time, the custody and government of the same, to such person or persons, as to him shall seem meet." We beg your Honor would be pleased to inform us, whether you still hold the command of that important fortress? You tell us, in your speech, that you are prevented from desiring us to make the usual establishment; from hence, we have grounds to apprehend, that the power, vested in you by the charter, is superseded by instruction. If the custody and government of that fortress, is now lodged with the military power, independent of the supreme civil magistrate, within this jurisdiction, it is so essential an alteration of the constitution, as must justly alarm a free people. We cannot, therefore, but be very earnestly solicitous of being clearly and explicitly made acquainted with the full import of the aforementioned order, as well as the grounds and facts upon which it is founded.

[The committee who reported the above, were, Mr. Hancock, Gen. Prebble, Col. Gerrish, and Capt. Farley.]

MESSAGE

FROM THE LIEUTENANT GOVERNOR TO THE HOUSE OF REPRESENTATIVES,
OCTOBER 16, 1770.

Gentlemen of the House of Representatives,

I AM not privy to any false representations, which might induce his Majesty's order, to which you refer, in your message to me, and which, you suppose, to imply a total want of confidence, and to carry in it evident marks of the royal displeasure. I am, nevertheless, ready to do every thing in my power, to enable you

to take the most effectual measures to clear up your own, and your
constituents innocence, and to recover his Majesty's favor.

It is my duty to acquaint his Majesty's principal Secretary of
State for America, with all such public transactions, as are worthy
of his Majesty's notice. In the beginning of May last, I enclosed
a copy of the answer of the House of Representatives to my message, of the 7th of April preceding. I did it without any comment, as I promised I would do. Soon after, I forwarded a printed
paper, containing the instructions, of the town of Boston, to their
Representatives. That message, and those instructions, without
any other representation, I have sufficient reason to believe, were
the immediate occasion of his Majesty's orders to me, to withdraw
from the Castle the garrison, in the pay of the province, and to
place there, a garrison of his Majesty's regular forces.

You recite in your message, which I am now answering, a paragraph of the charter, with which I am well acquainted, and which
I kept in my mind during the whole transaction, relative to the
exchange of the garrison, at his Majesty's Castle ; and you then
ask me, whether I still hold the command of that important fortress ? And, because I am prevented from desiring you to make
the usual establishment, you infer, that you have grounds to apprehend, that the power vested in me, by charter, is superseded
by instruction. This expression is somewhat equivocal. If you
mean no more, than that I have been instructed by his Majesty,
how to use that military authority, which is given me, by charter,
and by the royal commission, your inference is right, and such instructions I shall always observe ; but, if you intend that, by withdrawing a garrison from his Majesty's Castle, which was paid by
the province, and placing a garrison there, to be paid by the King,
in pursuance of instructions, received from him, I have divested
myself of the right given me, over this, in common with other forts
in the province, you have no grounds for your inference.   I have
not, in this instance, given up any part of your charter rights. I
never intend to do it in any other instance. On the other hand,
you may expect, that I will preserve every part of the King's prerogative.

I will take this occasion, to observe to you, that, as the ammunition and stores of war, lodged in the Castle, for his Majesty's
service, were purchased and intended for the general defence of
the province, as well as for the use of that particular fortress, I
think it necessary, either to continue the person, who had the immediate charge of those stores, or appoint some other person store-
keeper, to issue all stores, by my warrants or order, and to be
accountable to me. I must, also, retain another of the officers of
the former garrison, to receive all passes for outward bound vessels, and to make weekly return, to me, of all vessels, both outward and inward bound. This is so necessary a provision, for
preventing the breach of the acts of trade, that I dare not, upon

any consideration, omit it.   I must, therefore, recommend to you, to make a proper establishment of these two officers, until I may have opportunity of receiving a further signification of his Majesty's pleasure, concerning this garrison.

T. HUTCHINSON

====

MESSAGE

FROM THE HOUSE OF REPRESENTATIVES TO THE LIEUTENANT GOVERNOR, OCTOBER 23, 1770.

May it please your Honor,

In our message to your Honor, of the 13th instant, we desired you would be pleased to inform the House whether you still held the command of Castle William.   In answer to which you say, that, in withdrawing a garrison from his Majesty's Castle, which was paid by the province, and placing a garrison there, to be paid by the King, in pursuance of instructions from him, you have not given up any part of our charter rights.

This answer appears to the House to be somewhat equivocal. For your Honor may possibly differ with the House, in your construction of the clause in the charter, which we have recited.   By this clause, the Governor of the province is undoubtedly vested with the command of that fortress.   Your Honor may have been instructed to transfer that command to his Majesty's chief military officer in America, or any other person.   If that be the case, the power, which is vested in you, by the charter, is superseded by instructions.

A doubt in the House, respecting a matter of so very interesting a nature to the province, is the occasion of this repeated message to your Honor, to request that you would, in an explicit manner, assure us, whether you still hold the command of his Majesty's Castle William.

[The committee which prepared this message, were, Mr. S. Adams, Mr. J. Adams, Col. Warren, Mr. Hancock, and Col. Prescott.]

MESSAGE

FROM THE LIEUTENANT GOVERNOR TO THE HOUSE OF REPRESENTATIVES,
OCTOBER 23, 1770.

Gentlemen of the House of Representatives,

IN my answer to your message, of the 13th instant, I have told you, that, by withdrawing the garrison from Castle William, which was paid by the province, and placing a garrison there, to be paid by the King, in pursuance of instructions, received from him, you had no grounds to infer, that I have divested myself of the right given me, by charter, over this fort, in common with the other forts in the province.

I had no latent meaning in this, nor any other expression, in my answer. I intended it should convey this idea, that I was not, by the exchange of the garrison, divested of the right, and, consequently, that I still retain it, for it has never been suggested, that I have parted with it in any other way, nor do I know of any color for such suggestion.

I know of no ambiguity, in that clause of the charter, which you have recited in your first message to me. I shall be sorry, if the House shall put any construction upon it, different from what appears to me to be the plain sense of the words; but, I must govern myself by my own understanding, and choose to avoid any altercation concerning it.

The authority given me over the Castle, by his Majesty's commission, I have exercised, and continue to exercise, without any infringement of the rights of the people, by charter, or otherwise, and without any extension of the prerogative of the Crown beyond its just limits ; and, I doubt not, I shall be able to vindicate my conduct, if ever I shall be called to account for it.

T. HUTCHINSON.

MESSAGE

FROM THE COUNCIL TO THE LIEUTENANT GOVERNOR, OCTOBER 25, 1770.

May it please your Honor,

YOUR Honor having been pleased to make known to the Board, some part of a letter from the Earl of Hillsborough, and also the report of a committee of the Lords of Council, with his Majesty's order in Council, thereon—which report and order, greatly affecting the character of the Council of this province, and may, in their consequences, affect our charter right; we pray your

Honor to lay before this Board, an authentic copy of the said report and order, and so much of the said letter, as may concern either the Council or the province, that the Board may know the reasons on which they are grounded, and take such measures as shall be judged most advisable, to vindicate the character of the Council, and prevent any infringements on the charter rights of the province.

[The committee who waited on the Lieutenant Governor with the above message, reported verbally from his Honor, " that, by his instructions, he was strictly forbidden to give a copy of said letter, report, or order, or even to mention them, by speech or message, to either House."—It may be proper to observe here, that the aforesaid " report and order" were, in consequence of a *deposition* of A. Oliver, Esq. the Secretary, taken by request of Lieutenant Governor Hutchinson, and by him, with other papers, forwarded to England, to be laid before the Ministry ; which deposition states what was done by the Council, on the 6th of March, 1770, specially convened by the Lieutenant Governor, on account of the massacre of the 5th, when some of the British regular troops, then stationed in Boston, fired upon the citizens, and killed and wounded eleven of them. The deposition of the Secretary states, that the Council advised the Lieutenant Governor to order the troops to the barracks, at the Castle, as otherwise they would be destroyed ; that the commissioners also must remove from Boston, where their persons were not safe ; and that a plan had been formed by the people very generally, including men of property and influence, in the province, to have the troops and commissioners removed immediately. The deposition was so worded, as to bear the construction, and that perhaps most naturally, that such a plan was formed previously to the massacre ; whereas, the opinion of the Council really was, that the people were greatly exasperated, by the murder of their fellow citizens, and would not rest easy till the troops were removed from Boston to the Castle, or withdrawn wholly from the province. The deposition further states, that the minutes taken by the Secretary, of the doings and advice of Council, on the 6th, were by them, on the 7th, ordered to be altered ; because, though what took place was therein stated truly, yet, they were desirous it should be so expressed, as to be more favorable to them : the Secretary thus insinuating, that they were unwilling to have all they did and advised, appear precisely as it was ; but would have it receive a coloring which would still show their loyalty. And accordingly, in his said deposition, he recited the minutes, as taken the 6th, and then gave the same proceedings, as amended by the Council, on the 7th. The following report of the Council, on this subject, will give a correct view of the affair.]

REPORT

OF A COMMITTEE OF COUNCIL, MADE TO THE BOARD, OCTOBER 24, 1770, RE-
SPECTING THE REPRESENTATION MADE BY SECRETARY OLIVER OF THEIR
CONDUCT, MARCH SIXTH AND SEVENTH, 1770; AND BY THE BOARD UNANI-
MOUSLY ACCEPTED.

THE committee having considered the petition of Secretary
Andrew Oliver, and his affidavit, concerning the proceedings at the
Council, on the 6th and 7th of March last, annexed to a pamphlet
published in London, take occasion to make a few observations
upon them.

With regard to the said affidavit, several things are observable
from it.

1st. That what is there declared to be said by Mr. Tyler,* in
Council, is expressed in such a manner as to be generally understood to represent, that, antecedent to the unhappy affair of the
5th of March last, there had been a plan formed, by people of the
best characters among us, to remove the troops out of the town of
Boston; and after that, the commissioners.

2d. That divers gentlemen of the Council adopted what had
been so said.

3d. That the Secretary had, in his draft, expressed what had
been said in debate, at Council, in the terms in said affidavit recited; and that this form, or draft of his, was "allowed by the
Council, strictly to express the truth; but that it would not stand
well on the Council records; whereupon one of the gentlemen of
the Board prepared an amendment, which was substituted."

As to the first article, the plan therein mentioned, was, according to the affidavit, or deposition of the Secretary, intended to effect the removal of the troops, and the removal of the commissioners. With regard to the removal of the troops, Mr. Tyler, who
mentioned the said plan in Council, on the 6th of March last, declares, that he had uttered nothing in said Council, purporting
that any plan had been formed to remove the troops, previously to
their firing on the inhabitants; that he had no idea of a plan
formed for the removal of said troops, until the day after the shocking scene on the evening of the 5th of March; and that he then
meant to be understood, that the disposition of the people to remove the troops, was occasioned by the killing and wounding of
divers inhabitants of the town, and by the people's apprehensions
that the troops still had an unfriendly design against them. Mr.
Erving, Mr. Pitts, and Mr. Dexter,† declare, that they cannot recollect, neither do they believe, that any thing was said in Council by Mr. Tyler, purporting that any plan had been formed to re-

---

* R. Tyler, one of the Council.   † Members of the Council.

move the troops, previously to their firing on the inhabitants; but, that they understood him to mean, that the people were excited to such a measure, by the killing and wounding some of the inhabitants of the town, on the evening immediately preceding.

Mr. Danforth, and other gentlemen of the Board, then present in Council, have made, in substance, the same declaration. Mr. Cotton, the Secretary's deputy, and his assistant, Mr. Skinner, declared, that, when Mr. Tyler mentioned the plan aforesaid, they did not apprehend him to mean a plan, concerted before the 6th of March, and the Secretary, himself, has lately declared, before the Board, that he did not conceive Mr. Tyler to mean such a preconcerted plan; and that he never believed any such plan had been formed. All which declarations amount to a satisfactory proof, that what Mr. Tyler said in Council, did not convey the idea, that a plan had been formed to remove the troops, previous to their killing a number of the inhabitants.

With regard to a plan to remove the commissioners, Mr. Cotton declares, he heard Mr. Tyler say, that there was a plan to remove the troops from the town; and, that they would not stop there, but would remove the commissioners also. F. Skinner[*] declares, in substance, the same; as does also Capt. Caldwell.[*] The two first, however, say, that they did not apprehend Mr. Tyler meant a plan concerted before the 6th of March. With regard to this, Capt. Caldwell is not explicit.

Lieut. Col. Dalrymple[*] said nothing in his deposition, concerning the commissioners; but, afterwards, being asked whether he remembered that Mr. Tyler said, a part of the plan was to remove the commissioners out of Boston? he answered, that something of the kind was said by some one of the Council, during the debates, but he could not say, that it was Mr. Tyler.

This is the whole of what is declared on the positive side, relative to the commissioners. Two of these declarants, viz.: Messrs. Cotton and Skinner, say, they were called out, divers times, while the Council was sitting, and in the course of the proceedings; and Mr. Cotton infers from it, " that he cannot declare so fully as those who attended, without interruption." Capt. Caldwell did not go to the Council, till four o'clock in the afternoon of the 6th of March, and, therefore, cannot judge of what passed in Council, so well as those who attended both parts of the day; did not recollect, when he gave his deposition, that any thing had been said concerning the commissioners; and his answer, when afterwards asked, shews, he had only a general remembrance of something said about the commissioners. It is very probable, that what passed between the Lieutenant Governor and several of the Council, relative to the protection of the commissioners, as hereafter mentioned, was the thing which lay on his mind.

* Skinner was a Clerk to the Secretary.—Caldwell and Dalrymple, British Officers, called before the Governor and Council, to give their testimony.

It is not doubted, that these declarants understood Mr. Tyler, in the sense they have stated ; but, it is very probable, they might misapprehend him. It appears, by the deposition of Mr. Gray,* and others, that the Lieutenant Governor asked the Board, what protection there would be for the commissioners, if both regiments were ordered to the Castle ; and this, very probably, gave the occasion for mentioning the commissioners at all.   Mr. Tyler, upon that question, might express his sentiments on that head ; and, having so fair an opportunity, might express his sentiments also, concerning the commissioners themselves, and the low estimation in which they are held by people in general, not only here, but through the continent ; and, this being mixed with the subject of the day, viz. : the removal of the troops, might occasion, what he meant to say, relative to the troops only, to be understood by some, as relative to them and the commissioners also.   It is certain, that all the gentlemen of the Council, then present, have declared, on oath, they have no remembrance that Mr. Tyler said, there was a plan laid for the removal of the commissioners ; and, Mr. Gray adds, to this declaration, that he took particular notice of what Mr. Tyler did say.   Mr. Tyler, himself, on the most serious recollection, declares, on oath, that the assertion; that he said, " there was a plan formed to remove the commissioners, or, that it was any part of a plan to remove them," is a gross misrepresentation ; and that, in his best judgment, and firm belief, no plan to remove the troops, before their firing on the inhabitants of Boston ; or, at any time whatever, to remove the commissioners, ever was formed, or forming by the people, or any number of persons whatever.   He further declares, that, on the Lieutenant Governor's asking, in the Council, what will become of the commissioners, if the troops are removed, several of the gentlemen gave it as their opinion, that they would be safe, and always had been safe ; and, he verily believes, nothing was said to the contrary, by any one of the Council present.   Mr. Gray declares, " that, when the Lieutenant Governor asked the said question, he answered, that the commissioners would be as safe, without the troops, as with them ; for, that the people would never be so mad, as to offer them the least violence, when the troops could so easily be recalled, for their protection."   He further declares, " that one gentleman, at the Board, immediately seconded him, and assured his Honor of their safety ; and added, that he would pawn his life, they would receive no injury."

Mr. Danforth declares, he well remembers, that divers of the Council then declared, that, in their opinion, the commissioners might continue in town, in all safety, after the troops were removed ; and, that no one of the Council present, discovered an opinion diverse therefrom.

* Member of the Council.

Mr. Erving declares, that, he said at the Board, in the hearing of the Lieutenant Governor, on the 6th of March, that, in his opinion, the commis-ioners were safe in town, and never had been in danger; and, that he would pawn his life, they would remain safe, or words of the same import.

If the foregoing circumstances and declarations be duly considered, it will appear highly probable, that, if Mr. Tyler said any thing about the commissioners, it was misunderstood. And, this will appear still more so, if it be further remarked, that, on the contrary supposition, it must have been considered, as a reason for the troops remaining in town, had the commissioners been supposed to be in danger, as has been observed by several of the deponents; and the said deponents are persuaded, it would have been so considered by the Lieutenant Governor, and the commanding officer of the troops; and, consequently, have tended to defeat the end, which the Members of the Council, particularly Mr. Tyler, were aiming at. And, they further observe, that, had he mentioned it, as his opinion, there was a design of the people to remove the commissioners, it would have been so entirely contrary to the sentiments of the deponents, and, they doubt not, of every Member of the Council, present, except himself, that they verily believe, it must have produced such a dispute and opposition, as would not soon have been forgotten.

The second thing observable from the affidavit of the Secretary, is, that divers gentlemen of the Council, by referring expressly to it, adopted what Mr. Tyler had said, viz.: " that the people of the best characters among us, had formed a plan, not only to remove the troops, but the commissioners."

In contradiction to this, every gentleman of the Council, then present, deny that they adopted any such declaration. So far are they from adopting what is represented to have been said by Mr. Tyler, about a plan to remove the commissioners, that there is not one of them has the least remembrance of any thing said concerning a plan to remove the commissioners; and therefore, they could not refer to it, or in any sense whatever, adopt it. Mr. Hubbard and Mr. Russell,* declare, that, as they cannot recollect they heard a word from Mr. Tyler of any intention to remove the commissioners, so neither could they have adopted such a strange opinion, had it been advanced by any person whatever.

Mr. Erving, Mr. Dexter, and Mr. Pitts, declare the same, and add, that, according to their best remembrance, what was *really* said in Council, by Mr. Tyler, was not referred to by any other Member present, in such manner as that it could, with the least degree of propriety, be affirmed in general terms, as it is in the deposition of the said A. Oliver, " that they adopted what Mr. Tyler had said."

* Members of the Council.

Mr. Danforth, in his deposition, recites, that, " whereas in Mr. Oliver's affidavit it is asserted, that divers of the Council adopted what Mr. Tyler had said, by referring to it, and thereby excusing themselves from enlarging, (which assertion plainly imports that divers members of the Council assented to and adopted all that Mr. Oliver, in his affidavit, had represented to have been said by Mr. Tyler, relative to a plan formed to remove the commissioners, as well as the troops,) he, the deponent, declares, that although he had the like apprehensions Mr. Tyler had of the danger of further bloodshed, in case the troops should continue in town, yet, that he never adopted any sentiment, that a plan had been concerted to remove the commissioners, (or even the troops, by way of compulsion,) and, so far at least, as relates to the commissioners, this deponent is fully persuaded, that no Member of the Council, then present, did adopt the same ; inasmuch as he well remembers, that divers of them then declared, that, in their opinion, the commissioners might continue in town with all safety, after the troops were removed thence ; and no one of the Council, then present, discovered an opinion diverse therefrom."

From these depositions, and what went before, it appears, that the said gentlemen of the Council, were so far from adopting what the Secretary represents to have been said by Mr. Tyler, as to a plan to remove the commissioners, that there is not one of them has the least remembrance of any thing said about such a plan ; and therefore, they could not refer to it, or in any sense whatever, adopt it.

The third thing observable in the Secretary's affidavit, is what he declares about his draft expressing what had been said in debate at Council, " that it was allowed by the Council strictly to express the truth, but that it would not stand well on the Council records." This declaration represents the Council in a very odious light. It conveys to the world this idea, that they rejected his draft because it was true ; and that the truth of it made it unfit to be recorded in the Council books; "whereupon an amendment was substituted." To substitute an amendment, which alters the truth, is to substitute a falsehood. And as the said declaration suggests such a substitution, it implies a charge of falsehood on the gentlemen, who were present at that Council. But though the committee apprehend the Secretary did not intend any such charge, yet his words may probably be construed to imply it.

With regard to the said amendment, most of the gentlemen have expressed their sentiments in their respective depositions. Five of them declare, that the words made use of in the amendment, as recited by the Secretary, in his deposition, which were, the next morning, proposed in Council, to be substituted instead of the terms the Secretary had used in the minutes of the Council, taken the day before, these deponents then thought less liable to be misconstrued ; and that, by this alteration, the true meaning and intent of the Members of the Council, in what they had said on the preceding day, to the Lieutenant Governor, of the disposition of the people, would fully and fairly appear.

Mr. Danforth declares, that the said amendment was unanimously agreed to by the Members of the Council, then present, and contains the whole of what, after full debate and mature consideration, was by them adopted; and, (together with the advice given to the Lieutenant Governor, to use his influence that the troops might be removed,) was, as the deponent apprehends, the whole that could regularly be certified by the Secretary; as they were the only votes of the Council, that passed on that occasion.

The committee proceed to consider the Secretary's petitions to the Board, and to make some observations upon them.

In one of them he represents, that his deposition or affidavit, above mentioned, appears, by the tenor of it, to have been made merely to vindicate the Lieutenant Governor, in desiring that his Majesty's troops might be removed to Castle William, after the fatal catastrophe of the 5th of March, he having been called upon, by the Lieutenant Governor, to give a true relation of the proceedings, had in Council, on that affair. If the Lieutenant Governor desired the said deposition for his vindication, could he not have been vindicated without the Secretary's traducing the Council, and bringing into question the loyalty of the town of Boston, or the province? Was it not traducing the Council, to suggest that they rejected his draft, because it strictly expressed the truth? And was it not bringing into question the loyalty of the town or province, to suggest that a plan had been formed, by people of the best characters among us, to remove the troops and commissioners; and that divers of the Council adopted or allowed it to be true, that there was such a plan? Do these suggestions, and the declarations contained in the Secretary's deposition, in which he wholly omits what was said about the safety of the commissioners, comport with a true relation of the proceedings had in Council, on the above mentioned affair; which relation the Lieutenant Governor called upon him for?

The Secretary further represents, that, as holding his commission immediately from the King, who therein expresses his confidence in his fidelity, he could not consider himself as acting in breach of trust, in making said deposition, as he was called upon by the Commander in Chief, who is the King's Representative, to give a true relation of the proceedings had in Council, on that day.

Though the Secretary holds his commission immediately from the King, the commission constitutes him an officer of the province, to do the business appertaining to the office of Secretary; but does not give the Commander in Chief, notwithstanding he is the King's Representative in the province, any authority over him. By virtue of his commission, he is to do the proper business of Secretary; but could it be a part of such business, to take minutes at Council, of what all, or any of the Members, said in their debates? and afterwards to give a deposition of it, when called upon by the Commander in Chief ? If it was not a part of such business, for what purpose could he want to assist his memory, by taking the said minutes ? Could this be any proof of fidelity to the King ; or would it not be considered as a breach of trust ? Would not such an idea of the business of a Secretary, degrade him into the character of a spy or informer ? Would it not be inconsistent with the freedom of consultation and debate, and consequently with one of the most essential privileges and rights of Council ? And would it not, therefore, be subversive of every principle, which distinguishes a free government from despotism ? But, admitting that the Secretary, as the King's officer, is under obligation to take such minutes, at Council, and reduce them to a deposition, if desired by the King's Representative, (which is utterly denied,) yet it appears, by one of the Secretary's petitions to the Board, that he officiously, without the privity of any one, took the minutes of what was said in the debates of Council, on the 6th of March.

If the Secretary could think himself authorized to take such minutes, and give such deposition, was he not under the obligation of honor, and did not justice require him to communicate it to the Council, before he had completed and delivered it ? Had he done so, the mistakes, and the partial representations contained in it, might have been corrected, and his own honor and justice remained unimpeached.

It has been, for some time, justly complained of, that depositions, memorials, and every species of information, have been made and taken, and sent to England in a secret manner, and there made use of, to represent his Majesty's subjects here, in an odious light ; which has occasioned troops and naval armaments to be sent hither, to the great, and unjust annoyance and distress of his Majesty's subjects of this province. It was, therefore, the more extraordinary, that the Secretary, in the affair of his deposition, should act in the same secret manner ; especially, as it respected what had been said in Council ; about which, he could have easily informed himself from the Members, who, at the same time, had a right to know what he had represented concerning them. Whatever may have been designed, with regard to the operation of this deposition, the manifest tendency of it is, to give a most unfavorable, and, at the same time, a most unjust idea of the people here, and of the Council, in particular. As the said deposition represents the Council in an ill light, it would be no disagreeable present to Governor Bernard, to whom it was sent by the Lieutenant Governor, as he informed the Board. His Honor, at the same time, informed them, that he desired Governor Bernard to keep it to himself, unless his conduct, with regard to removing the troops, should be faulted ; in which case, it was to be made use of for his Honor's vindication. Whether it was used for that purpose, is uncertain. But, it is certain, that it was published in London, annexed, with other depositions, to a pamphlet, entitled " a *fair* account of the late unhappy disturbances at Boston, in New England ;" in which pamphlet and depositions, is given a very *unfair*, and, in all material circumstances, a very *false* account, of what is therein called, the late unhappy disturbance. The most material thing aimed at, in the said pamphlet, is, to obtrude, as truth, on the public, this falsehood, viz. : that a plan was here laid for the expulsion of the troops, prior to their firing on, and killing a number of the inhabitants of the town; and the principal, if not the only deposition, which, in any measure, tends to support such a charge, is the Secretary's.

The deposition has, in some degree, answered the purpose of the pamphlet writer or procurer; and is well calculated to answer the further purpose of Governor Bernard, to effect a change in the constitution of the Council, by giving a very disadvantageous idea of the Board, of the last year, from which will be formed the idea of the present Council, which includes the same Members as the last.

This deposition has been attended with circumstances which appear, in some degree, remarkable. It was taken the same day, on which most of the other depositions, annexed to the pamphlet, were taken, viz. : the 13th of March. They probably all went by Mr. Commissioner Robinson, who sailed for England, the 16th of March; and they are all published together, in the same pamphlet. Whether these circumstances are casual, or whether they indicate a mutual correspondence and communication between persons here, with regard to said depositions, there do not appear any sufficient means fully to determine.

The Secretary further represents, " how cautious he was in framing his deposition; and that he is confident he has been precise in setting down the very words used on the occasion, without adding any construction of his own." How cautious and precise the Secretary has been, especially in representing what was said about the commissioners, has fully appeared above. He not only gives an imperfect account of what he has represented, but, has wholly omitted all the declarations made at Council, relative to the commissioners, that they would be safe, though the troops should be removed; which has already sufficiently appeared.

The Secretary goes on to observe, " that the principal matter, wherein the testimony of divers (or rather of all) of said gentlemen, differs from his own, appears, to him, to be concerning what relates to the commissioners; with regard to which, he apprehends, his deposition is fully supported by the testimony of disinterested witnesses, then present."

The Secretary here suggests, that the gentlemen of the Council are interested, and, therefore, that their testimony, wherein it differs from that of his witnesses, who, he represents, as disinterested, must be invalidated." Seven gentlemen of the Council have given testimony, about what Mr. Tyler is represented to have said in Council, concerning the troops and commissioners. In this matter, it is evident, they are wholly disinterested. What inducement, then, could they have, to pervert the truth? How is their testimony, in this matter, invalidated? They may be stiled disinterested witnesses, as properly, as those produced by the Secretary; and, much more so, than two of them, who act under, and are dependent on the Secretary, for their continuance in office. The committee have been thus particular in this matter, that the true state of it might appear; and that, thereby, the pernicious consequences to the province, which, the Board apprehend, the Secretary's deposition may be attended with, may be prevented. So far as this matter stands related to the Council, it appears, that the Secretary's deposition exhibits to the world, a very dishonorable and injurious idea of them, by suggesting, " that, because his draft was allowed strictly to express the truth, it would not stand well on the Council record, and was, therefore, rejected by the Council." It appears, also, that the Secretary has, in a secret manner, taken minutes at Council, of what was said by the Members, in their debates; that he has subscribed his name to a paper, containing those minutes, and has taken his deposition before F. Hutchinson, Esq. to the truth of it; also, that the said paper and deposition have been sent, by the Lieutenant Governor, to Governor Bernard; and, that they have been since published, with other depositions, annexed to a pamphlet, designed to defame the province, with regard to the unhappy affair of the 5th of March.

The conduct of the Secretary, in this affair, is not only a breach of trust in him, and injurious to the character and honor of the Council, but is destructive of all freedom of speech and debate; and, consequently, a breach of privilege, the most essential privilege belonging to the Council, or that can belong to a deliberative body.

The committee, therefore, are humbly of opinion, that the honor of the Council requires the Board to adopt the following resolutions:

1. Resolved, That Andrew Oliver, Esq. Secretary of this province, by secretly taking minutes at Council, of what was said by the Members in their debates; also, by signing a paper, containing those minutes; and, further, by giving his deposition to the truth of it, has, in each, and all those instances, acted inconsistently with the duty of his office, and thereby is guilty of a breach of trust.

2. Resolved, That the said Andrew Oliver, Esq. inasmuch as such proceedings are destructive of all freedom of debate, is guilty of the breach of a most essential privilege of this Board.

3. Whereas the said Andrew Oliver, Esq. has suggested, in his said deposition, that, because his draft was allowed strictly to express the truth, it would not stand well on the Council records, and

and was, therefore, rejected by the Council. Resolved, That by such suggestion, he has injured and abused the Members composing the Council; and, by so doing, has reflected dishonor on this Board.

4. Resolved, That an attested copy of this report be sent to Mr. Agent Bollan, that he may make the best use thereof, he can, for the benefit of this province.

———

LETTER

FROM THE COUNCIL TO WILLIAM BOLLAN, ESQ. AGENT, IN ENGLAND, OCTOBER 30, 1770.

Sir,

WE are extremely sorry to find, by your letter of the   ; and otherwise, how unhappy the situation of our public affairs is, on the other side of the water; and that it is probable they will, in the next session of Parliament, be the subject matters of their inquiry, without our ever being notified to make answer to the charges exhibited against the province, or of defending the Council, in particular. This is so far from being constitutional, as, that perfect innocence is no protection in such a case. But yet, hard as it is, unconstitutional as it is, we make no doubt, that it will be the case, unless your active, vigorous efforts prevent it; which, from the experience of your former services, we are very confident will not be wanting. On, or about the 6th of July last, it is very likely you will find, that a committee of the Lords of Council, for plantation affairs, in their report, which was accepted by the Lords of Council, gave the following advice to his Majesty, that Castle William should be taken into his own hands, and garrisoned by his own troops; which hath since been done; the Castle delivered up; Capt. Phillips, the officers and privates, sent off, and now entirely in the hands of the regulars; that the place of rendezvous, for the King's ships, in North America, should be at Boston; accordingly, Com. Hood came from Halifax, with his squadron; he was soon relieved by the arrival of Com. Gambier. And now, at a time of profound peace, we have a greater number of men of war, in the harbor of Boston, than was known in time of war, since the first settlement of the country.

The following charges were likewise reported, and accepted by the Lords of Council, requesting his Majesty to lay the same before the Parliament, at their next session, really, that our constitution might be essentially altered, viz.:

" 1st. That seditious and libellous publications are encouraged,

35

and go unpunished, manifesting a design to stir up the people to acts of violence and opposition to the laws, and to the authority of Parliament. 2d. Goods, liable to duties, forcibly landed, without paying those duties; lawful seizures rescued by force; officers abused, and treated with violence, whilst doing their duty; illegal proceedings of the town of Boston, in their meetings of June 13th, and September 12th, 1768, and the Convention at Boston, September 22d;* a combination not to import goods from England; and the several resolutions and proceedings, in consequence thereof; the declarations and doctrines, inculcated by the House of Representatives, in their resolutions and messages to the Governor; the instructions of Boston to their Representatives;* the Council disposed to adopt those principles, and to countenance such illegal proceedings, evidently manifested, in their backwardness, to join with the Governor, in such measures as were necessary to prevent the same; their meeting, and acting as a Council of State, without a summons from the Governor, and without his presence, and printing their resolutions."

These are the charges, we conjecture, his Majesty, by advice of Council, will lay before the Parliament, in their next session; and, it is pretty certain, the Lieutenant Governor, in a letter from the Earl of Hillsborough, hath this account. A committee from the Council waited upon his Honor, for a copy of the letter, report, and order, so far as it respected the rights of the province and colony; but, the Lieutenant Governor told the committee, that, by his instructions, he was strictly forbid giving one, or even to mention them, by speech or message, to either House. These charges, the Lords of Council have looked into, and have adjudged to be facts. And, therefore, the Parliament is only to determine the punishment. Such a conduct as this, till of late, is not to be paralleled. How is English liberty lost! How precarious and uncertain is man's liberty, and, even his very life! For, if they, in this way, can take away the former, they may take away the latter. They may as constitutionally determine, that every Member of his Majesty's Council hath been guilty of high treason, and deny, that the Parliament would make an act for your punishment.† Surely, upon application for time allowed us to answer, they cannot deny you, unless corruption reigns without control. But still, while we think of the election of a Member for Middlesex, we need fear every thing. Wherefore, we will suggest a few things to you, relative to the charges aforesaid, so far as the charges respect the Council; we say, so far as they respect the Council; not, because we suppose the other charges true, and not to be answered; but, because the Council are not the proper persons to do it, and it might be taken amiss, if we should. As to

* See Appendix.

† This seems obscure, but it is so in the original.

the first, that seditious and libellous papers going unpunished, &c.; allowing that to be the case, where doth the fault lie? Not in the Council. Can they try and determine these matters? In this way, they have nothing to do with them. Why is there not a charge against the House of Lords, (which is the *summa curia*,) that they do not suppress those seditious and libellous publications at home? If we have any amongst us, there are fifty in England to one here. Must the English constitution, then, so far as it relates to the House of Lords, be altered, because they do not do that, which, by law, they cannot do; and, which, if they did, would be an infraction of the constitutional rights of Englishmen.

If such publications have taken place here, and no notice has been taken of them, where doth the fault lie? Surely in him who acts for the King, as his Attorney, in his not drawing indictments, summoning witnesses in support of the same, and then laying the whole before the Grand Jury; and, if he hath not done it, the fault is not in the Council, unless they had endeavored to prevent it, which is very far from being the case, as will presently be shown. It is very surprising, that administration should think so highly of the few disorders amongst us, when the provocations from themselves have been the sole cause of all. For us to be deprived of our rights, liberties, and privileges, purchased and defended by our ancestors, at the expense of so much treasure and blood, (and not by the Crown,) purchased by them, and granted to them, as an inheritance; and, in the struggle for the preservation of them, if the people should have gone a little too far, ought there not to have been an allowance made? Surely, they ought never to be magnified; nor could they so by any, but those " who strain at a gnat and swallow a camel;" who seek nothing so much, as the destruction of an injured, abused province, at all adventures. As to the Council being disposed to adopt these principles, and countenance such illegal proceedings, evidently manifested in their backwardness to join with the Governor, in such measures as were necessary to restrain and suppress them, there is nothing, that was ever invented, more groundless. After his Honor the Lieutenant Governor, the Secretary, Judge Trowbridge, and other very respectable gentlemen, were left out of the Council, Governor Bernard apprehended, that there was no duty, no loyalty left at the Council Board, and gave the prerogative up as lost; and this he often declared: We say, that after this, there was a message to both Houses, from the Governor, relative to a libel against him, published in one of the Boston newspapers. The House took it up of themselves; the *mobbish* Board, as he had represented them, chose a committee to take the message into consideration. The committee reported, which was unanimously accepted by the Council, and presented by the Board to the Governor, as their answer to his message. He was extremely pleased, and passed the highest panegyric upon the Council that could be

passed; assuring them, that he would write to the Secretary of
State, that he might acquaint his Majesty with the loyalty, duty,
and fidelity of his Council of the Massachusetts Bay; and, if he
was as good as his word, he did it; and his letter can be produced.   What he said of the Council then, was strictly true; for,
words could not express greater abhorrence of the libel, than that
answer conveyed.   Could a Council, which he is so fond of having now, have done more than they then did?

Again, can this charge on the Council be true, when he never
once desired a proclamation might issue, with advice of Council,
with, or without a reward, just as he was pleased to draw it, but
what the Council advised to it.   In many cases, this was done
immediately upon his hearing the story; and, if it was so far
against the province, as, that he could improve it to their prejudice, he never wanted faith to believe; for, immediately a Council was called, and advice moved for, that a proclamation might
issue, and, in many instances, that the Attorney General should
be directed to prosecute, and never once denied.   The Council,
in short, were so desirous that his Majesty's honor and prerogative might be preserved, and so afraid that he should take exceptions at the conduct of the Council, that, in sundry instances,
they went full far enough, when they advised to issue proclamations, and, at the same time, the matter complained of, was
scarcely worthy the notice of a single Justice of the Peace; and,
once or twice, when he obtained the advice of Council, no proclamation issued.   In these cases, we suppose, he did not think
we should have advised to a proclamation; but, then he intended
our refusal as a charge against the Council.

During his administration, there were proclamations issued, with
advice of Council; and yet, it is determined by the Lords of
Council, that the Massachusetts Council is backward to join the
Governor, in measures to prevent disorders; nay, adopt those
principles, and use measures to countenance them further.   Had
there been any Justices of the Peace, who Governor Bernard
thought failed in their duty, why did he not summon a general
Council, and ask their advice to remove them?   This, he never
did.   It was, therefore, time enough for him, or any one else, to
assert these as facts, when we had refused; which, we repeat, the
Council never did.

And, since the absence of Governor Bernard, how many proclamations have been issued?   Particularly, upon Mr. Hulton's, one
of the commissioners of the customs, complaint; or rather, on the
Council's first hearing, that a trespass was committed upon his
house, in a country town, about four miles from Boston, in the
night, when he and his family were a bed in it; though, at the
same time, the Council had no reason to think, there were twenty
persons present, when the trespass was committed, or, that it
would have been committed at all, had he been in Boston.   The

Council are unanimously of opinion, that the greater part of the town of Boston, that all the influential, leading men in it, were anxiously concerned to preserve the commissioners' persons from any insult or abuse, and their property, from the appearance of a trespass. Nay, we do not think the people of the town were disposed to injure their persons or property; but that, on the contrary, they would have been in perfect safety in Boston, had they continued there. We persuade ourselves, that the Lieutenant Governor will do the Council justice, touching these things of this nature, which have taken place during his administration. Our surprise, if possible, still rises, when we are charged with meeting, and acting as a Council of State, without a summons from the Governor, and without his presence, and printing our resolutions. We are put to a difficulty to make answer to this, as there is no truth, or even shadow of truth, in it. How can we prove a negative? Had there been mention made of any particular time and case, it would have eased us of this impossibility. We can guess only at this : there was an affair in our Legislative capacity, which would have been finished in a few minutes before the Governor prorogued the Court, which the Governor well knew. He did not, at that time, act, as he and all other Governors had done before a recess; namely, to ask the Council, if they had any thing further to do; but, instead, except by the Secretary, and one or two others, who were near him, ordered the House up; and, the Court was then prorogued, without our completing what we were upon, in our Legislative capacity; and, upon sundry remonstrances and arguments with the Governor, he permitted us to finish what we were then upon; and, after it was finished, we published it. We do not see any crime in this, nor even in our meeting together, when the Governor has laid a charge against the Council, even without his summons and presence. The necessity of the thing will justify such a conduct; otherwise, the Council of this province are, of all men, the most unhappy; more so, than any individual of his Majesty's subjects, in his extended dominions; and yet, we do positively declare, the Council never once met, as a Council of State, without his permission.

Upon the whole, considering that our charter differs from most others—they being of grace—ours not so, but for services to be done; and, therefore, in the nature of a deed, where there is a valuable consideration paid : The immense sums it cost our ancestors in coming over, and settling an howling wilderness, and purchasing the land of the natives; the many bloody wars they and we have been engaged in, all at our own cost, have now made it a fruitful field, which has been of such great advantage to England, both by our conquests, our fishery, our trade, and, what of the British manufactures have been consumed among us; so, that in every respect, we have exceeded the most sanguine hopes and expectations, for the real service of the Crown : We infer, that to deprive us of our charter, or the liberty of choosing Counsellors, which comes to the same thing, must be contrary to law, reason, and common equity. And, we doubt not, of your hearty concurrence with us, in using your best endeavors, to prevent the evils meditated and threatened; which, should they take place, will work the destruction of those rights, civil and religious, which, we think, have been dearly purchased, and never forfeited.

====

MESSAGE

FROM THE LIEUTENANT GOVERNOR TO THE TWO HOUSES,
NOVEMBER 2, 1770.

Gentlemen of the Council, and

Gentlemen of the House of Representatives,

It appears to me necessary, that I should inform you, that his Majesty's fifth instruction to the Governor, requires him to observe, that, in the passing of all laws, the style of enacting the same be, by the Governor, Council, and House of Representatives, and no other. This style has been conformed to, except, perhaps, in a particular instance or two, for near thirty years, without the least inconvenience.

It may save you time, and prevent increase of public charges, to let you know, that I cannot, upon any terms, depart from this instruction. If I could be made sensible, that it was the least damage to the province, I would humbly represent it to his Majesty.   T. HUTCHINSON.

====

MESSAGE

FROM THE HOUSE OF REPRESENTATIVES TO THE LIEUTENANT GOVERNOR,
NOVEMBER 6, 1770.

May it please your Honor,

In your message of the 2d instant, you are pleased to inform the two Houses, that "his Majesty's fifth instruction to the Governor, requires him to observe, that, in the passing of all laws, the style of enacting the same, be, by the Governor, Council, and House of Representatives, and no other." This House have taken the importance of the message into their serious consideration, and are of opinion, that the words, in General Court assembled, are not merely words of form, but of substance, and necessary to the validity of every act.

By the royal charter, the Governor and Council are vested with some powers severally, and jointly with other powers, of acting for certain purposes in their departments, when the General Court is not sitting; but, for the purpose of making laws and statutes, there is no power given, either to the Governor, Council, or House of Representatives, to act, but when they are assembled in General Court. No law, therefore, can be valid, unless it be enacted by the Governor, Council, and House of Representatives, when thus assembled; and this, we apprehend, must appear from the parchment roll, wherein the act is recorded; otherwise, the record itself is not complete, and it will become necessary to resort to dehors evidence, to prove a fact essential to the validity of the act, which is against the established rule, respecting records. We are warranted in this opinion, from the invariable use of the same style in all acts of Parliament; which universally contain that express averment, that they were passed by the several branches in Parliament assembled.

We cannot conceive any reason, why the words should be disagreeable to his Majesty; for, we must suppose it to be his pleasure, that all acts should pass in such form, as is necessary to make them effectual. We find the words, in General Court assembled, and by the authority of the same, constantly, and invariably used in the passing of laws, from the beginning of the charter until within thirty years past; if your Honor should conceive that exception was taken against the latter words only, in the clause, you would then conclude, that it was altogether through inadvertence, that the instruction was made so large as to extend to the former.

This House considers the words to be of substance, and necessary; and, as they cannot but be of opinion, that, upon further consideration, they will so appear to your Honor, they hope you will think yourself at liberty to admit them, in the passing of the bills to be laid before you; by which means, time may be saved, and an increase of public charges prevented.

[The committee were, Mr. Leonard, S. Adams, J. Adams, Maj. Hawley, and Mr. Ingersol.]

MESSAGE

Gentlemen of the House of Representatives,

In your message to me, of the 6th instant, you have declared yourselves of opinion, that the words, " in General Court assembled," are not merely words of form in our laws, but of substance, and necessary to the validity of every act. Had your opinion been well founded, I should have thought it surprising, as well as unfortunate, that such a discovery should, for thirty years together, have escaped the Members of the several General Assemblies, all the gentlemen of the law concerned in our Executive Courts, and all the inhabitants of the province in general. But, it appears to me, that there is not the least foundation for your opinion. The style of a law, which expresses the Governor, Council, and House of Representatives, expresses that authority, which, by charter, hath the power to make laws; and the same reason which you urge for adding the words, " in General Court assembled," will hold as well, for further adding, " by the King's writ;" " under the province seal;" " signed by the Governor;" " issued thirty days before the convening;" together with all the other requisites for forming a constitutional General Court; for, in all these cases, if the facts do not appear upon the roll, it may be necessary to make use of dehors evidence, as in the case, when the words, " in General Court assembled," are not inserted. But, I am of opinion, this sort of evidence never was, and, probably, never will, be necessary in either case.

You will not be able to support your assertion, that acts of Parliament universally contain this express averment, that they were passed by the several branches in Parliament assembled. Many ancient statutes, without this clause, are equally in force with modern statutes, which have the clause; and modern acts of this province, without the clause, you contend for, are equally in force with ancient acts which have that clause.

I am not acquainted with the special reason, which induced his Majesty to restrain the Governor from consenting to an act with this clause in it. Perhaps, it was merely because it was unnecessary and redundant. Be it as it may, I cannot depart from my instructions, nor make my humble application that it may be withdrawn, unless I could see that it is an abridgement of your rights, or tended to subject the province to inconvenience.

I cannot help, as you have given me occasion for it, putting you in mind, that you are now in the seventh week of the session, and that scarce any of the public business is yet completed. I doubt

not, the House in general, wish to return to their private affairs;
and, I have reason to think your constituents, in all parts of the
province, wish to see all obstructions to your giving greater despatch, removed. I must, therefore, repeat my recommendations
to you, that, in concurrence with the Council, who, I am very
sure, are disposed to do their part, you will prepare the business,
now before the Court, to be laid before me, that the session may
be brought to an end, as soon as possible.

T. HUTCHINSON.

MESSAGE

May it please your Honor,

WE have maturely considered your message to this House,
of the 8th instant; and, we cannot but observe, with great concern, that, by virtue of instructions to the King's Governor of the
province, we are reduced to the necessity of passing laws, in such
form, as to render them, in our opinion, ineffectual. The words,
in General Court assembled, we still consider to be so substantial,
that we are as much surprized, as your Honor suggests you should
be, if you apprehended our opinion was well founded, that such a
discovery should, during thirty years together, have escaped the
Members of the several General Assemblies, &c.

Your Honor is pleased to say, " it appears to you, there is not
the least foundation for our opinion ;" and, in another place, that
" you are of opinion, that this sort of evidence never was, and
never will, be necessary in either case." How far these opinions,
thus precisely given, considering your Honor's high rank in the
law, ought to be an authority to us, must be left to the world to
judge; but, if that authority should not be deemed of weight
enough, absolutely to decide the question, this House is of opinion, that the decision of impartial judges will not be in favor of
the sufficiency of the late style used in enacting our laws.

The House think it surprizing and unfortunate, that your Honor
should assert, that " the style of a law, which expresses the Governor, Council, and House of Representatives, expresses that authority, which, by charter, hath power to make laws." In order
to show, whether this assertion is true or not, we beg leave to
adduce the words of the charter. They are these, viz.: " We
will, and by these presents, for us, our heirs, and successors, do
ordain and grant, that there shall, and may be convened, held, and

S6

kept by the Governor, for the time being, upon every last Wednesday in the month of May, every year, forever; and at all such other times, as the Governor of our said province, shall think fit and appoint, a great and General Court or Assembly; which said great and General Court or Assembly, shall consist of the Governor and Council, or assistants, for the time being, and of such freeholders of our said province, or territory, as shall be, from time to time, elected, or deputed, by the major part of the freeholders, and other inhabitants of the respective towns or places, who shall be present at such elections, &c.; to which great and General Court or Assembly, to be held as aforesaid, we do hereby for us, our heirs, &c. give and grant full power and authority, from time to time, to direct, appoint, and declare, &c." And, afterwards, we find the same great and General Court or Assembly empowered in the following words, viz.: " and we do, of our further grace, &c. grant, establish, and ordain, for us, our heirs, and successors, that the great and General Court or Assembly of our said province, or territory, being convened as aforesaid, shall forever have full power and authority to erect and constitute judicatures and courts of records, or other courts," &c. And, afterwards, the Governor, and the great and General Court or Assembly, are empowered in the following words, viz.: "and we do further, for us, our heirs, and successors, give, and grant to the said Governor, and the great and General Court or Assembly of our said province, or territory, for the time being, full power and authority, from time to time, to make, ordain, and establish all manner of wholesome and reasonable orders, laws, statutes and ordinances," &c.

From whence it is certain and obvious, that the style of a law, which expresses the Governor, Council, and House of Representatives, does not express that authority, which, by charter, hath power to make laws; because, the Governor, Council, and House of Representatives, have no authority to make laws by charter, unless they are convened and held in General Court or Assembly. And, we may venture to submit to your own consideration, whether an act of the Governor, Council, and House of Representatives, would be valid, which should be passed by each of those branches, not in General Court assembled? Should a bill pass this House, and be sent up to the Board in the present session, and, after a prorogation of the General Court, be concurred by the Council, and consented to by the Governor, can there be the least foundation, or an opinion, that such bill could become a law?

The House is astonished to hear your Honor say, that " the same reason which we urge for adding the words, in General Court assembled, will hold as well, for further adding, by the King's writ; under the province seal; signed by the Governor; issued thirty days before the convening; together with all the other requisites for forming a constitutional General Court;" because, although the words, Governor, Council, and House of Representatives, only imply the King's writ, under the province seal, signed by the Governor, and issued thirty days before the convening, yet, it does not imply all the other requisites for forming a constitutional General Court; whereas, the Governor, Council, and House of Representatives, in General Court assembled, necessarily imply all these, and every other requisite; and, therefore, these appearing on the record, there can be no necessity of recurring to so great an absurdity, as evidence dehors, in support of a record of the highest nature. You have not denied, that it is a known and approved maxim of the law, that every record must prove itself without any dehors evidence; nor that an act of Parliament, or law of this province, is not a record of the highest nature; yet, you have given it as your opinion, that dehors evidence never was, and, probably, never will be necessary in either case; which seems to imply, that, if in any case it should be necessary, it may be admitted, or else, that every thing which is necessary, does appear upon the face of a law, without these words, in General Court assembled, notwithstanding the constant practice of Parliament, for more than five centuries, has been, to use equivalent words, which must, upon your principles, be perfectly unnecessary, redundant and nugatory.

Your Honor is pleased to say, we shall not be able to support our assertion, " that acts of Parliament universally contain the express averment, that they are passed by the several branches in Parliament assembled;" and, that " many ancient statutes, without this clause, are equally in force with modern statutes, which have the clause." How far our assertion can, or cannot be supported, we appeal to the statutes at large, to determine; and, we may venture to advance, that from the time of King Edward the First, under whose reign the present form of the Legislature took place, and the two Houses of Parliament were separated from each other, which is now five hundred years, to this day, there is scarcely a single statute without such an express averment. And, indeed, other expressions equivalent to such an averment, are used in almost all the statutes, that are more ancient than the reign of Edward the First. For example, in the statute of Merton, which was in the twentieth year of King Henry the Third, A.D. 1235, we find this averment, " it was provided in the court of our Lord, the King, holden at Merton, on Wednesday, &c. the twentieth year of the reign of King Henry, &c. before William, Archbishop of Canterbury, and others, his Bishops and suffragans, and before the greater part of the Earls and Barons of England, there being assembled, for the coronation of the said King, and Hellianor, the Queen, about which they were called, when it was treated for the commonwealth of the realm, upon the articles underwritten; thus, it was provided and granted, as well of the aforesaid Archbishop, Bishops, Earls, and Barons, as of the King himself, and others." And, in the statute of Marlbridge, which was in the fifty-second year of King Henry the Third. A.D. 1267, the averment is in these words : "the said King our Lord, providing for the better estate of his realm of England, and for the more speedy ministration of justice, as belongeth to the office of a King, the more discreet men of the realm being called together, as well of the higher, as of the lower estate, it was provided, agreed, and ordained," &c.

It is true, that Magna Charta, and Charta de Foresta, which have not such an express averment, are sometimes called statutes; but these are not only the most ancient monuments which are ever called statutes, and were made before any division of the Lords from the Commons; but they were originally intended to be charters, and were accordingly drawn in the form of charters, and executed under the seals of the Princes who gave them, and are considered, pleaded, and judged on, as we believe are all others which have not such an express averment, as parts of the common law, rather than as acts of Parliament. So that we are still of opinion, that there is no statute now in force, that is pleadable as an act of Parliament, which has not in it such an averment. Many ancient institutions are still in force, as rules of common law, which are not pleadable as acts of Parliament. When your Honor says, that modern acts of this province, without the clause we contend for, are equally in force with ancient acts, which have that clause, it is a manifest petition of the principle disputed between your Honor and the House, which the House can by no means allow.

You are pleased to inform us, that " you are not acquainted with the special reason which induced his Majesty to restrain the Governor from consenting to an act with this clause in it ;" where then is the freedom of the Governor of the province, if he is to govern twenty-eight years together, by positive instructions from other persons, at three thousand miles distance, without being able, in all that time, to discover any reasons for them ? The reasons which induced his Majesty's Ministers to dictate this instruction, and which induce Governors to be so fond of them, we fear, are very different from those suggested by your Honor; if the words are unnecessary and redundant, why does his Majesty consent to them in so many instances, every session of Parliament ? The true reason, we fear, is to reduce this province to the footing of little corporations in England, and, by degrees, to pare away, not only the appearance, but the substance of all authority, in the great and General Court of the province.

Upon the whole, it gives us great and just concern to find your Honor, not only determined, so scrupulously to adhere, even to the letter of this instruction, but declaring in your message, your present resolution not to make your humble application to his Majesty to withdraw it; so that the General Assembly is reduced to the hard alternative, either to forbear attempting to make any laws at all, however urgent the exigencies of the province may be, or to pass them in such an inartificial and barbarous style, that they may hereafter be drawn into question as insufficient, invalid, and void. For what reasonable assurance can we have, that some future corrupt administration, to effect some despotic measure, and to injure and destroy this province, may not move this exception to a multitude of our laws, that they are enacted in such a style, as that, from the face of them, compared with the charter, they appear to be invalid and void, and instruct the Governor not to consent to any law, to cure such defect and imperfection. Should such an exception be taken advantage of, by pleadings in our courts of law, how could even independent judges adjudge such laws, not conformable to the charter, to be valid ? And, if independent judges could not, what is to be expected from judges, whose commissions shall be during pleasure, when they shall know it to be the desire of administration here and at home, that such acts should be adjudged void.

Your Honor has taken occasion to put us in mind, in your message, that we were in the seventh week of the session, and that scarce any of the public business was then completed. Of this, we are very sensible, and have long wished to return to our private affairs. Had your Honor considered that the General Assembly has been, for these two years past, so interrupted by the chair, either by dissolutions or long prorogations, that they have had little or no time to advert to the internal concerns of the province, and so are, on that account, greatly in arrears, perhaps you would have spared this observation. We are, however, accountable to none but our constituents, for the time we spend in doing the part of the public business, which they have chosen us to transact; the great inconvenience of our sitting in this place, hath been the principal reason why the business has been so much retarded; the difficulty would have been, in some degree, less, if your Honor had been pleased to have taken your residence, where you had ordered the General Assembly to be held and kept. If your Honor is to judge, and not the Council and the House, with how much deliberation the importance of every case, relative to the general interest of the people, ought to be consulted, we pray your Honor to consider of what importance your promise was to both Houses, in your speech of the 25th of July last, that you would patiently wait the result of their debates, and give them no interruption therein. We doubt not but our constituents wish, as we do, to see all obstructions to our giving greater despatch, removed for the future; and, we believe, they are all sensible, that this in a great measure depends upon your Honor; we therefore repeat our earnest request, that you would be pleased to order the next session of this Assembly to be held at its ancient and established place, the Town House, in Boston, where the remaining part of the business of this year, may be completed with much greater despatch, and to better effect.

[Committee to present this, Mr. J. Adams, Maj. Hawley, Capt. Thayer, Mr. Porter, and Mr. Gardner.]

RESOLUTIONS

OF THE HOUSE OF REPRESENTATIVES, NOVEMBER 16, 1770.

WHEREAS his Honor the Lieutenant Governor of the province was pleased, by his Majesty's writ, to summon this great and General Court to meet at Harvard College, in Cambridge, on the last Wednesday in May last, and has never assigned any reason therefor, but that he was instructed by his Majesty so to do:

And, whereas this House did, at the then session, remonstrate to his Honor against the holding the said General Assembly out of the town of Boston; and, did also come into a resolution, " that notwithstanding there were matters of very great importance lying before the Assembly, which they were very desirous of entering upon and completing; nevertheless, it was by no means expedient to proceed to business, while the General Assembly was thus constrained to hold the session out of the town of Boston;" and did, thereupon, pray his Honor the Lieutenant Governor to remove the General Assembly to its ancient and usual seat, the Town House, in Boston:

And, whereas this House did afterwards resolve to adhere to the said former resolution; the reasons of which resolution, and the vote for adhering to the same, are set forth in the report of one committee of the House, made on the 6th, and of another committee, made on the 12th of June last:

And, whereas his Honor the Lieutenant Governor did, in his speech, at the next session of the General Assembly, on the 25th of July last, strongly recommend to the House to proceed to the public business; and, besides a repetition of much that he had before urged, was pleased to suggest, that, by the compact implied in accepting the charter, the General Assembly was obliged to do business wherever it should be convened; to which the House returned a full answer, in their message of the 31st of July; wherein, among other things, they say, that being thus convened, they were the sole judges of the proper time to do their part of the business of the province; and, that his Honor might as well, according to the Tresilian doctrine, prescribe to them what particular business they should do, and in what order, as control them in this point:

Resolved, That notwithstanding the great variety of arguments with which his Honor has labored the point, in his several speeches and messages, yet, it is clearly the opinion of the House, that they were within the bounds of the constitution, and fully supported and vindicated :

Nevertheless, inasmuch as his Honor the Lieutenant Governor, in his speech to both Houses, at the opening of the present session, was pleased to say, that there were matters of a very interesting nature to the province, which might be determined before we might have another opportunity of acting upon them :

And, in his message to this House, of the 4th of October, he was pleased further to say, that the state of this province would be laid before the Parliament at the ensuing session :

And, from credible intelligence from Great Britain, there is reason to apprehend, that administration are determined to have great alterations made in our valuable charter, if not wholly to vacate it ; and, at the same time, we had no agent to appear for us at the Court of Great Britain :

And, whereas it appeared to this House, that it was of the utmost importance to the province, to make inquiry into the causes of the public grievances, and seek a radical redress; and, particularly to be informed of the reasons of the garrison, at his Majesty's Castle William, in the pay of the province, being, since the last session, in a new and unprecedented manner, withdrawn, and the fortress surrendered to his Majesty's regular forces: For these, and other most weighty considerations, the House did, at the beginning of this session, resolve to proceed to the public business ; at the same time, in the strongest manner, remonstrating, and hereby ordering their protest to be entered on their journal, that they were constrained to proceed to business out of the town of Boston, from the most pressing necessity ; and, that it ought never to be drawn into precedent, but under the like necessity.

[Committee were, Mr. Wood, Mr. Hancock, Gen. Prebble, Mr. S. Adams, and Maj. Reed.]

MESSAGE

FROM THE HOUSE OF REPRESENTATIVES TO THE LIEUTENANT
GOVERNOR, NOVEMBER 20, 1770.

May it please your Honor,

In your message to this House, of the 23d of October, in answer to our repeated request, to be informed, whether you still hold the command of his Majesty's Castle William, you were pleased to say, "that in withdrawing the garrison, which was paid by the province, and placing a garrison there, to be paid by the King, in pursuance of instructions received from him, we had no grounds to infer, that you had divested yourself of the right given you, by charter, over that fort, in common with other forts in the province." Since which, we find, by the tenor of the orders given to Capt. Phillips, under your own hand, on the tenth day of September last, that you expressly directed him " to deliver the possession of that fort to Lieut. Col. Dalrymple, and to such detachment of the regular forces then on the island, as he should order;" which was done accordingly.

And, we also find, by the deposition of Mr. Stephen Hall, late chaplain of the garrison, whom your Honor directed to attend you, that afterwards, on the same day, being then at the Castle, your Honor personally delivered the keys of that fort to Lieut. Col. Dalrymple, as commanding officer; declaring that you did it, by " virtue of authority derived from his Majesty to govern this province, and, in consequence of express orders from the Earl of Hillsborough, to deliver the fort into the hands of the commanding officer of the King's troops then upon the island, to be garrisoned by such detachment, or detachments, as he should order." Yet, you are pleased, in the same message, to say, " the authority given you over the Castle by his Majesty's commission, you have exercised, and continue to exercise, without any infringement of the rights of the people by charter, or otherwise."

We consider all the powers and authority, given by the charter to the Governor of the province, to be grants for the benefit of the people, which cannot be resigned without injury to them. By the charter, the Governor, or Commander in Chief of the province, for the time being, hath the right to commit the custody and government of all forts within the province, to such person or persons, as to him shall seem meet. But your Honor has manifestly parted with that right, by vesting in Lieut. Col. Dalrymple, without any reservation, the right to commit the custody and government of Castle William to such person or persons, as to him shall seem meet. From which, it appears to this House, that you have made an absolute surrender of that fort to his Majesty's forces, with the most express resignation of your power of garrisoning the same, to Lieut. Col. Dalrymple. And though your Honor declared you did it by virtue of authority derived from his Majesty, to govern the province, yet you have no authority, either by the charter, or your commission, to delegate the power of garrisoning that Castle to any other person: the shew of the authority of the Governor, then held up, served only to make the surrender the more solemn and formal.

We further find, that Lieut. Col. Dalrymple accepted the keys of your Honor, expressly in consequence of orders from Gen. Gage, cautiously avoiding, as we conceive, recognizing any subordination to your Honor; and, as you have heretofore repeatedly declared, to our great astonishment, that you have no authority over the King's troops in the province, we have good grounds to infer, that you did divest yourself of the right given you by charter, over that fort; and the rather, because you informed us in your speech, at the opening of this session, that " you were prevented from desiring us to make the usual establishment for the same." And it is absurd to suppose, that you can have the command of a fort thus unreservedly surrendered to, and in full possession of such troops.

It appears to the House, that your Honor has, in this instance, merely in obedience to instructions, divested yourself of a power of governing, which, by the charter, is vested in you for the safety of the people; and, that it is a precedent of the most dangerous tendency. We do, therefore, in faithfulness to our constituents, warmly remonstrate against it as a very great grievance; and earnestly pray, that your Honor would, in tenderness to the rights of this people, take effectual measures, that the power of garrisoning his Majesty's Castle William, may be restored to the Governor of the province, to whom, by charter, it belongs.

[The committee, by whom this message was reported, consisted of S. Adams, Maj. Hawley, J. Adams, J. Hancock, Col. Worthington, J. Pickering, and Col. Warren.]

MESSAGE

FROM THE HOUSE OF REPRESENTATIVES TO THE LIEUTENANT GOVERNOR.

NOVEMBER 20, 1770.

May it please your Honor,

THE House of Representatives have heretofore viewed with concern, the deplorable state of the militia of this province; but, have hitherto refrained from any public mention of it, lest some misconstruction should be put upon it. But, by the last advices from Great Britain, the nations of Europe appear to be on the eve of a general war; and, perhaps, America may be the object in the eye of some of those nations. And, when some of the regiments within this province are destitute of field officers, and many companies without captains or subalterns, the arms of the militia, we fear, are deficient, and military discipline too much neglected.

Duty to his Majesty, and a regard to our own safety, constrain us to address your Honor, praying, that you would be pleased, as soon as may be, to fill up the vacancies in the several regiments, where such vacancies are, with such persons, as to your Honor shall seem meet; and, that your Honor would be pleased to use your endeavors, that the several officers carefully discharge the trust reposed in them; and, should any amendments in, or addition to the laws, for regulating the militia of this province, be thought needful at the next session of the General Court, the House of Representatives will cheerfully do all in their power, towards putting the militia on a respectable footing.

[The committee were, Mr. S. Adams, Capt. Heath, Mr. Porter, Capt. Brown, and Mr. Dennie.]

MESSAGE

FROM THE LIEUTENANT GOVERNOR TO THE HOUSE OF REPRESENTATIVES,
NOVEMBER 20, 1770.

Gentlemen of the House of Representatives,

On the 7th of this month I received a message from you, in which you informed me, that it was your opinion, a law without the words, in General Court assembled, in the enacting part, is not valid, and you offered several resolutions in support of your opinion. The next day I sent you an answer, in which I let you know my opinion, that a law, without those words in the enacting part, is valid, and I gave you several reasons to support this opinion. You thereupon sent for all the bills which lay before the Council, caused those words to be taken out, and you have since passed those bills, and divers others, to most of which I have given my assent, without the words. I had reason to think, that the majority of the House was convinced that the words were unnecessary, and, I expected, that I should hear nothing further upon the subject. I went to Cambridge on Saturday, the 17th, with an intention to prorogue the Court. Your committee soon attended me with another very long message, in which you again declare your opinion, that those words are necessary, and that impartial judges will not be in favor of the sufficiency of the late style used in enacting our laws.

I think your constituents will be surprised at your passing so great a number of laws, and declaring, immediately after, that you judge them all to be of no validity, which is doing all in your power, as a House of Representatives, to induce a refusal to submit not to them only, but to all other laws which have been made for near thirty years past. If I had been of opinion that those words are essential, I would either have refused my assent to the bills, lest a greater mischief should arise from defective laws, than from the want of them; or, if I had given my assent, I would certainly have done nothing which should prompt the people to deny the authority of them. To prevent this mischief, I am obliged to continue a controversy, which I wished to avoid, and to show that your last message does not better support your principle, than the former did. Previous to it, I will just observe, that I gave you no occasion to insinuate that I supposed my opinion would be an authority. You had expressed yourselves, in your message to me, in these words : " this House are of opinion," and, I did not imagine it would be deemed arrogance in me, to say, " I am of opinion" also ; which opinion carries the greatest, or whether either carries any authority, I have not determined.

You say, you think it surprising and unfortunate that I should assert, that " the style of a law which expresses the Governor, Council, and House of Representatives, expresses that authority, which, by charter, hath power to make laws ;" and you then recite divers paragraphs from the charter, and declare it to be " certain and obvious," that those words do not express that power, " because, unless the Governor, Council, and House of Representatives are convened and held in General Court or Assembly, they have no authority, by charter, to make laws ;" and you venture to submit to my own consideration, whether an act of the Governor, Council, and House of Representatives, would be valid, if passed by each of those branches not in General Court assembled, and add, " should a bill pass the House, and be sent up to the Board, in the present session, and, after a prorogation of the General Court, be concurred by the Council, and consented to by the Governor, can there be the least foundation for an opinion that such a bill could become a law ?"

You must give me leave, gentlemen, to be astonished in my turn ! You certainly have not thoroughly considered your own powers, and the nature of your political existence, otherwise, you must have discovered that there can be no act of the Governor, Council, and House of Representatives, except in General Court assembled. The words, " House of Representatives," in our laws, are technical, and used in an appropriated sense, and signify a body of men, who are an essential part of the General Court or Assembly, and which part can have no separate existence ; and, the instant the General Court or Assembly is dissolved, the House of Representatives is annihilated ; and, the instant the General Court is prorogued, there is a temporary cessation of the existence of the House, or, what is equivalent to it, an incapacity of exertion of any sort of powers ; and by all rules of Parliamentary proceedings, all your committees and delegated powers of every kind, end with the session ; and every act of the House, not made a complete act of the Legislature, by the concurrence of the other branches, becomes a nullity, and is considered as if it had never been. The orders and resolves of the House of Commons for imprisonment for the highest contempt, as soon as the Parliament is prorogued, lose their efficacy, and the offender is discharged. I know not any color you can have for greater authority within the province, than the House of Commons hath within the realm. If this be admitted, you may just as well suppose the Governor and Council to concur an act of a House of Representatives, which never existed, which is a palpable absurdity, as an act of a House after it ceases to exist, after every thing done, while it had an existence, is become a nullity. Seeing, then, that it is impossible for the Governor and Council to concur an act of the House of Representatives, after their union in General Court or Assembly ceases, and that the House of Representatives can have no existence, but as a part of the General Assembly; whenever the Governor and Council are named, as acting with the House of Representatives, it must be understood in their joint Legislative capacity; and, consequently, every act of the Governor, Council, and House of Representatives, must be an act of the Governor, Council, and House of Representatives "in General Court assembled,"

It would be easy to show, that all you have brought from the statutes, will not disprove what I advanced, viz. : that many ancient statutes are in force without the express averment you allege; and, I think it may likewise be made to appear, that the word "Commons" in acts of Parliament, are not analogous to the word "House of Representatives" in our provincial laws; and that, if it could be admitted, that additional words, or another mode of diction, would be more full and expressive, the use of a less expressive form of words, for near thirty years, without interruption, would, notwithstanding, be sufficient to establish the form, to give it a technical propriety, and to render all exceptions to it mere cavils.

I am sorry any time has been lost in a matter of so little consequence; because, I am not able to acquaint you with the "special" reason which induced the King to give his instruction, although I had let you know what I thought myself might be a sufficient reason; you charge, not me only, but all my predecessors, for twenty-eight years past, with governing, by positive orders from other persons, at three thousand miles distance, without being able to discover "any" reason for them; and, in your next paragraph, you express your concern, that I am determined so scrupulously to adhere to the letter of my instruction, as not to make my humble application to his Majesty to withdraw it; but you take no notice of the reason I give you, viz. : because it did not appear to me to abridge you of any of your rights, or to subject the province to any inconvenience. This is not the first time I have had occasion to complain of a partial and injurious representation of my messages, in order to give a more specious answer to them.

You had no reason to be displeased at my putting you in mind of the length of the session, for although you may be accountable to your constituents only, for the time you spend in doing the public business, you ought, nevertheless, to remember, that when much time is spent, and no business is done, my duty to your constituents requires that I should ease them of the burden you bring upon them, and put an end to the session, unless I can prevail with you to alter your measures and proceed to business. Of the thirteen weeks which the Court has sat since May, more than seven had passed before you entered upon business, so that the unusual length of your session cannot be attributed to former dissolutions or prorogations, especially, as the Court had time enough to have made up all arrears in the last spring session, nor have you been at all delayed by my not residing at Cambridge; the first day of the present session, I was prevented by tempestuous weather, but had I been present, I did not intend to have opened the Court until the next day.

Whether it was owing to my message, or to any other special motive, I cannot determine, but, immediately after, you discovered a resolution, and I thank you for it, to resist and remove all the unnecessary obstructions, which, from time to time, had been laid in your way; and you have done more business, notwithstanding all the alleged inconveniencies from the place of holding the Court, than I remember to have been done in the like space of time, since I have had any share in public affairs.

This morning your committee attended me with another message or remonstrance, relative to the exchange of the garrison at the Castle, to which I shall give no other answer, than that there is nothing in the orders I gave to Capt. Phillips, which does not perfectly consist with my retaining the command of the Castle, and my right to exchange the present garrison for the former, or any other, as I shall think proper; and, that Mr. Hall, the Chaplain, has not only not given you the form of words in which I committed the custody of the Castle, " according to the charter," to Col. Dalrymple, but has substituted words which carry a very different meaning; he has, however, with great modesty, declared, that he was not able to recollect the words, and could only recollect the impression they made upon his mind; and this reserve of his, not serving your purpose, you have industriously taken care to omit; and, I must further add, that the formality of delivering the keys has been the constant practice, when the Governor has committed the custody and government of that fort to any person, at three or four instances of which I have been present; and whenever he calls for them again, such person must deliver them.

Your other message, which respects the militia, is of great importance, and shall meet with all due attention; and I hope you will join with me in further effectual provision to enforce that due obedience to the orders of the Captain General, and of the military officers under him, which is absolutely necessary to render the militia of any service; which orders, in some late instances, have been disobeyed.

Upon the whole, gentlemen, I should do myself injustice, if I did not observe, that it gives me great satisfaction to reflect, that when you are, by every way in your power, seeking to impeach my conduct since I have been in the chair, you have been unsuccessful in every attempt. You will always endeavor in vain, to move me to give up to you any part of the prerogative of the Crown; I never will make any encroachment upon the rights of the people.   T. HUTCHINSON.

=====

MESSAGE

FROM HIS EXCELLENCY THE GOVERNOR TO THE TWO HOUSES,
APRIL 3, 1771.

Gentlemen of the Council, and

  Gentlemen of the House of Representatives,

SINCE we were last assembled in General Court, the tranquillity of his Majesty's dominions have been in great danger of being disturbed by the violent proceedings of the Spanish Governor of Buenos Ayres, in dispossessing his Majesty's subjects of their settlement at Port Egremont. I have received repeated assurances from the right honorable the Earl of Hillsborough, one of his Majesty's principal Secretaries of State, that, if matters should come to extremities, the security of his Majesty's dominions in America will be a principal object of his most gracious care and attention. A plan of augmentation of his Majesty's forces upon the British establishment, has already been determined upon, and his Majesty's pleasure has been signified to me, that I should exert my utmost endeavors to give efficacy and despatch to this plan, by assisting his Majesty's officers to raise such a number of recruits, as shall be sufficient to complete the several battalions, now serving in America. I have, with the advice of his Majesty's Council, issued my proclamation, inviting and requiring his Majesty's faithful subjects, in this province, to engage in, and promote, according to their several stations and capacities, a service so essential to their security and defence.

It appears probable, by the last intelligence from England, that satisfaction may have been made for this hostile act of the Spaniards; but, as I have received no authentic advice of it, and have no sufficient reason to suppose that the proposed plan of augmentation will be receded from, I shall persevere in giving encouragement to it; and if any act of legislation shall be found necessary, I will recommend it to you, and readily concur with you in it.

I have no particular interior business of the province now to lay before you. The stated season for the convening a new Assembly, agreeable to charter, being so near, I choose to refer to that time all matters, except such as are of immediate necessity, and will come before you, of course. If you will give the despatch which is requisite on your part, there shall be no delay on my part. I doubt not, as the most busy season of the year is just at hand, you wish to return to your respective homes as soon as may be.

I may not omit acquainting you, in form, that I have received his Majesty's commission, appointing me Captain General and Governor in Chief, in and over the province; that it has been published in the usual manner; that I have the most grateful sense of the honor done me by this appointment; and that it is my sincere desire and resolution to employ the powers, with which I am entrusted, for his Majesty's service, and for the best interest of the people; and I will cheerfully join, at all times, with the other branches of the Legislature, in such measures, as may tend completely to restore, and constantly to maintain, that state of order and tranquillity, upon which the prosperity of the province so much depends.   T. HUTCHINSON.

MESSAGE

FROM HIS EXCELLENCY THE GOVERNOR TO THE HOUSE OF REPRESENTATIVES, APRIL 5, 1771.*

Gentlemen of the House of Representatives,

As soon as you had opportunity for it, you appointed a committee to present me a verbal message, requesting me to remove the Court to its ancient and legal seat, the town of Boston. Immediately after, I sent for you to the Council Chamber, and there recommended to both Houses to proceed upon, and give despatch to such public business as, in the common course of our affairs, lay before them. I do not know how I could more fully have signified to you, that I declined complying with your request. But as this was not satisfactory, and you have sent me a second message, I must tell you, in the most explicit terms, that I cannot remove the Court to Boston.

I have done my endeavor, that all the obstructions to the Court's sitting in Boston, might be removed; but I have failed in my en-

---

* The House sent a verbal message to the Governor, on the first day of the session, requesting him to remove the Court to its ancient and usual seat, the Town House, in Boston. On the 5th, they sent another message, making a similar request.

deavor. One of these obstructions is your denying, in effect, the right reserved by the Crown, to convene the Court in such place as he thinks proper. If every other impediment was out of the way, whilst you continue to urge, that, by law, the Court must be held in Boston, I may not ask his Majesty's leave to carry you there. I should give up to the House of Representatives a right, which would have remained in the Crown, if no notice had been taken of it in the charter. I could even then have had no plea, if I had been called to answer, except my ignorance of the constitution; but, now it is expressly reserved, I should be wholly without excuse.

I am sensible there is business of great importance before the Court; but, I am less concerned whether you proceed to act upon it, because, it is but a short time before I shall be obliged, by charter, to meet a new Assembly; therefore, if you decline proceeding, I shall, without delay, put an end to the session.

T. HUTCHINSON.

MESSAGE

FROM THE HOUSE OF REPRESENTATIVES TO THE GOVERNOR,
APRIL 24, 1771.

May it please your Excellency,

THE House of Representatives have given all due attention to your speech to both Houses, at the opening of this session. The violent proceedings of the Spanish Governor of Buenos Ayres, in dispossessing his Majesty's subjects of their settlement at Port Egremont, has raised the indignation of all who have a just concern for the honor of the British Crown. Such an act of hostility, we conceive, could not but be followed with the most spirited resolution on the part of the British administration, to obtain a satisfaction fully adequate to the insult offered to his Majesty, and the injuries his subjects there have sustained. Your Excellency tells us, that it is probable, satisfaction may have been made for this hostile act of the Spaniards. If it is so, the public tranquillity of his Majesty's dominions, so far as it has been disturbed by this unwarrantable proceeding. is again restored; and, therefore, it seems to us reasonable to suppose. that the proposed plan of augmentation of troops, on the British establishment, is already receded from, which renders any consideration upon that subject, on our part, unnecessary.

We owe our gratitude to his Majesty, for his repeated assurances, expressed to your Excellency, by his Secretary of State, that the security of his dominions in America, will be a principal object of his most gracious care and attention. This province has frequently, in times past, expended much blood and treasure for the enlargement, as well as support, of those dominions. And, when our natural and constitutional rights and liberties, without which, no blessing can be secure to us, shall be fully restored, and established upon a firm foundation, as we shall then have the same reasons and motives therefor as heretofore, we shall not fail to continue those exertions, with the utmost cheerfulness, and to the extent of our ability.

As your Excellency has no particular interior business of the province to lay before us, it would have given us no uneasiness, if an end had been put to the present Assembly, rather than to have been again called to this place; and, we are unwilling to admit the belief, that when the season for calling a new Assembly, agreeable to the charter, shall arrive, your Excellency will continue an indignity, and a grievance so flagrant, and so repeatedly remonstrated by both Houses, as the deforcement of the General Assembly of its ancient and rightful seat.

Your Excellency is pleased to acquaint us in form, that you have received his Majesty's commission, appointing you Captain General and Commander in Chief in, and over the province. Your having had your birth and education in this province, and sustained the highest honors which your fellow subjects could bestow, cannot fail to be the strongest motives with your Excellency to employ those powers which you are now vested with, for his Majesty's real service, and the best interest of this people. The duties of the Governor and governed, are reciprocal; and by our happy constitution, their dependence is mutual. Nothing can more effectually produce and establish that order and tranquillity in the province, so often disturbed under the late unfortunate administration; nothing will tend more to conciliate the affections of this people, and ensure to your Excellency those aids, which you will constantly stand in need of, from their Representatives, than, as a wise and faithful administrator, to make use of the public power with a view only to the public welfare. And while your Excellency shall religiously regard the constitution of this province; while you shall maintain its fundamental laws, so necessary to secure the public tranquillity, you may be assured, that his Majesty's faithful Commons of this province, will never be wanting, in their utmost exertions, to support you in all such measures, as shall be calculated for the public good, and to render your administration prosperous and happy.

[Committee, Mr. S. Adams, Maj. Hawley, Mr. Hancock, Col. Worthington, Gen. Ruggles, and Mr. Greenleaf.]
38

MESSAGE

May it please your Excellency,

THE House of Representatives, after inquiry of the Secretary, cannot be made certain whether you have yet given your assent to two bills which were laid before your Excellency, early in this session ; the one, for granting the sum of five hundred and six pounds, for your services when Lieutenant Governor and Commander in Chief ; and the other, for granting the usual sum of thirteen hundred pounds, to enable your Excellency, as Governor, to carry on the affairs of this province.

And, as your Excellency was not pleased to give your assent to another bill, passed in the last session of this Assembly, for granting the sum of three hundred and twenty-five pounds for your services, when in the chair, as Lieutenant Governor, the House are apprehensive that you are under some restraint ; and, they cannot account for it upon any other principle, but your having provision for your support in some new and unprecedented manner. If the apprehensions of the House are not groundless, they are solicitous to be made certain of it, before an end is put to the present session ; and, think it their duty to pray your Excellency to inform them, whether any provision is made for your support, as Governor of this province, independent of his Majesty's Commons in it.

[The Committee by whom the above was reported, were, Mr. S. Adams, Col. Warren, Mr. Hancock, and Maj. Foster.]

MESSAGE

Gentlemen of the House of Representatives,

I COULD not, consistently with my duty to the King, give my assent to the bill passed the last session, for granting three hundred and twenty-five pounds for my support. Before the close of the present session, I shall assent to, or reject the bills which shall have passed the two Houses, as it shall appear to me the same duty requires of me.

You are solicitous to be informed, " whether any provision is made for my support, as Governor of the province, independent of his Majesty's Commons in it." By the expression, " his Majesty's Commons," I suppose, you would be understood to intend the House of Representatives. I must observe to you, that the King, Lords, and Commons, our supreme Legislature, have determined it to be expedient to enable his Majesty to make a certain and adequate provision for the support of the civil government in the colonies, as his Majesty shall judge necessary.

I will not enter into a dispute with you upon the propriety of this provision. It may not, however, be amiss to acquaint you, that I have not received the full instructions and other appendages to his Majesty's commission, which I have reason to expect. When I shall receive them, I will communicate such parts of them to the House of Representatives, as I shall think for his Majesty's service.

In the mean time, I am the only sufferer by declining or delaying my assent to any bills for my support ; and, I think your constituents will not blame me for being willing to avoid burdening them with this support, by the increase of the tax upon their polls and estates, while there is any probability that it may have been provided for in another way.

T. HUTCHINSON.

———

[In May, 1771, when the Members of the Court met in Cambridge, on the day of general election, the House of Representatives chose a committee, composed of Messrs. J. Otis, S. Adams, J. Hancock, and D. Leonard, to prepare a remonstrance to the Governor, against holding the Assembly in that place, as they had repeatedly done before. It is unnecessary to give the remonstrance, as it contains nothing but what had been urged before, on the subject. It was contended, that Boston was the only legal, constitutional, and convenient place for holding the General Court. The Council and House of Representatives, however, proceeded to the choice of Counsellors, all of whom were approved by the Governor, but J. Hancock, and J. Bowers.]

SPEECH

Gentlemen of the Council, and

    Gentlemen of the House of Representatives,

It is with pleasure that I now inform you, that the account, which I thought myself warranted to transmit to England, the last fall, of the general disposition in the people of the province, to promote order and a due submission to government, gave the greatest satisfaction to his Majesty, who has nothing more at heart, than to see his subjects in a state of happiness, peace, and prosperity. By making these the great objects of the administration, I shall advance the real interest of the province, and, at the same time to that duty to the King, which he requires of me.

The common interior business of the province, necessary to be acted upon at this session, I need not particularly point out to you. The state and circumstances of that part of the province, which lies to the east and north of Penobscot River, where settlements are every day making, by persons who have no color of title, I am required by the King, to recommend to your serious consideration. I think the people deceive themselves with a groundless expectation, of acquiring a title by force of possession. I know that his Majesty is displeased with such proceeding; and, I have reason to apprehend, that a longer neglect of effectual measures on our part, to prevent any further intrusions, and to remove those already made, will occasion the interposition of Parliament, to maintain and preserve the possession of this country or district, for the sake of his Majesty's timber, with which it is said to abound. I recommended this important business to the Assembly of the last year, at their session in September. The Council thought it necessary then to be acted upon, but the House referred it to the next session, and then let it drop without further notice.

The state of the militia deserves your consideration. A bill passed the two Houses the last year, in which the defects or failures, are attributed to the officers, and they are subjected to additional penalties. It did not appear to me that the officers, except in a few instances, were chargeable with neglect of duty. In general, the militia are backward in appearing upon military musters, and that subordination, which distinguished this government in the day of our forefathers, is lost; particularly, in the town of Boston, a company makes so small show upon a muster day, that the officers, who, I doubt not, are well disposed, and wish to do their duty, are under great discouragements. This is partly owing to the insufficiency of the fine for not attending common trainings;

and I leave you to consider, whether some provision is not also necessary to enforce obedience to the lawful commands or orders of the Captain General, and the officers under him, which is essential to a well regulated militia. As the laws now stand, I find it difficult to prevail with the most proper persons to take military commissions. If additional burdens and penalties are laid upon officers, their discouragements will increase in proportion.

I cannot help flattering myself, that the Assembly of this year, will be distinguished by a zealous regard to the interest of the province ; and I hope to be able to concur in sentiment with you upon all matters which may come before us.

T. HUTCHINSON.

MESSAGE

FROM HIS EXCELLENCY THE GOVERNOR TO THE HOUSE OF REPRESENTATIVES, MAY 30, 1771.

Gentlemen of the House of Representatives,

You may depend upon my representing to his Majesty, by the first vessels, the inconveniencies which you mention, in your message of yesterday,* to attend your sitting in any other place than the town of Boston. I am restrained from holding the Court there, without his Majesty's express leave. I will endeavor that every obstacle may be removed ; and, upon this, and every other occasion, to convince you that I am desirous not merely of preserving to you the enjoyment of all just rights and privileges, but of procuring every convenience, so far as shall consist with my duty to the King.   T. HUTCHINSON.

* The House had sent a message to the Governor, stating the inconveniencies of holding the General Court out of Boston, and remonstrating against the removal thereof from the ancient and usual place, as a grievance, both to the people and the Members of the Court.

PROTEST

OF THE HOUSE OF REPRESENTATIVES AGAINST CONVENING AND HOLDING
THE COURT OUT OF BOSTON, JUNE 19, 177L.*

HISTORY furnishes us with an instance of an act of Parliament passed, giving the force of laws to the King's proclamations: but this being directly subversive of the constitution, was soon repealed. Yet, since that period, an act has been labored for, to give the force of law to the King's instructions to the Governors of the colonies; and though it was not effected, some Governors have appeared to consider such instructions as laws, not only to themselves, but to the people. Whereas, nothing can be more clear, than that neither proclamation nor instruction ought to have any such force, either in regard to the Governor, or the subject here.

And, although it may be within the prerogative of the Crown, in cases of plain necessity, to summon a Parliament to some other place than Westminster; and so of a Governor of this province, in like cases of plain necessity, to convoke a General Assembly to some other place than Boston, its accustomed, ancient place, and where alone provision is made for it; yet, if a British King should call a Parliament, and keep it seven years in Cornwall, however his Ministry, as usual, might shift for themselves, their master, and his affairs, would be irretrievably embarrassed and ruined. And a Governor of this province, who, in order to harass the General Assembly into unconstitutional and unconscionable measures, should convene and hold them in the county of Berkshire or Lincoln, would render himself and his administration justly ridiculous and odious.

There is nothing more plainly to be distinguished, than power, right, and prerogative, and the abuse of such power, right, and prerogative. It is the King's prerogative, to pardon all crimes, from trespass to high treason; but if the King should pardon all criminals, there would be an end of his government. The Commons have the sole right to give and grant, or refuse to grant taxes; but if they should refuse to give any thing, there would be also an end of government. Should a King call a Parliament but once in seven years, and on its meeting, instantly dissolve it, and so repeatedly, a few such repetitions would ruin him, and be deemed a total dissolution of the social compact. Should a Governor of this province, annually convene a General Assembly, and before, or immediately after, the election of Counsellors, dissolve

---

* The committee who prepared this protest, were, Mr. J. Otis, Mr. Denny, Mr. Hancock, and Mr. Adams. The object of this protest being to show the danger of having instructions from the Ministry or Crown, superior to the authority given by the charter, rather than to complain of the Court's sitting in Cambridge, it is here inserted.

such Assembly, as the conduct would be similar, the inferences and consequences must also be alike ; for such exercises of the prerogative could not be deemed mistakes, but must be construed as voluntary and corrupt abuses of the prerogative, and a total perversion of the powers of which it consists. Such instances, it may be said, would be manifest abuses of power and prerogative ; and it is most clearly, in our opinion, an abuse of the power, vested by charter, in the Governor of this province, for him, from time to time, unnecessarily, or merely in obedience to an instruction, without exercising that judgment and discretion of his own, which, by charter, he is empowered, and is in duty bound to exercise for the good of the province, and not for the preservation of his place, to convene and hold the General Assembly out of the town of Boston ; which is not only its ancient, but also, on various accounts, the most convenient place ; more especially, as ample provision is there made for holding the Assembly, in costly and commodious buildings, and no part of the necessary provision is made in any other place in the province.

By the charter, the Governor, with other civil officers, is to be supported by the free gift of the General Assembly ; and, it would be dangerous for so important a trust as that of convening, adjourning, proroguing, or dissolving the General Assembly, to be placed in any one, who is not thus supported by the free grants of the people. The safety of the people requires, that every power should have a check ; by the charter, therefore, it is ordained, that the full power of convening, adjourning, proroguing, and dissolving the Assembly, shall be vested in the Governor, who is to reside within the province, and is, and ought to be, supported by the free grants of the people. The King, by the charter, has covenanted and granted, that the Governor shall exercise this power " as he shall think fit," or " judge necessary," and not another ; an endeavor, therefore, to restrain the Governor in the exercise of this power, is clearly an attempt to infringe and violate the charter. And the Governor, in our opinion, cannot, consistent with the trust and duty of his office, refuse or delay to hold the Assembly in the place which is evidently the most convenient, until he shall obtain " express leave," from the King or his Minister. It is so far forth suspending the effect, and depriving the people of the benefit of the royal grant made to them in the charter. To restrain the Governor in the free exercise of this power, at once reduces him to a mere machine ; and deprives us, not only of every charter right, but of all freedom. By such a restraint, a free Assembly would be subjugated to arbitrary edicts and mandates; for if an instruction is as obligatory on a Governor, as some contend for, or supersede the charter in one instance, it may in a thousand, or in all.

Upon the foregoing considerations, this House think it their indispensable duty, in discharge of the sacred trust reposed in them by their constituents, and for the sake of preserving and maintaining, as far as may be in their power, the free constitution of the province, in the most explicit manner, to protest, and they do accordingly protest, against all such doctrines, principles, and practices, as tend to establish either ministerial, or even royal instructions, as laws within the province.

And further, this House do particularly protest, and order the same to be entered on the journal, against the present manner of exercising the prerogative, in convening and holding the General Assembly at Harvard College, in Cambridge, merely by force of instructions, as an intolerable grievance, which ought speedily to be redressed.

It is notorious, that former Houses have borne this grievance with great moderation, in hopes it would not have been continued; and, although the present House is inclined to judge as candidly as possible, of the intentions of administration; yet, it is the clear opinion of the House, that, if after all the remonstrances that have been made against this grievance, it should not speedily be redressed, it will then become plain and obvious, that the power vested in the Governor, by the charter, for the good of the province, is wittingly perverted to a very different end.

====

ANSWER

OF THE HOUSE OF REPRESENTATIVES TO HIS EXCELLENCY'S SPEECH, AT
THE OPENING OF THE SESSION, JUNE 14, 1771.

May it please your Excellency,

THE House of Representatives have taken into consideration your speech to both Houses, at the opening of this session. Your Excellency is pleased to inform us, that you thought yourself warranted the last fall, to transmit to England, an account of the general disposition of the people of this province to promote order, and a due submission to government, which had given the greatest satisfaction to his Majesty. Your Excellency must be very sensible that the people of this province have always been disposed to promote order, and a due submission to constituional authority; and, therefore, we humbly conceive, there never was a time when your Excellency might not have been warranted to represent us in such a point of light, as would have given his Majesty the greatest satisfaction in that regard. The people, it is true, have been, and are still, with abundant reason, discontented with the acts of Parliament, for raising a revenue in America, without the free consent of their own Representatives; and, with other regulations which they justly apprehend to be not only oppressive, but destructive to their constitutional and charter rights. This uneasiness has been grossly misrepresented by the enemies of the province, as a mark of disaffection to his Majesty's government.

If your Excellency will be pleased to employ that influence, which your advanced station in the province now gives you, in effecting a redress of those great grievances, you will, in the opinion of this House, very substantially promote the real interest of the province, and establish order, happiness, peace, and prosperity; and thereby render the most acceptable service to the people, in a manner perfectly consistent with duty to his Majesty.

With regard to the settlements which your Excellency is pleased to inform us are every day making, on that part of the province, which lies to the east and north of Penobscot River, your Excellency is sensible that some of them are in consequence of grants made by the General Assembly of this province, agreeable to the royal charter; but if any other settlements are made there, without any color of title, the House apprehend that the charter, which is the first law of the province, provides a sufficient penalty of one hundred pounds sterling for every trespass on the King's woods; and, as his Majesty has been pleased, from time to time, to appoint a surveyor of his woods, with a power of substitution, whose duty it is to prevent any such intrusions, or remove them, if already made, the House are of opinion, that there can be no necessity, at present, of the interposition of this, or of any other Legislative act for that purpose.

The state of the militia of the province, is considered by this House, as a subject which requires the most serious attention. The Assembly of the last year, for the important purpose of better regulating the militia, prepared a bill, and laid it before your Excellency. We cannot agree with your Excellency, in the exceptions which you are pleased to mention against that bill. It is apparent, that a laudable ambition prevails among the people in many, if not all parts of the province, to excel in the military art; and we have observed with great satisfaction, a readiness in them to appear upon musters, and cheerfully to obey the lawful commands of such officers, as are desirous and capable of doing their duty. If, therefore, your Excellency shall have regard solely to the necessary qualifications of the persons who may be appointed to the military command, we cannot but promise ourselves, that the military spirit of the country will again be as conspicuous as it was in the days of our fore fathers, and thereby his Majesty's real service, and the safety of this province, greatly promoted.

We flatter ourselves, that the present Assembly will not be wanting in the same zealous regard for the real interest of the province, which distinguished the last and former Assemblies. Your Excellency may be assured, that this House will exert themselves to the utmost, in promoting the honor and service of his

Majesty, and in maintaining and supporting the rights and liberties of the people. These are the great ends of government; and, while we keep them in view, we shall have reason to expect your Excellency's concurrence with us in our determinations upon all matters of importance that shall come before the Assembly.

[The committee, by whom the above was reported, were, Mr. Hancock, Col. Bowers, Brig. Prebble, Mr. Ingersol, Mr. Hobson, Maj. Foster, and Mr. Adams.]

———

MESSAGE

FROM HIS EXCELLENCY THE GOVERNOR TO THE HOUSE OF REPRESENTATIVES, JULY 4, 1771.

Gentlemen of the House of Representatives,

THE Secretary has laid before me an engrossed bill, entitled an act for apportioning and assessing a tax of fifteen thousand pounds, &c. I find that this bill is of the same tenor with the acts, which of late years, have been annually passed by the General Court. By virtue of those acts, the assessors in several towns, have taxed the officers of the Crown, who have been resident in such towns, for the profits they receive from their commissions, although their offices have no peculiar relation to this province. I doubt whether this could be the intent of the former acts; but as this construction has been put upon them, I cannot sign another act in the same form, being expressly forbid by his Majesty's twenty-seventh instruction, from giving my consent to such an act, upon any pretence whatsoever. I cannot doubt of your being of the same sentiment with me, that such a general clause, as is now in the bill, which empowers the assessors to tax all commissions of profit, needs some qualification, and that it should extend no farther than to commissions which peculiarly relate to this province; otherwise any of his Majesty's servants, who may occasionally reside here for a short term, may be taxed for the profit which they receive from their commissions and places in Great Britain, and every other part of his Majesty's dominions.

T. HUTCHINSON.

MESSAGE

May it please your Excellency,

THE House of Representatives have taken into consideration, your Excellency's message of this day. The reason you are pleased to assign for withholding your assent to the tax bill, is surprising and alarming. We know of no commissioners of his Majesty's customs, nor of any revenue his Majesty has a right to establish in North America; we know and feel a tribute levied and extorted from those, who, if they have property, have a right to the absolute disposal of it.

By the royal charter, it is expressly granted, that the General Assembly shall have full power and authority to impose and levy proportionable and reasonable assessments, rates, and taxes, upon the estates and persons of all and every, the proprietors and inhabitants of this province. Hence, it plainly appears, that the power of raising and levying taxes, is vested in the General Assembly; and that power, which has the sole right of raising and levying taxes, has an uncontrolable right to order and direct, in what way and manner, and upon whom, such taxes shall be raised and levied. Therefore, for your Excellency to withhold your assent to this bill, merely by force of instruction, is effectually vacating the charter, and giving instructions the force of laws, within this province. And we are constrained to say, that your Excellency's present determination is to be governed by them, though this should be the consequence. We must further observe, that such a doctrine, if established, would render the Representatives of a free people, mere machines; and they would be reduced to this fatal alternative, either to have no taxes levied and raised at all, or to have them raised and levied in such a way and manner, and upon those, only, whom his Majesty pleases.

As to the operation of law, mentioned in your Excellency's message, the law of this province, at least in this respect, has rightly operated, as it ever ought to. And we know no reason, or any semblance of reason, why the commissioners, their superior or subordinate officers, who are equally protected with the other inhabitants, should be exempted from paying their full proportion of taxes for the support of government, within this province.

[The committee, by whom this message was prepared, were J. Otis, Capt. Thayer, Cc. Bowers, S. Adams, and Mr. Denny.]

MESSAGE

May it please your Excellency,

THE General Court, in their present session, having passed an act, to inquire into the rateable estates of this province, and the House of Representatives being very desirous to complete the same, as soon as may be, after the return of the lists; they therefore desire your Excellency would be pleased to give the Assembly an opportunity to come together the beginning of October next, for that purpose.

===

MESSAGE

Gentlemen of the House of Representatives,

I SHALL always consult his Majesty's service, as to the time of meeting the General Assembly, and govern myself accordingly.

T. HUTCHINSON.

===

MESSAGE

May it please your Excellency,

YOUR Excellency having refused to assent to the grants made at the last session of the General Court, to Mr. Bollan, and Mr. De Berdt, for their respective services in England, the two Houses, in faithfulness to themselves, and those they represent, are constrained to remonstrate to your Excellency on this subject; and for that purpose would observe, that self defence, whether it regards individuals or bodies of men, is the first law of nature; and, that in obedience to this law, this community, when its rights and liberties have been attacked, have, by their Representatives, at different times, appointed agents for their defence. Now, although it had been the usual practice for the Governor to be concerned in that appointment, yet, when circumstances became critical, and the dearest rights of the province were at stake—when the King's ministers appeared resolved to infringe those rights, and could influence the Governor, who was wholly in their power, to procure an agent to their mind, or to control the instructions that might be prepared for him, whereby the end and design of his appointment might be frustrated; when this was the case, it became fit and reasonable, that an agent, chosen by either House, and the instructions given him should be wholly independent of the Governor; and, consequently, it must be fit and reasonable, that the pay and support of such agent, should not be obstructed by the Governor.

The same reasoning is applicable to the appointment of the agent by the Council; with regard to which, it may be observed, that when heavy and repeated charges had been laid against them, by the late Governor, Sir Francis Bernard, of Nettleham, Baronet, designed and calculated not only to asperse their characters, but to affect the charter of the province, the necessity of the case required they should defend themselves against those charges. The right of defence, which is necessary to guard and preserve every other right, is founded in natural justice and common law, which do not suffer any one to be condemned, without being first heard, and their defence considered; and of this right they cannot be deprived, without being deprived at the same time of their political existence.

The Council are an order of men instituted by charter, and were censured by the said Governor, in their public capacity; a particular charge being made upon them, their sole authority was sufficient and proper to answer it; and the Council being a constituent part of the body politic, their defence was as necessary to the good of the whole, as the care and preservation of an essential part is to the body natural. The Council being an essential part of the body politic, or incorporated province, and their defence being necessary and beneficial to the whole, the province is chargeable to pay for such defence, and consequently, no Governor, or other person, can justly obstruct the payment.

The right of defence includes a right to all the means requisite and proper for that defence, and consequently, a right to appoint and support their own defender; without this, the freedom and benefit of defence would be taken away, where they cannot appear in their own persons.

From the foregoing observations, the two Houses think it appears, very manifestly, that they have a just and clear right, both jointly and separately, to appoint agents for themselves, without the concurrence of the Governor; and, that the great principle of self defence inherent in, and necessarily active, in all bodies capable of action, makes it unfit and unreasonable, that the Governor should refuse his assent to grants made to such agents, for their services to the province.

As the grants made at the last session, cannot operate, new grants have been made to the said agents, this present session, which now lie before your Excellency; to which grants, the two Houses hope, your Excellency will give your assent.

===

SPEECH

OF THE GOVERNOR TO THE TWO HOUSES, JULY 5, 1771.

Gentlemen of the Council, and
Gentlemen of the House of Representatives,

I HAVE continued the session longer than has been usual at this season of the year, that you might have the full time you desired for transacting the public and private business which came before you, and it gives me pleasure to reflect, that, in general, a good harmony has subsisted between the several branches of the Legislature. In some parts of your proceedings, I have not been able to concur in sentiment with you; particularly,

Gentlemen of the House of Representatives,

I cannot help disapproving of a certain instrument which you voted, in consequence of a message from me, and which you have caused to be entered upon your journal, and to be printed in the public newspapers. I am obliged to make some remarks upon it, before I put an end to the session, although it has not been addressed to me in the usual form. By this instrument, you protest, as you express it, first, against whatsoever tends to establish ministerial or royal instruction as laws within the province; and, secondly, against holding the Court in Cambridge, merely by force of instructions, as an intolerable grievance, which ought speedily to be redressed. The first part of your protest was altogether unnecessary, and can have no good effect, but may alarm the people when they are in no danger; for, by the tenor of my commission, notwithstanding I am required to follow the King's instructions, I am to make the charter and the laws of the province, the rule of my administration; and, upon these fundamentals, all my instructions are framed; and if ever you shall think that you have ground to accuse me of departing from the charter and the established laws, I promise you that I will not avail myself of an instruction for my justification or excuse; but, if I happen to differ from you upon the construction of the charter or your laws, you must allow me to govern myself by my own, rather than by your judgment.

The second part of your protest, appears to me, to be repugnant to what has been admitted for more than four score years, to be a part of your constitution; for, notwithstanding, you confine your protest to my removing the Court from Boston, by force of an instruction, you may, with equal reason, extend it to any act whatsoever done by force of instructions. I must deal plainly with you, gentlemen, and let you know that I cannot consider myself at liberty to depart from the King's instructions, in any matters, which are not repugnant to the charter and to the established laws; and it is not the preservation of my place which influences me, but a sense of my duty to the King, and the preservation of his just prerogative. It is a new doctrine advanced by the last Assembly, that the King, by reserving to himself the power of nominating and appointing a Governor, hath divested himself of the right of instructing him. If this had been the case, why did the Assembly, in 1692, thankfully receive Sir William Phips' commission, which was published at the same time with the charter, and which expressly required him to execute his trust, according to such powers and instructions, as he should receive, pursuant to the charter and to the established laws? Why has every Assembly since, until the Assembly of the last year, submitted, without any exception, to commissions of the same tenor? In the controversy with Governor Burnet, in 1728, the Assembly would not admit that his instructions should bind them, but they never pretended that they did not bind him.

Your observation, that, by the charter, the Governor is to convene the Court, from time to time, according to his discretion, or as he shall judge necessary, and, therefore, that the King's instruction ought not to control him, does not distinguish this case, because every power, where there is no special limitation, is to be exercised according to discretion, or as shall be judged necessary. I must further observe to you, that before the date of your charter, Governors in the plantations, were required to execute their trusts pursuant to the instructions they received from the Crown. When the Crown, by charter, reserves to itself the power of appointing a Governor, this reserve must be understood to mean a Governor under the like restrictions with other the King's Governors, unless there be further words to signify the contrary. I know of no such words in the charter.

His Majesty expects from me, on the one hand, that I make no invasion upon any of your rights; but, then, on the other hand, he enjoins me to give up no part of his prerogative. I know that the messages and resolves of the House the last year, which asserted, that the Governor is not held to the observance of this instruction, were very displeasing to the King; I am, therefore, under an additional obligation to bear my testimony against the like assertion.

I would not, however, have labored to explain points, so clear in themselves, if I was not apprehensive, that your constituents are liable to be prejudiced in favor of the proceedings of their Representatives, and that there is danger, if I had been silent, that this instrument would retard that quiet and contentment which, I doubt not, the gentlemen of the House, in general, who voted for it, wish to see fully restored.

I shall only observe upon your message presented me this day, in answer to my message to you of yesterday, that whatever may be the rights of the General Assembly, in matters of taxation, the Crown hath certainly reserved to itself the prerogative of disallowing every law of what nature soever; and as the disallowance of a tax act, after it is in part executed, would cause great perplexity, I think that his Majesty's instruction pointing out to you, through me, his servant, those parts of your tax acts which he disapproves of, should be considered as an instance of his tenderness and paternal regard to his subjects, and that it is not liable to the least exception. I shall transmit my messages, and this, your extraordinary answer, to be laid before his Majesty.

Gentlemen of the Council, and
        Gentlemen of the House of Representatives,

I have given my consent to the bills and votes which have passed the two Houses this session, as far as I could, consistent with my duty to the King, and with the interest of the province.

Upon mature consideration of the grants made to William Bollan, Esq. and to the executors of Dennys De Berdt, Esq. by the last Assembly, I refused my consent. I cannot yet see reason to alter my sentiments; and the objections to my signing the grants, made this session, to the same persons, to which your message of this forenoon refers, are rather increased than lessened.

                                T. HUTCHINSON.

====

LETTER

FROM ARTHUR LEE, ESQ.* TO THE SPEAKER OF THE HOUSE OF REPRESEN-
TATIVES, DATED LONDON, SEPTEMBER 22, 1771.

Sir,

        In obedience to the order of the House of Representatives, which you did me the honor of conveying to me, the 23d November, 1770, I have inquired at Dr. Franklin's lodgings, he himself being absent, for despatches from you; but I have found none. It

*Mr. Lee was of Virginia, and he was intimate with Dr. Franklin, then agent for the province, in England. He was a zealous advocate for the rights of the colonies, and strenuously opposed the arbitary measures of the British Ministry at that period.

shall continue to be my care to attend to the business of the province, till the Doctor's return.

It is now the dead time of the year, and nothing is passing worthy your attention. Parliament, without some unexpected emergency, will not meet till after Christmas.

The Commissary of Virginia is now here, with a view of prosecuting the scheme of an American Episcopate. He is an artful, though not an able man. You will consider, sir, in your wisdom, whether any measures on your side, may contribute to counteract this dangerous innovation. Regarding it as threatening the subversion both of our civil and religious liberties, it shall meet with all the opposition in my power.

With very great satisfaction I have learnt, from the late proceedings of the House, that you have determined to resist any new invasion of your rights, as well as to remonstrate against those that are already passed. It was such vigilance and perseverance in our illustrious ancestors, that redeemed our constitution when equally invaded; and, I trust in God, that these virtues in you will be crowned with the same success.

May the peace of God rest among you, to prosper your councils, and protect the province.

I have the honor to be your most obliged and faithful servant,

ARTHUR LEE.

No. 3, *Essex Court, Middle Temple.*

SPEECH

OF THE GOVERNOR TO THE TWO HOUSES, APRIL 8, 1772.

Gentlemen of the Council, and

Gentlemen of the House of Representatives,

I HAVE, from time to time, regularly transmitted the applications which have been made to me in former sessions, to convene the General Court in the town of Boston, together with the messages, resolves, and votes, of every kind, which have passed upon that subject, and they have all been laid before the King. This is all I could do, consistent with my duty; for, as I have before observed to you, I prorogued the Court to Cambridge, upon a signification of his Majesty's pleasure to that purpose, and I may not remove it to Boston without his Majesty's permission.

Our most gracious Sovereign is ever ready to afford a favorable attention to such petitions and requests of his subjects, as do not tend to injure the constitution, and are, in other respects, reasona-

40

ble to be granted; and if you had desired me to carry the Court to Boston, because it is the most convenient place, and the prerogative of the Crown to instruct the Governor to convene the Court at such place as his Majesty may think proper, had not been denied, I should have obtained leave to meet you at Boston, at this time; but I shall not be at liberty to do it, whilst this denial is persisted in. If you shall desist from it, and the removal of the Court to Boston, shall, for other reasons, be judged expedient, I have authority to acquaint you, that his Majesty will allow me to comply with your wishes.

I have received, in the recess of the Court, a letter from his Excellency William Tryon, Esq. Governor of his Majesty's province of New York, proposing, with great candor, measures for the settlement of the boundary line between the two provinces. The Secretary will lay a copy of this letter before you. I recommend the subject of it to your consideration, and shall be willing to contribute every thing in my power, to finish this long subsisting controversy.

Gentlemen of the House of Representatives,

Upon inquiry into the state of the treasury, I find there are surplusses of funds which have been established for the payment of sums borrowed for the charges of government in past years, and these, together with other unappropriated stocks, are more than equal to the sum which is necessary to satisfy the present demands upon the treasury, and to provide for the service of the advancing year.

The Treasurer will lay before you the state of the treasury, and an estimate of the sums requisite for its supply. It is with you, to originate such a bill as you shall judge proper.

Gentlemen of the Council, and
Gentlemen of the House of Representatives,

Much time is usually spent by the General Court in considering petitions for new trials at law, for leave to sell the real estates of persons deceased, by their executors, or administrators, and the real estates of minors, by their guardians. All such private business is properly cognizable by the established judicatories. If it be necessary that further powers should be given to such judicatories, or that new courts should be erected, I am willing to consent to any good and wholesome law, or laws, for those purposes. A legislative body, consisting of three distinct parts, the consent of each of which, is necessary to every valid act, is extremely improper for such decisions. The polity of the English government seldom admits of the exercise of this executive and judiciary power by the Legislature, and I know of nothing special in the government of this province, to give countenance to it.

There shall be no delay on my part, in the business of the session, and I will lay nothing unnecessary before you.

T. HUTCHINSON.

ANSWER

OF THE HOUSE OF REPRESENTATIVES TO THE GOVERNOR'S
SPEECH, APRIL 10, 1772.

May it please your Excellency,

THE House of Representatives have duly considered your
speech to both Houses, at the opening of this session. Your Excellency is pleased to acquaint us, that, " if we had desired you to
carry the Court to Boston, because it is the most convenient place ;
and the prerogative of the Crown to instruct the Governor to convene the Court at such place as his Majesty may think proper, had
not been denied ; you should have obtained leave to meet us in
Boston, at this time ; but that you shall not be at liberty to do so,
whilst this denial is persisted in."

We have maturely considered this point ; and are still firmly in
opinion, that such instruction is repugnant to the royal charter,
wherein the Governor is vested with the full power of adjournment, proroguing and dissolving the General Assembly, as he shall
judge necessary. Nothing in the charter, appears to us to afford
the least grounds to conclude, that a right is reserved to his Majesty of controling the Governor, in thus exercising this full power.
Nor indeed does it seem reasonable that there should ; for, it being impossible that any one, at the distance of three thousand miles,
should be able to foresee the most convenient time or place of holding the Assembly, it is necessary that such discretionary power
should be lodged with the Governor, who is, by charter, constantly
to reside within the province.

We are still earnestly desirous of the removal of this Assembly
to the Court House, in Boston ; and we are sorry that your Excellency's determination thereon, depends upon our disavowing
these principles ; because we cannot do it consistently with the
duty we owe our constituents. We are constrained to be explicit
at this time ; for if we should be silent, after your Excellency has
recommended it to us, as a necessary preliminary, to desist from
saying any thing upon this head, while we request your Excellency
for a removal of the Assembly, for reasons of convenience only,
it might be construed as tacitly conceding to a doctrine injurious to
the constitution, and in effect, as rescinding our own record, of
which we still deliberately approve.

The power of adjourning and proroguing the General Assembly, is a power in trust, to be exercised for the good of the province ; this House have a right to judge for themselves, whether it was thus exercised. We cannot avoid taking this occasion, freely to declare to your Excellency, that the holding of the Assembly in this place, without any good reason which we can conceive of, under the many and great inconveniences which this, and former Houses, have so fully set forth to your Excellency, is, in our opinion, an undue exercise of power ; and a very great grievance, which we still hope will soon be fully redressed.

Your Excellency may be assured, that this House will, with all convenient despatch, take into our most serious consideration, that part of your speech which concerns the establishment of a partition line between this province and the province of New York ; and that we will, with great candor, contribute every thing in our power, to accomplish the same equitable terms.

The other parts of your Excellency's speech, have had the proper attention of the House ; and we are determined, during the remainder of the session, which must be short, to consult his Majesty's real service—the true interest of the province.

[The Speaker, (Mr. Cushing,) Mr. S. Adams, Mr. Hobson, Capt. Heath, Maj. Foster, Mr. Ingersol, and Mr. Denny, wore the committee.]

SPEECH

OF THE GOVERNOR TO BOTH HOUSES, APRIL 25, 1772.

Gentlemen of the Council, and

  Gentlemen of the House of Representatives,

I THANK you for the despatch which you have given to the public business, and for that harmony, which has generally prevailed in the course of the present session.

I am sorry that there is any material point remaining, in which the several branches of the Legislature cannot yet agree. The opinion of the House of Representatives, declared in their message to me, that the removal of the Assembly from Boston, by force of an instruction from his Majesty, is an undue exercise of power, and a great grievance, differs widely from my own opinion on the prerogatives reserved by the Crown, and the duty required of the Governor, by the constitution.

In support of my opinion, I will lay before you, what appears to be the true spirit of the charter. I am not contending for victory, but I wish to satisfy you, that there is no room to suggest, that the King has been the cause of grievance to his subjects, by giving an instruction to the Governor, which, by the constitution, his Majesty had no authority to give. I am likewise desirous that my own conduct should appear in a favorable light to you, and to the good people of the province.

It may be proper then, to observe, that the first charter to the Massachusetts colony having been vacated, our ancestors, sensible of the necessity of some form of government, constitutionally derived from regal authority, humbly solicited the restoration of their charter, with such additional powers, as the Crown should think proper to grant; and thereupon, to use the words of the House of Representatives, in the year 1728, "their late Majesties King William and Queen Mary, of glorious memory, were graciously pleased to gratify the inhabitants here, and did grant to them certain powers, privileges, and franchises, to be used and employed for the benefit of the people; and, in the same grant, reserved other powers to be used and exercised by the Crown, or the Governors sent by it, agreeable to the directions and instructions contained in said grant, and their commissions, having reference for their better guidance and directions, to the several powers and authorities mentioned in the said charter."

It is further observable, that, by the first charter, the Crown had constituted a corporation in England, empowered to appoint, under its direction and instructions, Governors, and other officers, in the colony. By this second charter, the Crown reserves to itself the power of appointing and commissioning a Governor, and Lieutenant, or Deputy Governor. By their commissions, they were authorized to administer government, according to such instructions as should be given by the Crown, in pursuance of the charter, and of such reasonable laws as should be in force. Now, although I cannot conceive of this transaction, as properly speaking, a treaty or compact, yet, it may be proper to observe, that, after the charter and commissions had been made public, and matter of record in the province, the Governor and Council, with the Representatives of the people, not only acquiesced in, and acted by virtue of, powers and authorities thus derived, and thus limited by instructions, but by a law, or order, they required to be observed throughout the province, a day of solemn thanksgiving to Almighty God, for the distinguishing marks of royal favor in this settlement of government.

This has been the tenor of the commissions to all succeeding Governors ever since, and their instructions have been, from time to time, as there has been occasion for it, communicated to the Council and to the House of Representatives, sometimes at their request, and have been entered in their minutes and journals, and I never heard that the King's authority to give such instructions, was ever called in question, until within these two years. Instructions from the Crown have been, in fact, part of our constitution for fourscore years together.

I will now endeavor to shew that there has not been any exception taken to his Majesty's instruction, to remove the Assembly from the town of Boston, which will not equally avail against instructions in general, or in any other particular case whatsoever.

It has been said, that the Crown has parted with its prerogative of determining the time and place of convening the Assembly, and given it to the Governor, to be used as he shall judge necessary; therefore, an instruction which controls the Governor's discretion, the exercise of this power cannot be said to be an instruction in pursuance of the charter, and agreeable to the constitution.

I must observe to you, that all the powers which are given, by the charter, to the Governors, without the words, as he shall judge necessary, are as ample as those which are given with them, for the Governor is to exercise the general powers given him, according to his best discretion, which is, in other words, as he shall judge necessary. But, if you will attend to the charter, you will find a peculiar propriety in the use of the words, in that paragraph, for another purpose. The Governor is required to convene the Assembly, the last Wednesday in May, in every year, for the election of Counsellors, and this he must do, whether he judges it necessary or not; but then, he is empowered to adjourn, prorogue, and dissolve it, from time to time, as he shall judge necessary; which words are used merely to denote, that he is not confined to any other time of convening the Court, except the last Wednesday in May. What pretence then, can there be, to distinguish this from any other power, or what exercise of power can there be, pursuant to the charter, by force of an instruction, if this is not? If it be said, that, in other instances also, of power given to the Governor to use, according to his discretion, the King has parted with his prerogative, the reserve made by the Crown, to give instructions to the Governor, can, in no case whatsoever, have any effect. The fallacy of the whole argument, will appear from this distinction. Where the charter gives any privilege to the people, as in the case just mentioned, of an Assembly to be held every last Wednesday in May, and the like, in such cases, an instruction to restrain the Governor, may be said to be repugnant to the charter. Where it gives power to the Governor, to be used according to discretion, or, as he shall judge necessary, there an instruction to direct or guide, in the exercise of such power, is not repugnant, but pursuant to the charter. And there is no contradiction in it, for the Governor may very well be supposed to have general power of acting according to his own discretion, and, nevertheless, be subject in special instances, or on special occasions, to the control of royal wisdom or discretion.

It has been further urged, as an objection to this particular instruction, that the King, at the distance of three thousand miles, cannot foresee the proper time and place for convening the General Assembly. It is enough, for my present purpose, to observe, that his Majesty may have so full a knowledge of the state and circumstances of a particular town or place, as to be able to determine that it is not proper to convene the Assembly there. Upon such knowledge, I doubt not, this instruction was founded, and I have no reason to expect that any other instruction will ever be given, which cannot be as well justified.

There has been one more objection made to this exercise of the prerogative, viz.: That it is a power in trust, to be exercised for the good of the province, and the House of Representatives have a right to judge for themselves, whether it is thus exercised. If nothing more is intended, than, that the House of Representatives have a right to judge of the exercise of that, or any other part of the prerogative, and when they have any cause of complaint, to seek redress by representations to his Majesty, or in any constitutional way, I do not know that any body will deny it; but then, I know not to what purpose it is adduced. If it be intended, that, when the Governor, by his Majesty's order, convenes the Assembly at a time or place, which appears to them to be inconvenient or improper, they have, therefore, a right to refuse to appear, or refuse to proceed upon business, or that they have a right to continue to sit after the Governor has prorogued, or dissolved the Assembly, in their judgment, unreasonably or unnecessarily, will not this imply a contradiction? Is it not allowing a full power to do a thing, and, at the same time, admitting a power to defeat it, and prevent the full power from having any effect?

Thus, I think I have obviated all the objections which have been made to this instruction, in particular. I have already observed to you, that instructions, in general, are supported by your charter; I must now add, that, had no such express provision been made, they would have been unexceptionable and constitutional. The King is the head of the government, not only in the realm, but in the plantations. Local distance will not admit of the exercise of the royal authority in the plantations, by the King in person. This authority remains, notwithstanding, and, although it must be exercised by a substitute, yet, as much as may be of the royal guidance and influence, is to be preserved and maintained. This must be done by instructions for the general conduct of the Governor, and upon special occasions, as extraordinary unforeseen events may make them necessary.

But what benefit can we propose, if it should be admitted, that the Governor is not liable to be controled by instructions? The reserve in the royal commission is not made to deprive the people of any privilege, but to restrain the Governor from using, to their oppression or hurt, or to the diminution of the just prerogative of the Crown, that power and authority with which he is entrusted. Shall we be more safe with a Governor, left altogether to his own discretion, than with one who is under the control and guidance of our Sovereign? The House of Representatives, to which I have before referred you, thought not. In a message to the Governor, in the reign of his Majesty's royal grandfather, they very properly observe, " it is not reasonable we should confide in any Governor whatsoever, so much as in our gracious King, the common father of all his people, who is known to delight in nothing so much, as in their happiness; and whose interest and glory, and that of his royal progeny, are inseparable from the prosperity and welfare of his people; whereas, neither the prosperity nor adversity of a people, affect a Governor's interest, when he has once left them."

We have abundant reason, to adopt the same language and sentiment in the reign of his present Majesty, who has nothing more at heart, than the happiness and prosperity of his subjects, in all parts of his dominions.

In conformity to the charter, which limits the time of your continuance, I am now obliged to dissolve an Assembly, which has discovered a very good disposition to such measures as tend to promote the prosperity of the province. I have great reason to believe, the people of the province in general, are in the same disposition, and that I shall meet a new Assembly, as well inclined to the like measures. T. HUTCHINSON.

―

SPEECH

OF THE GOVERNOR TO THE TWO HOUSES, MAY 28, 1772.

Gentlemen of the Council, and

Gentlemen of the House of Representatives,

In conformity to the powers and privileges granted by the royal charter, you have been convened at this place, in order to the election of Counsellors for the ensuing year; and this business being finished, you have now an opportunity of proceeding to the consideration of such other public affairs as may properly come before you. In every measure, as far as shall consist with my duty to the King, and with the welfare and prosperity of the province, I will cheerfully concur with you.

I have nothing in special command from his Majesty, to lay before you. Most of you are so well acquainted with the usual business of the General Assembly, at this annual session, that I need not particularly point it out to you.

I transmitted, by the first opportunity, to his Excellency the

Governor of New York, a copy of the act of the last Assembly, appointing commissaries, in order to the settlement of the line between the two provinces. I doubt not I shall soon receive an answer, and be able to communicate it to you. In the course of the session I shall probably propose to you, by message, the consideration of some other public matters, for which, at present, I am not fully prepared. **T. HUTCHINSON.**

ANSWER

May it please your Excellency,

THE House of Representatives have deliberately considered your speech at the opening of this session. Your Excellency is pleased to say, that, " in conformity to the powers and privileges granted by the royal charter, we have been convened at this place, in order to the election of Counsellors for the ensuing year." It is a charter right, that a General Assembly shall be convened on the last Wednesday in May, annually, for the choice of Counsellors ; but the convening and holding the General Assembly at Harvard College, in Cambridge, is a measure very grievous to us ; and it requires the greatest degree of candor, to suppose it to be for the good of the people, which is the sole end for which the powers vested in you, by the charter, were granted.

The Town House, in Boston, is the accustomed ancient place for holding the General Assembly, and where alone provision is made for it. It does not appear to us, that there was any necessity for convening the Assembly in this place, nor can we conceive of any for continuing it here. Without such necessity, the continuing the Assembly in any other place than the Town House, in Boston, will be a very great grievance, and an undue exercise of your power. And, as we cannot, without the greatest inconvenience, proceed to the consideration of the public business in this place, which is very pressing, and greatly in arrears, by reason of the prorogations the last year, we are constrained to lay before your Excellency, our earnest request, that you would be pleased to remove the Assembly, to the Town House, in Boston, where we may, with the greatest advantage and despatch, transact all such public matters as are now before us, together with such others, as your Excellency shall propose for our consideration.

41

MESSAGE

Gentlemen of the House of Representatives,

I AGREE with you that the powers vested in me, by charter, are to be exercised for the good of the people, and I have made this the great object of my administration. I wish to avoid every thing which shall appear to you to be grievous; and, although I cannot agree with you, that, unless there be a necessity of holding the Court in some other place than the town of Boston, it must, therefore, be a grievance to remove it from thence; yet, I will take the subject matter of your message into consideration, and if it shall not appear to me necessary for his Majesty's service, and the good of the province, to continue the Court in some other place than the town of Boston, I will comply with your desire and remove it there. If it shall appear to me necessary to continue it in some other place, although, by the constitution, I am made the judge of that necessity, yet, I will endeavor by another message, to convince you of it, that you may proceed in your business, with the greater satisfaction.   T. HUTCHINSON.

===

MESSAGE

Gentlemen of the House of Representatives,

As I wish to have a just understanding of every expression in any message which comes to me from the House of Representatives, I must desire you to acquaint me, whether, when you say in your message of the 29th May, that it does not appear to you there was any necessity of convening the Assembly at Cambridge, you intend my convening it there when I first removed it from Boston, or my convening it there the present year. As soon as I am ascertained of this, I shall be ready to give you a full answer to your message.   T. HUTCHINSON.

ANSWER

OF THE HOUSE OF REPRESENTATIVES TO THE GOVERNOR,
JUNE 3, 1772.

May it please your Excellency,

In answer to your message of this day, this House beg leave to say, that they judge the intention of the expression, particularly referred to by your Excellency, as well as of all other expressions in their message of the 29th of May, to be sufficiently clear and plain, and, therefore, it is altogether needless to make any explanation of them; and hope your Excellency will not delay to give a full answer to that message.

—

MESSAGE

FROM HIS EXCELLENCY THE GOVERNOR TO THE HOUSE OF
REPRESENTATIVES, JUNE 3, 1772.

Gentlemen of the House of Representatives,

I must govern myself by the measure, not of your understanding, but my own. What appears to you to be sufficiently plain, appears to me to be doubtful and equivocal. As it may be construed one way or the other, so in complying with your desire, founded upon this, among other reasons, I should, or should not, conform to the instructions of the King, whose servant I am. As reserved as you have been in your message to me, I will be unreserved and open with you. Whilst you dispute the authority by which I removed the Court from Boston, I do not intend to carry it thither again; and whensoever I shall receive his Majesty's instructions for exercising the just prerogative of the Crown, in any case, I will observe them without violation in any degree; and when your intention in any message appears to me uncertain, and you refuse to make it certain, I think it will be a sufficient justification for my refusal to do any thing in consequence of such message, so long as the uncertainty remains.

T. HUTCHINSON.

MESSAGE

May it please your Excellency,

THE House of Representatives beg leave to acquaint your Excellency, that a motion was made on the first Friday of this session, to assign a time for the consideration of a suitable grant for the support of his Majesty's Governor of the province. But, it being suggested to the House, that your Excellency was not pleased, the last year, to give your consent to a bill, which passed both Houses of Assembly, in their first session, for granting the sum of thirteen hundred pounds for the support of your Excellency, the House thought proper to direct the attendance of the Secretary, to give information touching this matter, who, expressly said, that your Excellency did not give your consent to said bill.

This House is wholly at a loss to account for that measure, unless provision is made for the support of your Excellency, otherwise than by the grants and acts of the General Assembly of the province.

By the royal charter, it is incumbent upon the General Assembly to make adequate provision for the support of his Majesty's government of this province, and every act for the making such provision, is to be originated by the House of Representatives.

The support of his Majesty's Governor of the province, is an important part of the support of his Majesty's government here.

If provision is made for the support of your Excellency, otherwise than by the grants and acts of the General Assembly, it is absolutely requisite that this House should be acquainted with it. They, therefore, pray, that your Excellency would be pleased to inform them, whether provision is made for the support of your Excellency, as Governor of this province, in any way and manner, other than has been heretofore used and practised, to wit, by the grants and acts of the General Assembly ; and, if it is so, in what way and manner that provision is made.

MESSAGE

Gentlemen of the House of Representatives,

BY inspecting the journal of the proceedings of the House of Representatives, in April, 1771, you will find, that, in answer to a message from the House, I then observed, that his Majesty has been enabled, by an act of Parliament, to make a certain and adequate provision for the support of the civil government in the colonies, as his Majesty shall judge necessary.

I am now able to acquaint you, that his Majesty has been graciously pleased to make provision for my support, in the station, in which he has thought fit to place me; and, as this is judged to be an adequate support, I must conclude it cannot be his Majesty's pleasure, that, without his special permission, which has not yet been signified to me, I should accept of any grant from the province, in consideration of the ordinary government services done, or to be done, by me.   T. HUTCHINSON.

[The General Court was then adjourned to Boston, to meet on the 16th.]

MESSAGE

FROM THE GOVERNOR TO THE HOUSE OF REPRESENTATIVES,
JULY 10, 1772.

Gentlemen of the House of Representatives,

I AM informed, that, in consequence of my answer to your message of the 6th of June, you have passed certain votes, or resolves, which you have ordered to be entered upon your journals. It may be of importance to his Majesty's service, that I should have as early knowledge, as may be, of the proceedings of the House of Representatives, especially in matters of this nature, I must desire you to direct, that I be furnished with an attested copy of such votes or resolves, from your journals, if any such have been ordered to be entered there.   T. HUTCHINSON.

REPORT AND RESOLUTIONS

ADOPTED BY THE HOUSE OF REPRESENTATIVES, JULY 10, 1772.*

THAT the making provision for the support of the Governor of the province, independent of the grants and acts of the General

---

* This report was made on the 4th, but was ordered to lie for a revision. The committee, by whom this report, and the message of same date, were prepared, consisted of the Speaker, Maj. Hawley, Mr. S. Adams, Col. Worthington, Mr. Hancock, Col. Williams, Capt. Heath, Col. Warren, and Col. Bowers.

Assembly, is, in the opinion of the committee, an infraction upon the rights granted to the inhabitants, by the royal charter, and in derogation of the constitution.

The charter of this province, is a most solemn contract, not only between King William and Queen Mary, by whom it was granted, of the one part, and the inhabitants of the province, of the other; but also between the heirs and successors of their royal Majesties, and the successors of the said inhabitants forever. This appears from the very words and tenor of the charter.

By the said charter, it is established and ordained, "That there shall be one Governor, to be, from time to time, appointed and commissioned by the King:" and, it is also herein expressly granted, that "the General Assembly shall have full power and authority to impose and levy reasonable rates and taxes for the support of his Majesty's government of the province;" of which, the support of the Governor is a most material and important part.

That the great and General Court or Assembly, of this province, is, by the charter, vested with the exclusive right of judging what is an adequate support of his Majesty's government of this province, and of determining in what way and manner, provision for that purpose shall be made, appears not only from the natural and obvious sense and meaning of the words and terms of the charter, but from the constant and uninterrupted usage and practice upon that charter, for more than eighty years, from the time when it was granted.

That the support of the Governor is part of the support of the government of the province, not only has been the constant sense of the General Assemblies of this province; but it also appears, from the act of the British Parliament, referred to in his Excellency's message, and his Majesty's determination therein; for in the message, his Excellency informs the House, that he had observed in his answer to a message of a former House, "that his Majesty had been enabled, by an act of Parliament, to make a certain and adequate provision for the support of civil government in the colonies." And in this message he declares, that "he is able to acquaint the House, that his Majesty has been graciously pleased to make provision for his support in the station, in which he has thought fit to place him;" by which, his Excellency cannot be understood to intend any other than his station as Governor of this province. And by the connexion of the several parts of the message, it is most plainly to be inferred, that his Excellency would acquaint the House, that his Majesty had made that provision in consequence of, and by the power vested in him, by an act of Parliament, which enabled him to make provision for the support of the civil government of the colonies. So that, unless it should be supposed that his Majesty himself hath mistaken the true sense of the act, it is evidently the opinion of the British Parliament, that the support of a Governor is part of the support of the government of a colony.

That the power and authority of providing for the support of the Governor, should be vested in the General Assembly, is necessary to preserve the freedom of the constitution. For, if the King, who has the absolute power of appointing and commissioning the Governor, shall also have the power of judging and determining what shall be a reasonable and adequate support for him, and of the ways and means of making provision for that purpose, there remains no check at all upon the power, devolved by charter, on the Crown. And a power without a check, is, so far forth, destructive of the freedom of the constitution.

Moreover, this is a most dangerous innovation, as it affords a precedent for future more extensive evil of the same kind. For, with equal reason, may the Crown take and exercise the power of judging and determining what shall be an adequate support for every other part of civil government, and the ways and means of making provision therefor; which would take away the freedom of the constitution, and establish arbitrary government within the province.

Although it may not be affirmed, that the Governor, by being altogether dependent upon the Crown for his support, becomes positively vested with any new powers which were not granted to him by the charter, or that his department in government is enlarged, yet, the relation he before stood in to the people, by his dependence on them, is altered. That check upon the exercise of the powers that are vested in him, by the charter, which was evidently designed to remain in the General Assembly, is annihilated; and he may, if he pleases, exercise even his constitutional powers, in such a manner as shall be injurious and oppressive to the people, without restraint. He is, therefore, a Governor, not dependent upon the people, as the charter prescribes, and, consequently not, in that respect, such a Governor as the people consented to, at the granting thereof.

The support of government, and the means of its defence, ought to depend, and, in all free governments, it does depend upon the grants of the people, made by Representatives of their own free election, and the acts of the Legislative. And adequate provision is thus made for these purposes, as is judged and determined by the Representatives of the people to be reasonable; proportioned to their abilities, and the station and merit of those who are entrusted with the administration. This has been claimed as the undoubted right of the Parliament and people of England, and so adjudged, for many ages past.

As it is clearly the right of the Legislative of this province, the General Assembly have always made adequate provision for the support of the Governor. The advice, therefore, given to his Majesty, to take upon himself the payment of his Governor, must have been grounded upon false information, or proceeded from a temper inimical to the good people of this province. Whatever may have been the design of administration, it is a measure, whereby, not only the just right of the General Assembly of this province is rescinded, but the highest indignity is thrown upon it; as though it was either not disposed to make adequate provision for, or not the competent judges ' of, the support of the government, upon which the safety and welfare of the people depends.

For these reasons, the committee beg leave, further to report the following resolutions, for the consideration and acceptance of the House.

Whereas, in and by the charter of this province, the full power and authority to impose and levy proportionable and reasonable rates and taxes upon the estates and persons of all and every the proprietors and inhabitants of the province, for his Majesty's service, in the necessary defence and support of his government therein, is vested in the General Assembly; and the rates and taxes by them imposed and levied for the purposes aforesaid, are to be disposed of, according to such acts as are, or shall be in force therein:

And, whereas the support of his Majesty's Governor of the province, is one material and most important part of the support of his Majesty's government therein:

1. Resolved, That, by virtue of the full power and authority granted by the charter as aforesaid, the General Assembly is the constituted judge of the adequate support of his Majesty's Governor, and the rates and taxes necessary to be imposed and levied for that purpose; therefore,

2. Resolved, That the imposing and levying rates and taxes, and making provision for the support of the Governor, otherwise than by the grants and acts of the General Assembly, is an infraction upon the charter in a material point, whereby a most important trust is wrested out of the hands of the General Assembly, and it is deprived of a most important part of Legislative power and authority vested therein by the charter, and necessary for the good and welfare of the province, and the support and government thereof.

3. Resolved, That the General Assembly of this province, hath ever since the charter was granted, from time to time, by their own grants and acts, made suitable and adequate provision for the support of his Majesty's Governor thereof.

4. Resolved, That the Governor's having and receiving his support independent of the grants and acts of the General Assembly, is a dangerous innovation, which renders him a Governor not dependent on the people, as the charter has prescribed, and consequently, not, in that respect, such a Governor as the people consented to, at the granting thereof. It destroys that mutual check and dependence, which each branch of the Legislative ought to have upon the others, and the balance of power which is essential

to all free governments. And this House do most solemnly protest, that the innovation is an important change of the constitution, and exposes the province to a despotic administration of government.

And, whereas, the General Assembly hath, from the beginning, made ample provision for the support of his Majesty's Governor:

5. Resolved, That the advice given to his Majesty, that it was necessary for his Majesty's service, and the good and welfare of this province, that certain and adequate provision should be made for the support of the Governor thereof, otherwise than as has been the invariable practice, by the grants and acts of the General Assembly, was, in the opinion of this House, either grounded on false information, or it proceeded from a temper inimical, as well to his Majesty, as to the people of this province.

6. Resolved, That a message go up to his Excellency the Governor, assuring him, that this House is ready to make him the usual annual grant, and other ordinary provision for his support; provided, his Excellency will accept the same, in full consideration " of the ordinary services of government done, or to be done, by him;" and praying his Excellency, that if he is determined in his opinion, that he cannot, " without his Majesty's special permission, accept of any grant from the province," for his support, as Governor thereof, he would make application to his Majesty, that he would be graciously pleased to give further order, that his Excellency may, without restraint, receive his whole support from this government, according to ancient and invariable usage.

MESSAGE

FROM THE HOUSE OF REPRESENTATIVES TO THE GOVERNOR,
JULY 10, 1772,

May it please your Excellency,

THE House of Representatives, after the most deliberate consideration of your message of the 13th June, are of opinion, that the making provision for your Excellency's support in the station, in which his Majesty has been pleased to place you, as Governor of this province, independent of the grants and acts of the General Assembly, and your Excellency's receiving the same, is an infraction on the rights granted to the inhabitants of the province, by the royal charter, and in derogation of the freedom of the civil constitution. This House is ready, with cheerfulness, to make the usual annual grant, and other ordinary provision ; provided

42

your Excellency will receive the same for your whole support, as Governor of the province.

Your Excellency has been pleased to signify to the House, your opinion, that you cannot, without his Majesty's special permission, receive any grant from the province, for your support, as Governor. If your Excellency is fully determined in this opinion, we pray you to make application to his Majesty, that he would be graciously pleased to give further orders, whereby you may, without any restraint, receive your support from this government, according to ancient and invariable usage.

=====

MESSAGE

FROM THE GOVERNOR TO THE HOUSE OF REPRESENTATIVES,
JULY 13, 1772.

Gentlemen of the House of Representatives,

I THINK it incumbent on me, to put you in mind of the ruinous state of the Province House, with the yards, out houses, and appendages. I imagine it must cost double the sum to repair it the next year, as will be sufficient at present, and it is most probable, that I shall not be able to keep my family there another winter. It would be most agreeable to my inclination, to reside wholly at my house in the country, and it is for the convenience of the inhabitants of the town of Boston, and other persons who occasionally come there, and have public business to transact, that I spend so much of my time in Boston. When the house provided for the Governor, is not in a tenantable repair, I think there can be no exception, if I change the place of my residence.

T. HUTCHINSON.

=====

MESSAGE

FROM THE HOUSE OF REPRESENTATIVES TO THE GOVERNOR,
JULY 14, 1772.

May it please your Excellency,

IN answer to your message of yesterday, this House beg leave to observe, that they are not unapprized that the Province House is out of repair, and that expense might be saved, by making such repairs as are necessary, as soon as may be. But, that building was procured for the residence of a Governor, whose whole support was to be provided for by the grants and acts of the General Assembly, according to the tenor of the charter; and, it is the opinion of this House, that it never was expected by any Assembly of this province, that it would be appropriated for the residence of any Governor, for whose support, adequate provision should be made in another way. Upon this consideration, we cannot think it our duty to make any repairs, at this time.

Your Excellency may be assured, that this House is far from being influenced by any personal disrespect. Should the time come, which we hope for, when your Excellency shall think yourself at liberty to accept of your whole support from this province, according to ancient and invariable usage, we doubt not, but you will then find the Representatives of this people ready to provide for your Excellency a house, not barely tenantable, but elegant. In the mean time, as your Excellency receives from his Majesty a certain and adequate support, we cannot have the least apprehensions that you will be so far guided by your own inclination, as that you will make any town in the province the place of your residence, but where it shall be most conducive to his Majesty's service, and the good and welfare of the people.

[The committee who reported this message, were, Maj. Hawley, Mr. Ingersol, Mr. Adams, Mr. Bacon, and Capt. Heath.]

MESSAGE

FROM THE GOVERNOR TO THE HOUSE OF REPRESENTATIVES,
JULY 14, 1772.

Gentlemen of the House of Representatives,

In consequence of my message to you, of the 10th instant, you have caused to be laid before me the report of a committee, accepted, and ordered to be entered upon your journals. This report contains certain resolves or declarations, which, as I conceive, are not well founded, but, on the contrary, tend to alter the constitutional dependence of this colony upon the Crown, and upon the Supreme Legislative authority of Great Britain.

The sum of those resolves or declarations, may be comprized in a few words. You have declared, that the support made for the Governor, by other powers than the legislative authority of this province, is a material infraction upon the charter; that the Governor is thereby rendered not dependent on the people, as the charter has prescribed, and consequently not, in that respect, such

a Governor as the people consented to; that the mutual check and
dependence of the branches of the Legislature is destroyed, and
the province exposed to a despotic administration. 'You have
likewise asserted, that the Assemblies, ever since the charter, have
made adequate provision for the support of the Governor; that the
advice to his Majesty to make provision for this support, proceeded from false information, or from a temper inimical to his Majesty, and to the people of this province, and you have desired me
to make application to his Majesty, that I may, without restraint,
receive my whole support from this government, according to ancient and invariable usage.

In support of these declarations, you have first alleged, that the
charter is a solemn contract between King William and Queen
Mary, and their successors, on the one part, and the inhabitants
of this province forever, on the other. If you meant no more by
a solemn contract, than what is implied between the Crown as the
grantor of certain powers and privileges, and the inhabitants of
the colony as the grantees, by which they acquire a right to the
use of those powers and privileges, until the charter in whole, or
in part, shall be legally vacated, I would take no exception; but
when you afterwards allege, that, by virtue of this contract, a
power devolved on the Crown, of appointing a Governor, there is
too great room to apprehend, that some may suppose this contract
to be something of the nature of the *pacta conventa*, or covenants
settled by treaty, between two independent states, which supposition would have such a dangerous tendency, that it is necessary
for me to define very particularly, the nature of a charter from the
Crown, upon the principles of the English constitution, and to remind you of the particular circumstances which attended the grant
of your charter.

It is a part of the prerogative of the Crown, as well as of the
power and authority of Parliament, to constitute corporations or
political bodies, and to grant to such bodies a form of government,
and powers of making and carrying into execution such laws, as
from their local, or other circumstances, may be necessary, the
Supreme Legislative authority of the British dominions always remaining entire, notwithstanding. Now, in order to share in the
benefit of this authority, our ancestors, by their agents, did not
propose a treaty, nor any thing of the nature of the *pacta conventa*,
which I have before mentioned, but, as subjects of England, first
petitioned to Parliament, that by a legislative act, their vacated
charter might be restored, and failing of success, afterwards to
use the words of the present charter, " made their humble application to King William and Queen Mary, that they would be graciously pleased to incorporate their subjects in the colony, and to
grant and confirm to them such powers, privileges, and franchises,
as, in their royal wisdom, should be thought most conducing to
their interest and service, and to the welfare and happy state of

their subjects in New England." The powers thus granted, were not, as you strangely allege, devolved on the Crown by our ancestors, but passed from the Crown to its subjects. By this charter, a General Court, or Assembly, is constituted, and among other powers granted to the Assembly, are those of making laws, not repugnant to the laws of England, and imposing rates and taxes for the service of the Crown, in the necessary defence and support of the Government. You have taken pains to prove what would not have been denied, that the support of the Governor must be included in the support of the government; and you say, that, by the grant of full power to raise taxes, you have acquired an exclusive right of supporting the Governor, and, therefore, the support of the Governor by the Crown, must be an infraction upon the charter. Consider, gentlemen, where this argument will carry you. The same clause which empowers the Assembly to tax the people for the support, empowers it also to tax for the defence of government. The defence and support of government are, in their nature, duties, attended with burdens, rather than privileges; the powers given to the Assembly to tax, are in order to compel to the performance of these duties. Can it be supposed, that this grant of power to compel the people to submit to this burden of taxes, for the defence of the government, should exclude the Crown from affording its aid for this defence, when it shall be necessary. If you are in danger of being attacked by a foreign power, has the Crown deprived itself of the right of ordering a fleet for your defence, and must the colony be lost to this power, and would you, in that case, refuse this aid, because you have an exclusive right of defending the government yourselves? Your charter gives you equal right to this objection in the case of defence, as in the case of support.

Should not so heavy a charge against the Crown, as that of making an infraction upon your charter, and wresting out of your hands, powers vested in you, have had something more than this shadow of an argument for its support? a support so feeble, that I have no need to call to my aid the act of Parliament, which enables the Crown to do what has been done, and which, if your claim from the charter had been better founded than it is, would have been sufficient to have rendered it of no effect.

If you fail of this exclusive right of supporting the Governor, your assertions that the charter prescribes a Governor dependent upon the people, and that you have not, in that respect, such a Governor as the people consented to, is altogether without foundation.

You are equally unfortunate in your notions of the mutual check and dependence which each branch of the Legislature ought to have upon the other, as also in the nature of a free government, and of the English constitution.

The mutual check which each branch of the Legislature ought

to have upon the other, consists in the necessity of the concurrence of all the branches, in order to a valid act; and when any
one branch withholds this concurrence, it is properly a check upon
the other two.   So far as this may be said to be a dependence, I
agree with you, but this is not sufficient for your purpose, for the
same check will remain in each branch when the salary of the
Governor is paid by the Crown, as when it is paid by the province.
Now this check does not affect that freedom and independence in
each branch, which is the glory of the English constitution, and
which will not admit that any one should be compelled by the
others to any act against its judgment.   If I should violate this
freedom and independence of the Council, or House of Representatives, I should justly incur his Majesty's displeasure.   Is it not
reasonable, that the Governor should be entitled to the like share
of freedom and independence, in the exercise of his judgment with
the other branches ?   That independence which cannot consist
with a free government, and which the English constitution abhors,
and which may properly be termed despotism, is a freedom in
those who are vested with executive and judiciary powers, from
the restraint of known established laws, and a liberty of acting
according to their own will and pleasure.   This restraint, in your
constitution, will remain the same, whether the Governor receives
his salary from the Crown, or from the province.   Thus, by confounding the sense and meaning of the words, check and dependence, you have given a plausible appearance to your argument.
This is an artifice which has often been made use of by writers in
newspapers, with design to give false notions of government, and
to stir up discontent and disorder ; but I am far from attributing
any such design to the Members of the House of Representatives
in general.

Let me add, that the English constitution is founded upon these
principles of freedom.   The King, Lords, and Commons, have this
mutual check upon each other ; they are, notwithstanding, altogether free and independent, and, that this freedom may be preserved entire in the Crown, we find, that ever since the hereditary
revenues have ceased, a revenue, known by the name of the civil
list, has been established among the first acts of every reign, not
temporary, or from year to year, but during the life or administration of the Prince upon the throne.   I have reason to think, that
if the Governors of this colony may be made equally secure of an
adequate provision for their support, the Crown will never interpose.

You find the same spirit of freedom run through the several offices in the English government.   The salaries of such persons as
are entrusted with the executive and judiciary powers, do not
depend upon grants made by the House of Commons, in proportion
to their abilities, station, and merit, as you say it is essential to a
free government that they should do, but certain fixed salaries and

emoluments are annexed to their offices. Indeed, nothing can be more dissonant than your system from the spirit of the English constitution.

You have made a forced construction of a clause in your charter, and have then made a very essential change in your constitution, that it may agree with this construction.

By your charter, the legislative power consists of three branches, and the consent of the Governor is expressly declared to be essential to every valid act of government. You say, notwithstanding, that he is constitutionally dependent upon the people for his support, and that this dependence is intended as a check. This check must be by withholding his support, when, in some case or other, he shall refuse to act, or act contrary, in your judgment, to the duty of his station. If he gives up his own judgment, and conforms to yours, does not the act in such case cease to be the act of the Governor, and become the act of the House of Representatives, and will it not thus, so far destroy one branch of the constitution.

Let me add further, if a Governor departs from his own judgment and conscience, is he not highly criminal, and will not the House of Representatives, which compels him to it, be at least equally guilty with him?

I am sensible, that when all other exceptions to this representation of your constitution are taken away, you will ask what security have we then against the oppression of a Governor? The answer is obvious. The law and the constitution are your security; if we depart from them, there is a power superior to him, to which he is accountable for his maleadministration. This is all the redress which can consist with the nature of a subordinate government.

No state of government is perfect; if we have all that perfection which the state we are in will admit of, we have no reason to complain. Indeed, we have no reason to fear redress from any oppression. So tender has been our most gracious Sovereign of the rights of his subjects, that, although I should humbly hope for royal forgiveness in case of inattention to some points, of no great importance, which might affect the prerogative, yet, I may not expect the forgiveness of any wilful invasion of your liberties.

If, when you declare that the Assemblies, ever since the charter, have made an adequate provision for the support of the Governor, you intend a provision suitable to the dignity of his station, and not merely such, as in the judgment of the House, the particular merits of the Governor might require, you will not be able to maintain your assertion; on the contrary, it evidently appears, that in some instances the support of the Governor has been delayed until he has complied with the measures of the Assembly, and in others, defalcations have been made from it, in order to effect the same purpose.

If you had known the provision made for the support of the Governor, to have been, as it probably was, in consequence of the advice of his Majesty's Privy Council, you would not have declared that such advice was grounded upon false information, or proceeded from a temper inimical to his Majesty, and to the people of this province.

After thus declaring my opinion of your proceedings, and giving you my reasons in support of such opinion, you will not expect that I should make my application to his Majesty, agreeable to one of your resolves, and to your message, by your committee, to allow me to receive my whole support from this government. Your votes or resolves, I must transmit, to be laid before his Majesty.

I have had repeated occasion to make my humble application, that the doings of the House of Representatives may be considered in the most favorable light.

I will do the same upon this occasion. From my personal knowledge of the majority of the Members of the House, who voted for the acceptance of this report, I am well assured that they have not done it from sinister views and purposes, but, that they have been induced to form an erroneous opinion of the rights and powers of the several branches of this Legislature. I wish that this may palliate what it is not in my power to justify or excuse.

T. HUTCHINSON.

===

SPEECH

OF THE GOVERNOR TO THE TWO HOUSES, JANUARY 6, 1773.

Gentlemen of the Council, and

    Gentlemen of the House of Representatives,

I HAVE nothing in special command from his Majesty to lay before you at this time; I have general instructions to recommend to you, at all times, such measures as may tend to promote that peace and order, upon which your own happiness and prosperity, as well as his Majesty's service, very much depend. That the government is at present in a disturbed and disordered state, is a truth too evident to be denied. The cause of this disorder, appears to me equally evident. I wish I may be able to make it appear so to you, for then, I may not doubt that you will agree with me in the proper measures for the removal of it. I have pleased myself, for several years past, with hopes, that the cause would cease of itself, and the effect with it, but I am disappointed; and I may not any longer, consistent with my duty to the King, and my regard to the interest of the province, delay communicating my sentiments to you upon a matter of so great importance. I shall be explicit, and treat the subject without reserve. I hope you will receive what I have to say upon it, with candor, and, if you shall not agree in sentiments with me, I promise you, with candor, likewise, to receive and consider what you may offer in answer.

When our predecessors first took possession of this plantation, or colony, under a grant and charter from the Crown of England, it was their sense, and it was the sense of the kingdom, that they were to remain subject to the supreme authority of Parliament. This appears from the charter itself, and from other irresistible evidence. This supreme authority has, from time to time, been exercised by Parliament, and submitted to by the colony, and hath been, in the most express terms, acknowledged by the Legislature, and, except about the time of the anarchy and confusion in England, which preceded the restoration of King Charles the Second, I have not discovered that it has been called in question, even by private or particular persons, until within seven or eight years last past. Our provincial or local laws have, in numerous instances, had relation to acts of Parliament, made to respect the plantations in general, and this colony in particular, and in our Executive Courts, both Juries and Judges have, to all intents and purposes, considered such acts as part of our rule of law. Such a constitution, in a plantation, is not peculiar to England, but agrees with the principles of the most celebrated writers upon the law of nations, that " when a nation takes possession of a distant country, and settles there, that country, though separated from the principal establishment, or mother country, naturally becomes a part of the state, equally with its ancient possessions."

So much, however, of the spirit of liberty breathes through all parts of the English constitution, that, although from the nature of government, there must be one supreme authority over the whole, yet this constitution will admit of subordinate powers with Legislative and Executive authority, greater or less, according to local and other circumstances. Thus we see a variety of corporations formed within the kingdom, with powers to make and execute such by-laws as are for their immediate use and benefit, the members of such corporations still remaining subject to the general laws of the kingdom. We see also governments established in the plantations, which, from their separate and remote situation, require more general and extensive powers of legislation within themselves, than those formed within the kingdom, but subject, nevertheless, to all such laws of the kingdom as immediately respect them, or are designed to extend to them ; and, accordingly, we, in this province have, from the first settlement of it, been left to the exercise of our Legislative and Executive powers, Parliament occa-

43

sionally, though rarely, interposing, as in its wisdom has been judged necessary.

Under this constitution, for more than one hundred years, the laws both of the supreme and subordinate authority were in general, duly executed; offenders against them have been brought to condign punishment, peace and order have been maintained, and the people of this province have experienced as largely the advantages of government, as, perhaps, any people upon the globe; and they have, from time to time, in the most public manner expressed their sense of it, and, once in every year, have offered up their united thanksgivings to God for the enjoyment of these privileges, and, as often, their united prayers for the continuance of them.

At length the constitution has been called in question, and the authority of the Parliament of Great Britain to make and establish laws for the inhabitants of this province has been, by many, denied. What was at first whispered with caution, was soon after openly asserted in print; and, of late, a number of inhabitants, in several of the principal towns in the province, having assembled together in their respective towns, and have assumed the name of legal town meetings, have passed resolves, which they have ordered to be placed upon their town records, and caused to be printed and published in pamphlets and newspapers. I am sorry that it is thus become impossible to conceal, what I could wish had never been made public. I will not particularize these resolves or votes, and shall only observe to you in general, that some of them deny the supreme authority of Parliament, and so are repugnant to the principles of the constitution, and that others speak of this supreme authority, of which the King is a constituent part, and to every act of which his assent is necessary, in such terms as have a direct tendency to alienate the affections of the people from their Sovereign, who has ever been most tender of their rights, and whose person, crown, and dignity, we are under every possible obligation to defend and support. In consequence of these resolves, committees of correspondence are formed in several of those towns, to maintain the principles upon which they are founded.

I know of no arguments, founded in reason, which will be sufficient to support these principles, or to justify the measures taken in consequence of them. It has been urged, that the sole power of making laws is granted, by charter, to a Legislature established in the province, consisting of the King, by his Representative the Governor, the Council, and the House of Representatives; that, by this charter, there are likewise granted, or assured to the inhabitants of the province, all the liberties and immunities of free and natural subjects, to all intents, constructions and purposes whatsoever, as if they had been born within the realms of England;

that it is part of the liberties of English subjects, which has its foundation in nature, to be governed by laws made by their consent in person, or by their representative; that the subjects in this province are not, and cannot be represented in the Parliament of Great Britain, and, consequently, the acts of that Parliament cannot be binding upon them.

I do not find, gentlemen, in the charter, such an expression as sole power, or any words which import it. The General Court has, by charter, full power to make such laws, as are not repugnant to the laws of England. A favorable construction has been put upon this clause, when it has been allowed to intend such laws of England only, as are expressly declared to respect us. Surely then this is, by charter, a reserve of power and authority to Parliament to bind us by such laws, at least, as are made expressly to refer to us, and consequently, is a limitation of the power given to the General Court. Nor can it be contended, that, by the limits of free and natural subjects, is to be understood an exemption from acts of Parliament, because not represented there, seeing it is provided by the same charter, that such acts shall be in force; and if they that make the objection to such acts, will read the charter with attention, they must be convinced that this grant of liberties and immunities is nothing more than a declaration and assurance on the part of the Crown, that the place, to which their predecessors were about to remove, was, and would be considered as part of the dominions of the Crown of England, and, therefore, that the subjects of the Crown so removing, and those born there, or in their passage thither, or in their passage from thence, would not become aliens, but would, throughout all parts of the English dominions, wherever they might happen to be, as well as within the colony, retain the liberties and immunities of free and natural subjects, their removal from, or not being born within the realm notwithstanding. If the plantations be part of the dominions of the Crown, this clause in the charter does not confer or reserve any liberties, but what would have been enjoyed without it, and what the inhabitants of every other colony do enjoy where they are without a charter. If the plantations are not the dominions of the Crown, will not all that are born here, be considered as born out of the liegeance of the King of England, and, whenever they go into any parts of the dominions, will they not be deemed aliens to all intents and purposes, this grant in the charter notwithstanding?

They who claim exemption from acts of Parliament by virtue of their rights as Englishmen, should consider that it is impossible the rights of English subjects should be the same, in every respect, in all parts of the dominions. It is one of their rights as English subjects, to be governed by laws made by persons, in whose election they have, from time to time, a voice; they remove from the kingdom, where, perhaps, they were in the full exercise of this right, to the plantations, where it cannot be exercised, or where the exercise of it would be of no benefit to them. Does it follow that the government, by their removal from one part of the dominions to another, loses its authority over that part to which they remove, and that they are freed from the subjection they were under before; or do they expect that government should relinquish its authority because they cannot enjoy this particular right? Will it not rather be said, that by this, their voluntary removal, they have relinquished for a time at least, one of the rights of an English subject, which they might, if they pleased, have continued to enjoy, and may again enjoy, whensoever they will return to the place where it can be exercised?

They who claim exemption, as part of their rights by nature, should consider that every restraint which men are laid under by a state of government, is a privation of part of their natural rights; and of all the different forms of government which exist, there can be no two of them in which the departure from natural rights is exactly the same. Even in case of representation by election, do they not give up part of their natural rights when they consent to be represented by such person as shall be chosen by the majority of the electors, although their own voices may be for some other person? And is it not contrary to their natural rights to be obliged to submit to a representative for seven years, or even one year, after they are dissatisfied with his conduct, although they gave their voices for him when he was elected? This must, therefore, be considered as an objection against a state of government, rather than against any particular form.

If what I have said shall not be sufficient to satisfy such as object to the supreme authority of Parliament over the plantations, there may something further be added to induce them to an acknowledgment of it, which, I think, will well deserve their consideration. I know of no line that can be drawn between the supreme authority of Parliament and the total independence of the colonies: it is impossible there should be two independent Legislatures in one and the same state; for, although there may be but one head, the King, yet the two Legislative bodies will make two governments as distinct as the kingdoms of England and Scotland before the union. If we might be suffered to be altogether independent of Great Britain, could we have any claim to the protection of that government, of which we are no longer a part? Without this protection, should we not become the prey of one or the other powers of Europe, such as should first seize upon us? Is there any thing which we have more reason to dread than independence? I hope it never will be our misfortune to know, by experience, the difference between the liberties of an English colonist, and those of the Spanish, French, or Dutch.

If then, the supremacy of Parliament over the whole British dominions shall no longer be denied, it will follow that the mere exercise of its authority can be no matter of grievance. If it has been, or shall be exercised in such way and manner as shall appear to be grievous, still this cannot be sufficient ground for immediately denying or renouncing the authority, or refusing to submit to it. The acts and doings of authority, in the most perfect form of government, will not always be thought just and equitable by all the parts of which it consists; but it is the greatest absurdity, to admit the several parts to be at liberty to obey, or disobey, according as the acts of such authority may be approved, or disapproved of by them, for this necessarily works a dissolution of the government. The manner, then, of obtaining redress, must be by representations and endeavors, in such ways and forms, as the established rules of the constitution prescribe or allow, in order to make any matters, alleged to be grievances, appear to be really such; but, I conceive it is rather the mere exercise of this authority, which is complained of as a grievance, than any heavy burdens which have been brought upon the people by means of it.

As contentment and order were the happy effects of a constitution, strengthened by universal assent and approbation, so discontent and disorder are now the deplorable effects of a constitution, enfeebled by contest and opposition. Besides divisions and animosities, which disturb the peace of towns and families, the law in some important cases cannot have its course; offenders ordered, by advice of his Majesty's Council, to be prosecuted, escape with impunity, and are supported and encouraged to go on offending; the authority of government is brought into contempt, and there are but small remains of that subordination, which was once very conspicuous in this colony, and which is essential to a well regulated state.

When the bands of government are thus weakened, it certainly behoves those with whom the powers of government are entrusted, to omit nothing which may tend to strengthen them.

I have disclosed my sentiments to you without reserve. Let me entreat you to consider them calmly, and not be too sudden in your determination. If my principles of government are right, let us adhere to them. With the same principles, our ancestors were easy and happy for a long course of years together, and I know of no reason to doubt of your being equally easy and happy. The people, influenced by you, will desist from their unconstitutional principles, and desist from their irregularities, which are the consequence of them; they will be convinced that every thing which is valuable to them, depend upon their connexion with their parent state; that this connexion cannot be carried in any other way, than such as will also continue their dependence upon the supreme authority of the British dominions; and that, notwithstanding this dependence, they will enjoy as great a proportion of those, to which they have a claim by nature, or as Englishmen, as can be enjoyed by a plantation or colony.

If I am wrong in my principles of government, or in the inferences which I have drawn from them, I wish to be convinced of
my error. Independence, I may not allow myself to think that
you can possibly have in contemplation. If you can conceive of
any other constitutional dependence than what I have mentioned,
if you are of opinion, that upon any other principles our connexion
with the state from which we sprang, can be continued, communicate your sentiments to me with the same freedom and unreserv-
edness, as I have communicated mine to you.

I have no desire, gentlemen, by any thing I have said, to preclude you from seeking relief, in a constitutional way, in any
cases in which you have heretofore, or may hereafter suppose that
you are aggrieved ; and, although I should not concur with you in
sentiment, I will, notwithstanding, do nothing to lessen the
weight which your representations may deserve. I have laid before you what I think are the principles of your constitution ; if
you do not agree with me, I wish to know your objections ; they
may be convincing to me, or I may be able to satisfy you of the
insufficiency of them. In either case, I hope we shall put an end
to those irregularities, which ever will be the portion of a government where the supreme authority is controverted, and introduce
that tranquillity, which seems to have taken place in most of the
colonies upon the continent.

The ordinary business of the session, I will not now particularly
point out to you. To the enacting of any new laws, which may
be necessary for the more equal and effectual distribution of justice, or for giving further encouragement to our merchandize,
fishery, and agriculture, which, through the divine favor, are already in a very flourishing state, or for promoting any measures,
which may conduce to the general good of the province, I will
readily give my assent or concurrence.   T. HUTCHINSON.

ANSWER

OF THE COUNCIL TO THE SPEECH OF GOVERNOR HUTCHINSON,
OF JANUARY 6......JANUARY 25, 1773.

May it please your Excellency,

THE Board have considered your Excellency's speech to both
Houses, with the attention due to the object of it ; and, we hope,
with the candor you were pleased to recommend to them. We
thank you for the promise, that, " if we shall not agree with you
in sentiment, you will, with candor, likewise receive and consider
what we may offer in answer."

Your speech informs the two Houses, that this government is at present in a disturbed and disordered state; that the cause of this disorder is the unconstitutional principles adopted by the people, in questioning the supreme authority of Parliament; and that the proper measure for removing the disorder, must be the substituting of contrary principles.

Our opinion on these heads, as well as on some others, proper to be noticed, will be obvious, in the course of the following observations.

With regard to the present disordered state of the government, it can have no reference to tumults or riots; from which this government is as free as any other, whatever. If your Excellency meant, only, that the province is discontented, and in a state of uneasiness, we should entirely agree with you; but you will permit us to say, that we are not so well agreed in the cause of it. The uneasiness, which was a general one, throughout the colonies, began when you inform, the authority of Parliament was first called in question, viz. about seven or eight years ago. Your mentioning that particular time, might have suggested to your Excellency the true cause of the origin and continuance of that uneasiness.

At that time, the stamp act, then lately made, began to operate; which, with some preceding and succeeding acts of Parliament, subjecting the colonies to taxes, without their consent, was the original cause of all the uneasiness which has happened since; and has also occasioned an inquiry into the nature and extent of the authority, by which they were made. The late town meetings in several towns, are instances of both. These are mentioned by your Excellency, in proof of a disordered state. But, though we do not approve of some of their resolves, we think they had a clear right to instruct their Representatives in any subject they apprehended to be of sufficient importance to require it; which necessarily implies a previous consideration and expression of their minds on that subject, however mistaken they may be concerning it.

When a community, great or small, think their rights and privileges infringed, they will express their uneasiness in a variety of ways; some of which, may be highly improper and criminal. So far as any of an atrocious nature have taken place, we would express our abhorrence of them; and, as we have always done, hitherto, we shall continue to do every thing in our power, to discourage and suppress them. But it is in vain to hope that this can be done effectually, so long as the cause of the uneasiness exists. Your Excellency will perceive that the *cause* you assign, is, by us, supposed to be an *effect*, derived from the original cause, above mentioned; the removal of which, will remove its effects.

To obtain this removal, we agree with you in the method pointed out in your speech, where you say, " the manner of obtaining redress must be by representation, and endeavors, in such ways and forms as the constitution allows, in order to make any matters alleged to be grievances, appear to be really such.

This method has been pursued repeatedly. Petitions to Parliament have gone from the colonies, and from this colony in particular; but without success. Some of them, in a former Ministry, were previously shewn to the Minister, who, as we have been informed, advised the Agents to postpone presenting them to the House of Commons, till the first reading of the bill they referred to; when, being presented, a rule of the House against receiving petitions on money bills, was urged for rejecting them, and they were rejected, accordingly; and other petitions, for want of formality, or whatever was the reason, have had the same fate. This we mention, not by way of censure on that honorable House, but in some measure to account for the conduct of those persons, who, despairing of redress, in a constitutional way, have denied the just authority of Parliament; concerning which, we shall now give our own sentiments, intermixed with observations on those of your Excellency.

You are pleased to observe, that when our predecessors first took possession of this colony, under a grant and charter from the Crown of England, it was their sense, and the sense of the whole kingdom, that they were to remain subject to the supreme authority of Parliament; and to prove that subjection, the greater part of your speech is employed.

In order to a right conception of this matter, it is necessary to guard against any improper idea of the term *supreme* authority. In your idea of it, your Excellency seems to include *unlimited* authority; for, you are pleased to say, that you know of no line which can be drawn between the supreme authority of Parliament, and the real independence of the colonies. But if no such line can be drawn, a denial of that authority, in any instance whatever, implies and amounts to a declaration of total independence. But if supreme authority, includes unlimited authority, the subjects of it are emphatically slaves; and equally so, whether residing in the colonies, or Great Britain. And, indeed, in this respect, all the nations on earth, among whom government exists in any of its forms, would be alike conditioned, excepting so far as the mere grace and favor of their Governors might make a difference, for from, the nature of government there must be, as your Excellency has observed, one supreme authority over the whole.

We cannot think, that when our predecessors took possession of this colony, it was their sense, or the sense of the kingdom, that they were to remain subject to the supreme authority of Parliament in this idea of it. Nor can we find, that this appears from the charter; or, that such authority has ever been exercised by Parliament, submitted to by the colony, or acknowledged by the Legislature.

Supreme, or unlimited authority, can with fitness, belong only to the Sovereign of the universe ; and that fitness is derived from the perfection of his nature. To such authority, directed by infinite wisdom and infinite goodness, is due both active and passive obedience ; which, as it constitutes the happiness of rational creatures, should, with cheerfulness, and from choice, be unlimitedly paid by them. But, this can be said with truth, of no other authority whatever. If, then, from the nature and end of government, the supreme authority of every government is limited, the supreme authority of Parliament must be limited ; and the inquiry will be, what are the limits of that authority, with regard to this colony ? To fix them with precision, to determine the exact lines of right and wrong in this case, as in some others, is difficult ; and we have not the presumption to attempt it. But we humbly hope, that, as we are personally and relatively, in our public and private capacities, for ourselves, for the whole province, and posterity, so deeply interested in this important subject, it will not be deemed arrogance to give some general sentiments upon it, especially as your Excellency's speech has made it absolutely necessary.

For this purpose, we shall recur to those records which contain the main principles on which the English constitution is founded ; and from them make such extracts as are pertinent to the subject.

Magna Charta declares, that no aid thall be imposed in the kingdom, unless by the Common Council of the kingdom, except to redeem the King's person, &c. And that all cities, boroughs, towns, and ports, shall have their liberties and free customs ; and shall have the Common Council of the kingdom, concerning the assessment of their aids, except in the cases aforesaid.

The statute of the 34th of Edward I. *de tallio non concedendo*, declares, that no tallage or aid should be laid or levied by the King or his heirs, in the realm, without the good will and assent of the Archbishops, Bishops. Earls, Barons, Knights, Burgesses, and others, the freemen of the commonalty of this realm. A statute of the 25th Edward III. enacts, that from thenceforth, no person shall be compelled to make any loans to the King, against his will, because such loans were against reason and the franchise of the land.

The petition of rights in the 3d of Charles I. in which are cited the two foregoing statutes, declares, that, by those statutes, and other good laws and statutes of the realm, his Majesty's subjects inherited this freedom, that they should not be compelled to contribute to any tax, tallage, aid, or other like charge, not set by common consent of Parliament.

And the statute of the 1st of William III. for declaring the rights and liberties of the subject, and settling the succession of the Crown, declares, that the levying of money for, or to the use of the Crown, by pretence of prerogative, without grant of Parliament for longer time, or in any other manner than the same is, or shall be granted, is illegal.

44

From these authorities, it appears an essential part of the English constitution, that no tallage, or aid, or tax, shall be laid or levied without the good will and assent of the freedom of the commonalty of the realm. If this could be done without their assent, their property would be in the highest degree precarious; or rather they could not, with fitness, be said to have any property at all. At best, they would be only the holders of it for the use of the Crown, and the Crown be the real proprietor. This would be vassalage in the extreme, from which the generous nature of Englishmen have been so abhorrent, that they have bled with freedom in defence of this part of their constitution, which has preserved them from it; and influenced by the same generosity, they can never view with disapprobation, any lawful measures taken by us for the defence of our own constitution, which entitles us to the same rights and privileges with themselves. These were derived to us from common law, which is the inheritance of all his Majesty's subjects; have been recognized by acts of Parliament, and confirmed by the province charter, which established its constitution; and which charter, has been recognized by acts of Parliament also. This act was made in the second year of the reign of his late Majesty George II. for the better preservation of his Majesty's woods in America, in which is recited the clause of the charter, reserving for the use of the royal navy, all trees suitable for masts; and on this charter is grounded the succeeding enacting clause of the act; and thus is the charter implicitly confirmed by act of Parliament. From all which it appears, that the inhabitants of this colony are clearly entitled to all the rights and privileges of free and natural subjects; which certainly must include that most essential one, that no aid or taxes be levied on them, without their own consent, signified by their Representatives.

But, from the clause in the charter, relative to the power granted to the General Court, to make laws not repugnant to the laws of England, your Excellency draws this inference, that surely this is, by charter, a reserve of power and authority to Parliament, to bind us by such laws, at least, as are made to refer to us, and consequently is a limitation of the power given to the General Court. If it be allowed, that, by that clause there was a reserve of power to Parliament, to bind the province, it was only by such laws as were in being at the time the charter was granted; for, by the charter, there is nothing appears to make it refer to any parliamentary laws, that should be afterwards made; and therefore, it will not support your Excellency's inference.

The grant of power to the General Court to make laws, runs thus—"full power and authority, from time to time, to make and ordain, and establish, all manner of wholesome and reasonable laws, orders, statutes and ordinances, directions and instructions, either with penalties or without, so as the same be not repugnant or contrary to the laws of this our realm of England, as they shall judge to be for the good and welfare of our said province." We humbly conceive an inference very different from your Excellency's, and a very just one too, may be drawn from this clause, if attention be given to the description of the orders and laws that were to be made. They were to be wholesome, reasonable, and for the good and welfare of the province; and in order that they might be so, it is provided, that they be not repugnant or contrary to the laws of the realm, which were then in being; by which proviso, all the liberties and immunities of free and natural subjects within the realm, were more effectually secured to the inhabitants of the province, agreeable to another clause in the charter, whereby those liberties and immunities are expressly granted to them; and accordingly, the power of the General Court is so far limited, that they shall not make orders and laws to take away or diminish those liberties and immunities.

This construction appears to us a just one, and perhaps may appear so to your Excellency, if you will please to consider, that, by another part of the charter, effectual care was taken for preventing the General Assembly passing of orders and laws repugnant to, or that in any way might militate with acts of Parliament then or since made, or that might be exceptionable in any other respect whatever; for the charter reserves to his Majesty the appointment of the Governor, whose assent is necessary in the passing of all orders and laws; after which, they are to be sent to England, for the royal approbation or disallowance; by which double control, effectual care is taken to prevent the establishment of any improper orders or laws, whatever. Besides, your Excellency is sensible that letters patent must be construed one part with another, and all the parts of them together, so as to make the whole harmonize and agree. But your Excellency's construction of the paragraph empowering the General Court to make orders and laws, does by no means harmonize and agree with the paragraph granting liberties and immunities; and therefore, we humbly conceive, is not to be admitted: whereas on the other construction, there is a perfect harmony and agreement between them. But supposing your Excellency's inference just, that by said former paragraph, considered by itself, are reserved to Parliament, power and authority to bind us by laws made expressly to refer us, does it consist with justice and equity, that it should be considered a part, and urged against the people of this province, with all its force, and without limitation; and at the same time, the other paragraph, which they thought secured to them the essential rights and privileges of free and natural subjects, be rendered of no validity.

If the former paragraph (in this supposed case) be binding on this people, the latter must be binding on the Crown, which thereby became guarantee of those rights and privileges, or it must be supposed that one party is held by a compact, and the other not; which supposition is against reason and against law; and therefore, destroys the foundation of the inference. Supposing it well founded, however, it would not from thence follow, that the charter intended such laws as should subject the inhabitants of this province to taxes, without their consent; for, (as it appears above) it grants to them all the rights and liberties of free and natural subjects; of which, one of the most essential is, a freedom from all taxes not consented to by themselves. Nor could the parties, either grantor or grantees, intend such laws. The royal grantor could not, because his grant contradicts such intention, and because it is inconsistent with every idea of royalty and royal wisdom, to grant what it does not intend to grant. And it will be readily allowed, that the grantees could not intend such laws; not only on account of their inconsistency with the grant, but because their acceptance of a charter, subjecting them to such laws, would be voluntary slavery.

Your Excellency next observes, " that it cannot be contended, that, by the liberties of free and natural subjects, is to be understood an exemption from acts of Parliament, because not represented there, seeing it is provided by the charter, that such acts shall be in force." If the observations we have made above, and our reasoning on them be just, it will appear, that no such provision is made in the charter; and, therefore, that the deductions and inferences derived from the supposition of such provision, are not well founded. And with respect to representation in Parliament, as it is one of the essential liberties of free and natural subjects, and properly makes those who enjoy it, liable to parliamentary acts, so in reference to the inhabitants of this province, who are entitled to all the liberties of such subjects, the impossibility of their being duly represented in Parliament, does clearly exempt them from all such acts, at least, as have been or shall be made by Parliament, to tax them; representation and taxation being, in our opinion, constitutionally inseparable.

This grant of liberties and immunities, your Excellency informs us, " is nothing more than a declaration and assurance on the part of the Crown, that the place to which our predecessors were about to remove, was, and would be considered, as part of the dominions of the Crown; and, therefore, that the subjects, so removing, would not become aliens, but would, both without and within the colony, retain the liberties and immunities of free and natural subjects."

The dominion of the Crown over this country, before the arrival of our predecessors, was merely ideal. Their removal hither, realized that dominion, and has made the country valuable both to the Crown and nation, without any cost to either of them, from that time to this. Even in the most distressed state of our predecessors, when they expected to be destroyed by a general conspiracy and incursion of the Indian natives, they had no assistance from them. This grant then of liberties, which is the only consideration they received from the Crown, for so valuable an acquisition to it, instead of being violated by military power, or explained away by nice inferences and distinctions, ought in justice, and with a generous openness and freedom, to be acknowledged by every Minister of the Crown, and preserved sacred from every species of violation.

"If the plantations be part of the dominions of the Crown, this clause in the charter, granting liberties and immunities, does not," your Excellency observes, "confer or reserve any liberties, but what would have been enjoyed without it; and what the inhabitants of every other colony do enjoy, where they are without a charter." Although the colonies. considered as part of the dominions of the Crown, are entitled to equal liberties. the inhabitants of this colony, think it a happiness, that those liberties are confirmed and secured to them by a charter; whereby the honor and faith of the Crown are pledged, that those liberties shall not be violated. And for protection in them, we humbly look up to his present Majesty, our rightful and lawful Sovereign, as children to a father, able and disposed to assist and relieve them; humbly imploring his Majesty, that his subjects of this province, ever faithful and loyal, and ever accounted such, till the stamp act existed, and who, in the late war, and upon all other occasions, have demonstrated that faithfulness and loyalty, by their vigorous and unexampled exertions in his service, may have their grievances redressed, and be restored to their just rights.

Your Excellency next observes, "that it is impossible the rights of English subjects should be the same in every respect, in all parts of the dominions," and instances in the right of "being governed by laws made by persons, in whose election they have a voice." When "they remove from the kingdom to the plantations, where it cannot be enjoyed," you ask, "will it not be said, by this voluntary removal, they have relinquished, for a time at least, one of the rights of an English subject, which they might, if they pleased, have continued to enjoy, and may again enjoy, whenever they will return to the place where it can be exercised?"

When English subjects remove from the kingdom to the plantations, with their property, they not only relinquish that right *de facto*, but it ought to cease in the kingdom *de jure*. But it does not from thence follow, that they relinquish that right in reference to the plantation or colony, to which they remove. On the contrary, having become inhabitants of that colony, and qualified according to the laws of it, they can exercise that right, equally with the other inhabitants of it. And their right, on like conditions, will travel with them through all the colonies, wherein a Legislature, similar to that of the kingdom, is established. And therefore, in this respect, and, we suppose, in all other essential respects, it is not impossible the rights of English subjects should be the same in all parts of the dominions, under a like form of Legislature.

This right of representation, is so essential and indisputable, in regard of all laws for levying taxes, that a people under any form of government, destitute of it, is destitute of freedom : of that degree of freedom, for the preservation of which, government was instituted ; and without which, government degenerates into despotism. It cannot, therefore, be given up, or taken away, without making a breach in the essential rights of nature.

But your Excellency is pleased to say, " that they who claim exemption as part of their rights by nature, should consider that every restraint which men are laid under by a state of government, is a privation of part of their natural rights. Even in case of representation by election, do they not give up part of their natural rights, when they consent to be represented by such persons as shall be chosen by the majority of the electors, although their own voices may be for some other person. And is it not contrary to their natural rights, to be obliged to submit to a representation for seven years, or even one year, after they are dissatisfied with his conduct, although they gave their voices for him, when he was elected ? This must, therefore, be considered as an objection against a state of government, rather than against any particular form."

Your Excellency's premises are true, but we do not think your conclusion follows from them. It is true, that every restraint of government is a privation of natural right ; and the two cases you have been pleased to mention, may be instances of that privation. But, as they arise from the nature of society and government ; and as government is necessary to secure other natural rights, infinitely more valuable, they cannot, therefore, be considered as an objection, either against a state government, or against any particular form of it.

Life, liberty, property, and the disposal of that property, with our own consent, are natural rights. Will any one put the other in competition with these ; or infer, that, because those others must be given up in a state of government, these must be given up also ? The preservation of these rights, is the great end of government. But is it probable, they will be effectually secured by a government, which the proprietors of them, have no part in the direction of, and over which, they have no power or influence, whatever ! Hence, is deducible representation, which being necessary to preserve these invaluable rights of nature, is itself, for that reason, a natural right, coinciding with, and running into that great law of nature, self preservation.

Thus have we considered the most material parts of your Excellency's speech, and, agreeable to your desire, disclosed to you our sentiments on the subject of it. " Independence," as you have rightly judged, " we have not in contemplation." We cannot, however, adopt your principles of government, or acquiesce in all the inferences you have drawn from them.

We have the highest respect for that august body, the Parliament, and do not presume to prescribe the exact limits of its authority ; yet, with the deference which is due to it, we are humbly of opinion, that, as all human authority is, in the nature of it, and ought to be, limited, it cannot, constitutionally, extend, for the reasons we have suggested, to the levying of taxes, in any form, on his Majesty's subjects in this province.

In such principles as these, our predecessors were easy and happy, and in the due operation of such, their descendants, the present inhabitants of this province, have been easy and happy : but they are not so now. Their uneasiness and unhappiness are occasioned by acts of Parliament, and regulations of government, which lately, and within a few years past, have been made. And this uneasiness and unhappiness, both in the cause and effects of them, though your Excellency seems, and can only seem, to be of a different opinion, have extended, and continue to extend, to all the colonies, throughout the continent.

It would give us the highest satisfaction, to see happiness and tranquillity restored to the colonies, and, especially to see, between Great Britain and them, an union established on such an equitable basis, as neither of them shall ever wish to destroy. We humbly supplicate the sovereign arbiter and superintendant of human affairs, for these happy events.

[Hon. J. Bowdoin, H. Gray, J. Otis, and S. Hall, were the committee of Council, who prepared the above.]

ANSWER

OF THE HOUSE OF REPRESENTATIVES TO THE SPEECH OF THE
GOVERNOR, OF SIXTH JANUARY......JANUARY 26, 1773.

May it please your Excellency,

Your Excellency's speech to the General Assembly, at the opening of this session, has been read with great attention in this House.

We fully agree with your Excellency, that our own happiness, as well as his Majesty's service, very much depends upon peace and order ; and we shall at all times take such measures as are consistent with our constitution, and the rights of the people, to promote and maintain them. That the government at present is in a very disturbed state, is apparent. But we cannot ascribe it to the people's having adopted unconstitutional principles, which seems to be the cause assigned for it by your Excellency. It appears to us, to have been occasioned rather by the British House of Commons assuming and exercising a power inconsistent with the freedom of the constitution, to give and grant the property of the colonists, and appropriate the same without their consent.

It is needless for us to inquire what were the principles that induced the councils of the nation to so new and unprecedented a measure. But, when the Parliament, by an act of their own, expressly declared, that the King, Lords, and Commons, of the nation " have, and of right ought to have full power and authority to make laws and statutes of sufficient force and validity, to bind the colonies and people of America, subjects of the Crown of Great Britain, in all cases whatever," and in consequence hereof, another revenue act was made, the minds of the people were filled with anxiety, and they were justly alarmed with apprehensions of the total extinction of their liberties.

The result of the free inquiries of many persons, into the right of the Parliament, to exercise such a power over the colonies, seems, in your Excellency's opinion, to be the cause, of what you are pleased to call the present " disturbed state of the government;" upon which, you " may not any longer, consistent with your duty to the King, and your regard to the interest of the province, delay communicating your sentiments." But that the principles adopted in consequence hereof, are unconstitutional, is a subject of inquiry. We know of no such disorders arising therefrom, as are mentioned by your Excellency. If Grand Jurors have not, on their oaths, found such offences, as your Excellency, with the advice of his Majesty's Council, have ordered to be prosecuted, it is to be presumed, they have followed the dictates of good conscience. They are the constitutional judges of these matters, and it is not to be supposed, that moved from corrupt principles, they have suffered offenders to escape a prosecution, and thus supported and encouraged them to go on offending. If any part of authority shall, in an unconstitutional manner, interpose in any matter, it will be no wonder if it be brought into contempt; to the lessening or confounding of that subordination, which is necessary to a well regulated state. Your Excellency's representation that the bands of government are weakened. we humbly conceive to be without good grounds; though we must own, the heavy burdens unconstitutionally brought upon the people, have been, and still are universally, and very justly complained of, as a grievance.

You are pleased to say, that, " when our predecessors first took possession of this plantation, or colony, under a grant and charter from the Crown of England, it was their sense, and it was the sense of the kingdom, that they were to remain subject to the supreme authority of Parliament;" whereby we understand your Excellency to mean, in the sense of the declaratory act of Parliament afore mentioned, in all cases whatever. And, indeed, it is difficult, if possible, to draw a line of distinction between the universal authority of Parliament over the colonies, and no authority at all. It is, therefore, necessary for us to inquire how it appears, for your Excellency has not shown it to us, that when, or at the time that our predecessors took possession of this plantation, or colony, under a grant and charter from the Crown of England, it was their sense, and the sense of the kingdom, that they were to remain subject to the authority of Parliament. In making this inquiry, we shall, according to your Excellency's recommendation, treat the subject with calmness and candor, and also with a due regard to truth.

Previous to a direct consideration of the charter granted to the province or colony, and the better to elucidate the true sense and meaning of it, we would take a view of the state of the English North American continent at the time, when, and after possession was first taken of any part of it, by the Europeans. It was then possessed by heathen and barbarous people, who had, nevertheless, all that right to the soil, and sovereignty in and over the lands they possessed, which God had originally given to man. Whether their being heathen, inferred any right or authority to christian princes, a right which had long been assumed by the Pope, to dispose of their lands to others, we will leave to your Excellency, or any one of understanding and impartial judgment, to consider. It is certain, they had in no other sense, forfeited them to any power in Europe. Should the doctrine be admitted, that the discovery of lands owned and possessed by pagan people, gives to any christian prince a right and title to the dominion and property, still it is vested in the Crown alone. It was an acquisition of foreign territory, not annexed to the realm of England, and, therefore, at the absolute disposal of the Crown. For we take it to be a settled point, that the King has a constitutional prerogative, to dispose of and alienate, any part of his territories not annexed to the realm. In the exercise of this prerogative, Queen Elizabeth granted the first American charter ; and, claiming a right by virtue of discovery, then supposed to be valid, to the lands which are now possessed by the colony of Virginia, she conveyed to Sir Walter Rawleigh, the property, dominion, and sovereignty thereof, to be held of the Crown, by homage, and a certain render, without any reservation to herself, of any share in the Legislative and Executive authority. After the attainder of Sir Walter, King James the I. created two Virginian companies, to be governed each by laws, transmitted to them by his Majesty, and not by the Parliament, with power to establish, and cause to be made, a coin to pass current among them ; and vested with all liberties, franchises and immunities, within any of his other dominions, to all intents and purposes, as if they had been abiding and born within the realm. A declaration similar to this, is contained in the first charter of this colony, and in those of other American colonies, which shows that

45

the colonies were not intended, or considered to be within the realm of England, though within the allegiance of the English Crown. After this, another charter was granted by the same King James, to the Treasurer and Company of Virginia, vesting them with full power and authority, to make, ordain, and establish, all manner of orders, laws, directions, instructions, forms and cere-monies of governments, and magistracy, fit and necessary, and the same to abrogate, &c. without any reservation for securing their subjection to the Parliament, and future laws of England. A third charter was afterwards granted by the same King, to the Treasurer and Company of Virginia, vesting them with power and authority to make laws, with an addition of this clause, " so, al-ways, that the same be not contrary to the laws and statutes of this our realm of England." The same clause was afterwards copied into the charter of this and other colonies, with certain va-riations, such as, that these laws should be " consonant to reason," " not repugnant to the laws of England," " as nearly as conve-niently may be to the laws, statutes and rights of England," &c. These modes of expression, convey the same meaning, and serve to show an intention, that the laws of the colonies should be as much as possible, conformable in the spirit of them, to the princi-ples and fundamental laws of the English constitution, its rights and statutes then in being, and by no means to bind the colonies to a subjection to the supreme authority of the English Parliament. And that this is the true intention, we think it further evident from this consideration, that no acts of any colony Legislative, are ever brought into Parliament for inspection there, though the laws made in some of them, like the acts of the British Parliament, are laid before the King for his dissent or allowance.

We have brought the first American charters into view, and the state of the country when they were granted, to show, that the right of disposing of the lands was, in the opinion of those times, vested solely in the Crown; that the several charters conveyed to the grantees, who should settle upon the territories therein grant-ed, all the powers necessary to constitute them free and distinct states; and that the fundamental laws of the English constitution should be the certain and established rule of legislation, to which, the laws to be made in the several colonies, were to be, as nearly as conveniently might be, conformable, or similar, which was the true intent and import of the words, " not repugnant to the laws of England," " consonant to reason," and other variant expres-sions in the different charters. And we would add, that the King, in some of the charters, reserves the right to judge of the conso-nance and similarity of their laws with the English constitution. to himself, and not to the Parliament; and, in consequence thereof, to affirm, or within a limited time, disallow them.

These charters, as well as that afterwards granted to Lord Bal-timore, and other charters, are repugnant to the idea of Parlia-mentary authority; and, to suppose a Parliamentary authority over the colonies, under such charters, would necessarily induce that solecism in politics, *imperium in imperio.* And the King's repeatedly exercising the prerogative of disposing of the American territory by such charters, together with the silence of the nation thereupon, is an evidence that it was an acknowledged prerogative.

But, further to show the sense of the English Crown and nation, that the American colonists, and our predecessors in particular, when they first took possession of this country, by a grant and charter from the Crown, did not remain subject to the supreme authority of Parliament, we beg leave to observe, that when a bill was offered by the two Houses of Parliament to King Charles the I granting to the subjects of England, the free liberty of fishing on the coast of America, he refused his royal assent, declaring as a reason, that " the colonies were without the realm and jurisdiction of Parliament."

In like manner, his predecessor, James the I. had before declared, upon a similar occasion, that " America was not annexed to the realm, and it was not fitting that Parliament should make laws for those countries." This reason was, not secretly, but openly declared in Parliament. If, then, the colonies were not annexed to the realm, at the time when their charters were granted, they never could be afterwards, without their own special consent, which has never since been had, or even asked. If they are not now annexed to the realm, they are not a part of the kingdom, and consequently not subject to the Legislative authority of the kingdom. For no country, by the common law, was subject to the laws or to the Parliament, but the realm of England.

We would, if your Excellency pleases, subjoin an instance of conduct in King Charles the II. singular indeed, but important to our purpose, who, in 1679, framed an act for a permanent revenue for the support of Virginia, and sent it there by Lord Culpepper, the Governor of that colony, which was afterwards passed into a law, and " enacted by the King's most excellent Majesty, by, and with the consent of the General Assembly of Virginia." If the King had judged that colony to be a part of the realm, he would not, nor could he, consistently with Magna Charta, have placed himself at the head of, and joined with any Legislative body in making a law to tax the people there, other than the Lords and Commons of England.

Having taken a view of the several charters of the first colony in America, if we look into the old charter of this colony, we shall find it to be grounded on the same principle; that the right of disposing the territory granted therein, was vested in the Crown, as being that Christian Sovereign who first discovered it, when in the possession of heathens; and that it was considered as being not within the realm, but being only within the Fee and Seignory of the King. As, therefore, it was without the realm of England, must not the King, if he had designed that the Parliament should have had any authority over it, have made a special reservation for that purpose, which was not done ?

Your Excellency says, " it appears from the charter itself, to have been the sense of our predecessors, who first took possession of this plantation, or colony, that they were to remain subject to the authority of Parliament." You have not been pleased to point out to us, how this appears from the charter, unless it be in the observation you make on the above mentioned clause, viz.: "that a favorable construction has been put upon this clause, when it has been allowed to intend such laws of England only, as are expressly made to respect us," which you say, " is by charter, a reserve of power and authority to Parliament, to bind us by such laws, at least, as are made expressly to refer to us, and consequently is a limitation of the power given to the General Court." But, we would still recur to the charter itself, and ask your Excellency, how this appears, from thence, to have been the sense of our predecessors ? Is any reservation of power and authority to Parliament thus to bind us, expressed or implied in the charter ? It is evident, that King Charles the I. the very Prince who granted it, as well as his predecessor, had no such idea of the supreme authority of Parliament over the colony, from their declarations before recited. Your Excellency will then allow us, further to ask, by what authority, in reason or equity, the Parliament can enforce a construction so unfavorable to us. *Quod ab initio injustum est, nullum potest habere juris effectum,* said Grotius. Which, with submission to your Excellency, may be rendered thus : whatever is originally in its nature wrong, can never be *sanctified*, or made right by *repetition* and use.

In solemn agreements, subsequent restrictions ought never to be allowed. The celebrated author, whom your Excellency has quoted, tells us, that, " neither the one or the other of the interested, or contracting powers, hath a right to interpret at pleasure." This we mention, to show, even upon a supposition, that the Parliament had been a party to the contract, the invalidity of any of its subsequent acts, to explain any clause in the charter ; more especially to restrict or make void any clause granted therein to the General Court. An agreement ought to be interpreted " in such a manner as that it may have its effect." But, if your Excellency's interpretation of this clause is just, " that it is a reserve of power and authority to Parliament to bind us by such laws as are made expressly to refer to us," it is not only " a limitation of the power given to the General Court" to legislate, but it may, whenever the Parliament shall think fit, render it of no effect; for it puts it in the power of Parliament, to bind us by as many laws as they please, and even to restrain us from making any laws at all. If your Excellency's assertions in this, and the next succeeding part of your speech, were well grounded, the conclusion would be undeniable, that the charter, even in this clause, " does not confer or reserve any liberties," worth enjoying, " but what would have been enjoyed without it ;" saving that, within any of his Majesty's dominions, we are to be considered barely as not aliens. You are pleased to say, it cannot " be contended, that by the liberties of free and natural subjects," (which are expressly granted in the charter, to all intents, purposes and constructions, whatever) " is to be understood, an exemption from acts of Parliament, because not represented there ; seeing it is provided by the same charter, that such acts shall be in force." If, says an eminent lawyer, " the King grants to the town of D. the same liberties which London has, this shall be intended the like liberties." A grant of the liberties of free and natural subjects, is equivalent to a grant of the same liberties. And the King, in the first charter to this colony, expressly grants, that it " shall be construed, reputed and adjudged in all cases, most favorably on the behalf and for the benefit and behoof of the said Governor and Company, and their successors— any matter, cause or thing, whatsoever, to the contrary notwithstanding." It is one of the liberties of free and natural subjects, born and abiding within the realm, to be governed, as your Excellency observes, " by laws made by persons, in whose elections they, from time to time, have a voice." This is an essential right. For nothing is more evident, than, that any people, who are subject to the unlimited power of another, must be in a state of abject slavery. . It was easily and plainly foreseen, that the right of representation in the English Parliament, could not be exercised by the people of this colony. It would be impracticable, if consistent with the English constitution. And for this reason, that this colony might have and enjoy all the liberties and immunities of free and natural subjects within the realm, as stipulated in the charter, it was necessary, and a Legislative was accordingly constituted within the colony ; one branch of which, consists of Representatives chosen by the people, to make all laws, statutes, ordinances, &c. for the well ordering and governing the same, not repugnant to the laws of England, or, as nearly as conveniently might be, agreeable to the fundamental laws of the English constitution. We are, therefore, still at a loss to conceive, where your Excellency finds it " provided in the same charter, that such acts," viz. acts of Parliament, made expressly to refer to us, " shall be in force" in this province. There is nothing to this purpose, expressed in the charter, or in our opinion, even implied in it. And surely it would be very absurd, that a charter, which is evidently formed upon a supposition and intention, that a colony is and should be considered as not within the realm ; and declared by the very Prince who granted it, to be not within the jurisdiction of Parliament, should yet provide, that the laws which the same Parliament should make, expressly to refer to that colony, should be in force therein. Your Excellency is pleased to ask, " does it follow, that the government, by their (our ancestors) removal from one part of the dominions to another, loses its authority over that part to which they remove ; and that they are freed from the subjection they were under before ?" We answer, if that part of the King's dominions, to which they removed, was not then a part of the realm, and was never annexed to it, the Parliament lost no authority over it, having never had such authority ; and the emigrations were consequently freed from the subjection they were under before their removal. The power and authority of Parliament, being constitutionally confined within the limits of the realm, and the nation collectively, of which alone it is the representing and Legislative Assembly. Your Excellency further asks, " will it not rather be said, that by this, their voluntary removal, they have relinquished, for a time, at least, one of the rights of an English subject, which they might, if they pleased, have continued to enjoy, and may again enjoy, whenever they return to the place where it can be exercised ?" To which we answer ; they never did relinquish the right to be governed by laws, made by persons in whose election they had a voice. The King stipulated with them, that they should have and enjoy all the liberties of free and natural subjects, born within the realm, to all intents, purposes and constructions, whatsoever ; that is, that they should be as free as those, who were to abide within the realm : consequently, he stipulated with them, that they should enjoy and exercise this most essential right, which discriminates freemen from vassals, uninterruptedly, in its full sense and meaning ; and they did, and ought still to exercise it, without the necessity of returning, for the sake of exercising it, to the nation or state of England.

We cannot help observing, that your Excellency's manner of reasoning on this point, seems to us, to render the most valuable clauses in our charter unintelligible : as if persons going from the realm of England, to inhabit in America, should hold and exercise there a certain right of English subjects ; but, in order to exercise it in such manner as to be of any benefit to them, they must *not inhabit* there, but return to the place where alone it can be exercised. By such construction, the words of the charter can have no sense or meaning. We forbear remarking upon the absurdity of a grant to persons born without the realm, of the same liberties which would have belonged to them, if they had been born within the realm.

Your Excellency is disposed to compare this government to the variety of corporations, formed within the kingdom, with power to make and execute by-laws, &c. ; and, because they remain subject to the supreme authority of Parliament, to infer, that this colony is also subject to the same authority : this reasoning appears to us not just. The members of those corporations are resident within the kingdom ; and residence subjects them to the authority of Parliament, in which they are also represented ; whereas the people of this colony are not resident within the realm.

The charter was granted, with the express purpose to induce them to reside without the realm; consequently, they are not represented in Parliament there. But, we would ask your Excellency, are any of the corporations, formed within the kingdom, vested with the power of erecting other subordinate corporations? of enacting and determining what crimes shall be capital? and constituting courts of common law, with all their officers, for the hearing, trying and punishing capital offenders with death? These and many other powers vested in this government, plainly show, that it is to be considered as a corporation, in no other light, than as every state is a corporation. Besides, appeals from the courts of law here, are not brought before the House of Lords; which shows, that the peers of the realm, are not the peers of America: but all such appeals are brought before the King in council, which is a further evidence, that we are not within the realm.

We conceive enough has been said, to convince your Excellency, that, " when our predecessors first took possession of this plantation, or colony, by a grant and charter from the Crown of England, it *was not*, and never had been the sense of the kingdom, that they were to remain subject to the supreme authority of Parliament. We will now, with your Excellency's leave, inquire what *was* the sense of our ancestors, of this very important matter.

And, as your Excellency has been pleased to tell us, you have not discovered, that the supreme authority of Parliament has been called in question, even by private and particular persons, until within seven or eight years past; except about the time of the anarchy and confusion in England, which preceded the restoration of King Charles the II. we beg leave to remind your Excellency of some parts of your own history of Massachusetts Bay. Therein we are informed of the sentiments of " persons of influence," after the restoration; from which, the historian tells us, some parts of their conduct, that is, of the General Assembly, " may be pretty well accounted for." By the history, it appears to have been the opinion of those persons of influence, " that the subjects of any prince or state, had a natural right to remove to any other state, or to another quarter of the world, unless the state was weakened or exposed by such remove; and, even in that case, if they were deprived of the right of all mankind, liberty of conscience, it would justify a separation, and upon their removal, their subjection determined and ceased." That " the country to which they had removed, was claimed and possessed by independent princes, whose right to the lordship and sovereignty thereof had been acknowledged by the Kings of England," an instance of which is quoted in the margin. " That they themselves had actually purchased, for valuable consideration, not only the soil, but the dominion, the lordship and sovereignty of those princes;" without which purchase, " in the sight of God and men, they had no right or title to what they possessed." They had received a charter of incorporation from the King, from whence arose a new kind of subjection, namely, "a voluntary, civil subjection;" and by this compact, "they were to be governed by laws made by themselves." Thus it appears to have been the sentiments of private persons, though persons by whose sentiments the public conduct was influenced, that their removal was a justifiable separation from the mother state, upon which, their subjection to that state, determined and ceased. The supreme authority of Parliament, if it had then ever been asserted, must surely have been called in question, by men who had advanced such principles as these.

The first act of Parliament, made expressly to refer to the colonies, was after the restoration. In the reign of King Charles the II. several such acts passed. And the same history informs us, there was a difficulty in conforming to them; and the reason of this difficulty is explained in a letter of the General Assembly to their Agent, quoted in the following words; "they apprehended them to be an invasion of the rights, liberties and properties of the subjects of his Majesty, in the colony, they not being represented in Parliament, and according to the usual sayings of the learned in the law, the laws of England were bounded within the four seas, and did not reach America: However, as his Majesty had signified his pleasure, that those acts should be observed in the Massachusetts, they had made provision, by a law of the colony, that they should be strictly attended." Which provision, by a law of their own, would have been superfluous, if they had admitted the supreme authority of Parliament. In short, by the same history it appears, that those acts of Parliament, as such, were disregarded; and the following reason is given for it: "It seems to have been a general opinion, that acts of Parliament had no other force, than what they derived from acts made by the General Court, to establish and confirm them."

But, still further to show the sense of our ancestors, respecting this matter, we beg leave to recite some parts of a narrative, presented to the Lords of Privy Council, by Edward Randolph, in the year 1676, which we find in your Excellency's collection of papers lately published. Therein it is declared to be the sense of the colony, "that no law is in force or esteem there, but such as are made by the General Court; and, therefore, it is accounted a breach of their privileges, and a betraying of the liberties of their commonwealth, to urge the observation of the laws of England." And, further, "that no oath shall be urged, or required to be taken by any person, but such oath as the General Court hath considered, allowed and required." And, further, "there is no notice taken of the act of navigation, plantation or any other laws, made in England for the regulation of trade." "That the government would make the world believe, they are a free state, and do act in all matters accordingly." Again, "these magistrates ever reserve to themselves, a power to alter, evade and disannul any law or command, not agreeing with their humor, or the absolute authority of their government, acknowledging no superior." And, farther, " he (the Governor) freely declared to me, that the laws made by your Majesty and your Parliament, obligeth them in nothing, but what consists with the interests of that colony; that the Legislative power and authority is, and abides in them solely." And in the same Mr. Randolph's letter to the Bishop of London, July 14, 1682, he says, " this independency in government is claimed and daily practised." And your Excellency being then sensible, that this was the sense of our ancestors, in a marginal note, in the same collection of papers, observes, that, " this, viz. the provision made for observing the acts of trade, is very extraordinary, for this provision was an act of the colony, declaring the acts of trade shall be in force there." Although Mr. Randolph was very unfriendly to the colony, yet, as his declarations are concurrent with those recited from your Excellency's history, we think they may be admitted, for the purpose for which they are now brought.

Thus we see, from your Excellency's history and publications, the sense our ancestors had of the jurisdiction of Parliament, under the first charter. Very different from that, which your Excellency in your speech, apprehends it to have been.

It appears by Mr. Neal's History of New England, that the agents, who had been employed by the colony to transact its affairs in England, at the time when the present charter was granted, among other reasons, gave the following for their acceptance of it, viz. " The General Court has, with the King's approbation, as much power in New England, as the King and Parliament have in England; they have all English privileges, and can be touched by no law, and by no tax but of their own making." This is the earliest testimony that can be given of the sense our predecessors had of the supreme authority of Parliament, under the present charter. And it plainly shows. that they, who having been freely conversant with those who framed the charter, must have well understood the design and meaning of it, supposed that the terms in our charter, " full power and authority," intended and were considered as a sole and exclusive power, and that there was no " reserve in the charter, to the authority of Parliament, to bind the colony" by any acts whatever.

Soon after the arrival of the charter, viz. in 1692, your Excellency's history informs us, " the first act" of this Legislative, was a sort of Magna Charta, asserting and setting forth their general privileges, and this clause was among the rest; " no aid, tax, tallage, assessment, custom, loan, benevolence, or imposition whatever, shall be laid, assessed, imposed, or levied on any of their Majesty's subjects, or their estates, on any pretence whatever, but by the act and consent of the Governor, Council, and Representa-

46

tives of the people assembled in General Court." And though this act was disallowed, it serves to show the sense which the General Assembly, contemporary with the granting the charter, had of their sole and exclusive right to legislate for the colony. The history says, " the other parts of the act were copied from Magna Charta ;" by which, we may conclude that the Assembly then construed the words, " not repugnant to the laws," to mean, conformable to the fundamental principles of the English constitution. And it is observable, that the Lords of Privy Council, so lately as in the reign of Queen Anne, when several laws enacted by the General Assembly were laid before her Majesty for her allowance, interpreted the words in this charter, " not repugnant to the laws of England," by the words, " as nearly as conveniently may be agreeable to the laws and statutes of England." And her Majesty was pleased to disallow those acts, not because they were repugnant to any law or statute of England, made expressly to refer to the colony, but because divers persons, by virtue thereof, were punished, without being tried by their peers in the ordinary " courts of law," and " by the ordinary rules and known methods of justice," contrary to the express terms of Magna Charta, which was a statute in force at the time of granting the charter, and declaratory of the rights and liberties of the subjects within the realm.

You are pleased to say, that " our provincial or local laws have, in numerous instances, had relation to acts of Parliament, made to respect the plantations, and this colony in particular." The authority of the Legislature, says the same author who is quoted by your Excellency, " does not extend so far as the fundamentals of the constitution. They ought to consider the fundamental laws as sacred, if the nation has not in very express terms, given them the power to change them. For the constitution of the state ought to be fixed ; and since that was first established by the nation, which afterwards trusted certain persons with the Legislative power, the fundamental laws are excepted from their commission." Now the fundamentals of the constitution of this province, are stipulated in the charter ; the reasoning, therefore, in this case, holds equally good. Much less, then, ought any acts or doings of the General Assembly, however numerous, to neither of which your Excellency has pointed us, which barely relate to acts of Parliament made to respect the plantations in general, or this colony in particular, to be taken as an acknowledgment of this people, or even of the Assembly, which inadvertently passed those acts, that we are subject to the supreme authority of Parliament ; and with still less reason are the decisions in the executive courts to determine this point. If they have adopted that " as part of the rule of law," which, in fact, is not, it must be imputed to inattention or error in judgment, and cannot justly be urged as an alteration or restriction of the Legislative authority of the province.

Before we leave this part of your Excellency's speech, we would observe, that the great design of our ancestors, in leaving the kingdom of England, was to be freed from a subjection to its spiritual laws and courts, and to worship God according to the dictates of their consciences. Your Excellency, in your history observes, that their design was " to obtain for themselves and their posterity, the liberty of worshipping God in such manner as appeared to them most agreeable to the sacred scriptures." And the General Court themselves declared in 1651, that " seeing just cause to fear the persecution of the then Bishop, and high commission for not conforming to the ceremonies of those under their power, they thought it their safest course, to get to this outside of the world, out of their view, and beyond their reach." But, if it had been their sense, that they were still to be subject to the supreme authority of Parliament, they must have known that their design might, and probably would be frustrated ; that the Parliament, especially considering the temper of those times, might make what ecclesiastical laws they pleased, expressly to refer to them, and place them in the same circumstances with respect to religious matters, to be relieved from which, was the design of their removal ; and we would add, that if your Excellency's construction of the clause in our present charter is just, another clause therein, which provides for liberty of conscience for all christians, except papists, may be rendered void by an act of Parliament made to refer to us, requiring a conformity to the rites and mode of worship in the church of England, or any other.

Thus we have endeavored to show the sense of the people of this colony under both charters ; and, if there have been in any late instances a submission to acts of Parliament, it has been, in our opinion, rather from inconsideration, or a reluctance at the idea of contending with the parent state, than from a conviction or acknowledgment of the Supreme Legislative authority of Parliament.

Your Excellency tells us, " you know of no line that can be drawn between the supreme authority of Parliament and the total independence of the colonies." If there be no such line, the consequence is, either that the colonies are the vassals of the Parliament, or that they are totally independent. As it cannot be supposed to have been the intention of the parties in the compact, that we should be reduced to a state of vassalage, the conclusion is, that it was their sense, that we were thus independent. " It is impossible," your Excellency says, " that there should be two independent Legislatures in one and the same state." May we not then further conclude, that it was their sense, that the colonies were, by their charters, made distinct states from the mother country ? Your Excellency adds, " for although there may be but one head, the King, yet the two Legislative bodies will make two governments as distinct as the kingdoms of England and Scotland, before the union." Very true, may it please your Excellency ;

and if they interfere not with each other, what hinders, but that being united in one head and common Sovereign, they may live happily in that connection, and mutually support and protect each other? Notwithstanding all the terrors which your Excellency has pictured to us as the effects of a total independence, there is more reason to dread the consequences of absolute uncontroled power, whether of a nation or a monarch, than those of a total independence. It would be a misfortune " to know by experience, the difference between the liberties of an English colonist and those of the Spanish, French, and Dutch: and since the British Parliament has passed an act, which is executed even with rigor, though not voluntarily submitted to, for raising a revenue, and appropriating the same, without the consent of the people who pay it, and have claimed a power of making such laws as they please, to order and govern us, your Excellency will excuse us in asking, whether you do not think we already experience too much of such a difference, and have not reason to fear we shall soon be reduced to a worse situation than that of the colonies of France, Spain, or Holland?

If your Excellency expects to have the line of distinction between the supreme authority of Parliament, and the total independence of the colonies drawn by us, we would say it would be an arduous undertaking, and of very great importance to all the other colonies; and therefore, could we conceive of such a line, we should be unwilling to propose it, without their consent in Congress.

To conclude, these are great and profound questions. It is the grief of this House, that, by the ill policy of a late injudicious administration, America has been driven into the contemplation of them. And we cannot but express our concern, that your Excellency, by your speech, has reduced us to the unhappy alternative, either of appearing by our silence to acquiesce in your Excellency's sentiments, or of thus freely discussing this point.

After all that we have said, we would be far from being understood to have in the least abated that just sense of allegiance which we owe to the King of Great Britain, our rightful Sovereign; and should the people of this province be left to the free and full exercise of all the liberties and immunities granted to them by charter, there would be no danger of an independence on the Crown. Our charters reserve great power to the Crown in its Representative, fully sufficient to balance, analogous to the English constitution, all the liberties and privileges granted to the people. All this your Excellency knows full well; and whoever considers the power and influence, in all their branches, reserved by our charter, to the Crown, will be far from thinking that the Commons of this province are too independent.

This answer was reported by Mr. S. Adams, Mr. Hancock,

Maj. Hawley, Col. Bowers, Mr. Hobson, Maj. Foster, Mr. Phillips, and Col. Thayer.]

MESSAGE

May it please your Excellency,

THE House of Representatives having directed the Secretary to inform them, whether you have been pleased to give your assent to the grants lately made to the Justices of the Superior Court of Judicature, &c. and it appearing that your Excellency has not yet done it, it is their request, that you would be pleased to make known to them the difficulty (if any there be) in your Excellency's mind, which prevents your assenting to said grants.

The people without doors are universally alarmed with the report that salaries are fixed to the offices of the said Justices, by order of the Crown ; and an unusual delay to confirm the grants now made, is judged by this House to be a sufficient apology for this inquiry.

MESSAGE

Gentlemen of the House of Representatives,

I HAVE received information, that his Majesty has been pleased to order, that salaries shall be allowed to the Justices of the Superior Court, and that such salaries shall continue so long as those Justices shall reside within the province, and whilst they are absent from it, with his Majesty's leave ; but I have no information that any warrants for the payment of such salaries have been issued. I, therefore, did not give an immediate assent to the grants which you have made for their services the year past, as the warrants, if they should hereafter be transmitted, may include part of the same time for which your grants are made, but thought it most advisable to consider of some precaution, to prevent all claim from the province for any services, for which the Justices may also be entitled to a salary from the King. I hope, therefore, a short delay, which has been occasioned by a regard to your interest, as well as by a sense of my duty to his Majesty, will not be thought unnecessary. T. HUTCHINSON.

MESSAGE

May it please your Excellency,

Your message of the 4th instant, informs this House, that his Majesty has been pleased to order that salaries shall be allowed to the Justices of the Superior Court of this province.

We conceive that no Judge, who has a due regard to justice, or even to his own character, would choose to be placed under such an undue bias as they must be under, in the opinion of this House, by accepting of, and becoming dependent for their salaries upon the Crown.

Had not his Majesty been misinformed, with respect to the constitution and appointment of our Judges, by those who advised to this measure, we are persuaded, he would never have passed such an order; as he was pleased to declare, upon his accession to the throne, that " he looked upon the independence and uprightness of the Judges, as essential to the impartial administration of justice, as one of the best securities of the rights and liberties of his subjects, and as most conducive to the honor of the Crown."

Your Excellency's precaution to prevent all claim from the province for any services, for which the Justices may also be entitled to a salary from the King, is comparatively, of very small consideration with us.

When we consider the many attempts that have been made, effectually to render null and void those clauses in our charter, upon which the freedom of our constitution depends, we should be lost to all public feeling, should we not manifest a just resentment. We are more and more convinced, that it has been the design of administration, totally to subvert the constitution, and introduce an arbitrary government into this province; and we cannot wonder that the apprehensions of this people are thoroughly awakened.

We wait with impatience to know, and hope your Excellency will very soon be able to assure us, that the Justices will utterly refuse ever to accept of support, in a manner so justly obnoxious to the disinterested and judicious part of the good people of this province, being repugnant to the charter, and utterly inconsistent with the safety of the rights, liberties, and properties of the people.

[The committee who reported this message, were, Mr. S. Adams, Mr. Pickering, Mr. Phillips, Mr. Hancock, Mr. Heath, Mr. Foster, and Mr. Denny.]

—

MESSAGE

FROM THE HOUSE OF REPRESENTATIVES TO THE GOVERNOR,
FEBRUARY 16, 1773.

May it please your Excellency,

THE House of Representatives think it of the last importance, to wait on your Excellency, and pray that you would be pleased to inform them, whether your Excellency can now satisfy the House, that the Justices of the Superior Court have refused, or will refuse, to accept of their support from the Crown; a matter which appears to have filled the minds of the good people of this province, with the greatest anxiety; and a determination of which, in the affirmative, will tend to promote his Majesty's service, and the peace and happiness of the people.

—

MESSAGE

FROM THE GOVERNOR TO THE HOUSE OF REPRESENTATIVES,
FEBRUARY 16, 1773.

Gentlemen of the House of Representatives,

I MOST certainly am not able to inform you, that the Justices of the Superior Court have refused, or will refuse, to accept of their support from the Crown. All that I thought necessary for me to do, before I gave my assent to the grants which you had made, was the taking proper caution to prevent their being entitled to a salary from the province, after a salary from the Crown should commence, if the warrants for the payment of such salary should hereafter be received.   T. HUTCHINSON.

SPEECH

Gentlemen of the Council, and

 Gentlemen of the House of Representatives,

THE proceedings of such of the inhabitants of the town of Boston, as assembled together, and passed and published their resolves or votes, as the act of the town, at a legal town meeting, denying, in the most express terms, the supremacy of Parliament, and inviting every other town and district in the province, to adopt the same principle, and to establish committees of correspondence, to consult upon proper measures to maintain it, and the proceedings of divers other towns, in consequence of this invitation, appeared to me to be so unwarrantable, and of such a dangerous nature and tendency, that I thought myself bound to call upon you in my speech at opening the session, to join with me in discountenancing and bearing a proper testimony against such irregularities and innovations.

I stated to you fairly and truly, as I conceived, the constitution of the kingdom and of the province, so far as relates to the dependence of the former upon the latter; and I desired you, if you differed from me in sentiments, to show me, with candor, my own errors, and to give your reasons in support of your opinions, so far as you might differ from me. I hoped that you would have considered my speech by your joint committees, and have given me a joint answer; but, as the House of Representatives have declined that mode of proceeding, and as your principles in government are very different, I am obliged to make separate and distinct replies. I shall first apply myself to you,

Gentlemen of the Council,

The two first parts of your answer, which respect the disorders occasioned by the stamp act, and the general nature of supreme authority, do not appear to me to have a tendency to invalidate any thing which I have said in my speech; for, however the stamp act may have been the immediate occasion of any disorders, the authority of Parliament was, notwithstanding, denied, in order to justify or excuse them. And, for the nature of the supreme authority of Parliament, I have never given you any reason to suppose, that I intended a more absolute power in Parliament, or a greater degree of active or passive obedience in the people, than what is founded in the nature of government, let the form of it be what it may. I shall, therefore, pass over those parts of your answer, without any other remark. I would also have saved you the trouble of all those authorities which you have brought to show, that all taxes upon English subjects, must be levied by virtue of the act, not of the King alone, but in conjunction with the Lords and Commons, for I should very readily have allowed it; and I should as readily have allowed, that all other acts of legislation must be passed by the same joint authority, and not by the King alone.

Indeed, I am not willing to continue a controversy with you, upon any other parts of your answer. I am glad to find, that independence is not what you have in contemplation, and that you will not presume to prescribe the exact limits of the authority of Parliament, only, as with due deference to it, you are humbly of opinion, that, as all human authority in the nature of it is, and ought to be limited, it cannot constitutionally extend, for the reasons you have suggested, to the levying of taxes, in any form, on his Majesty's subjects of this province.

I will only observe, that your attempts to draw a line as the limits of the supreme authority in government, by distinguishing some natural rights, as more peculiarly exempt from such authority than the rest, rather tend to evince the impracticability of drawing such a line; and, that some parts of your answer seem to infer a supremacy in the province, at the same time that you acknowledge the supremacy of Parliament; for otherwise, the rights of the subjects cannot be the same in all essential respects, as you suppose them to be, in all parts of the dominions, " under a like form of Legislature."

From these, therefore, and other considerations, I cannot help flattering myself, that, upon more mature deliberation, and in order to a more consistent plan of government, you will choose rather to doubt of the expediency of Parliament's exercising its authority in cases that may happen, than to limit the authority itself, especially, as you agree with me in the proper method of obtaining a redress of grievances by constitutional representations, which cannot well consist with a denial of the authority to which the representations are made; and from the best information I have been able to obtain, the denial of the authority of Parliament, expressly, or by implication, in those petitions to which you refer, was the cause of their not being admitted, and not any advice given by the Minister to the Agents of the colonies. I must enlarge, and be more particular in my reply to you,

Gentlemen of the House of Representatives.

I shall take no notice of that part of your answer, which attributes the disorders of the province, to an undue exercise of the power of Parliament; because you take for granted, what can by no means be admitted, that Parliament had exercised its power without just authority. The sum of your answer, so far as it is pertinent to my speech, is this.

You allege that the colonies were an acquisition of foreign territory, not annexed to the realm of England; and, therefore, at the

47

absolute disposal of the Crown ; the King having, as you take it, a constitutional right to dispose of, and alienate any part of his territories, not annexed to the realm; that Queen Elizabeth accordingly conveyed the property, dominion, and sovereignty of Virginia, to Sir Walter Raleigh, to be held of the Crown by homage and a certain render, without reserving any share in the legislative and executive authority ; that the subsequent grants of America were similar in this respect ; that they were without any reservation for securing the subjection of the colonists to the Parliament, and future laws of England ; that this was the sense of the English Crown, the nation, and our predecessors, when they first took possession of this country ; that if the colonies were not then annexed to the realm, they cannot have been annexed since that time ; that if they are not now annexed to the realm, they are not part of the kingdom ; and, consequently, not subject to the legislative authority of the kingdom ; for no country, by the common law, was subject to the laws or to the Parliament, but the realm of England.

Now, if this foundation shall fail you in every part of it, as I think it will, the fabric which you have raised upon it must certainly fall.

Let me then observe to you, that as English subjects, and agreeable to the doctrine of feudal tenure, all our lands and tenements are held mediately, or immediately of the Crown, and although the possession and use, or profits, be in the subject, there still remains a dominion in the Crown. When any new countries are discovered by English subjects, according to the general law and usage of nations, they become part of the state, and, according to the feudal system, the lordship or dominion, is in the Crown ; and a right accrues of disposing of such territories, under such tenure, or for such services to be performed, as the Crown shall judge proper ; and whensoever any part of such territories, by grant from the Crown, becomes the possession or property of private persons, such persons, thus holding, under the Crown of England, remain, or become subjects of England, to all intents and purposes, as fully, as if any of the royal manors, forests, or other territory, within the realm, had been granted to them upon the like tenure. But, that it is now, or was, when the plantations were first granted, the prerogative of the Kings of England to alienate such territories from the Crown, or to constitute a number of new governments, altogether independent of the sovereign legislative authority of the English empire, I can by no means concede to you. I have never seen any better authority to support such an opinion, than an anonymous pamphlet, by which, I fear, you have too easily been misled ; for I shall presently show you, that the declarations of King James the I. and of King Charles the I. admitting they are truly related by the author of this pamphlet, ought to have no weight with you ; nor does the cession or restoration, upon a treaty of peace, of countries which have been lost or acquired in war, militate with these principles; nor may any particular act of power of a prince, in selling, or delivering up any part of his dominions to a foreign prince or state, against the general sense of the nation, be urged to invalidate them; and, upon examination, it will appear, that all the grants which have been made of America, are founded upon them, and are made to conform to them, even those which you have adduced in support of very different principles.

You do not recollect, that prior, to what you call the first grant by Queen Elizabeth to Sir Walter Raleigh, a grant had been made by the same Princess, to Sir Humphrey Gilbert, of all such countries as he should discover, which were to be of the allegiance of her, her heirs and successors; but he dying in the prosecution of his voyage, a second grant was made to Sir Walter Raleigh, which, you say, conveyed the dominion and sovereignty, without any reserve of legislative or executive authority, being held by homage and a render. To hold by homage, which implies fealty, and a render, is descriptive of soccage tenure as fully, as if it had been said to hold as of our manor of East Greenwich, the words in your charter. Now, this alone was a reserve of dominion and sovereignty in the Queen, her heirs and successors; and, besides this, the grant is made upon this express condition, which you pass over, that the people remain subject to the Crown of England, the head of that legislative authority, which, by the English constitution, is equally extensive with the authority of the Crown, throughout every part of the dominions. Now, if we could suppose the Queen to have acquired, separate from her relation to her subjects, or in her natural capacity, which she could not do, a title to a country discovered by her subjects, and then to grant the same country to English subjects, in her public capacity as Queen of England, still, by this grant, she annexed it to the Crown. Thus by not distinguishing between the Crown of England, and the Kings and Queens of England, in their personal or natural capacities, you have been led into a fundamental error, which must prove fatal to your system. It is not material, whether Virginia reverted to the Crown by Sir Walter's attainder, or whether he never took any benefit from his grant, though the latter is most probable, seeing he ceased from all attempts to take possession of the country after a few years trial. There were, undoubtedly, divers grants made by King James the I. of the continent of America, in the beginning of the seventeenth century, and similar to the grant of Queen Elizabeth, in this respect, that they were dependent on the Crown. The charter to the Council at Plymouth, in Devon, dated November 3, 1620, more immediately respects us, and of that we have the most authentic remains.

By this charter, upon the petition of Sir Ferdinando Gorges, a corporation was constituted, to be, and continue by succession, forever in the town of Plymouth aforesaid, to which corporation, that part of the American continent, which lies between 40 and 48 degrees of latitude, was granted, to be held of the King, his heirs and successors, as of the manor of East Greenwich, with powers to constitute subordinate governments in America, and to make laws for such governments, not repugnant to the laws and statutes of England. From this corporation, your predecessors obtained a grant of the soil of the colony of Massachusetts Bay, in 1627, and in 1628, they obtained a charter from King Charles the I. making them a distinct corporation, also within the realm, and giving them full powers within the limits of their patent, very like to those of the Council of Plymouth, throughout their more extensive territory.

We will now consider what must have been the sense of the King, of the nation, and of the patentees, at the time of granting these patents. From the year 1602, the banks and sea coasts of New England had been frequented by English subjects, for catching and drying cod fish. When an exclusive right to the fishery was claimed, by virtue of the patent of 1620, the House of Commons was alarmed, and a bill was brought in for allowing a free fishery; and, it was upon this occasion, that one of the Secretaries of State declared, perhaps, as his own opinion, that the plantations were not annexed to the Crown, and so were not within the jurisdiction of Parliament. Sir Edwin Sandys, who was one of the Virginia Company, and an eminent lawyer, declared, that he knew Virginia had been annexed, and was held of the Crown, as of the manor of East Greenwich, and he believed New England was so also; and so it most certainly was. This declaration, made by one of the King's servants, you say, shewed the sense of the Crown, and, being not secretly, but openly declared in Parliament, you would make it the sense of the nation also, notwithstanding your own assertion, that the Lords and Commons passed a bill, that shewed their sense to be directly the contrary. But if there had been full evidence of express declarations made by King James the I. and King Charles the I. they were declarations contrary to their own grants, which declare this country to be held of the Crown, and, consequently, it must have been annexed to it. And may not such declarations be accounted for by other actions of those princes, who, when they were soliciting the Parliament to grant the duties of tonnage and poundage, with other aids, and were, in this way, acknowledging the rights of Parliament, at the same time were requiring the payment of those duties, with ship money, &c. by virtue of their prerogative?

But to remove all doubts of the sense of the nation, and of the patentees of this patent, or charter, in 1620, I need only refer you to the account published by Sir Ferdinando Gorges himself, of the proceedings in Parliament upon this occasion. As he was the most active Member of the Council of Plymouth, and, as he relates what came within his own knowledge and observation, his narrative, which has all the appearance of truth and sincerity, must carry conviction with it. He says, that soon after the patent was passed, and whilst it lay in the Crown Office, he was summoned to appear in Parliament, to answer what was to be objected against it; and the House being in a committee, and Sir Edward Coke, that great oracle of the law, in the chair, he was called to the bar, and was told by Sir Edward, that the House understood that a patent had been granted to the said Ferdinando, and divers other noble persons, for establishing a colony in New England, that this was deemed a grievance of the Commonwealth, contrary to the laws, and to the privileges of the subject, that it was a monopoly, &c. and he required the delivery of the patent into the House. Sir Ferdinando Gorges made no doubt of the authority of the House, but submitted to their disposal of the patent, as, in their wisdom, they thought good; "not knowing, under favor, how any action of that kind could be a grievance to the public, seeing it was undertaken for the advancement of religion, the enlargement of the bounds of our nation, &c. He was willing, however, to submit the whole to their honorable censures." After divers attendances, he imagined he had satisfied the House, that the planting a colony, was of much more consequence, than a simple disorderly course of fishing. He was, notwithstanding, disappointed; and, when the public grievances of the kingdom were presented by the two Houses, that of the patent for New England was the first. I do not know how the Parliament could have shewn more fully the sense they then had of their authority over this new acquired territory; nor can we expect better evidence of the sense which the patentees had of it, for I know of no historical fact, of which we have less reason to doubt.

And now, gentlemen, I will shew you how it appears from our charter itself, which you say, I have not yet been pleased to point out to you, except from that clause, which restrains us from making laws repugnant to the laws of England; that it was the sense of our predecessors, at the time when the charter was granted, that they were to remain subject to the supreme authority of Parliament.

Besides this clause, which I shall have occasion further to remark upon, before I finish, you will find, that, by the charter, a grant was made, of exemption from all taxes and impositions upon any goods imported into New England, or exported from thence into England, for the space of twenty-one years, except the custom of five per cent. upon such goods, as, after the expiration of seven years, should be brought into England. Nothing can be more plain, than that the charter, as well as the patent to the Council of Plymouth, constitutes a corporation in England, with powers to create a subordinate government or governments within the plantation, so that there would always be subjects of taxes and impositions both in the kingdom and in the plantation. An exemption for twenty-one years, implies a right of imposition after the expiration of the term, and there is no distinction between the kingdom and the plantation. By what authority then, in the understanding of the parties, were those impositions to be laid ? If any, to support a system, should say by the King, rather than to acknowledge the authority of Parliament, yet this could not be the sense of one of our principal patentees, Mr. Samuel Vassal, who, at that instant, 1628, the date of the charter, was suffering the loss of his goods, rather than submit to an imposition laid by the King, without the authority of Parliament; and to prove, that a few years after, it could not be the sense of the rest, I need only to refer you to your own records for the year 1642, where you will find an order of the House of Commons, conceived in such terms, as discover a plain reference to this part of the charter, after fourteen years of the twenty-one were expired. By this order, the House of Commons declare, that all goods and merchandize exported to New England, or imported from thence, shall be free from all taxes and impositions, both in the kingdom and New England, until the House shall take further order therein to the contrary. The sense which our predecessors had of the benefit which they took from this order, evidently appears from the vote of the General Court, acknowledging their humble thankfulness, and preserving a grateful remembrance of the honorable respect from that high court, and resolving, that the order sent unto them, under the hand of the Clerk of the honorable House of Commons, shall be entered among their public records, to remain there unto posterity. And, in an address to Parliament, nine years after, they acknowledge, among other undeserved favors, that of taking off the customs from them.

I am at a loss to know what your ideas could be, when you say, that if the plantations are not part of the realm, they are not part of the kingdom, seeing the two words can properly convey but one idea, and they have one and the same signification in the different languages from whence they are derived. I do not charge you with any design; but the equivocal use of the word realm, in several parts of your answer, makes them perplexed and obscure. Sometimes you must intend the whole dominion, which is subject to the authority of Parliament; sometimes only strictly the territorial realm to which other dominions are, or may be annexed. If you mean that no countries, but the ancient territorial realm, can, constitutionally, be subject to the supreme authority of England, which you have very incautiously said, is a rule of the common law of England; this is a doctrine which you will never be able to support. That the common law should be controled and changed by statutes, every day's experience teaches, but that the common law prescribes limits to the extent of the Legislative power, I believe has never been said upon any other occasion. That acts of Parliaments, for several hundred years past, have respected countries, which are not strictly within the realm, you might easily have discovered by the statute books. You will find acts for regulating the affairs of Ireland, though a separate and distinct kingdom. Wales and Calais, whilst they sent no Representatives to Parliament, were subject to the like regulations ; so are Guernsey, Jersey, Alderney, &c. which send no Members to this day. These countries are not more properly a part of the ancient realm, than the plantations, nor do I know they can more properly be said to be annexed to the realm, unless the declaring that acts of Parliament shall extend to Wales, though not particularly named, shall make it so, which I conceive it does not, in the sense you intend.

Thus, I think, I have made it appear that the plantations, though not strictly within the realm, have, from the beginning, been constitutionally subject to the supreme authority of the realm, and are so far annexed to it, as to be, with the realm and the other dependencies upon it, one entire dominion ; and that the plantation, or colony of Massachusetts Bay in particular, is holden as feudatory of the imperial Crown of England. Deem it to be no part of the realm, it is immaterial ; for, to use the words of a very great authority in a case, in some respects analogous, " being feudatory, the conclusion necessarily follows, that it is under the government of the King's laws and the King's courts, in cases proper for them to interpose, though (like Counties Palatine) it has peculiar laws and customs, *jura regalia*, and complete jurisdiction at home."

Your remark upon, and construction of the words, not repugnant to the laws of England, are much the same with those of the Council ; but, can any reason be assigned, why the laws of England, as they stood just at that period, should be pitched upon as the standard, more than at any other period ? If so, why was it not recurred to, when the second charter was granted, more than sixty years after the first ? It is not improbable, that the original intention might be a repugnancy in general, and a *fortiori*, such laws as were made more immediately to respect us, but the statute of 7th and 8th of King William and Queen Mary, soon after the second charter, favors the latter construction only ; and the province agent, Mr. Dummer, in his much applauded defence of the charter, says, that, then a law in the plantations may be said to be repugnant to a law made in Great Britain, when it flatly contradicts it, so far, as the law made there, mentions and relates to the plantations. But, gentlemen, there is another clause, both in the first and second charter, which, I think, will serve to explain this, or to render all dispute upon the construction of it unnecessary. You are enabled to impose such oaths only, as are warrantable by, or not repugnant to the laws and statutes of the realm. I believe you will not contend, that these clauses must mean such oaths only, as were warrantable at the respective times when the charters were granted. It has often been found necessary, since the date of the charters, to alter the forms of the oaths to the government by acts of Parliament, and such alterations have always been conformed to in the plantations.

Lest you should think that I admit the authority of King Charles the II. in giving his assent to an act of the Assembly of Virginia, which you subjoin to the authorities of James the I. and Charles the I. to have any weight, I must observe to you, that I do not see any greater inconsistency with Magna Charta, in the King's giving his assent to an act of a subordinate Legislature immediately, or in person, than when he does it mediately by his Governor or Substitute; but, if it could be admitted, that such an assent discovered the King's judgment that Virginia was independent, would you lay any stress upon it, when the same King was, from time to time, giving his assent to acts of Parliament, which inferred the dependence of all the colonies, and had by one of those acts, declared the plantations to be inhabited and peopled by his Majesty's subjects of England?

I gave you no reason to remark upon the absurdity of a grant to persons born within the realm, of the same liberties which would have belonged to them, if they had been born within the realm; but rather guarded against it, by considering such grant as declaratory only, and in the nature of an assurance, that the plantations would be considered as the dominions of England. But is there no absurdity in a grant from the King of England, of the liberties and immunities of Englishmen to persons born in, and who are to inhabit other territories than the dominions of England; and would such grant, whether by charter, or other letters patent, be sufficient to make them inheritable, or to entitle them to the other liberties and immunities of Englishmen, in any part of the English dominions?

As I am willing to rest the point between us, upon the plantations having been, from their first discovery and settlement under the Crown, a part of the dominions of England, I shall not take up any time in remarking upon your arguments, to show, that since that time, they cannot have been made a part of those dominions.

The remaining parts of your answer, are principally intended to prove, that under both charters, it hath been the sense of the people, that they were not subject to the jurisdiction of Parliament, and, for this purpose, you have made large extracts from the history of the colony. Whilst you are doing honor to the book, by laying any stress upon its authority, it would have been no more than justice to the author, if you had cited some other passages, which would have tended to reconcile the passage in my speech, to the history. I have said, that except about the time of the anarchy, which preceded the restoration of King Charles the II. I have not discovered that the authority of Parliament had been called in question, even by particular persons. It was, as I take it, from the principles imbibed in those times of anarchy, that the persons of influence, mentioned in the history, disputed the authority of

Parliament, but the government would not venture to dispute it. On the contrary, in four or five years after the restoration, the government declared to the King's commissioners, that the act of navigation had been for some years observed here, that they knew not of its being greatly violated, and that such laws as appeared to be against it, were repealed. It is not strange, that these persons of influence, should prevail upon a great part of the people to fall in, for a time, with their opinions, and to suppose acts of the colony necessary to give force to acts of Parliament. The government, however, several years before the charter was vacated, more explicitly acknowledged the authority of Parliament, and voted that their Governor should take the oath required of him, faithfully to do, and perform all matters and things, enjoined him by the acts of trade. I have not recited in my speech, all these particulars, nor had I them all in my mind; but, I think, I have said nothing inconsistent with them. My principles in government, are still the same, with what they appear to be in the book, you refer to; nor am I conscious, that by any part of my conduct, I have given cause to suggest the contrary.

Inasmuch, as you say, that I have not particularly pointed out to you the acts and doings of the General Assembly, which relate to acts of Parliament; I will do it now, and demonstrate to you, that such acts have been acknowledged by the Assembly, or submitted to by the people.

From your predecessors removal to America, until the year 1640, there was no session of Parliament; and the first short session, of a few days only, in 1640, and the whole of the next session, until the withdraw of the King, being taken up in the disputes between the King and the Parliament, there could be no room for plantation affairs. Soon after the King's withdraw, the House of Commons passed the memorable order of 1642; and, from that time to the restoration, this plantation seems to have been distinguished from the rest; and the several acts and ordinances, which respected the other plantations, were never enforced here; and, possibly, under color of the exemption, in 1642, it might not be intended they should be executed.

For fifteen or sixteen years after the restoration, there was no officer of the customs in the colony, except the Governor, annually elected by the people, and the acts of trade were but little regarded; nor did the Governor take the oath required of Governors, by the act of the 12th of King Charles the II. until the time which I have mentioned. Upon the revolution, the force of an act of Parliament was evident, in a case of as great importance, as any which could happen to the colony. King William and Queen Mary were proclaimed in the colony, King and Queen of England, France, and Ireland, and the dominions thereunto belonging, in the room of King James; and this, not by virtue of an act of the colony, for no such act ever passed, but by force of an act of Parliament, which

48

altered the succession to the Crown, and for which, the people waited several weeks, with anxious concern. By force of another act of Parliament, and that only, such officers of the colony as had taken the oaths of allegiance to King James, deemed themselves at liberty to take, and accordingly did take, the oaths to King William and Queen Mary. And that I may mention other acts of the like nature together, it is by force of an act of Parliament, that the illustrious house of Hanover succeeded to the throne of Britain and its dominions, and by several other acts, the forms of the oaths have, from time to time, been altered; and, by a late act, that form was established which every one of us has complied with, as the charter, in express words, requires, and makes our duty. Shall we now dispute, whether acts of Parliament have been submitted to, when we find them submitted to, in points which are of the very essence of our constitution? If you should disown that authority, which has power even to change the succession to the Crown, are you in no danger of denying the authority of our most gracious Sovereign, which I am sure none of you can have in your thoughts?

I think I have before shewn you, gentlemen, what must have been the sense of our predecessors, at the time of the first charter; let us now, whilst we are upon the acts and doings of the Assembly, consider what it must have been at the time of the second charter. Upon the first advice of the revolution, in England, the authority which assumed the government, instructed their agents to petition Parliament to restore the first charter, and a bill for that purpose, passed the House of Commons, but went no further. Was not this owning the authority of Parliament? By an act of Parliament, passed in the first year of King William and Queen Mary, a form of oaths was established, to be taken by those Princes, and by all succeeding Kings and Queens of England, at their coronation; the first of which is, that they will govern the people of the kingdom, and the dominions thereunto belonging, according to the statutes in Parliament agreed on, and the laws and customs of the same. When the colony directed their agents to make their humble application to King William, to grant the second charter, they could have no other pretence, than, as they were inhabitants of part of the dominions of England; and they also knew the oath the King had taken, to govern them according to the statutes in Parliament. Surely, then, at the time of this charter, also, it was the sense of our predecessors, as well as of the King and of the nation, that there was, and would remain, a supremacy in the Parliament. About the same time, they acknowledge, in an address to the King, that they have no power to make laws repugnant to the laws of England. And, immediately after the assumption of the powers of government, by virtue of the new charter, an act was passed to revive, for a limited time, all the local laws of the colonies of Massachusetts Bay and New Plymouth, respectively, not repugnant to the laws of England.   And, at the same session, an act passsed, establishing naval officers, in several ports of the province, for which, this reason is given ; that all undue trading, contrary to an act of Parliament, made in the 15th year of King Charles the II. may be prevented in this, their Majesty's province.   The act of this province, passed so long ago as the second year of King George the I. for stating the fees of the custom house officers, must have relation to the acts of Parliament, by which they are constituted ; and the provision made in that act of the province, for extending the port of Boston to all the roads, as far as Cape Cod, could be for no other purpose, than for the more effectual carrying the acts of trade into execution.   And, to come nearer to the present time, when an act of Parliament had passed, in 1771, for putting an end to certain unwarrantable schemes, in this province, did the authority of government, or those persons more immediately affected by it, ever dispute the validity of it ?   On the contrary, have not a number of acts been passed in the province, the burdens to which such persons were subjected, might be equally apportioned ; and have not all those acts of the province been very carefully framed, to prevent their militating with the act of Parliament ?   I will mention, also, an act of Parliament, made in the first year of Queen Anne, although the proceedings upon it, more immediately respected the Council. By this act, no office, civil or military, shall be void, by the death of the King, but shall continue six months, unless suspended, or made void, by the next successor.   By force of this act, Governor Dudley continued in the administration six months from the demise of Queen Anne, and immediately after, the Council assumed the administration, and continued it, until a proclamation arrived from King George, by virtue of which, Governor Dudley reassumed the government.   It would be tedious to enumerate the addresses, votes and messages, of both the Council and House of Representatives, to the same purpose.   I have said enough to shew that this government has submitted to Parliament, from a conviction of its constitutional supremacy, and this not from inconsideration, nor merely from reluctance at the idea of contending with the parent state.

If, then, I have made it appear, that both by the first and second charters, we hold our lands, and the authority of government, not of the King, but of the Crown of England, that being a dominion of the Crown of England, we are consequently subject to the supreme authority of England.   That this hath been the sense of this plantation, except in those few years when the principles of anarchy, which had prevailed in the kingdom, had not lost their influence here ; and if, upon a review of your principles, they shall appear to you to have been delusive and erroneous, as I think they must, or, if you shall only be in doubt of them, you certainly will not draw that conclusion, which otherwise you might do, and which I am glad you have hitherto avoided ; especially when you consider the obvious and inevitable distress and misery of independence upon our mother country, if such independence could be allowed or maintained, and the probability of much greater distress, which we are not able to foresee.

You ask me, if we have not reason to fear we shall soon be reduced to a worse situation than that of the colonies of 'France, Spain, or Holland. I may safely affirm that we have not ; that we have no reason to fear any evils from a submission to the authority of Parliament, equal to what we must feel from its authority being disputed, from an uncertain rule of law and government. For more than seventy years together, the supremacy of Parliament was acknowledged, without complaints of grievance. The effect of every measure cannot be foreseen by human wisdom. What can be expected more, from any authority, than, when the unfitness of a measure is discovered, to make it void ? When, upon the united representations and complaints of the American colonies, any acts have appeared to Parliament, to be unsalutary, have there not been repeated instances of the repeal of such acts ? We cannot expect these instances should be carried so far, as to be equivalent to a disavowal, or relinquishment of the right itself. Why, then, shall we fear for ourselves, and our posterity, greater rigor of government for seventy years to come, than what we, and our predecessors have felt, in the seventy years past.

You must give me leave, gentlemen, in a few words, to vindicate myself from a charge, in one part of your answer, of having, by my speech, reduced you to the unhappy alternative of appearing, by your silence, to acquiesce in my sentiments, or of freely discussing this point of the supremacy of Parliament. I saw, as I have before observed, the capital town of the province, without being reduced to such an alternative, voluntarily, not only discussing but determining this point, and inviting every other town and district in the province to do the like. I saw that many of the principal towns had followed the example, and that there was imminent danger of a compliance in most, if not all the rest, in order to avoid being distinguished. Was not I reduced to the alternative of rendering myself justly obnoxious to the displeasure of my Sovereign, by acquiescing in such irregularities, or of calling upon you to join with me in suppressing them ? Might I not rather have expected from you an expression of your concern, that any persons should project and prosecute a plan of measures, which would lay me under the necessity of bringing this point before you ? It was so far from being my inclination, that nothing short of a sense of my duty to the King, and the obligations I am under to consult your true interest, could have compelled me to it.

Gentlemen of the Council, and
  Gentlemen of the House of Representatives,

We all profess to be the loyal and dutiful subjects of the King of Great Britain. His Majesty considers the British empire as one entire dominion, subject to one supreme legislative power ; a due submission to which, is essential to the maintenance of the rights, liberties and privileges of the several parts of this dominion. We have abundant evidence of his Majesty's tender and impartial regard to the rights of his subjects ; and I am authorised to say, that " his Majesty will most graciously approve of every constitutional measure that may contribute to the peace, the happiness, and prosperity of his colony of Massachusetts Bay, and which may have the effect to shew to the world, that he has no wish beyond that of reigning in the hearts and affections of his people."

T. HUTCHINSON.

ANSWER

OF THE COUNCIL TO THE SPEECH OF GOVERNOR HUTCHINSON, OF FEBRUARY SIXTEENTH ......FEBRUARY 25, 1773.

May it please your Excellency,

As a small part only of your Excellency's last speech to both Houses, is addressed to the Board, there are but a few clauses on which we shall remark.

With regard to the disorders that have arisen, your Excellency and the Board, have assigned different causes. The cause you are pleased to assign, together with the disorders themselves, we suppose to be effects, arising from the stamp act, and certain other acts of Parliament. If we were not mistaken in this, which you do not assert, it so far seems to invalidate what is said in your speech, on that head.

We have taken notice of this only, because it stands connected with another matter, on which we would make a few further observations. What we refer to, is the general nature of supreme authority. We have already offered reasons, in which your Excellency seems to acquiesce, to shew that, though the term *supreme*, sometimes carries with it the idea of *unlimited* authority, it cannot, in that sense, be applied to that which is human. What is usually denominated the supreme authority of a nation, must nevertheless be limited in its acts to the objects that are properly or constitutionally cognizable by it. To illustrate our meaning, we beg leave to quote a passage from your speech, at the opening of the session, where your Excellency says, " so much of the spirit of liberty breathes through all parts of the English constitution, that, although from the nature of government, there must be one supreme authority over the whole, yet, this constitution will admit of subordinate powers, with legislative and executive authority, greater or less, according to local and other circumstances." This is very true, and implies that the legislative and executive authority granted to the subordinate powers, should extend and operate, as far as the grant allows; and that, if it does not exceed the limits prescribed to it, and no forfeiture be incurred, the supreme power has no rightful authority to take away or diminish it, or to substitute its own acts, in cases wherein the acts of the subordinate power can, according to its constitution, operate. To suppose the contrary, is to suppose, that it has no property in the privileges granted to it; for, if it holds them at the will of the supreme power, which it must do, by the above supposition, it can have no property in them. Upon which principle, which involves the contradiction, that what is granted, is, in reality, not granted, no subordinate power can exist. But, as in fact, the two powers are not incompatible, and do subsist together, each restraining its acts to their constitutional objects, can we not from hence, see how the supreme power may supervise, regulate, and make general laws for the kingdom, without interfering with the privileges of the subordinate powers within it? And also, see how it may extend its care and protection to its colonies, without injuring their constitutional rights? What has been here said, concerning supreme authority, has no reference to the manner in which it has been, in fact, exercised; but is wholly confined to its general nature. And, if it conveys any just idea of it, the inferences that have been, at any time, deduced from it, injurious to the rights of the colonists, are not well founded; and have, probably, arisen from a misconception of the nature of that authority.

Your Excellency represents us, as introducing a number of authorities, merely to shew, that "all taxes upon English subjects, must be levied by virtue of the act, not of the King alone, but in conjunction with the Lords and Commons;" and, are pleased to add, that "you should very readily have allowed it; and you should as readily have allowed, that all other acts of legislation, must be passed by the same joint authority, and not by the King alone." Your Excellency "would have saved us the trouble of all those authorities;" and, on our part, we should have been as willing to have saved your Excellency the trouble of dismembering our argument, and from thence, taking occasion to represent it in a disadvantageous light, or rather, totally destroying it.

In justice to ourselves, it is necessary to recapitulate that argument, adduced to prove the inhabitants of this province are not, constitutionally, subject to Parliamentary taxation. In order thereto, we recurred to Magna Charta, and other authorities. And the argument abridged, stands thus: that, from those authorities, it appears an essential part of the English constitution, "that no tallage, or aid, or tax, shall be laid or levied, without the good will and assent of the freemen of the commonalty of the realm." That, from common law, and the province charter, the inhabitants of this province are clearly entitled to all the rights of free and natural subjects, within the realm. That, among those rights, must be included the essential one just mentioned, concerning aids and taxes; and therefore, that no aids or taxes can be levied on us, constitutionally, without our own consent, signified by our Representatives. From whence, the conclusion is clear, that therefore, the inhabitants of this province are not, constitutionally, subject to Parliamentary taxation.

We did not bring those authorities to shew the tax acts, or any other acts of Parliament, in order to their validity, must have the concurrence of King, Lords, and Commons; but to shew, that it has been, at least from the time of Magna Charta, an essential right of free subjects within the realm, to be free from all taxes, but such as were laid with their own consent. And it was proper to shew this, as the rights and liberties, granted by the province charter, were to be equally extensive, to all intents and purposes, with those enjoyed by free and natural subjects within the realm. Therefore, to shew our own right in relation to taxes, it was necessary to shew the rights of freemen within the realm, in relation to them; and for this purpose, those authorities were brought, and not impertinently, as we humbly apprehend. Nor have we seen reason to change our sentiments with respect to this matter, or any other contained in our answer to your Excellency's speech.

In the last clause of your speech, your Excellency informs the two Houses, " you are authorised to say, that his Majesty will most graciously approve of every constitutional measure, that may contribute to the peace, the happiness and prosperity of his colony of Massachusetts Bay." We have the highest sense of his Majesty's goodness in his gracious disposition to approve of such measures, which, as it includes his approbation of the constitutional rights of his subjects of this colony, manifests his inclination to protect them in those rights; and to remove the incroachments that have been made upon them. Of this act of royal goodness, they are not wholly unworthy, as in regard to loyalty, duty, and affection to his Majesty, they stand among the foremost of his faithful subjects.

[The committee who prepared this answer, were, Mr. Bowdoin, Col. Otis, Mr. Dexter, Col. Ward, and Mr. Spooner.]

ANSWER

OF THE HOUSE OF REPRESENTATIVES TO THE SPEECH OF THE
GOVERNOR, OF FEBRUARY SIXTEENTH......MARCH 2, 1773.

May it please your Excellency,

In your speech, at the opening of the present session, your Excellency expressed your displeasure, at some late proceedings of the town of Boston, and other principal towns in the province. And, in another speech to both Houses, we have your repeated exceptions at the same proceedings, as being " unwarrantable," and of a dangerous nature and tendency; " against which, you thought yourself bound to call upon us to join with you in bearing a proper testimony." This House have not discovered any principles advanced by the town of Boston, that are unwarrantable by the constitution; nor does it appear to us, that they have " invited every other town and district in the province, to adopt their principles." We are fully convinced, that it is our duty to bear our testimony against " innovations, of a dangerous nature and tendency;" but, it is clearly our opinion, that it is the indisputable right of all, or any of his Majesty's subjects, in this province, regularly and orderly to meet together, to state the grievances they labor under; and, to propose, and unite in such constitutional measures, as they shall judge necessary or proper, to obtain redress. This right has been frequently exercised by his Majesty's subjects within the realm; and, we do not recollect an instance, since the happy revolution, when the two Houses of Parliament have been called upon to discountenance, or bear their testimony against it, in a speech from the throne.

Your Excellency is pleased to take notice of some things, which we " allege," in our answer to your first speech; and, the observation you make, we must confess, is as natural, and undeniably true, as any one that could have been made; that, " if our foundation shall fail us in every part of it, the fabric we have raised upon it, must certainly fall." You think this foundation will fail us; but, we wish your Excellency had condescended to a consideration of what we have " adduced in support of our principles." We might then, perhaps, have had some things offered for our conviction, more than bare affirmations; which, we must beg to be excused, if we say, are far from being sufficient, though they came with your Excellency's authority, for which, however, we have a due regard.

Your Excellency says, that, " as English subjects, and agreeable to the doctrine of the feudal tenure, all our lands are held mediately, or immediately, of the Crown." We trust, your Excellency does not mean to introduce the feudal system in its perfection;

which, to use the words of one of our greatest historians, was " a state of perpetual war, anarchy, and confusion, calculated solely for defence against the assaults of any foreign power; but, in its provision for the interior order and tranquillity of society, extremely defective. A constitution, so contradictory to all the principles that govern mankind, could never be brought about, but by foreign conquest or native usurpation." And, a very celebrated writer calls it, " that most iniquitous and absurd form of government, by which human nature was so shamefully degraded." This system of iniquity, by a strange kind of fatality, " though originally formed for an encampment, and for military purposes only, spread over a great part of Europe ;" and, to serve the purposes of oppression and tyranny, " was adopted by princes, and wrought into their civil constitutions ;" and, aided by the canon law, calculated by the Roman Pontiff, to exalt himself above all that is called God, it prevailed to the almost utter extinction of knowledge, virtue, religion, and liberty from that part of the earth. But, from the time of the reformation, in proportion as knowledge, which then darted its rays upon the benighted world, increased, and spread among the people, they grew impatient under this heavy yoke ; and the most virtuous and sensible among them, to whose steadfastness, we, in this distant age and climate, are greatly indebted, were determined to get rid of it ; and, though they have in a great measure subdued its power and influence in England, they have never yet totally eradicated its principles.

Upon these principles, the King claimed an absolute right to, and a perfect estate in, all the lands within his dominions ; but, how he came by this absolute right and perfect estate, is a mystery which we have never seen unravelled, nor is it our business or design, at present, to inquire. He granted parts or parcels of it to his friends, the great men, and they granted lesser parcels to their tenants. All, therefore, derived their right and held their lands, upon these principles, mediately or immediately of the King ; which Mr. Blackstone, however, calls, " in reality, a mere fiction of our English tenures."

By what right, in nature and reason, the christian princes in Europe, claimed the lands of heathen people, upon a discovery made by any of their subjects, is equally mysterious. Such, however, was the doctrine universally prevailing, when the lands in America were discovered ; but, as the people of England, upon those principles, held all the lands they possessed, by grants from the King, and the King had never granted the lands in America to them, it is certain they could have no sort of claim to them. Upon the principles advanced, the lordship and dominion, like that of the lands in England, was in the King solely ; and a right from thence accrued to him, of disposing such territories, under such tenure, and for such services to be performed, as the King or Lord thought proper. But how the grantees became subjects of England, that is, the supreme authority of the Parliament, your Excellency has not explained to us. We conceive that upon the feudal principles, all power is in the King; they afford us no idea of Parliament. " The Lord was in early times, the Legislator and Judge over all his feudatories," says Judge Blackstone. By the struggle for liberty in England, from the days of King John, to the last happy revolution, the constitution has been gradually changing for the better ; and upon the more rational principles, that all men. by nature, are in a state of equality in respect of jurisdiction and dominion, power in England has been more equally divided. And thus, also. in America, though we hold our lands agreeably to the feudal principles of the King ; yet our predecessors wisely took care to enter into compact with the King, that power here should also be equally divided, agreeable to the original fundamental principles of the English constitution, declared in Magna Charta, and other laws and statutes of England, made to confirm them.

Your Excellency says, " you can by no means concede to us that it is now, or was, when the plantations were first granted, the prerogative of the Kings of England, to constitute a number of new governments, altogether independent of the sovereign authority of the English empire." By the feudal principles, upon which you say " all the grants which have been made of America, are founded, the constitutions of the Emperor, have the force of law." If our government be considered as merely feudatory, we are subject to the King's absolute will, and there is no authority of Parliament, as the sovereign authority of the British empire. Upon these principles, what could hinder the King's constituting a number of independent governments in America ? That King Charles the I. did actually set up a government in this colony, conceding to it powers of making and executing laws, without any reservation to the English Parliament, of authority to make future laws binding therein, is a fact which your Excellency has not disproved, if you have denied it. Nor have you shewn that the Parliament or nation objected to it ; from whence we have inferred that it was an acknowledged right. And we cannot conceive, why the King has not the same right to alienate and dispose of countries acquired by the discovery of his subjects, as he has to "restore, upon a treaty of peace, countries which have been acquired in war," carried on at the charge of the nation; or to " sell and deliver up any part of his dominions to a foreign Prince or state, against the general sense of the nation ;" which is " an act of power," or prerogative, which your Excellency allows. You tell us, that, " when any new countries are discovered by English subjects, according to the general law and usage of nations, they become part of the state. The law of nations is, or ought to be, founded on the law of reason. It was the saying of Sir Edwin Sandis, in the great case of the union of the realm of

Scotland with England, which is applicable to our present purpose, that " there being no precedent for this case in the law, the law is deficient ; and the law being deficient, recourse is to be had to custom ; and custom being insufficient, we must recur to natural reason ;" the greatest of all authorities, which, he adds, " is the law of nations." The opinions, therefore, and determinations of the greatest Sages and Judges of the law in the Exchequer Chamber, ought not to be considered as decisive or binding, in our present controversy with your Excellency, any further, than they are consonant to natural reason. If, however, we were to recur to such opinions and determinations, we should find very great authorities in our favor, to show, that the statutes of England are not binding on those who are not represented in Parliament there. The opinion of Lord Coke, that Ireland was bound by statutes of England, wherein they were named, if compared with his other writings, appears manifestly to be grounded upon a supposition, that Ireland had, by an act of their own, in the reign of King John, consented to be thus bound ; and, upon any other supposition, this opinion would be against reason ; for consent only gives human laws their force. We beg leave, upon what your Excellency has observed of the colony becoming a part of the state, to subjoin the opinions of several learned civilians, as quoted by a very able lawyer in this country. " Colonies," says Puffendorf, " are settled in different methods ; for, either the colony continues a part of the Commonwealth it was set out from, or else is obliged to pay a dutiful regard to the mother Commonwealth, and to be in readiness to defend and vindicate its honor, and so is united by a sort of unequal confederacy ; or, lastly, is erected into a separate Commonwealth, and assumes the same rights, with the state it descended from." And, King Tullius, as quoted by the same learned author, from Grotius, says, " we look upon it to be neither truth nor justice, that mother cities, ought, of necessity, and by the law of nature, to rule over the colonies."

Your Excellency has misinterpreted what we have said, " that no country, by the common law, was subject to the laws or the Parliament, but the realm of England ;" and, are pleased to tell us, " that we have expressed ourselves incautiously." We beg leave to recite the words of the Judges of England, in the before mentioned case, to our purpose. " If a King go out of England with a company of his servants, allegiance remaineth among his subjects and servants, although he be out of his realm, whereto his laws are confined." We did not mean to say, as your Excellency would suppose, that " the common law prescribes limits to the extent of the Legislative power," though, we shall always affirm it to be true, of the law of reason and natural equity. Your Excellency thinks, you have made it appear, that the " colony of Massachusetts Bay is holden as feudatory of the imperial Crown of England ;" and, therefore, you say, " to use the words of a very great authority in a case, in some respects analogous to it," being feudatory, it necessarily follows, that " it is under the government of the King's laws." Your Excellency has not named this authority; but, we conceive his meaning must be, that being feudatory, it is under the government of the King's laws absolutely ; for, as we have before said, the feudal system admits of no idea of the authority of Parliament; and this would have been the case of the colony, but for the compact with the King in the charter.

Your Excellency says, that " persons thus holding under the Crown of England, remain, or become subjects of England," by which, we suppose your Excellency to mean, subject to the supreme authority of Parliament, " to all intents and purposes, as fully, as if any of the royal manors, &c. within the realm, had been granted to them upon the like tenure." We apprehend, with submission, your Excellency is mistaken in supposing that our allegiance is due to the Crown of England. Every man swears allegiance for himself, to his own King, in his natural person. " Every subject is presumed by law to be sworn to the King, which is to his natural person," says Lord Coke. Rep. on Calvin's case. " The allegiance is due to his natural body;" and, he says, " in the reign of Edward II. the Spencers, the father and the son, to cover the treason hatched in their hearts, invented this damnable and damned opinion, that homage and oath of allegiance was more by reason of the King's Crown, that is, of his politic capacity, than by reason of the person of the King ; upon which opinion, they inferred execrable and detestable consequents." The Judges of England, all but one, in the case of the union between Scotland and England, declared, that " allegiance followeth the natural person, not the politic ;" and, " to prove the allegiance to be tied to the body natural of the King, and not to the body politic, the Lord Coke cited the phrases of divers statutes, mentioning our natural liege Sovereign." If, then, the homage and allegiance is not to the body politic of the King, then it is not to him as the head, or any part of that Legislative authority, which your Excellency says, " is equally extensive with the authority of the Crown throughout every part of the dominion ;" and your Excellency's observations thereupon, must fail. The same Judges mention the allegiance of a subject to the Kings of England, who is out of the reach and extent of the laws of England, which is perfectly reconcileable with the principles of our ancestors, quoted before from your Excellency's history, but, upon your Excellency's principles, appears to us to be an absurdity. The Judges, speaking of a subject, say, " although his birth was out of the bounds of the kingdom of England, and out of the reach and extent of the laws of England, yet, if it were within the allegiance of the King of England, &c. Normandy, Aquitain, Gascoign, and other places, within the limits of France, and, consequently, out of the realm or bounds of the kingdom of England, were in subjection to the Kings of England." And the Judges say, "*Rex et Regnum*, be not so relatives, as a King can be King but of one kingdom, which clearly holdeth not, but that his kingly power extending to divers nations and kingdoms, all owe him equal subjection, and are equally born to the benefit of his protection ; and, although he is to govern them by their distinct laws, yet any one of the people coming into the other, is to have the benefit of the laws, wheresoever he cometh." So they are not to be deemed aliens, as your Excellency in your speech supposes, in any of the dominions, all which accords with the principles our ancestors held. " And he is to bear the burden of taxes of the place where he cometh, but living in one, or for his livelihood in one, he is not be taxed in the other, because laws ordain taxes, impositions, and charges, as a discipline of subjection, particularized to every particular nation." Nothing, we think, can be more clear to our purpose than this decision of Judges, perhaps as learned, as ever adorned the English nation, or in favor of America, in her present controversy with the mother state.

Your Excellency says, that, by " our not distinguishing between the Crown of England, and the Kings and Queens of England, in their personal or natural capacities, we have been led into a fundamental error." Upon this very distinction we have availed ourselves. We have said, that our ancestors considered the land, which they took possession of in America, as out of the bounds of the kingdom of England, and out of the reach and extent of the laws of England ; and, that the King also, even in the act of granting the charter, considered the territory as not within the realm ; that the King had an absolute right in himself to dispose of the lands, and that this was not disputed by the nation ; nor could the lands, on any solid grounds, be claimed by the nation ; and, therefore, our ancestors received the lands, by grant, from the King ; and, at the same time, compacted with him, and promised him homage and allegiance, not in his public or politic, but natural capacity only. If it be difficult for us to show how the King acquired a title to this country in his natural capacity, or separate from his relation to his subjects, which we confess, yet we conceive, it will be equally difficult for your Excellency to show how the body politic and nation of England acquired it. Our ancestors supposed it was acquired by neither ; and, therefore, they declared, as we have before quoted from your history, that saving their actual purchase from the natives, of the soil, the dominion, the lordship, and sovereignty, they had in the sight of God and man, no right and title to what they possessed. How much clearer then, in natural reason and equity, must our title be, who hold estates dearly purchased at the expense of our own, as well as our ancestors labor, and defended by them with treasure and blood.

Your Excellency has been pleased to confirm, rather than deny or confute, a piece of history, which, you say, we took from an anonymous pamphlet, and by which you "fear we have been too easily misled." It may be gathered from your own declaration, and other authorities, besides the anonymous pamphlet, that the House of Commons took exception, not at the King's having made an absolute grant of the territory, but at the claim of an exclusive right to the fishery on the banks and sea coast, by virtue of the patent. At this you say, " the House of Commons was alarmed, and a bill was brought in for allowing a free fishery." And, upon this occasion, your Excellency allows, that " one of the Secretaries of State declared, that the plantations were not annexed to the Crown, and so were not within the jurisdiction of Parliament." If we should concede to what your Excellency supposes might possibly, or, " perhaps," be the case, that the Secretary made this declaration, " as his own opinion," the event showed that it was the opinion of the King too ; for it is not to be accounted for upon any other principle, that he would have denied his royal assent to a bill, formed for no other purpose, but to grant his subjects in England, the privilege of fishing on the sea coasts in America. The account published by Sir Ferdinando Gorges himself, of the proceedings of Parliament on this occasion, your Excellency thinks, will remove all doubt, of the sense of the nation, and of the patentees of this patent or charter, in 1620. " This narrative," you say, " has all the appearance of truth and sincerity," which we do not deny ; and, to us, it carries this conviction with it, that " what was objected" in Parliament, was the exclusive claim of fishing only. His imagining that he had satisfied the House, after divers attendances, that the planting a colony was of much more consequence than a simple disorderly course of fishing, is sufficient for our conviction. We know that the nation was at that time alarmed with apprehensions of monopolies ; and, if the patent of New England was presented by the two Houses as a grievance, it did not show, as your Excellency supposes, " the sense they then had of their authority over this new acquired territory," but only their sense of the grievance of a monopoly of the sea.

We are happy to hear your Excellency say, that " our remarks upon, and construction of the words, not repugnant to the laws of England, are much the same with those of the Council." It serves to confirm us in our opinion, in what we take to be the most important matter of difference between your Excellency and the two Houses. After saying, that the statute of 7th and 8th of William and Mary favors the construction of the words, as intending such laws of England as are made more immediately to respect us, you tell us, that " the province Agent, Mr. Dummer, in his much applauded defence, says, that, then a law of the plantations may be said to be repugnant to a law made in Great Britain, when it flatly contradicts it, so far as the law made there, mentions and relates to the plantations." This is plain and obvious to common sense, and, therefore, cannot be denied. But, if your Excellency would read a page or two further in that excellent defence, you will see that he mentions this as the sense of the phrase, as taken from an act of Parliament, rather than as the sense he would choose himself to put upon it; and, he expressly designs to show, in vindication of the charter, that, in that sense of the words, there never was a law made in the plantations repugnant to the laws of Great Britain. He gives another construction, much more likely to be the 'true intent of the words, namely, " that the patentees shall not presume, under color of their particular charters, to make any laws inconsistent with the great charter, and other laws of England, by which the lives, liberties, and properties of Englishmen are secured." This is the sense in which our ancestors understood the words; and, therefore, they are unwilling to conform to the acts of trade, and disregarded them till they made provision to give them force in the colony, by a law of their own; saying, that " the laws of England did not reach America; and those acts were an invasion of their rights, liberties, and properties," because they were not " represented in Parliament." The right of being governed by laws, which were made by persons, in whose election they had a voice, they looked upon as the foundation of English liberties. By the compact with the King, in the charter, they were to be as free in America, as they would have been if they had remained within the realm; and, therefore, they freely asserted, that they " were to be governed by laws made by themselves, and by officers chosen by themselves." Mr. Dummer says, " it seems reasonable enough to think that the Crown," and, he might have added, our ancestors, " intended by this injunction to provide for all its subjects, that they might not be oppressed by arbitrary power; but being still subjects, they should be protected by the same mild laws, and enjoy the same happy government, as if they continued within the realm." And, considering the words of the charter in this light, he looks upon them as designed to be a fence against oppression and despotic power. But the construction which your Excellency puts upon the words, reduces us to a state of vassalage, and exposes us to oppression and despotic power, whenever a Parliament shall see fit to make laws for that purpose, and put them in execution.

We flatter ourselves, that, from the large extracts we have made from your Excellency's history of the colony, it appears evidently, that under both charters, it hath been the sense of the people and of the government, that they were not under the jurisdiction of Parliament. We pray you again to turn to those quotations, and our observations upon them; and we wish to have your Excellncy's judicious remarks. When we adduced that history, to prove that the sentiments of private persons of influence, four or five years after the restoration, were very different from what your Excellency apprehended them to be, when you delivered your speech, you seem to concede to it, by telling us, " it was, as you take it, from the principles imbibed in those times of anarchy, (preceding the restoration,) that they disputed the authority of Parliament ;" but, you add, " the government would not venture to dispute it." We find in the same history, a quotation from a letter of Mr. Stoughton, dated seventeen years after the restoration, mentioning " the country's not taking notice of the acts of navigation, to observe them." And it was, as we take it, after that time, that the government declared, in a letter to their Agents, that they had not submitted to them ; and they ventured to "dispute" the jurisdiction, asserting, that they apprehended the acts to be an invasion of the rights, liberties, and properties of the subjects of his Majesty in the colony, they not being represented in Parliament, and that " the laws of England did not reach America." It very little avails in proof, that they conceded to the supreme authority of Parliament, their telling the Commissioners, " that the act of navigation had for some years before, been observed here; that they knew not of its being greatly violated ; and that, such laws as appeared to be against it, were repealed." It may as truly be said now, that the revenue acts are observed by some of the people of this province ; but it cannot be said that the government and people of this province have conceded, that the Parliament had authority to make such acts to be observed here. Neither does their declaration to the Commissioners, that such laws as appeared to be against the act of navigation, were repealed, prove their concession of the authority of Parliament, by any means, so much as their making provision for giving force to an act of Parliament within this province, by a deliberate and solemn act or law of their own, proves the contrary.

You tell us, that " the government, four or five years before the charter was vacated, more explicitly," that is, than by a conversation with the Commissioners, " acknowledged the authority of Parliament, and voted, that their Governor should take the oath required of him, faithfully to do and perform all matters and things enjoined him by the acts of trade." But does this, may it please your Excellency, show their explicit acknowledgment of the authority of Parliament ? Does it not rather show directly the contrary ? For, what could there be for their vote, or authority, to require him to take the oath already required of him, by the act of Parliament, unless both he, and they, judged that an act of Parliament was not of force sufficient to bind him to take such oath ? We do not deny, but, on the contrary, are fully persuaded, that your Excellency's principles in governments are still of the same with what they appear to be in the history ; for, you there say, that " the passing this law, plainly shows the wrong sense they had of the relation they stood in to England." But we are from hence convinced, that your Excellency, when you wrote the history, was of our mind in this respect, that our ancestors, in passing the law, discovered their opinion, that they were without the jurisdiction of Parliament; for it was upon this principle alone, they shewed the wrong sense they had in your Excellency's opinion, of the relation they stood in to England.

Your Excellency, in your second speech, condescends to point out to us the acts and doings of the General Assembly, which relates to acts of Parliament, which, you think, "demonstrates that they have been acknowledged by the Assembly, or submitted to by the people;" neither of which, in our opinion, shows that it was the sense of the nation, and our predecessors, when they first took possession of this plantation, or colony, by a grant and charter from the Crown, that they were to remain subject to the supreme authority of the English Parliament.

Your Excellency seems chiefly to rely upon our ancestors, after the revolution, "proclaiming King William and Queen Mary, in the room of King James," and taking the oaths to them, "the alteration of the form of oaths, from time to time," and finally, "the establishment of the form, which every one of us has complied with, as the charter, in express terms requires, and makes our duty." We do not know that it has ever been a point in dispute, whether the Kings of England were *ipso facto* Kings in, and over, this colony, or province. The compact was made between King Charles the I. his heirs and successors, and the Governor and company, their heirs and successors. It is easy, upon this principle, to account for the acknowledgment of, and submission to King William and Queen Mary, as successors of Charles the I. in the room of King James; besides, it is to be considered, that the people in the colony, as well as in England, had suffered under the tyrant James, by which, he had alike forfeited his right to reign over both. There had been a revolution here, as well as in England. The eyes of the people here, were upon William and Mary; and the news of their being proclaimed in England, was, as your Excellency's history tells us, "the most joyful news ever received in New England." And, if they were not proclaimed here, "by virtue of an act of the colony," it was, as we think may be concluded from the tenor of your history, with the general or universal consent of the people, as apparently, as if "such act had passed." It is consent alone, that makes any human laws binding; and as a learned author observes, a purely voluntary submission to an act, because it is highly in our favor and for our benefit, is in all equity and justice, to be deemed as not at all proceeding from the right we include in the Legislators, that they, thereby obtain an authority over us, and that ever hereafter, we must obey them of duty. We would observe, that one of the first acts of the General Assembly of this province, since the present charter, was an act, requiring the taking the oaths mentioned in an act of Parliament, to which you refer us. For what purpose was this act of the Assembly passed, if it was the sense of the Legislators that

50

the act of Parliament was in force in the province ? And, at the same time, another act was made for the establishment of other oaths necessary to be taken; both which acts have the royal sanction, and are now in force. Your Excellency says, that when the colony applied to King William for a second charter, they knew the oath the King had taken, which was to govern them according to the statutes in Parliament, and (which your Excellency here omits,) the laws and customs of the same. By the laws and customs of Parliament, the people of England freely debate and consent to such statutes as are made by themselves, or their chosen Representatives. This is a law, or custom, which all mankind may justly challenge as their inherent right. According to this law, the King has an undoubted right to govern us. Your Excellency, upon recollection, surely will not infer from hence, that it was the sense of our predecessors that there was to remain a supremacy in the English Parliament, or a full power and authority to make laws binding upon us, in all cases whatever, in that Parliament where we cannot debate and deliberate upon the necessity or expediency of any law, and, consequently, without our consent ; and, as it may probably happen, destructive of the first law of society, the good of the whole. You tell us, that " after the assumption of all the powers of government, by virtue of the new charter, an act passed for the reviving, for a limited time, all the local laws of the Massachusetts Bay and New Plymouth respectively, not repugnant to the laws of England. And, at the same session, an act passed establishing naval officers, that all undue trading, contrary to an act of Parliament, may be prevented." Among the acts that were then revived, we may reasonably suppose, was that, whereby provision was made to give force to this act of Parliament, in the province. The establishment, therefore, of the naval officers, was to aid the execution of an act of Parliament, for the observance of which, within the colony, the Assembly had before made provision, after free debates, with their own consent, and by their own act.

The act of Parliament, passed in 1741, for putting an end to several unwarrantable schemes, mentioned by your Excellency, was designed for the general good ; and, if the validity of it was not disputed, it cannot be urged as a concession of the supreme authority, to make laws binding on us in all cases whatever. But, if the design of it was for the general benefit of the province, it was, in one respect. at least greatly complained of, by the persons more immediately affected by it ; and to remedy the inconvenience, the Legislative of this province, passed an act, directly militating with it ; which is the strongest evidence, that although they may have submitted. *sub silentio*, to some acts of Parliament, that they conceived might operate for their benefit, they did not conceive themselves bound by any of its acts. which, they judged, would operate to the injury even of individuals.

Your Excellency has not thought proper, to attempt to confute the reasoning of a learned writer on the laws of nature and nations, quoted by us, on this occasion, to shew that the authority of the Legislature does not extend so far as the fundamentals of the constitution. We are unhappy in not having your remarks upon the reasoning of that great man ; and, until it is confuted, we shall remain of the opinion, that the fundamentals of the constitution being excepted from the commission of the Legislators, none of the acts or doings of the General Assembly, however deliberate and solemn, could avail to change them, if the people have not, in very express terms, given them the power to do it ; and, that much less ought their acts and doings, however numerous, which barely refer to acts of Parliament made expressly to relate to us, to be taken as an acknowledgment, that we are subject to the supreme authority of Parliament.

We shall sum up our own sentiments in the words of that learned writer, Mr. Hooker, in his Ecclesiastical Policy, as quoted by Mr. Locke. " The lawful power of making laws to command whole political societies of men, belonging so properly to the same entire societies, that for any prince or potentate of what kind soever, to exercise the same of himself, and not from express commission, immediately and personally received from God, is no better than mere tyranny. Laws, therefore, they are not, which public approbation hath not made so ; for laws human, of what kind soever, are available by consent." " Since men, naturally, have no full and perfect power to command whole politic multitudes of men, therefore, utterly without our consent, we could in such sort, be at no man's commandment living. And to be commanded, we do not consent, when that society, whereof we be a party, hath at any time before consented." We think your Excellency has not proved, either that the colony is a part of the politic society of England, or that it has ever consented that the Parliament of England or Great Britain, should make laws binding upon us, in all cases, whether made expressly to refer to us or not.

We cannot help, before we conclude, expressing our great concern, that your Excellency has thus repeatedly, in a manner, insisted upon our free sentiments on matters of so delicate a nature and weighty importance. The question appears to us, to be no other, than, whether we are the subjects of absolute unlimited power, or of a free government, formed on the principles of the English constitution. If your Excellency's doctrine be true, the people of this province hold their lands of the Crown and people of England ; and their lives, liberties, and properties, are at their disposal, and that, even by compact and their own consent. They were subject to the King as the head *alterius populi* of another people, in whose Legislative they have no voice or interest. They are, indeed, said to have a constitution and a Legislative of their own : but your Excellency has explained it into a mere phantom; limited, controled, superseded, and nullified, at the will of another. Is this the constitution which so charmed our ancestors, that, as your Excellency has informed us, they kept a day of solemn thanksgiving to Almighty God when they received it? And were they men of so little discernment, such children in understanding, as to please themselves with the imagination, that they were blessed with the same rights and liberties which natural born subjects in England enjoyed, when, at the same time, they had fully consented to be ruled and ordered by a Legislative, a thousand leagues distant from them, which cannot be supposed to be sufficiently acquainted with their circumstances, if concerned for their interest, and in which, they cannot be in any sense represented?

[The committee who reported the above, were, Mr. Cushing, (the Speaker,) Mr. S. Adams, Mr. Hancock, Mr. Phillips, Maj. Foster, Col. Bowers, Mr. Hobson, Col. Thayer, and Mr. Denny.]

RESOLUTIONS

OF THE HOUSE OF REPRESENTATIVES, RESPECTING THE SALARIES OF THE
JUSTICES OF THE SUPERIOR COURT, MARCH 3, 1773.

WHEREAS, by an act of the British Parliament, made and passed in the sixth year of his present Majesty's reign, it is declared, that the King, Lords, and Commons, in Parliament assembled, have ever had, and of right ought to have, full power and authority to make laws and statutes, of sufficient force and validity, to bind the colonies and people of America, subjects of the Crown of Great Britain, in all cases whatever; and, afterwards, the same Parliament made and passed an act for levying duties in America, with the express purpose of raising a revenue, and to enable his Majesty to appropriate the same for the necessary charges of the administration of justice, and the support of civil government in such colonies, where it shall be judged necessary, and towards further defraying the expenses of defending, protecting, and securing said dominions: And, his Majesty has been pleased, by virtue of the last mentioned act, to appropriate a part of the revenue, thus raised, against the consent of the people, in providing for the support of the Governor of the province; and from his Excellency's message, of the 4th of February, we cannot but conclude, that provision is made also for the support of the Judges of the Superior Court of Judicature, independent of the grants and acts of the General Assembly, contrary to invariable usage of this province; therefore,

Resolved, That the admitting of any authority to make laws, binding on the people of this province, in all cases whatever, saving the General Court or Assembly, is inconsistent with the spirit of our free constitution, and is repugnant to one of the most essen-. tial clauses in our charter, whereby the inhabitants are entitled to all the liberties of free and natural born subjects, to all intents, constructions, and purposes whatever, as if they had been born within the realm of England. It reduces the people to the absolute will and disposal of a Legislature, in which they can have no voice, and who may make it their interest to oppress and enslave them.

Resolved, That by the royal charter aforesaid, " the General Court or Assembly, hath full power and authority to impose and levy proportionable and reasonable assessments, rates and taxes, upon the estates and persons, of all and every the proprietors and inhabitants of the province, to be issued and disposed of, by warrant, under the hand of the Governor, with the advice and consent of the Council, for his Majesty's service, in the necessary defence and support of the government of the province, and the protection and preservation of the inhabitants there, according to such acts as are, or shall be, in force, within the province." And the making provision for the support of the Governor and Judges, otherwise than by the grants and acts of the General Court, or Assembly, is a violent breach of the most important clause in the charter: the support of government, in which their support is included, being one of the principal purposes, for which the clause was inserted.

And, whereas, the independence, as well as the uprightness of the Judges of the land, is essential to the impartial administration of justice, and one of the best securities of the rights, liberty, and property of the people; therefore,

Resolved, That the making the Judges of the land independent of the grants of the people, and altogether dependent on the Crown, as they will be, if, while they thus hold their commissions during pleasure, they accept of salaries from the Crown, is unconstitutional, and destructive of that security, which every good member of civil society, has a just right to be assured of, under the due execution of the laws; and is directly the reverse of the constitution, and appointment of the Judges in Great Britain.

Resolved, That the dependence of the Judges of the land on the Crown, for their support, tends, at all times, especially, while they hold their commissions during pleasure, to the subversion of justice and equity, and to introduce oppression and despotic power.

Resolved, As the opinion of this House, that while the Justices of the Superior Court hold their commissions during pleasure, any one of them who shall accept of, and depend upon the pleasure of the Crown for his support, independent of the grants and acts of the General Assembly, will discover to the world, that he has not a due sense of the importance of an impartial administration of justice, that he is an enemy to the constitution, and has it in his heart to promote the establishment of an arbitrary government in the province.

———

LETTER

Province of Massachusetts Bay, June 29, 1773.

MY LORD,

THE reestablishment of the union and harmony, which formerly subsisted between Great Britain and her colonies, is earnestly to be wished by the friends of both. As your Lordship is one of them, the two Houses of the Assembly of this province, beg leave to address you. The original causes of the interruption of that union and harmony, may probably be found in the letters sent from hence to administration, and to other gentlemen of influence in Parliament, since the appointment of Sir Francis Bernard to the government of this province. And there is great reason to apprehend, that he and his coadjutors, originally recommended and laid the plans for establishing the American revenue, out of which, they expected large stipends and appointments for themselves, and which, through their instrumentality, has been the occasion of all the evils which have since taken place. When we had humbly addressed his Majesty, and petitioned both Houses of Parliament, representing our grievance, and praying for the repeal of the revenue acts, the like instruments, and probably the same, exerted themselves to prevent those petitions being laid before his Majesty and the Parliament, or to frustrate the prayer of them. Of this, we have just had some new and unexpected evidence, from original letters of Governor Hutchinson and Lieutenant Governor Oliver; in which the former, particularly and expressly, by his letter of the 10th of December, 1768, endeavored, in cooperation with Governor Bernard, to frustrate a petition of a number of the Council, for a repealing of those acts, and to procure his Majesty's censure on the petitions : and the letters of the latter, by the disadvantageous idea conveyed by them, of the two Houses of Assembly, manifestly tended to create a prejudice against any petitions coming from a body of such a character. And his letter of the 11th of May, 1768, in particular, mentions the petitions of the House of Representatives to his Majesty, and their letters to divers noble Lords. with such circumstances as had a tendency to defeat the petition and render the letters of no effect.

It is now manifest, my Lord, what practices and arts have been used, to mislead administration, both in the first proposal of American revenue acts, and in the continuance of them. But when they had lost their force, and there appeared, under the influence of your Lordship, a disposition in Parliament to repeal these acts, his Excellency Governor Hutchinson, in his speech, at the opening of the last session of the General Court, was pleased to throw out new matter for contention and debate; and to call on the two Houses, in such a manner, as amounted to little short of a *challenge* to answer him. Into such a dilemma were they brought by the speech, that they were under a necessity of giving such answers to it as they did, or of having their conduct construed into an acquiescence with the doctrines contained in it, which would have been an implicit acknowledgment, that the province was in a state of subjection, differing very little from slavery. The answers were the effect of necessity; and this necessity occasioned great grief to the two Houses.

The people of this province, my Lord, are true and faithful subjects of his Majesty, and think themselves happy in their connexion with Great Britain. They would rejoice at the restoration of the harmony and good will that once subsisted between the parent state and them. But it is in vain to expect this happiness, during the continuance of their grievances, and while their charter rights, one after another, are wrested from them. Among these rights, is the supporting of the officers of the Crown, by grants from the Assembly; and in an especial manner, the supporting of the Judges in the same way, on whose judgment the province is dependent, in the most important cases of life, liberty and property. If warrants have not yet been, or if they already have been issued, we earnestly beg the favor of your Lordship's interposition to suppress, or recal them.

If your Lordship should condescend to ask, what are the measures of restoring the harmony so much desired, we should answer, in a word, that we are humbly of opinion, if things were brought to the general state, in which they stood at the conclusion of the late war, it would restore the happy harmony, which, at that time subsisted. Your Lordship's appointment to be principal Secretary of State, for the American department, has given the colonies the highest satisfaction. They think it a happy omen; and that it will be productive of American tranquillity, consistent with their rights, as British subjects. The two Houses humbly hope for your Lordship's influence to bring about such a happy event; and, in the mean time, they can, with full confidence, rely on your Lordship, that the machinations of Sir Francis Bernard, and other known enemies of the peace of Great Britain and her colonies, will not be suffered to prevent or delay it.

This letter, which has been agreed upon by both Houses, is, in their name, and by their order, signed and transmitted to your

Lordship, by, my Lord, your Lordship's most obedient and very humble servant,   THOMAS FLUCKER, *Secretary.*

===

[The Governor's speech, at the opening of the session, on the last Wednesday of May, 1773, related entirely to the settling of the boundary line, between Massachusetts and New York. The Counsellors chosen, were all approved, except Jerathmeel Bowers, William Phillips, and John Adams.]

===

RESOLUTIONS.

On motion of Mr. S. Adams, the following Resolutions were adopted, 110 to 4, May 28, 1773.

WHEREAS the Speaker hath communicated to this House, a letter from the truly respectable House of Burgesses, in his Majesty's ancient colony of Virginia, enclosing a copy of the resolves entered into by them, on the 12th of March last, and requesting that a committee of this House may be appointed, to communicate, from time to time, with a corresponding committee, then appointed by the said House of Burgesses, in Virginia:

And, whereas this House is fully sensible of the necessity and importance of a union of the several colonies in America, at a time when it clearly appears, that the rights and liberties of all are systematically invaded; in order that the joint wisdom of the whole, may be employed in consulting their common safety:

Resolved, That this House have a very grateful sense of the obligations they are under to the House of Burgesses, in Virginia, for the vigilance, firmness and wisdom, which they have discovered, at all times, in support of the rights and liberties of the American colonies; and do heartily concur with them in their said judicious and spirited resolves.

Resolved, That a standing committee of correspondence and inquiry, be appointed, to consist of fifteen Members, any eight of whom, to be a quorum; whose business it shall be, to obtain the most early and authentic intelligence, of all such acts and resolutions of the British Parliament, or proceedings of administrations as may relate to, or affect the British colonies in America; and to keep up, and maintain, a correspondence and communication with our sister colonies, respecting these important considerations; and the result of such their proceedings, from time to time, to lay before the House.

Resolved, That it be an instruction to the said committee, that they do, without delay, inform themselves particularly of the principles and authority, on which was constituted a court of inquiry, held in Rhode Island; said to be vested with powers to transport persons accused of offences, committed in America, to places beyond the seas, to be tried.*

Resolved, That the said committee be further instructed to prepare and report to this House, a draft of a very respectful answer to the letter, received from the Speaker of the honorable House of Burgesses, of Virginia; and another, to a letter received from the Speaker of the honorable House of Representatives, of the colony of Rhode Island; also, a circular letter to the Speakers of the several other Houses of Assembly, on this continent; enclosing the aforesaid resolves, and requesting them to lay the same before their respective Assemblies, in confidence, that they will readily and cheerfully comply with the wise and salutary resolves of the House of Burgesses, in Virginia.

[The committee of correspondence, chosen in pursuance of the resolves aforesaid, were, Mr. Cushing, (the Speaker,) Mr. S. Adams, Hon. John Hancock, Mr. William Phillips, Capt. William Heath, Hon. Joseph Hawley, James Warren, Esq. R. Derby, Jun: Esq. Mr. Elbridge Gerry, J. Bowers, Esq. Jedediah Foster, Esq. Daniel Leonard, Esq. Capt. T. Gardner, Capt. Jonathan Greenleaf, and J. Prescott, Esq.]

LETTER

FROM THE HOUSE OF REPRESENTATIVES, ADDRESSED TO THE SPEAKERS OF THE SEVERAL HOUSES OF ASSEMBLY, ON THE CONTINENT.

Boston, June 3, 1773.

SIR,

THE House of Representatives, of this province, being earnestly attentive to the controversy between Great Britain and the colonies, and considering that the authority claimed and exercised by Parliament, on the one side, and by the General Assemblies of this continent, on the other, greatly militates, and is productive of this unhappy contention, think it of the utmost importance to the welfare of both, and particularly of the colonies, that the constitutional powers and rights of each, be inquired into, delineated and fully ascertained.

---

* In consequence of burning the Gaspee, a British armed vessel, which had greatly harrassed the navigation of Rhode Island, a court of inquiry was appointed, under the great seal of England, to be holden at Newport. They met once and again, but finally dissolved, without doing any thing important. It was supposed, that many persons, suspected of burning the Gaspee, would have been sent to England for trial.

51

That his Majesty's subjects of America, are entitled to the same rights and liberties as those of Great Britain, and that these ought, in justice, by the constitution, to be as well guaranteed and secured, to the one, as to the other, are too apparent to be denied.

It is, by this House, humbly conceived, to be likewise undeniable, that the authority assumed, and now forcibly exercised by Parliament, over the colonies, is utterly subversive of freedom in the latter; and that, while his Majesty's loyal subjects in America, have the mortification, daily, to see new abridgements of their rights and liberties, they have not the least security for those, which at present remain. Were the colonists only affected by a Legislative, subject to their control, they would, even then, have no other security than belongs to them by the laws of nature, and the English constitution; but, should the authority, now claimed by Parliament, be fully supported by power, or submitted to by the colonies, it appears to this House, that there will be an end to liberty in America; and that the colonists will then change the name of freemen, for that of slaves.

In order to adjust and settle these important concerns, the free and magnanimous Burgesses of Virginia, have proposed a method for uniting the councils of its sister colonies; and it appearing to this House, to be a measure very wise and salutary, is cheerfully received and heartily adopted.

With great respect for your honorable Assembly, and in confidence, that a matter which so nearly affects the safety of each colony, will be assisted by its wise councils, permit this House to enclose a copy of resolutions, lately entered into here; and to request you to communicate the same at a convenient opportunity.

THOMAS CUSHING, *Speaker.*

[June 2, 1773, the galleries having been cleared, by a vote of the House, Mr. S. Adams observed, "that he perceived the minds of the people were much agitated by a report, that letters, of an extraordinary nature, had been written and sent to England, greatly to the prejudice of this province: that he had obtained certain letters, with different signatures, with the consent of the gentleman, from whom he received them, that they should be read in the House, under certain restrictions, namely, that the said letters be neither printed nor copied, in whole, or in part,"—and he accordingly offered them for the consideration of the House. A vote then passed, that the letters be read; and they were read accordingly: being signed, Thomas Hutchinson, Andrew Oliver, Charles Paxton, Robert Auchmuty, &c. The whole House was then resolved into a committee, to take said letters into consideration, and the House adjourned to the afternoon. Mr. Hancock, from the committee of the whole House, reported, that the committee were of opinion, the tendency and design of the said letters, was to over-throw the constitution of this government, and to introduce arbitrary power into the province ; and the report was accepted, 101 to 5.   A committee of nine, was thereupon chosen, to consider what was proper to be done, in reference to the letters aforesaid ; and the Speaker, (Mr. Cushing,) Mr. Adams, Mr. Hancock, Mr. Gorham, Mr. Pickering, Maj. Hawley, Col. Warren, Mr. Payne and Maj. Foster, were chosen.]

MESSAGE

FROM THE GOVERNOR TO THE HOUSE OF REPRESENTATIVES,

JUNE 3, 1773.

Gentlemen of the House of Representatives,

I AM informed, that certain private letters, said to have been wrote by me, to a gentleman in England, lately deceased, were yesterday laid before your House ; and, that you have come into a resolution, or vote, that they tend to subvert the constitution.

I have never wrote any public or private letter, with such intention, and am not conscious of any letter, which can have such an effect. Before you take any further proceedings, I must desire, that a transcript of the proceedings of yesterday, be laid before me, and that I may be informed to what letters they refer, in order to my considering what steps are proper for me to take upon the occasion.   T. HUTCHINSON.

MESSAGE

FROM THE HOUSE OF REPRESENTATIVES TO THE GOVERNOR,

JUNE 5, 1773.

May it please your Excellency,

IN answer to your message, of the third of June, the House of Representatives have resolved, that the dates of certain letters, now before them, referred to in the message, together with a transcript of the proceedings of the House thereon, as requested by your Excellency, be laid before you.

And, as your Excellency has been pleased, in your message to say, that you have never wrote any public or private letter, with an intention to subvert the constitution, it is the desire of this House, that your Excellency would be pleased to order, that copies be laid before us, of such letters as your Excellency has written, of those dates, relating to the public affairs of this province; together with such other letters, as your Excellency shall think proper.

[The committee, who prepared this message, were, Mr. Hancock, Mr. Adams, Mr. Gerry, Mr. Pickering and Maj. Hawley.]

MESSAGE

FROM THE GOVERNOR TO THE HOUSE OF REPRESENTATIVES, JUNE 9, 1773.

Gentlemen of the House of Representatives,

By your committee, you have laid before me the dates of six original letters, with my signature to them, which have been brought into your House, and read, together with other letters from several other persons. You have also laid before me, an extract from the journal of your proceedings, by which it appears, you are of opinion, that the tendency and design of the letters, thus read, was to overthrow the constitution of this government, and to introduce arbitrary power into the province.

I find, by the dates of the letters with my signature, that, if genuine, they must be private letters, wrote to a gentleman in London, since deceased; that all, except the last, were wrote many months before I came to the chair; that they were wrote, not only with that confidence, which is always implied in a friendly correspondence, by private letters, but that they are expressly confidential; notwithstanding which, they contain nothing more respecting the constitution of the colonies in general, than what is contained in my speeches to the Assembly, and what I have published in a more extensive manner to the world; and there is not one passage in them, which was ever intended to respect, or which, as I am well assured, the gentleman to whom they were wrote, ever understood to respect, the particular constitution of this government, as derived from the charter.

I am at a loss for what purpose you desire the copies of my letters, the originals of which, you have in your hands. If it is with a view to make them public, the originals are more proper for that purpose than the copies. I think it would be very improper, and out of character in me, to lay my private letters before you, at your request; my public ones, I am restrained from laying before you, without express leave from his Majesty. Thus much, however, I may assure you, that it has not been the tendency and design of them to subvert the constitution of this government, but rather to preserve it entire; and I have reason to think, they have not been altogether ineffectual to that purpose.

T. HUTCHINSON.

MESSAGE

FROM THE HOUSE OF REPRESENTATIVES TO THE COUNCIL, JUNE 15, 1773.

May it please the Honorable Board,

THERE are certain letters, which have been laid before the House, signed Thomas Hutchinson, Andrew Oliver, Charles Paxton, and Robert Auchmuty, containing matters that nearly affect the interest of this province, and some, particularly refer to the conduct of the honorable Board; therefore, the House have ordered copies of the said letters, to be laid before the honorable Board, that they may take such order thereon, as they shall judge proper. The originals are, at present, in the hands of a committee of the House; but if the Board are desirous of it, they may have them to compare with the copies.

RESOLVES

OF THE HOUSE OF REPRESENTATIVES, RESPECTING THE LETTERS OF THE GOVERNOR, LIEUTENANT GOVERNOR, AND OTHERS, JUNE 16, 1773.

RESOLVED, That the letters, signed Thomas Hutchinson, and those signed Andrew Oliver, now under the consideration of this House, appear to be the genuine letters of the present Governor and Lieutenant Governor of this province, whose hand writing and signatures are well known to many of the Members of this House; and, that they contain aggravated accounts of facts, and misrepresentations; and, that one manifest design of them, was, to represent the matters they treat of, in a light, highly injurious to this province, and the persons against whom they were wrote.

Resolved, That, though the letters aforesaid, signed Thomas Hutchinson, are said. by the Governor, in his message to this House, of June 9th, to be "private letters, wrote to a gentleman in London, since deceased;" and "that all, except the last, were wrote many months before he came to the chair; yet, they were wrote by the present Governor, when he was Lieutenant Governor and Chief Justice of this province, who has been represented abroad, as eminent for his abilities, as for his exalted station ; and was under no official obligation to transmit intelligence of such matters as are contained in said letters ; and, that they, therefore, must be considered, by the person to whom they were sent, as documents of solid intelligence ; and, that this gentleman in London, to whom they were wrote, was then a Member of the British Parliament, and one who was very active in American affairs ; and therefore, that these letters, however secretly wrote, must naturally be supposed to have, and really had, a public operation.

Resolved, That these " private letters," being wrote " with express confidence of secrecy," was only to prevent the contents of them being known here, as appears by said letters ; and this rendered them the more injurious in their tendency, and really insidious.

Resolved, That the letters, signed Thomas Hutchinson, considering the person by whom they were wrote, the matters they expressly contain, the express reference in some of them, for " full intelligence," to Mr. Hallowell, a person deeply interested in the measures so much complained of, and recommendatory notices of divers other persons, whose emoluments arising from our public burdens, might excite them to unfavorable representations of us, the measures they suggest, the temper in which they were wrote, the manner in which they were sent, and the person to whom they were addressed ; had a natural and efficacious tendency to interrupt and alienate the affections of our most gracious Sovereign, King George the III. from this, his loyal and affectionate province; to destroy that harmony and good will between Great Britain and this colony, which every friend to either, would wish to establish ; to excite the resentment of the British administration against this province ; to defeat the endeavors of our agents and friends to serve us, by a fair representation of our state of grievances ; to prevent our humble and repeated petitions from reaching the royal ear of our common Sovereign ; and to produce the severe and destructive measures which have been taken against this province, and others still more so, which have been threatened.

Resolved, That the letters, signed Andrew Oliver, considering the person by whom they were wrote, the matters they expressly contain, the measures they suggest, the temper in which they were wrote, the manner in which they were sent, and the person to whom they were addressed, had a natural and efficacious tendency to interrupt and alienate the affections of our most gracious Sovereign, King George the III. from this, his loyal and affectionate province ; to destroy that harmony and good will between Great Britain and this colony, which every friend to either, would wish to establish ; to excite the resentment of the British administration against this province ; to defeat the endeavors of our agents and friends to serve us, by a fair representation of our state of grievances; to prevent our humble and repeated petitions from having the desired effect; and to produce the severe and destructive measures which have been taken against this province, and others still more so, which have been threatened.

Resolved, As the opinion of this House, that it clearly appears from the letters aforesaid, signed Thomas Hutchinson, and Andrew Oliver, that it was the desire and endeavor of the writers of them, that certain acts of the British Parliament, for raising a revenue in America, might be carried into effect by military force; and by introducing a fleet and army into his Majesty's loyal province, to intimidate the minds of his subjects here, and prevent every constitutional measure to obtain the repeal of those acts, so justly esteemed a grievance to us, and to suppress the very spirit of freedom.

Resolved, That it is the opinion of this House, that, as the salaries lately appointed for the Governor, Lieutenant Governor, and Judges of this province, directly repugnant to the charter, and subversive of justice, are founded on this revenue; and, as those letters were wrote with a design, and had a tendency to promote and support that revenue, therefore, there is great reason to suppose the writers of those letters, were well knowing to, suggested, and promoted the enacting said revenue acts, and the establishments founded on the same.

Resolved, That while the writer of these letters, signed Thomas Hutchinson, has been thus exerting himself, by his " secret confidential correspondence," to introduce measures, destructive of our constitutional liberty, he has been practising every method among the people of this province, to fix in their minds an exalted opinion of his warmest affection for them, and his unremitted endeavors to promote their best interest at the Court of Great Britain.

Resolved, As the opinion of this House, that by comparing these letters, signed Thomas Hutchinson, with those, signed Andrew Oliver, Charles Paxton, and Nathan Rogers, and, considering what has since, in fact taken place, conformable thereto, that it is manifest, there has been, for many years past, measures contemplated, and a plan formed, by a set of men, born and educated among us, to raise their own fortunes, and advance themselves to posts of honor and profit, not only to the destruction of the charter and constitution of this province, but at the expense of the rights and liberties of the American colonies. And, it is further the opinion of this House, that the said persons have been some of the chief instruments in the introduction of a military force into the province, to carry their plans into execution; and, therefore, they have been, not only greatly instrumental of disturbing the peace and harmony of the government, and causing, and promoting great discord and animosities, but are justly chargeable with the great corruption of morals, and all that confusion, misery and bloodshed, which have been the natural effects of the introduction of troops.

Whereas, for many years past, measures have been taken by the British administration, very grievous to the good people of this province, which this House have now reason to suppose, were promoted, if not originally suggested, by the writers of these letters; and many efforts have been made, by the people, to obtain the redress of their grievances:

Resolved, That it appears to this House, that the writers of these letters, have availed themselves of disorders, that naturally arise in a free government, under such oppressions, as arguments to prove, that it was, originally, necessary such measures should have been taken, and that they should now be continued and increased.

Whereas, in the letter, signed Charles Paxton, dated Boston Harbor, June 20, 1768, it is expressly declared, that, " unless we have immediately two or three regiments, it is the opinion of all the friends of government, that Boston will be in open rebellion:"

Resolved, That this is a most wicked and injurious representation, designed to inflame the minds of his Majesty's Ministers and the nation, and to excite in the breast of our Sovereign, a jealousy of his loyal subjects of said town, without the least grounds therefor, as enemies of his Majesty's person and government.

Whereas certain letters, signed by two private persons, viz.: Thomas Moffat, and George Rome, have been laid before the House, which letters contain many matters, highly injurious to government and to the national peace:

Resolved, That it has been the misfortune of this government, from the earliest period of it, from time to time, to be secretly traduced, and maliciously represented to the British Ministry, by persons, who were neither friendly to this colony, nor to the English constitution:

Resolved, That the House have just reason to complain of it, as a very great grievance, that the humble petitions and remonstrances of the Commons of this province, are not allowed to reach the hand of our most gracious Sovereign, merely because they are presented by an agent, to whose appointment, the Governor, with whom our chief dispute may subsist, doth not consent; while the partial and inflammatory letters of individuals, who are greatly interested in the revenue acts, and the measures taken to carry them into execution, have been laid before administration, attended to, and determined upon, not only to the injury of the reputation of the people, but to the depriving them of their invaluable rights and liberties.

Whereas, this House are humbly of opinion, that his Majesty will judge it to be incompatible with the interest of his Crown, and the peace and safety of the good people of this, his loyal province, that persons should be continued in places of high trust and authority in it, who are known to have, with great industry, though secretly, endeavored to undermine, alter, and overthrow the constitution of the province : therefore,

Resolved, That this House is bound, in duty to the King and their constituents, humbly to remonstrate to his Majesty, the conduct of his Excellency Thomas Hutchinson, Esquire, Governor, and the Honorable Andrew Oliver, Esquire, Lieutenant Governor of this province ; and to pray that his Majesty would be pleased to remove them forever from the government thereof.

MESSAGE

FROM THE GOVERNOR TO THE HOUSE OF REPRESENTATIVES,
JUNE 21, 1773.

Gentlemen of the House of Representatives,

I PERCEIVE, with concern, for the honor and reputation of the. province, that you have passed, and caused to be published, a number of votes or resolves, in which you have, in an unparalleled and most injurious manner, determined the intentions and designs of the Governor, in certain private letters, wrote several years since, the originals of which, as alleged, have, by some means or other, come into your possession.

Whilst I was the subject of the debates, occasioned by the letters, I did not think it advisable, to give you any interruption. Now, that you have come to your determination, I must remind you, that you are near to the close of the fourth week of the session, and, that you have done little, or none, of the business of the Court.

To prevent all unnecessary burden upon your constituents, by too long a session, I must desire you to give despatch to such matters as lie before you, or are proper to be acted upon by you.

T. HUTCHINSON.

MESSAGE

FROM THE HOUSE OF REPRESENTATIVES TO THE GOVERNOR,
JUNE 24, 1773.

May it please your Excellency,

THE House have maturely considered your message, of the 21st instant, and fully apprehend, that had we not passed, and

52

caused to be published, the votes and resolves upon the letters, referred to in your message, we should have betrayed a total want of a proper attention, not only to the honor and reputation of the province, but the true interest of our constituents, however unparalleled and injurious your Excellency, is pleased to represent them ; and, we can assure your Excellency that this House came possessed of those letters in a manner truly honorable. Had your Excellency duly considered that those letters contained matters of a very extraordinary nature, and that we have already passed upon divers matters of a public, as well as a private nature, you would have judged it needless to have reminded us, that we are near the close of the fourth week of the session : We are, however, answerable to none but our constituents, for the time we spend in doing that part of the public business, which they have chosen us to transact; and, we are clearly of opinion, that we are, at present, the sole judges of the time that is necessary for us to take, in deliberating and determining upon all matters, that may properly come under our consideration.

EXTRACT

FROM THE GOVERNOR'S MESSAGE TO THE TWO HOUSES, JANUARY 26, 1774.

Gentlemen of the Council, and

    Gentlemen of the House of Representatives,

THE judicial proceedings of the Governor and Council, as the Supreme Court of Probate, and, as the Court for determining in cases of marriage and divorce, having been impeded in many instances, where the opinion of the Governor has been different from that of the majority of Councellors present, the Governor having always considered his consent as necessary to every judicial act. In the year 1771, I stated the arguments, as well against, as for the claim of the Governor ; and his Majesty having been pleased to order the case thus stated, to be laid before the Lords of his Majesty's most honorable Privy Council, I am now able to inform you, that it has been signified to me, to be his Majesty's pleasure, that I do acquiesce in the determination of the majority of Councellors present, voting as a Court for proving wills and administration, and deciding controversies concerning marriage and divorce, although I should differ in opinion from that majority. This order more immediately respects the Council ; nevertheless, the tender regard which his Majesty has shewn for the interest and convenience of his subjects, in a construction of the charter, different from what had been made by all his Governors, ever since its first publication, make it proper for me to communicate the order to both Houses.

I am required to signify to you his Majesty's disapprobation of the appointment of committees of correspondence, in various instances, which sit and act, during the recess of the General Court, by prorogation.   T. HUTCHINSON.

EXTRACT

FROM THE ANSWER OF THE HOUSE OF REPRESENTATIVES TO THE GOVERNOR, FEBRUARY 5, 1774.

May it please your Excellency,

It affords great satisfaction to this House, to find, that his Majesty has been pleased to put an end to an undue claim, heretofore made by the Governors of this province, grounded upon a supposition, that the consent of the chair was necessary to the validity of the judicial acts of the Governor and Council. Whereby their proceedings, when sitting as the Supreme Court of Probate, and as the Court for determining in cases of marriage and divorce, have been so often impeded. The royal order, that the Governor shall acquiesce in the determination of the majority of the Council, respects not the Council only, but the body of the people of this province. And his Majesty has therein shewed his regard to justice, as well as the interest and convenience of his subjects, in rescuing a clause in the charter, from a construction, which, in the opinion of this House, was repugnant to the express meaning and intent of the charter, inconsistent with the idea of a Court of Justice, and dangerous to the rights and property of the subject.

Your Excellency is pleased to inform the two Houses, that you are required to signify to them his Majesty's disapprobation of the appointment of committees of correspondence, in various instances, which sit and act, during the recess of the General Court by prorogation. You are not pleased to explain to us the grounds and reasons of his Majesty's disapprobation; until we shall have such explanation laid before us, a full answer to this part of your speech will not be expected from us. We cannot, however, omit saying upon this occasion, that while the common rights of the American subjects, continue to be attacked in various instances, and, at times when the several Assemblies are not sitting, it is highly necessary that they should correspond with each other, in order to unite in the most effectual means for the obtaining a redress of their grievances. And, as the sitting of the General Assemblies in this, and most of the colonies, depends upon the pleasure of the Governors, who hold themselves under the direction of administration, it is to be expected, that the meeting of the Assemblies will be so ordered, as that the intention proposed by a correspondence between them, will be impracticable, but by committees, to sit and act, in the recess. We would, moreover, observe, that as it has been the practice for years past, for the Governor, and Lieutenant Governor of this province, and other Officers of the Crown, at all times, to correspond with Ministers of State, and persons of distinction and influence in the nation, in order to concert and carry on such measures of the British administration, as have been deemed by the colonists to be grievous to them, it cannot be thought unreasonable, or improper, for the colonists to correspond with their agents, as well as with each other, to the end, that their grievances may be so explained to his Majesty, as that, in his justice, he may afford them necessary relief. As this province has heretofore felt the great misfortune of the displeasure of our Sovereign, by means of misrepresentations, permit us further to say, there is room to apprehend that his Majesty has, in this instance, been misinformed; and, that there are good grounds to suspect, that those who may have misinformed him, have had in meditation further measures destructive to the colonies, which they were apprehensive, would be defeated by means of committees of correspondence, sitting and acting, in the recess of the respective Assemblies.

It must be pleasing to the good people of this province, to find, that the heavy debt which had been incurred by their liberal aids, through the course of the late war, for the subduing his Majesty's inveterate enemies, and extending his territory and dominion in America, is so nearly discharged. Whenever the House of Representatives shall deem it incumbent upon them to provide for any future charges, it will be done, as it ought, by such ways and means, as, after due deliberation, to them shall seem meet.

In the mean time, this House will employ the powers with which they are entrusted, in supporting his Majesty's just authority in the province, according to the royal charter, and in despatching such public business, as now properly lies before us. And, while we pursue such measures, as tend, by God's blessing, to the redress of grievances, and to the restoration and establishment of the public liberty, we persuade ourselves, that we shall, at the same time, as far as in us lies, most effectually secure the tranquillity and good order of the government, and the great end for which it was instituted, the safety and welfare of the people.

[The committee, by whom the foregoing was reported, were, the Speaker, Mr. S. Adams, Mr. Hancock, Col. Warren, Col. Thayer, Col. Bowers, and Capt. Derby.]

MESSAGE

OF THE GOVERNOR TO BOTH HOUSES, FEBRUARY 24, 1774.

Gentlemen of the Council, and
  Gentlemen of the House of Representatives,

HAVING received discretionary leave from the King, to go to England, I think it proper to acquaint you with this instance of his Majesty's most gracious condescension; and, that I intend to avail myself of it, as soon as his service will admit.

I must desire you to give all the despatch possible, to such necessary public business, as may yet lie before you; for, I must soon, by an adjournment or prorogation, give the Court a recess, that I may attend to that preparation for my voyage, which his Majesty's service, and my personal affairs require.

T. HUTCHINSON.

SPEECH

OF GOVERNOR GAGE TO THE TWO HOUSES, MAY 26, 1774.*

Gentlemen of the Council, and
  Gentlemen of the House of Representatives,

HIS Majesty, having been pleased to appoint me, Governor and Captain General of his province of the Massachusetts Bay, and my commission having been read and published, I have met you, for the election of Councellors, for the ensuing year; on which business, you have been convened agreeably to your charter. And, as that work is finished, you will proceed as you shall judge, to the consideration of such other matters, as may properly come before you, and that you judge ought to be entered upon, previous to the first of next month. And you may be assured, that I shall, with pleasure, concur with you, to the utmost of my power, in all matters that tend to the welfare and prosperity of the province.

I make mention of the first of next month, because, I have the King's particular commands, for holding the General Court at Salem, from that day, till his Majesty shall have signified his royal will and pleasure, for holding it again at Boston.

---

* Gen. Gage, had then been lately appointed Governor of this province. When a list of the gentlemen, elected Councellors, was presented to him, he objected to James Bowdoin, John Winthrop, Timothy Danielson, Benjamin Austin, William Phillips, Michael Farley, James Prescott, John Adams, Norton Quincy, Jerathmeel Bowers, Enoch Freeman, and Jedediah Foster.

The honor of my appointment, to the command of this government, being so lately conferred, and the time since I took it upon me, so very short, I have not, at present, any matter to lay before you, farther than to acquaint you, that the treasurer having informed me, that sufficient provision is made for the redemption of the government securities, that are now, and will become due in June, 1775, you will have no other burden upon you, but to supply the treasury, for the support of government, for the ensuing year.

THO. GAGE.

=

ANSWER

OF THE COUNCIL TO THE GOVERNOR'S SPEECH, JUNE 9, 1774.

May it please your Excellency,

YOUR speech to the two Houses, at the opening of the session, has been duly considered. His Majesty having been pleased to appoint you to the government of this province, we take this opportunity to wait on you, with our congratulations, on that occasion. Your Excellency has arrived, at a juncture, when the harmony between Great Britain and the colonies is greatly interrupted; whereby your station, though elevated, must needs be rendered less agreeable to you, than otherwise it would have been. But, if you should be the happy instrument of restoring, in any measure, that harmony, and of extricating the province from their present embarrassments, you will, doubtless, consider these happy effects as more than a compensation for any inconveniences arising to you from the peculiar circumstances of the times. His Majesty's faithful Council will, on all occasions, cheerfully cooperate with your Excellency, in every attempt for accomplishing those desirable ends.

We wish your Excellency every felicity. The greatest, of a political nature, both to yourself and the province, is, that your administration, in the principles and general conduct of it, may be a happy contrast to that of your two immediate predecessors. It is irksome to us to censure any one, but we are constrained to say, that there is the greatest reason to apprehend, that from their machinations, both in concert and apart, are derived the origin and progress of the disunion between Great Britain and the colonies, and the present distressed state of the province; a province, to which, the latter of them, in an especial manner, owed his best services, and whose liberties and rights, he was under every obligation of duty and gratitude to support.

The inhabitants of this colony, claim no more than the rights of Englishmen, without diminution or abridgment. These, as it will be our indispensable duty. so it shall be our constant endeavor, to maintain, to the utmost of our power, in perfect consistence, however, with the truest loyalty to the Crown; the just prerogatives of which, your Excellency will find this Board ever zealous to support.

Permit us, sir, on this occasion, to express the firmest confidence, that, under their present grievances, the people of this province, will not, in vain, look to your Excellency, for your paternal aid and assistance: and, as the great end of government is the good of the people, that your experience and abilities will be applied to attain that end. The steady pursuit of which, at the same time it ensures their confidence and esteem, will be a source of the truest enjoyment, self approbation. We thank your Excellency, for the assurance you have given, that you will, with pleasure, concur with the two Houses, to the utmost of your power, in all matters that tend to the welfare and prosperity of the province; and your Excellency may be assured, that we shall contribute every thing on our part, to promote measures of so salutary a tendency.

[The committee, appointed to present the above to the Governor, reported, that, when the chairman had proceeded as far as that part of the address, which expressed a wish, " that his administration might be a happy contrast to that of his two immediate predecessors," the Governor desired the chairman not to proceed any further, as he could not receive an address, which reflected so highly on his predecessors; but, that he would assign his reasons to the Council, in writing.]

MESSAGE

FROM THE GOVERNOR TO THE COUNCIL, JUNE 14, 1774.

Gentlemen of the Council,

I cannot receive an address, which contains indecent reflections on my predecessors, who have been tried, and honorably acquitted, by the Lords of the Privy Council, and their conduct approved by the King. I consider the address as an insult upon his Majesty, and the Lords of the Privy Council, and an affront to myself. THO. GAGE.

" On the 17th of June, the Governor directed the Secretary to acquaint the two Houses, it was his pleasure the General Assembly should be dissolved; and to declare the same dissolved accordingly. The Secretary went to the Court House, and finding the door of the Representative's Chamber locked, directed the Messenger to go in, and acquaint the Speaker, that the Secretary had a message from his Excellency to the honorable House, and desired he might be admitted, to deliver it. The Messenger soon returned, and said he had acquainted the Speaker, who mentioned it to the House; and their orders were, to keep the door fast. Whereupon, the following proclamation was published on the stairs leading to the Representative's Chamber, in presence of a number of the Members of the House, and divers other persons; and immediately after in Council." 　　*Extract from Journal of Gen. Court.*

Province of Massachusetts Bay.

BY THE GOVERNOR......A PROCLAMATION FOR DISSOLVING THE GENERAL COURT.

WHEREAS, the proceedings of the House of Representatives, in the present session of the General Court, make it necessary for his Majesty's service, that the said General Court should be dissolved; I have, therefore, thought fit to dissolve the said General Court; and the same is hereby dissolved accordingly; and the Members thereof, are discharged from any further attendance.

Given under my hand, at Salem, the 17th day of June, 1774, in the fourteenth year of his Majesty's reign. 　　THO. GAGE.

By his Excellency's command,

THO. FLUCKER, *Secretary.*

God save the King.

[Before the General Court separated, they elected five delegates, to meet such as should be chosen by the other colonies, to convene at Philadelphia, to consider the critical and alarming situation of the country. They met in September, 1774, and delegates from all the other provinces, (except Georgia, which, however, soon afterwards joined the confederacy,) convened there, at that period, and formed the first Continental Congress. The following gentlemen were appointed delegates : Thomas Cushing, Samuel Adams, Robert T. Paine, James Bowdoin, and John Adams. And as the General Court was dissolved, it was also proposed to have a Provincial Congress, or meeting of deputies, from every town in this state. Deputies were accordingly chosen, and met at Salem, October 7th, 1774. An adjournment was immediately voted, to Concord. John Hancock, was chosen President, and Benjamin Lincoln, Secretary. A committee was appointed, to consider the state of the province, consisting of the following gentlemen, viz. the President, Joseph Hawley, Dr. Joseph Warren, Samuel Dexter, Col. Ward, Col. Warren, Capt. Heath, Col. Lee, Dr. Church, Dr. Holtan, Mr. Gerry, Col. Tyng, Capt. Robinson, Maj. Foster, and Mr. Gorham. The day following, the committee reported a message to Gov. Gage, which was accepted ; and is as follows :]

MESSAGE

FROM THE PROVINCIAL CONGRESS, SITTING AT CONCORD, TO HIS EXCELLENCY GOVERNOR GAGE.

May it please your Excellency,

THE delegates, from the several towns, in the province of Massachusetts Bay, convened in Congress, beg leave to address you. The distressed and miserable state of the province, occasioned by the intolerable grievances and oppressions to which the people are subjected, and the danger and destruction to which they are exposed, of which your Excellency must be sensible, and the want of a General Assembly, have rendered it indispensably necessary to collect the wisdom of the province, by their delegates, in this Congress, to concert some adequate remedy for preventing impending ruin, and providing for the public safety.

It is with the utmost concern, we see your hostile preparations, which have spread such alarm through the province, and the whole continent, as threaten to involve us in all the confusion and horrors of civil war : and, while we contemplate an event so deeply to be regretted by every good man, it must occasion the surprise and astonishment of all mankind, that such measures are pursued, against a people, whose love of order, attachment to Britain, and loyalty to their prince, have ever been truly exemplary. Your Excellency must be sensible, that the sole end of government is the protection and security of the people: whenever, therefore, that power, which was originally instituted to effect these important and valuable purposes, is employed to harrass and enslave the people ; in this case, it becomes a curse, rather than a blessing.

53

The most painful apprehensions are excited in our minds, by the measures now pursuing; the rigorous execution of the (Boston) port bill, with improved severity, must certainly reduce the capital and its numerous dependences to a state of poverty and ruin. The acts for altering the charter,* and the administration of justice in the colony, are manifestly designed to abridge this people of their rights, and to license murders; and, if carried into execution, will reduce them to slavery. The number of troops in the capital, increased by daily accessions drawn from the whole continent, together with the formidable and hostile preparations, which you are now making on Boston Neck, in our opinion, greatly endanger the lives, liberties, and property, not only of our brethren in the town of Boston, but of this province in general. Permit us to ask your Excellency, whether an inattentive and unconcerned acquiescence to such alarming, such menacing measures, would not evidence a state of insanity? Or, whether the delaying to take every possible precaution for the security of this province, would not be the most criminal neglect in a people, heretofore rigidly and justly tenacious of their constituted rights?

Penetrated with the most poignant concern, and ardently solicitous to preserve union and harmony between Great Britain and the colonies, necessary to the well-being of both, we entreat your Excellency to remove that brand of contention, the fortress at the entrance of Boston. We are much concerned, that you should have been induced to construct it, and thereby, causelessly excite such a spirit of resentment and indignation, as now generally prevails.

We assure you, that the good people of this colony, never have had the least intention to do any injury to his Majesty's troops; but, on the contrary, most earnestly desire, that every obstacle to treating them as fellow subjects, may be immediately removed: but are constrained to tell your Excellency, that the minds of the people will never be relieved, till those hostile works are demolished. And we request you, as you regard his Majesty's honor and interest, the dignity, and happiness of the empire, and the peace and welfare of this province, that you immediately desist from the fortress, now constructing at the south entrance into the town of Boston, and restore the pass to its natural state.

---

* In June of this year, an act of Parliament was passed, revoking that part of the charter, which allowed the Representatives of the people to elect Councellors; and the King, with the advice of his Ministers, was empowered to appoint them; and, in August, he accordingly appointed others, commonly called mandamus counsellors; being wholly independent of the people, and holding their office of the Crown, they were likely to be fit instruments of oppression and tyranny.

ADDRESS

OF THE PROVINCIAL CONGRESS TO THE INHABITANTS OF THE TOWNS AND
DISTRICTS OF MASSACHUSETTS BAY, DECEMBER 4, 1774.

Friends and Brethren,

AT a time when the good people of this colony were deprived
of their laws, and the administration of justice; when the cruel
oppressions brought on their capital had stagnated almost all their
commerce; when a standing army was illegally posted among us,
for the express purpose of enforcing submission to a system of
tyranny; and, when the General Court was, with the same design,
prohibited to sit; we were chosen, and empowered by you, to assemble, and consult upon measures necessary for our common
safety and defence. With much anxiety for the common welfare,
we have attended this service, and upon the coolest deliberation,
have adopted the measures recommended to you.

We have still confidence in the wisdom, justice, and goodness
of our Sovereign, as well as in the integrity, humanity, and good
sense of the nation. And, if we had a reasonable expectation, that
the truth of facts would be made known in England, we should
entertain the most pleasing hopes, that the measures concerted,
by the colonies, jointly and severally, would procure a full redress
of our grievances: but, we are constrained in justice to you, to
ourselves, and posterity, to say, that the incessant and unrelenting
malice of our enemies has been so successful, as to fill the Court
and kingdom of Great Britain, with falsehood and calumnies concerning us, and excite the most bitter and groundless prejudices
against us; that the sudden dissolution of Parliament, and the
hasty summons for a new election, gives us reason to apprehend,
that a majority of the House of Commons will be again elected,
under the influence of an arbitrary Ministry; and, that the general tenor of our intelligence from Great Britain, with the frequent
reinforcements of the army and navy at Boston, excites the strongest jealousy, that the system of colony administration, so unfriendly to the protestant religion, and destructive of American
liberty, is still to be pursued, and attempted with force, to be
carried into execution.

You are placed, by Providence, in a post of honour, because it
is a post of danger; and while struggling for the noblest objects,
the liberties of our country, the happiness of posterity, and rights
of human nature, the eyes, not only of North America and the
whole British empire, but of all Europe, are upon you. Let us
be, therefore, altogether solicitous, that no disorderly behavior,
nothing unbecoming our character, as Americans, as citizens, and
christians, be justly chargeable to us.

Whoever, with a small degree of attention, contemplates the commerce between Great Britain and America, will be convinced, that a total stoppage thereof, will soon produce in Great Britain such dangerous effects, as cannot fail to convince the Ministry, the Parliament, and people, that it is their interest and duty to grant us relief. Whoever considers the number of brave men inhabiting North America, well know, that a general attention to military discipline, must so establish their rights and liberties, as under God, to render it impossible for an arbitrary Minister of Britain, to destroy them. These are facts, which our enemies are apprized of, and if they will not be influencd by principles of justice, to alter their cruel measures towards America, these ought to lead them thereto. They, however, hope to effect by stratagem, what they may not obtain by power, and are using arts, by the assistance of base scribblers, who undoubtedly receive their bribes, and by many other means, to raise doubts and divisions throughout the colonies.

To defeat their wicked designs, we think it necessary for each town to be particularly careful, strictly to execute the plans of the Continental and Provincial Congress ; and, while it censures its own individuals, counteracting those plans, that it be not deceived, or diverted from its duty by rumors, should any take place, to the prejudice of other communities. Your Provincial Congresses, we have reason to hope, will hold up the towns, if any should be so lost, as not to act their parts ; and none can doubt, that the Continental Congress will rectify errors, should any take place, in any colony, through the subtilty of our enemies. Surely, no arguments can be necessary, to excite you to the most strict adherence to the American Association, since the minutest deviation in one colony, especially in this, will probably be misrepresented in the others, to discourage their general zeal and perseverance, which, however, we assure ourselves, cannot be effected.

While the British Ministry are suffered, with a high hand, to tyrannise over America, no part of it, we presume, can be negligent in guarding against the ravages threatened by the standing army,. now in Boston ; these troops will, undoubtedly, be employed in attempts to defeat the association, which our enemies cannot but fear; will eventually defeat them; and, so sanguinary are those, our enemies, as we have reason to think, so thirsty for the blood of this innocent people, who are only contending for their rights, that we should be guilty of the most unpardonable neglect, should we not apprize you of your danger, which appears to us imminently great, and ought, attentively, to be guarded against. The improvement of the militia in general, in the art military, has been therefore thought necessary, and strongly recommended by this Congress. We now think, that particular care should be taken by the towns and districts in this colony, that each of the minute men, not already provided therewith, should be immediately equipped with an effective fire arm, bayonet, pouch, knapsack, thirty rounds of cartridges and ball, and, that they be disciplined three times a week, and oftener, as opportunity may offer.

To encourage these, our worthy countrymen, to obtain the skill of complete soldiers, we recommend it to the towns, and districts, forthwith to pay their own minute men a reasonable consideration for their services; and, in case of a general muster, their further services must be recompensed by the province. An attention to discipline in the militia, in general, is, however, by no means to be neglected.

With the utmost cheerfulness, we assure you, of our determination to stand or fall, with the liberties of America; and while we humbly implore the sovereign disposer of all things, to whose divine Providence, the rights of his creatures cannot be indifferent, to correct the errors, and alter the measures of an infatuated Ministry, we cannot doubt of his support, even in the extreme difficulties, which we all may have to encounter. May all means devised, for our safety, by the general Congress of America, and Assemblies, or Conventions of the colonies, be resolutely executed, and happily succeeded; and may this injured people be reinstated in the full exercise of their rights, without the evils and devastations of civil war.

[Other documents might have been given, which would be interesting to the people of Massachusetts, and of the kind promised in the proposal, for publishing this volume. But, the controversy respecting the extent of the rights of the colonies, for many years maintained, *chiefly* by the Legislature, and individual citizens of Massachusetts, had, at this period, become general through the provinces; and, a Continental Congress, having been appointed, and convened, to consider the political condition of the country, it is not necessary to give any further proceedings of the people of this State. It is true, also, that all important events, subsequent to 1774, are preserved in various public journals, to which the future historian of America, may easily have access.]

CONTENTS.

CONTENTS. **423**